Numerical Optimization and Algorithms: 3rd Edition

Numerical Optimization and Algorithms: 3rd Edition

Guest Editors

Dunhui Xiao

Shuai (Steven) Li

MDPI

Basel • Beijing • Wuhan • Barcelona • Belgrade • Novi Sad • Cluj • Manchester

Guest Editors
Dunhui Xiao
School of Mathematical Sciences
Tongji University
Shanghai
China

Shuai (Steven) Li
Faculty of Information Technology and Electrical Engineering
University of Oulu
Oulu
Finland

Editorial Office
MDPI AG
Grosspeteranlage 5
4052 Basel, Switzerland

This is a reprint of the Special Issue, published open access by the journal *Algorithms* (ISSN 1999-4893), freely accessible at: https://www.mdpi.com/journal/algorithms/special_issues/YVBNUO5ER1.

For citation purposes, cite each article independently as indicated on the article page online and as indicated below:

Lastname, A.A.; Lastname, B.B. Article Title. *Journal Name* **Year**, *Volume Number*, Page Range.

ISBN 978-3-7258-6960-2 (Hbk)
ISBN 978-3-7258-6961-9 (PDF)
https://doi.org/10.3390/books978-3-7258-6961-9

Contents

About the Editors

Dunhui Xiao

Dunhui Xiao is a Professor at the School of Mathematical Sciences, Tongji University, and a recipient of the National High-Level Overseas Young Talent Award. He serves as the Vice Director of the Information Office (concurrent) and Head of the Computational Mathematics Division at Tongji University. Additionally, he is an Executive Member of the 11th Standing Committee of the Computational Mathematics Division of the Chinese Mathematical Society, a Standing Member of the AI Practical Applications Society, a Committee Member of Shanghai CSIAM, and the Vice Director of the Tongji Branch of the Zhangjiang Institute for Mathematical Research. He obtained his PhD from Imperial College London, where he conducted his post-doc research as well. Then, he worked as a lecturer at Swansea University's Zienkiewicz Centre for Computational Engineering, one of the birthplaces of the finite element method.

He has led multiple national and international research projects, including those funded by the UK's EPSRC, Royal Society, and China's national funding agencies. He serves as a reviewer for multiple academic journals and funding agencies, including the UK Research Councils, ERC in Europe and the Ministry of Science and Technology in China. His research focuses on model order reduction, data-driven models, physics-data hybrid computational models, data assimilation, domain decomposition, and computational fluid dynamics.

Shuai (Steven) Li

Shuai (Steven) Li is currently a Full Professor with the Faculty of Information Technology and Electrical Engineering (ITEE), University of Oulu, and also an Adjunct Professor with the VTT-Technology Research Center of Finland. Steven's main research interests are nonlinear optimization and intelligent control with their applications to robotics. He has published over 200 SCI-indexed journal papers (including more than 90 on IEEE transactions) in peer reviewed journals. Steven is available for supervising both master and PhD students. PhD graduates from his group are now working in leading universities in Hong Kong, India, and China as professors. Steven is a Fellow of IET (Institution of Engineering and Technology), a Fellow of BCS (British Computer Society) and a Fellow of IMA (Institute of Mathematics and its Applications).

algorithms

MDPI

Article

The Computability of the Channel Reliability Function and Related Bounds

Holger Boche [1] and Christian Deppe [2,*]

[1] Theoretical Information Technology, Technical University of Munich, 80333 Munich, Germany; boche@tum.de
[2] Institute for Communications Technology, Technische Universität Braunschweig, 38106 Brunswick, Germany
* Correspondence: christian.deppe@tu-bs.de

Abstract: The channel reliability function is a crucial tool for characterizing the dependable transmission of messages across communication channels. In many cases, the only upper and lower bounds of this function are known. We investigate the computability of the reliability function and its associated functions, demonstrating that the reliability function is not Turing computable. This also holds true for functions related to the sphere packing bound and the expurgation bound. Additionally, we examine the R_∞ function and zero-error feedback capacity, as they are vital in the context of the reliability function. Both the R_∞ function and the zero-error feedback capacity are not Banach–Mazur computable.

Keywords: Turing computability; channel reliability function; zero-error feedback capacity

1. Introduction

In [1], C. Shannon established the foundations of information theory by characterizing the key mathematical properties of communication channels. For a transmission rate R that is less than the channel capacity C, the probability of erroneous decoding with respect to an optimal code decreases exponentially as the code length $n \in \mathbb{N}$ increases. Shannon introduced the channel reliability function $E(R)$ as being the exponent governing this exponential decrease in relation to the transmission rate R.

A major goal in information theory is to find a closed-form expression for the channel reliability function. This expression should be computable and fully determined by the parameters of the communication task. Naturally, we must define what constitutes a closed-form expression. In [2], Chow, and in [3], Borwein and Crandall discuss different approaches to defining closed-form expressions. All of the various representations satisfy the requirement that the corresponding functions can be computed algorithmically using a digital computer. This can be achieved with great precision, depending on the inputs within their domain of definition.

Shannon's characterization of the capacity for message transmission via the discrete memoryless channel (DMC) in [1], Ahlswede's characterization of the capacity for message transmission via the multiple access channel in [4], and Ahlswede and Dueck's characterization of the identification capacity for DMCs in [5] are all significant examples of closed-form solutions using elementary functions. These provide important instances of the computability of the corresponding performance functions, as defined in the previous context. The precise definition of computability, as outlined by Turing, is presented in Section 2.

Lovász's characterization of the zero-error capacity for the pentagram also represents a closed-form number according to Chow's definition in [2], which can be computed

 https://doi.org/10.3390/a18060361

algorithmically—an outcome that is desirable. However, the characterization of the zero-error capacity for a cyclical heptagon remains an open problem. Moreover, it is still unclear whether the zero-error capacities of DMCs can take computable values for computable channels. Additionally, the algorithmic computability of the broadcast capacity region is still uncertain.

In the age of artificial intelligence, it is increasingly important to determine whether a digital computer can solve a given problem or compute a given function. Since every function that can be computed by a digital computer can also be computed by a Turing machine (as will be discussed in more detail below), this question is reduced to asking whether a function is computable. It is therefore crucial to distinguish between determining how to compute the zero-error capacity and whether it is computable at all. In this work, we focus on the latter: the computability of the zero-error capacity.

The Lovász ϑ-function for graphs was analyzed in [6] from three distinct research perspectives related to various graph invariants. This investigation resulted in new insights into the Shannon capacity of graphs, observations on cospectral and nonisomorphic graphs, and bounds on graph invariants while also serving as a tutorial in zero-error information theory and algebraic graph theory. Further observations on the Lovász ϑ-function are provided by the author in [7].

In this paper, we provide a negative answer to the question of whether the channel reliability function and several related bounds are algorithmically computable by Turing machines.

Significant research has been conducted on the channel reliability function, but many aspects of its behavior remain unresolved (see surveys [8] and [9]). In fact, a complete characterization of the channel reliability function is still unknown for binary-input binary-output channels. As a result, considerable efforts have been made to derive computable lower and upper bounds for the function (see [10–12]).

Determining the behavior of the channel reliability function across the entire interval $(0, C)$ is a challenging problem. Various approaches have attempted to compute the reliability function algorithmically by constructing sequences of upper and lower bounds. The first significant contribution in this direction was made by Shannon, Gallager, and Berlekamp in [13].

A fundamental question that arises is whether the reliability function can be computed in this manner. To investigate this, we employ the framework of Turing computability [14]. In general, a function is considered Turing computable if there exists an algorithm capable of computing it. The Turing machine serves as the most fundamental and powerful model of computation, underpinning theoretical computer science. Unlike physical computers, which have practical constraints, a Turing machine is an abstract mathematical construct that can be rigorously analyzed using formal mathematical methods.

It is important to note that the Turing machine represents the ultimate performance limit of current digital computers, including supercomputers. A Turing machine models an algorithm or a program, where computation consists of step-by-step manipulation of symbols or characters that are read from and written to a memory tape according to a set of rules. These symbols can be interpreted in various ways, including as numbers. To perform computations on abstract sets, the elements of the set must be encoded as strings of symbols on the tape. This approach allows Turing computability to be defined for real and complex numbers.

The use of digital computers to compute approximations of channel capacities or channel reliability functions has been a prominent topic in information theory. The computation of channel capacity for discrete memoryless channels (DMCs) is a convex optimization problem, and in 1972, an algorithm for approximating the capacity of a DMC on digital computers was independently published in [15] and [16].

Even for binary symmetric channels with rational crossover probabilities (excluding the case $p = \frac{1}{2}$), the channel capacity is a transcendental number. As a result, despite the relative simplicity of these channels, their capacity can only be approximated with finite precision by digital computers. In contrast to the problem of computing channel capacity, determining the behavior of the channel reliability function over the entire interval $(0, C) \subset \mathbb{R}$ is a significantly more complex task. A common approach to this challenge involves considering sequences of upper and lower bounds for $E(R)$ (see [13]).

In general, the *channel reliability function* is a well-studied topic in information theory. Originally introduced and analyzed for discrete memoryless channels (DMCs), the concept has since been significantly extended to various other scenarios and channel models. In [17], the reliability function of a DMC was studied at rates above capacity. Subsequent refinements and theoretical bounds were proposed, such as the Poor–Verdú upper bound addressed in [18]. Extensions beyond DMCs include continuous channels and channels with feedback or secrecy constraints. For instance, upper bounds for Gaussian channels were developed in [19], while the role of feedback in Poisson and Gaussian channels was explored in [20,21]. The impact of signal constraints was analyzed in [22], and improved Gaussian channel bounds were proposed in [23]. Secrecy considerations and cost constraints were incorporated into the analysis of the reliability and secrecy functions in [24]. The reliability function in the presence of side information, as in the Gelfand–Pinsker channel, was considered in [25]. More recently, a new upper bound for DMCs was given in [26], and noisy feedback for binary symmetric channels was studied in [27]. These developments culminated in the analysis of reliability functions in quantum communication settings. Foundational work includes [28,29], and recent advancements include [30].

In this work, we explore whether it is possible to compute the channel reliability function in this manner using a mathematically rigorous formalization of computability. Specifically, our analysis is based on the theory of Turing machines and recursive functions.

In many cases, there is no direct characterization of the behavior of a general function over an abstract set in terms of an algorithm on a Turing machine. Consequently, a common strategy is to approximate the function successively using a sequence of computable upper and lower bounds, for which an algorithm is available. One can then ask the weaker question of whether it is possible to approximate the function in a computable manner. This requires computable sequences of computable upper and lower bounds. This approach is also necessary for the reliability function, and we conducted this analysis. Unfortunately, our results show that the channel reliability function is not a Turing computable performance function when the channel is considered as input.

We also examine several other closely related functions, including the R_∞ function, the sphere packing bound function, the expurgation bound function, and the zero-error feedback capacity, all of which are closely tied to the reliability function. We treat all of these functions as functions of the channel.

As envisioned, the sixth generation (6G) of mobile networks will introduce a wide range of new features [31]. These innovations bring new challenges to the design of wireless communication systems. Specifically, the Tactile Internet will enable not only the control of data but also the manipulation of physical and virtual objects [31]. With such applications, there arises an increased need to ensure the trustworthiness of the system and its services [32,33].

6G will impose more diverse and demanding quality-of-service (QoS) requirements on network resilience, reliability, service availability, and delay [31]. The channel reliability function plays a vital role in the reliability and delay performance analysis of communication systems. It is therefore of interest to explore whether the reliability and delay performance of communication systems can be verified automatically on digital hardware [33]. Analyzing the channel reliability function with respect to Turing computability becomes crucial in this context. The question of Turing computability for performance functions is a central issue in information theory, as closed-form expressions are only known for a few performance functions. It is therefore important to compute corresponding performance functions on available computers with provable performance, ensuring the strict requirements for future communication systems [31,33].

The structure of this paper is as follows. In Section 2, we begin by presenting the basic definitions and known results that will be used throughout the paper. Section 3 focuses on the R_∞ function. We examine the decidability of connected sets with the R_∞ function and demonstrate that only an approximation from below is possible. This has implications for the sphere packing bound, and we show that it is not a Turing computable performance function.

In Section 4, we analyze the reliability function and prove that it is also not Turing computable. The same result holds for the expurgation bound. In Section 5, we investigate the zero-error feedback capacity, which is closely related to the R_∞ function. We first address a question posed by Alon and Lubetzky in [34] regarding the zero-error capacity with feedback, specifically for the case without feedback (which was examined in [35]). We then show that the zero-error feedback capacity is not Banach–Mazur computable and cannot be approximated by computable increasing sequences of computable functions. Additionally, we characterize the superadditivity of the zero-error feedback capacity and demonstrate that the R_∞ function is additive.

In Section 6, we analyze the behavior of the expurgation bound rates. Finally, we conclude by summarizing the implications of our results for the channel reliability function. Our findings indicate that, in general, there cannot be a simple recursive closed-form expression for the channel reliability function over a very precise interval.

Some of the results in this paper were presented at the IEEE International Symposium on Information Theory in Espoo, as noted in [36].

2. Definitions and Basic Results

2.1. Basic Concepts of Computability Theory

In this section, we present the basic definitions and results from computability theory that are necessary for this work. We begin with the fundamental definitions of computability, starting with the concept of a Turing machine [14].

A Turing machine serves as a mathematical model for what we intuitively understand as computation machines. In this sense, they provide an abstract idealization of modern-day computers. Any algorithm that can be executed by a real-world computer can, in principle, be simulated by a Turing machine, and vice versa. However, unlike real-world computers, Turing machines are not constrained by limitations such as energy consumption, computation time, or memory size. Furthermore, all computation steps on a Turing machine are assumed to be executed flawlessly, with no possibility of error.

Recursive functions, more specifically known as *μ-recursive functions*, form a special subset of the set $\bigcup_{n=0}^{\infty}\left\{f : \mathbb{N}^n \hookrightarrow \mathbb{N}\right\}$, where the symbol "$\hookrightarrow$" denotes a *partial mapping*. The set of recursive functions provides an alternative characterization of the notion of computability. Turing machines and recursive functions are equivalent in the following sense: a function $f : \mathbb{N}^n \hookrightarrow \mathbb{N}$ is computable by a Turing machine if and only if it is a partial recursive function.

Next, we introduce several key definitions from *computable analysis* [37–39], which we will apply in the subsequent sections.

Definition 1. *A sequence of rational numbers* $\{r_n\}_{n\in\mathbb{N}}$ *is called a computable sequence if there exist recursive functions* $a, b, s : \mathbb{N} \to \mathbb{N}$ *with* $b(n) \neq 0$ *for all* $n \in \mathbb{N}$ *and*

$$r_n = (-1)^{s(n)} \frac{a(n)}{b(n)}, \quad n \in \mathbb{N}.$$

Definition 2. *We say that a computable sequence* $\{r_n\}_{n\in\mathbb{N}}$ *of rational numbers converges effectively, i.e., computably, to a number* x*, if a recursive function* $a : \mathbb{N} \to \mathbb{N}$ *exists such that* $|x - r_n| < \frac{1}{2^N}$ *for all* $N \in \mathbb{N}$ *and all* $n \in \mathbb{N}$ *with* $n \geq a(N)$ *applies.*

We can now introduce computable numbers.

Definition 3. *A real number* x *is said to be computable if there exists a computable sequence of rational numbers* $\{r_n\}_{n\in\mathbb{N}}$*, such that* $|x - r_n| < 2^{-n}$ *for all* $n \in \mathbb{N}$*. We denote the set of computable real numbers using* $\mathbb{R}_c$*.*

Next, we need suitable subsets of the natural numbers.

Definition 4. *A set* $A \subset \mathbb{N}$ *is called recursive if there exists a recursive function* f*, such that* $f(x) = 1$ *if* $x \in A$ *and* $f(x) = 0$ *if* $x \in A^c$*, where* A^c *stands for the complement set of* A*.*

Definition 5. *A set* $A \subset \mathbb{N}$ *is recursively enumerable if there exists a recursive function whose domain is exactly* A*.*

Remark 1. *For the definition of recursive and partial recursive functions, see [37]. Recursive functions* $f : \mathbb{N} \to \mathbb{N}$ *are the building blocks to develop the framework for computing theory on rational numbers, on real numbers, and on related functions defined over these number fields. This theory captures exactly what can be achieved in theory with digital computers in these number fields. We next introduce the concept of computable performance functions on the basis of computability theory. It is important to note that computability theory formalizes exactly what is computable with perfect digital computers.*

2.2. Basic Concepts of Information Theory

To define the reliability function and its related functions, we first need the definition of a discrete memoryless channel. In the theory of transmission, the receiver must be in a position to successfully decode all the messages transmitted by the sender.

Let $\mathcal{X}$ be a finite alphabet, and denote the set of all probability distributions on $\mathcal{X}$ using $\mathcal{P}(\mathcal{X})$. We define the set of computable probability distributions, $\mathcal{P}_c(\mathcal{X})$, as the subset of $\mathcal{P}(\mathcal{X})$ consisting of all distributions $P \in \mathcal{P}(\mathcal{X})$ for which $P(x) \in \mathbb{R}_c$ holds for all $x \in \mathcal{X}$.

Furthermore, for finite alphabets $\mathcal{X}$ and $\mathcal{Y}$, let $\mathcal{CH}$ denote the set of all conditional probability distributions (or channels) $P_{Y|X} : \mathcal{X} \to \mathcal{P}(\mathcal{Y})$. We define $\mathcal{CH}_c$ as the set of computable conditional probability distributions, i.e., those for which $P_{Y|X}(\cdot|x) \in \mathcal{P}_c(\mathcal{Y})$ holds for every $x \in \mathcal{X}$.

Let $M \subset CH_c(\mathcal{X}, \mathcal{Y})$. We call M semi-decidable if and only if there is a Turing machine TM_M that either stops or computes forever, depending on whether $W \in M$ is true. This means TM_M exactly accepts the elements of M, and for an input $W \in M^c = CH_c(\mathcal{X}, \mathcal{Y}) \setminus M$, it computes forever.

Definition 6. *A discrete memoryless channel (DMC) is a triple* $(\mathcal{X}, \mathcal{Y}, W)$*, where* $\mathcal{X}$ *is the finite input alphabet,* $\mathcal{Y}$ *is the finite output alphabet, and* $W(y|x) \in CH(\mathcal{X}, \mathcal{Y})$*, with* $x \in \mathcal{X}$*,* $y \in \mathcal{Y}$*. The probability that a sequence* $y^n \in \mathcal{Y}^n$ *is received if* $x^n \in \mathcal{X}^n$ *was sent is defined by*

$$W^n(y^n|x^n) = \prod_{j=1}^{n} W(y_j|x_j).$$

Definition 7. *A (deterministic) block code* $\mathcal{C}(n)$ *with rate R and block length n consists of*

- *A message set* $\mathcal{M} = \{1, 2, ..., M\}$ *with* $M = 2^{nR} \in \mathbb{N}$*;*
- *An encoding function* $e : \mathcal{M} \to \mathcal{X}^n$*;*
- *aAdecoding function* $d : \mathcal{Y}^n \to \mathcal{M}$*.*

We call such a code an (R, n)*-code.*

Definition 8. *Let* $(\mathcal{X}, \mathcal{Y}, W)$ *be a DMC. Using* $\mathcal{C}(n)$*, we denote a block code with the block length n and message set* $\mathcal{M}$*.*

1. *The individual message probability of error is defined by the conditional probability of error, given that message* $m \in \mathcal{M}$ *is transmitted:*

$$P_e(\mathcal{C}(n), W, m) = Pr\{d(Y^n) \neq m | X^n = e(m)\}.$$

2. *We define the average probability of error by*

$$P_{e,\text{av}}(\mathcal{C}(n), W) = \frac{1}{|\mathcal{M}|} \sum_{m \in \mathcal{M}} P_e(\mathcal{C}(n), W, m).$$

   $P_{e,\text{av}}(W, R, n)$ *denotes the minimum error probability* $P_{e,\text{av}}(\mathcal{C}(n), W)$ *over all block codes* $\mathcal{C}(n)$ *of block length n and with message set* $\mathcal{M} = 2^{nR}$*.*

3. *We define the maximal probability of error by*

$$P_{e,\max}(\mathcal{C}(n), W) = \max_{m \in \mathcal{M}} P_e(\mathcal{C}(n), W, m).$$

   $P_{e,\max}(W, R, n)$ *denotes the minimum error probability* $P_{e,\max}(\mathcal{C}(n), W)$ *over all block codes* $\mathcal{C}(n)$ *of block length n and with message set* $\mathcal{M} = 2^{nR}$*.*

4. *The Shannon capacity for a channel* $W \in CH(\mathcal{X}, \mathcal{Y})$ *is defined by*

$$C(W) := \sup\{R : \lim_{n \to \infty} P_{e,\max}(W, R, n) = 0\}.$$

5. *The zero-error capacity for a channel* $W \in CH(\mathcal{X}, \mathcal{Y})$ *is defined by*

$$C_0(W) := \sup\{R : P_{e,\max}(W, R, n) = 0 \textit{ for some } n\}.$$

Remark 2. *For R with* $C_0(W) < R < C(W)$*, there exists* $A(W, R), B(W, R) \in \mathbb{R}^+$*, such that*

$$2^{-nA(W,R)+o(1)} \leq P_{e,\max}(W, R, n) \leq 2^{-nB(W,R)+o(1)}.$$

We also define the discrete memoryless channel with noiseless feedback (DMCF). By this, we mean that, in addition to the DMC, there exists a return channel that sends the element of $\mathcal{Y}$ actually received back from the receiving point to the transmitting point. It is assumed that this information is received at the transmitting point before the next letter is sent and can therefore be used to choose the next letter to be sent. We assume that this feedback is noiseless. We denote the feedback capacity of a channel W by $C^{FB}(W)$ and the zero-error feedback capacity by $C_0^{FB}(W)$. Shannon proved in [40] that $C(W) = C^{FB}(W)$.

This is, in general, not true for the zero-error capacity. We see that the zero-error (feedback) capacity is related to the reliability function, which we analyze in this paper. It is defined as follows.

Definition 9. *The channel reliability function (error exponent) is defined by*

$$E(W,R) = \limsup_{n\to\infty} -\frac{1}{n}\log_2 P_{e,\max}(W,R,n). \tag{1}$$

Remark 3. *We make use of the common convention that* $\log_2 0 := -\infty$.

Remark 4. *We need the* lim sup *in* (1), *because it is not known whether the limit value, i.e., the limts on the right-hand side of* (1), *exist.*

The first simple observation is that for $R > C(W)$, we have $E(W,R) = 0$, and if $C_0(W) > 0$ for $0 \le R < C_0(W)$, we have $E(W,R) = +\infty$. One well-known upper bound is the sphere packing bound, which can be defined as follows (see [10]).

Definition 10. *Let $\mathcal{X},\mathcal{Y}$ be finite alphabets, and $(\mathcal{X},\mathcal{Y},W)$ be a DMC. Then, for all $R \in (0,C(W))$, we define the sphere packing bound function:*

$$E_{SP}(W,R) = \sup_{\rho>0}\max_{P\in\mathcal{P}(\mathcal{X})}\left(-\log\sum_y\left(\sum_x P(x)W(y|x)^{\frac{1}{1+\rho}}\right)^{1+\rho} - \rho R\right). \tag{2}$$

Theorem 1 (Fano 1961, Shannon, Gallager, Berlekamp 1967)**.** *For any DMC W and for all $R \in (0,C(W))$, it holds that*

$$E(W,R) \le E_{SP}(W,R).$$

The sphere packing upper bound is an important upper bound. The following two lower bounds of the reliability function are also very important. In [41], the random coding bound was defined as follows:

Definition 11. *Let $\mathcal{X},\mathcal{Y}$ be finite alphabets, and $(\mathcal{X},\mathcal{Y},W)$ be a DMC. Then, for all $R \in (0,C(W))$, we define the random coding bound function as*

$$E_r(W,R) = \max_{0\le\rho\le1} E_0(W,\rho) - \rho R, \text{ where} \tag{3}$$

$$E_0(\rho) = \max_{P\in\mathcal{P}(\mathcal{X})}\left[-\log\sum_y\left(\sum_x P(x)W(y|x)^{1/(1+\rho)}\right)^{1+\rho}\right]. \tag{4}$$

Theorem 2. *Let $\mathcal{X},\mathcal{Y}$ be finite alphabets and $(\mathcal{X},\mathcal{Y},W)$ be a DMC; then,*

$$E(W,R) \ge E_r(W,R).$$

Gallager also defined in [41] the k-letter expurgation bound as follows:

Definition 12. *Let $\mathcal{X},\mathcal{Y}$ be finite alphabets and $(\mathcal{X},\mathcal{Y},W)$ be a DMC; then, for all $R \in (0,C(W))$, we define the k-letter expurgation bound function:*

$$E_{ex}(W,R,k) = \sup_{\rho \geq 1} E_x(\rho,k) - \rho R \tag{5}$$

$$E_x(\rho,k) = -\frac{\rho}{k} \log \min_{P_{X^k} \in \mathcal{P}(\mathcal{X}^k)} Q^k(\rho, P_{X^k}) \tag{6}$$

$$Q^k(\rho, P_{X^k}) = \sum_{x^k, x'^k} P_{X^k}(x^k) P_{X^k}(x'^k) g_k(x^k, x'^k)^{\frac{1}{\rho}} \tag{7}$$

$$g_k(x^k, x'^k) = \sum_{y^k} \sqrt{W^k(y^k|x^k) W^k(y^k|x'^k)}. \tag{8}$$

Theorem 3. *Let $\mathcal{X}, \mathcal{Y}$ be finite alphabets and $(\mathcal{X}, \mathcal{Y}, W)$ be a DMC. Then, for all $R \in (0, C(W))$, we have*

$$E(W,R) \geq \lim_{k \to \infty} E_{ex}(W,R,k). \tag{9}$$

The inequality in (9) follows from Fekete's lemma.

The smallest value of R, at which the convex curve $E_{SP}(W,R)$ meets its supporting line of slope -1, is called the critical rate and is denoted by R_{crit} [9]. For the certain interval $[R_{crit}, C]$, the random coding lower bound corresponds to the sphere packing upper bound. The channel reliability function is therefore known for this interval. The channel reliability function is generally not known for the interval $[0, R_{crit}]$. For the interval $[0, R_{crit}]$, there are also better lower bounds than the random coding lower bound. $R_\infty(W)$ is the infimum of all rates $\underline{R}$ such that $E_{SP}(W, \underline{R})$ is finite on the open interval $(\underline{R}, C(W))$. $C_0(W) \leq R_\infty(W)$ applies if $C_0(W) > 0$. The following representation of R_∞ exists (see [9]):

$$R_\infty(W) = \min_{Q \in \mathcal{P}(\mathcal{Y})} \max_{x \in \mathcal{X}} \log_2 \frac{1}{\sum_{y: W(y|x) > 0} Q(y)}. \tag{10}$$

There exist alphabets $\mathcal{X}, \mathcal{Y}$ and channels $W \in \mathcal{CH}$ such that $C_0(W) = 0$ while $R_\infty(W) > 0$.

Moreover, for the zero-error feedback capacity C_0^{FB}, it holds that $C_0^{FB}(W) = R_\infty(W)$ whenever $C_0(W) > 0$. However, if $C_0(W) = 0$, there exists a channel W for which $C_0^{FB}(W) = 0$ while $R_\infty(W) > 0$ (see [9]).

For the zero-error feedback capacity, the following is known.

Theorem 4 (Shannon 1956, [40]). *Let $W \in \mathcal{CH}(\mathcal{X}, \mathcal{Y})$; then,*

$$C_0^{FB}(W) = \begin{cases} 0 & \text{if } C_0(W) = 0 \\ \max_{P \in \mathcal{P}(\mathcal{X})} \min_y \log_2 \frac{1}{\sum_{x: W(y|x) > 0} P(x)} & \text{otherwise.} \end{cases} \tag{11}$$

2.3. Lower and Upper Bounds on the Reliability Function for the Typewriter Channel

As mentioned before, Shannon, Gallager, and Berlekamp assumed in [13] that the expurgation is bound tight. Katsman, Tsfasman, and Vladut showed in [42] a counterexample for the symmetric q-ary channel when $q \geq 49$. Dalai and Polyanskiy found a simpler counterexample in [43]. They showed that the conjecture is already wrong for the q-ary typewriter channel for $q \geq 4$. We would like to briefly present their results here.

Definition 13. *Let $\mathcal{X} = \mathcal{Y} = \mathbb{Z}_q$ and $0 \leq \epsilon \leq \frac{1}{2}$. The typewriter channel W_ϵ is defined by*

$$W_\epsilon(y|x) = \begin{cases} 1 - \epsilon & y = x \\ \epsilon & y = x + 1 \mod q. \end{cases} \tag{12}$$

The extension of the channel W_ϵ^n is defined by

$$W_\epsilon^n(y^n|x^n) = \prod_{k=1}^{n} W_\epsilon(y_i|x_i). \tag{13}$$

For the reliability function of this channel, the interval $(C_0(W_\epsilon), C(W_\epsilon))$ is of interest. The capacity of a typewriter channel W_ϵ has the formula

$$C(W_\epsilon) = \log(q) - h_2(\epsilon),$$

where h_2 is the binary entropy function. Shannon showed in [40] that $C_0(W_\epsilon)$ is positive if $q \geq 4$. He showed that for even q, it holds that $C_0(W_\epsilon) = \log\left(\frac{q}{2}\right)$. It is difficult to get a formula for odd q. Lovász proved in [44] that Shannon's lower bound for $q = 5$: $C_0(W_\epsilon) = \log\sqrt{5}$ is tight. For general odd q, Lovász proved

$$C_0(W_\epsilon) \leq \log \frac{\cos(\pi q)}{1 + \cos(\pi q)} q.$$

It is only known for $q = 5$ that this bound is tight. In general, this is not true. For special q, there are special results outlined in [44–47].

Dalai and Polyanskiy provide upper and lower bounds on the reliability function in [43]. They observed that the zero-error capacity of the pentagon can be determined by a careful study of the expurgated bound.

They present an improved lower bound for the case of even and odd q, showing that it also is a precisely shifted version of the expurgated bound for the BSC. Their result also provides a new elementary disproof of the conjecture suggested in [13] that the expurgated bound is asymptotically tight when computed on arbitrarily large blocks. Furthermore, in [43], Dalai and Polyanskiy present a new upper bound for the case of odd q based on the minimum distance of codes. They use Delsarte's linear programming method [48] (see also [49]), combining the construction used by Lovász [44] for bounding the graph capacity with the construction used by McEliece–Rodemich–Rumsey–Welch [50] for bounding the minimum distance of codes in Hamming spaces. In the special case $\epsilon = 1/2$, they give another improved upper bound for the case of odd q, following the ideas of Litsyn [51] and Barg–McGregor [52], which in turn are based on estimates for the spectra of codes originated by Kalai–Linial [53].

2.4. Computable Channels and Computable Performance Functions

We need further basic concepts for computability. We want to investigate the function $E(W,R)$ and the upper bounds like $E_{SP}(W,R)$ and $E_{ex}(W,R)$ for $k \in \mathbb{N}$ as functions of W and R. These functions are generally only well defined for fixed channels W on subintervals of $[0, C(W)]$ as functions depending on R. For example, for $W \in CH(\mathcal{X},\mathcal{Y})$ with $C_0(W) > 0$, $E(W,R)$ is infinite for $R < C_0(W)$. Hence, $E(W,R)$ must be examined and computed as a function of R on the interval $(C_0(W), C(W)]$. Similar statements also apply to the other functions that have already been introduced. We now fix non-trivial alphabets $\mathcal{X},\mathcal{Y}$ and the corresponding set $CH_c(\mathcal{X},\mathcal{Y})$ of the computable channels and $R \in \mathbb{R}_c$.

Definition 14 (Turing computable channel function). *We call a function $f : CH_c(\mathcal{X},\mathcal{Y}) \to \mathbb{R}_c$ a Turing computable channel function if there is a Turing machine that converts any program for the representation of $W \in CH_c(\mathcal{X},\mathcal{Y})$ into a program for the computation of $f(W)$—that is, $f(W) = TM_f(W)$, $W \in CH_c(\mathcal{X},\mathcal{Y})$.*

We want to determine whether there is a closed form for the channel reliability function. For this, we need the following definition, which we discuss in more detail in Remark 5 below.

Definition 15 (Turing computable performance function). *Let $\perp$ be a symbol. We call a function $F : \mathcal{CH}(\mathcal{X},\mathcal{Y})_c \times \mathbb{R}_c^+ \to \mathbb{R}_c \cup \{\perp\}$ a Turing computable performance function if there are two Turing computable channel functions $\underline{f}$ and $\overline{f}$ with $\underline{f}(W) \le \overline{f}(W)$ for $W \in \mathcal{CH}_c(\mathcal{X},\mathcal{Y})$, and a Turing machine TM_F, which is defined for input $R \in \mathbb{R}_c^+$ and $W \in \mathcal{CH}_c(\mathcal{X},\mathcal{Y})$. The Turing machine TM_F stops for the variables $R \in \mathbb{R}_c^+$ and $W \in \mathcal{CH}_c(\mathcal{X},\mathcal{Y})$ and any representation for W and R as input if and only if $R \in (\underline{f}(W), \overline{f}(W))$ and the Turing machine TM_F delivers $F(W,R) = TM_F(W,R)$. If $R \notin (\underline{f}(W), \overline{f}(W))$, then TM_F does not stop.*

Remark 5. *The requirement for function $F : \mathcal{CH}(\mathcal{X},\mathcal{Y})_c \times \mathbb{R}_c^+ \to \mathbb{R}_c \cup \{\perp\}$ to be a Turing computable performance function is relatively weak. For example, let us take W and R as inputs. Then, the interval $(\underline{f}(W), \overline{f}(W))$ is computed first. If R is now in the interval $((\underline{f}(W), \overline{f}(W))$, then the Turing machine TM_F must stop for the input (W,R) and deliver the result for $F(W,R)$. We impose no requirements on the behavior of the Turing machine for input W and $R \notin (\underline{f}(W), \overline{f}(W))$. In particular, the Turing machine TM_F does not have to stop for the input (W,R) in this case.*

Take, for example, any Turing computable function $G : \mathcal{CH}(\mathcal{X},\mathcal{Y})_c \times \mathbb{R}_c^+ \to \mathbb{R}_c \cup \{\perp\}$ with the corresponding Turing machine TM_G. Furthermore, let $\underline{TM} : \mathcal{CH}_c(\mathcal{X},\mathcal{Y}) \to \mathbb{R}_c$ and $\overline{TM} : \mathcal{CH}_c(\mathcal{X},\mathcal{Y}) \to \mathbb{R}_c$ be any two TMs, so that $\underline{TM}(W) \le \overline{TM}(W)$ always holds for all $W \in \mathcal{CH}_c(\mathcal{X},\mathcal{Y})$. Then, the following Turing machine $TM : \mathcal{CH}_c(\mathcal{X},\mathcal{Y}) \times \mathbb{R}_c \to \mathbb{R}_c \cup \{\perp\}$ defines a Turing computable performance function.

1. *For any input $W \in \mathcal{CH}_c(\mathcal{X},\mathcal{Y})$ and $R \in \mathbb{R}_c$, first compute $\underline{f}(W) = \underline{TM}(W)$ and $\overline{f}(W) = \overline{TM}(W)$.*
2. *Compute the following two tests in parallel:*
   - *(a) Use the Turing machine $TM_{>\underline{f}(W)}$ and test $R > \underline{f}(W)$ using $TM_{>\underline{f}(W)}$ for input $R \in \mathbb{R}_c$.*
   - *(b) Use the Turing machine $TM_{<\overline{f}(W)}$ and test $R < \overline{f}(W)$ using $TM_{<\overline{f}(W)}$ for input $R \in \mathbb{R}_c$.*

   Let these two tests run until both Turing machines stop. If both Turing machines stop in 2, then compute $G(W,R)$ and set $TM(W,R) = G(W,R)$.

TM actually generates a Turing computable performance function, and the Turing machine TM stops for the input (W,R) if and only if $R \in (\underline{f}(W), \overline{f}(W))$ applies. Then, it gives the value $G(W,R)$ as output. This follows from the fact that the Turing machine $TM_{>\underline{f}(W)}$ stops for input $R \in \mathbb{R}_c$ if and only if $R > \underline{f}(W)$. The second Turing machine $TM_{<\overline{f}(W)}$ from 2 stops exactly when $R < \overline{f}(W)$, i.e. the Turing machine TM in 2., which simulates $TM_{>\underline{f}(W)}$ and $TM_{<\overline{f}(W)}$ in parallel, stops exactly when $R \in (\underline{f}(W), \overline{f}(W))$ applies.

Remark 6. *Using the above approach, we can try, for example, to find upper and lower bounds for the channel reliability function by allowing general Turing computable functions $G : \mathcal{CH}(\mathcal{X},\mathcal{Y})_c \times \mathbb{R}_c^+ \to \mathbb{R}_c \cup \{\perp\}$ and algorithmically determine the interval from $\mathbb{R}_c^+$ for which the function $G(W,\cdot)$ delivers lower or upper bounds for the channel reliability function.*

Definition 16 (Banach–Mazur computable channel function). *We call $f : \mathcal{CH}_c(\mathcal{X},\mathcal{Y}) \to \mathbb{R}_c$ a Banach–Mazur computable channel function if every computable sequence $\{W_r\}_{r\in\mathbb{N}}$ from $\mathcal{CH}_c(\mathcal{X},\mathcal{Y})$ is mapped by f into a computable sequence from $\mathbb{R}_c$.*

For practical applications, it is necessary to have performance functions that satisfy Turing computability. Depending on W, the channel reliability function or the bounds for this function should be computed. This computation is carried out by an algorithm that also receives W as input. This means that the algorithm should also be recursively dependent on W; otherwise, a special algorithm would have to be developed for each W (depending on W but not recursively dependent), since the channel reliability function for this channel, or a bound for this function, is computed.

It is now clear that when defining the Turing computable performance function, the Turing computable channel functions $\underline{f}, \overline{f}$ cannot be dispensed with, because the channel reliability function depends on the specific channel and the permissible rate region for which the function can be computed. For $\overline{f}$, one often has the representation $\overline{f}(W) = C(W)$ with $W \in \mathcal{CH}_c(\mathcal{X}, \mathcal{Y})$. For $\underline{f}$, the choice $\underline{f}(W) = C_0(W)$ with $W \in \mathcal{CH}_c(\mathcal{X}, \mathcal{Y})$ for the channel reliability function is a natural choice, because the channel reliability function is only useful for this interval. (We note that we showed in [35] that $C_0(W)$ is not Turing computable in general.)

For the Turing computability of the channel reliability function or corresponding upper and lower bounds, it is therefore a necessary condition that the dependency of the relevant rate intervals on W be Turing computable—that is, recursive.

Remark 7. *As noted in the Introduction, very few closed-form expressions for performance functions are known in information theory. Even for relatively simple scenarios, such as secure message transmission over a wiretap channel with an active jammer, closed-form solutions are not available (see [54–56]). Existing methods in information theory provide convergent multi-letter sequences for determining capacity. While these sequences enable the investigation of important properties of the capacity (see [54,57,58]), they are not yet suitable for direct numerical computation of the capacity. This is due to the reliance on Fekete's lemma to prove the existence of the limit of these sequences. However, it was shown in [59] that Fekete's lemma is not constructive, meaning no algorithm can effectively compute the associated limit values.*

Moreover, the problem of finding simple optimizers for performance functions is generally not algorithmically solvable [60,61]. For instance, the Blahut–Arimoto algorithm can be used to compute an infinite sequence of input distributions that converge to an optimal distribution. However, there is no way to halt the process based on a reliable approximation error, making it impossible to stop the computation at a specific point (see [60,61]).

3. Results for the Rate Function R_∞ and Applications on the Sphere Packing Bound

In this section, we analyze the function R_∞ and its implications for the sphere packing bound. Specifically, we demonstrate that R_∞ is not a Turing computable performance function.

We begin by expressing $R_\infty(W)$ as

$$R_\infty(W) = \min_{Q \in \mathcal{P}(\mathcal{Y})} \max_{x \in \mathcal{X}} \log_2 \frac{1}{\sum_{y: W(y|x) > 0} Q(y)}. \tag{14}$$

From this, we derive the equivalent representations:

$$
\begin{aligned}
R_\infty(W) &= \min_{Q\in\mathcal{P}(\mathcal{Y})}\max_{x\in\mathcal{X}}\log_2\frac{1}{\sum_{y:W(y|x)>0}Q(y)}\\
&= \min_{Q\in\mathcal{P}(\mathcal{Y})}\log_2\frac{1}{\min_{x\in\mathcal{X}}\sum_{y:W(y|x)>0}Q(y)}\\
&= \log_2\min_{Q\in\mathcal{P}(\mathcal{Y})}\frac{1}{\min_{x\in\mathcal{X}}\sum_{y:W(y|x)>0}Q(y)}\\
&= \log_2\frac{1}{\max_{Q\in\mathcal{P}(\mathcal{Y})}\min_{x\in\mathcal{X}}\sum_{y:W(y|x)>0}Q(y)}\\
&= \log_2\frac{1}{\Psi_\infty(W)},
\end{aligned}
$$

where

$$\Psi_\infty(W) = \max_{Q\in\mathcal{P}(\mathcal{Y})}\min_{x\in\mathcal{X}}\sum_{y:W(y|x)>0}Q(y). \tag{15}$$

In summary, the following holds true: let $\mathcal{X},\mathcal{Y}$ be arbitrary non-trivial finite alphabets; then, for $W\in\mathcal{CH}_c(\mathcal{X},\mathcal{Y})$

$$R_\infty(W) = \log_2\frac{1}{\Psi_\infty(W)}. \tag{16}$$

Lemma 1. *It holds that*

$$R_\infty : \mathcal{CH}_c(\mathcal{X},\mathcal{Y}) \to \mathbb{R}_c.$$

Proof. Let W be fixed. We consider the vector $\begin{pmatrix}Q(1) & \cdots & Q(|\mathcal{Y}|)\end{pmatrix}^{\mathrm{T}}$ of the convex set

$$\mathcal{M}_{Prob} = \{u\in\mathbb{R}^{|\mathcal{Y}|} : u = \begin{pmatrix}u_1\\ \vdots\\ u_{|\mathcal{Y}|}\end{pmatrix}, u_l \geq 0, l = 1,\ldots,|\mathcal{Y}|, \sum_l u_l = 1\}.$$

$G(u) := \min_x \sum_{y:W(y|x)>0} u_y$ is a computable continuous function on $\mathcal{M}_{Prob}$. Thus, for $\Psi_\infty(W) = \max_{u\in\mathcal{M}_{Prob}} G(u)$, we always have $\Psi_\infty(W)\in\mathbb{R}_c$ with $\Psi_\infty(W) > 0$, and thus $R_\infty(W)\in\mathbb{R}_c$. □

Remark 8. *We do not know whether $C_0 : \mathcal{CH}_c(\mathcal{X},\mathcal{Y}) \to \mathbb{R}_c$ holds for any finite $\mathcal{X},\mathcal{Y}$. This statement holds for $\max\{|\mathcal{X}|,|\mathcal{Y}|\}\leq 5$, but the general case is open.*

For finite alphabets $\mathcal{X},\mathcal{Y}$ and $\lambda\in\mathbb{R}_c$ with $\lambda > 0$, we want to analyze the set

$$\{W\in\mathcal{CH}_c(\mathcal{X},\mathcal{Y}) : R_\infty(W) > \lambda\}.$$

To accomplish this, we refer to the proof of Theorem 23 in [35]. Along the same lines, one can show that the following holds true:

Theorem 5. *Let $\mathcal{X},\mathcal{Y}$ be non-trivial finite alphabets. For all $\lambda\in\mathbb{R}_c$ with $0 < \lambda < \log_2(\min\{|\mathcal{X}|,|\mathcal{Y}|\})$, the set*

$$\{W\in\mathcal{CH}_c(\mathcal{X},\mathcal{Y}) : R_\infty(W) > \lambda\}$$

is not semi-decidable.

The following theorem can be derived from a combination of the proof of Theorem 5 and Theorem 24 in [35]. The proof is carried out in the same way as the proof of Theorem 24 in [35].

Theorem 6. *Let $\mathcal{X},\mathcal{Y}$ be non-trivial finite alphabets. The function $R_\infty : CH_c(\mathcal{X},\mathcal{Y}) \to \mathbb{R}$ is not Banach–Mazur computable.*

We now prove a stronger result then what we were able to show for C_0 in [35] so far. We show that the analogous question, like the question in [34] for C_0 for the function R_∞, can be answered positively.

We need a concept of distance for $W_1, W_2 \in CH(\mathcal{X},\mathcal{Y})$. Therefore, for fixed and finite alphabets $\mathcal{X},\mathcal{Y}$, we define the distance between W_1 and W_2 based on the total variation distance

$$d_C(W_1,W_2) = \max_{x\in\mathcal{X}} \sum_{y\in\mathcal{Y}} |W_1(y|x) - W_2(y|x)|. \tag{17}$$

Definition 17. *A function $f : CH(\mathcal{X},\mathcal{Y}) \to \mathbb{R}$ is called computable continuously if the following are true:*

1. *f is sequentially computable, i.e., f maps every computable sequence $\{W_n\}_{n\in\mathbb{N}}$ with $W_n \in CH_c(\mathcal{X},\mathcal{Y})$ into a computable sequence $\{f(W_n)\}_{n\in\mathbb{N}}$ of computable numbers,*
2. *f is effectively uniformly continuous, i.e., there is a recursive function $d : \mathbb{N} \to \mathbb{N}$ such that for all $W_1, W_2 \in CH_c(\mathcal{X},\mathcal{Y})$ and all $N \in \mathbb{N}$ with $d_C(W_1,W_2) \le \frac{1}{d(N)}$, it holds that $|f(W_1) - f(W_2)| \le \frac{1}{2^N}$.*

Theorem 7. *Let $\mathcal{X},\mathcal{Y}$ be finite alphabets with $|\mathcal{X}| \ge 2$ and $|\mathcal{Y}| \ge 2$. There exists a computable sequence of computable continuous functions $\{F_N\}_{N\in\mathbb{N}}$ on $CH_c(\mathcal{X},\mathcal{Y})$ with*

1. *$F_N(W) \ge F_{N+1}(W)$ with $W \in CH(\mathcal{X},\mathcal{Y})$ and $N \in \mathbb{N}$,*
2. *$\lim_{N\to\infty} F_N(W) = R_\infty(W)$ for all $W \in CH(\mathcal{X},\mathcal{Y})$.*

Proof. We consider the function

$$\Phi_N(W) = \max_{Q\in\mathcal{P}(\mathcal{Y})} \min_{x\in\mathcal{X}} \sum_{y\in\mathcal{Y}} \frac{NW(y|x)}{1+NW(y|x)} Q(y)$$

for $N \in \mathbb{N}$. For all $x \in \mathcal{X}$ we have for all $Q \in \mathcal{P}(\mathcal{Y})$

$$\sum_{y\in\mathcal{Y}} \frac{NW(y|x)}{1+NW(y|x)} Q(y) \le \sum_{y\in\mathcal{Y}:W(y|x)>0} Q(y), \tag{18}$$

and for all $N \in \mathbb{N}$, we have for all $x \in \mathcal{X}$ and $Q \in \mathcal{P}(\mathcal{Y})$

$$\sum_{y\in\mathcal{Y}} \frac{NW(y|x)}{1+NW(y<x)} Q(y) \le \sum_{y\in\mathcal{Y}:W(y|x)>0} \frac{(N+1)W(y|x)}{1+(N+1)W(y|x)} Q(y). \tag{19}$$

Φ_N is a computable continuous function, and $\{\Phi_N\}_{N\in\mathbb{N}}$ is a computable sequence of computable continuous functions. So,

$$F_N(W) = \log_2 \frac{a}{\Phi_N(W)},$$

for $N \in \mathbb{N}$ and $W \in CH(\mathcal{X},\mathcal{Y})$. F_N satisfies all properties of the theorem, and point 1 is shown.

It holds

$$\begin{aligned} & \left| \sum_{y\in\mathcal{Y}:W(y|x)>0} Q(y) - \sum_{y\in\mathcal{Y}} \frac{NW(y|x)}{1+NW(y|x)} Q(y) \right| \\ = & \left| \sum_{y\in\mathcal{Y}:W(y|x)>0} \frac{1}{1+NW(y|x)} Q(y) \right| \\ \leq & \frac{1}{1+N\min_{y\in\mathcal{Y}:W(y|x)>0} W(y|x)}. \end{aligned}$$

Therefore , we have

$$\begin{aligned} \sum_{y\in\mathcal{Y}:W(y|x)>0} Q(y) \leq & \frac{1}{1+N\min_{y\in\mathcal{Y}:W(y|x)>0} W(y|x)} \\ & + \sum_{y\in\mathcal{Y}} \frac{NW(y|x)}{1+NW(y|x)} Q(y). \end{aligned} \tag{20}$$

Because of (18), we have

$$\Phi_N(W) \leq \Psi_\infty(W)$$

for all $W \in \mathcal{C}H_c(\mathcal{X},\mathcal{Y})$. (20) yields

$$\begin{aligned} \sum_{y\in\mathcal{Y}:W(y|x)>0} Q(y) \leq & \frac{1}{1+N\min_{x\in\mathcal{X}}\left(\min_{y\in\mathcal{Y}:W(y|x)>0} W(y|x)\right)} \\ & + \sum_{y\in\mathcal{Y}} \frac{NW(y|x)}{1+NW(y|x)} Q(y). \end{aligned}$$

So,

$$\begin{aligned} \min_{x\in\mathcal{X}} \sum_{y\in\mathcal{Y}:W(y|x)>0} Q(y) \leq & \frac{1}{1+N\min_{x\in\mathcal{X}}\left(\min_{y\in\mathcal{Y}:W(y|x)>0} W(y|x)\right)} \\ & + \min_{x\in\mathcal{X}} \sum_{y\in\mathcal{Y}} \frac{NW(y|x)}{1+NW(y|x)} Q(y) \end{aligned}$$

and

$$\Psi_\infty(W) \leq \frac{1}{1+N\min_{x\in\mathcal{X}}\left(\min_{y\in\mathcal{Y}:W(y|x)>0} W(y|x)\right)} + \Phi_N(W)$$

holds. So, we have

$$0 \leq \Psi_\infty(W) - \Phi_N(W) \leq \frac{1}{1+N\min_{x\in\mathcal{X}}\left(\min_{y\in\mathcal{Y}:W(y|x)>0} W(y|x)\right)}.$$

□

We now want to prove that the corresponding question in [34] can be answered positively for R_∞.

Theorem 8. *Let $\mathcal{X},\mathcal{Y}$ be finite alphabets with $|\mathcal{X}| \geq 2$ and $|\mathcal{Y}| \geq 2$. For all $\lambda \in \mathbb{R}_c$ with $0 < \lambda < \log_2(\min\{|\mathcal{X}|,|\mathcal{Y}|\})$, the set*

$$\{W \in \mathcal{C}H_c(\mathcal{X},\mathcal{Y}) : R_\infty(W) < \lambda\}$$

is semi-decidable.

Proof. We use the computable sequences of computable continuous functions F_N from Theorem 7. It holds that

$$W \in \{W \in \mathcal{CH}_c(\mathcal{X},\mathcal{Y}) : R_\infty(W) < \lambda\}$$

if and only if there is an N_0 such that $F_{N_0} < \lambda$ holds. As in the proof of Theorem 28 from [35], we now use the construction of a Turing machine $TM_{R_\infty,<\lambda}$, which exactly accepts the set

$$\{W \in \mathcal{CH}_c(\mathcal{X},\mathcal{Y}) : R_\infty(W) < \lambda\}.$$

□

We now consider the approximability "from below" (this can be seen as a kind of reachability). We have shown that $R_\infty(\cdot)$ can always be represented as a limit value of monotonically decreasing computable sequences of computable continuous functions. From this, it can be concluded that the sequence is then also a computable sequence of Banach–Mazur computable functions. We now have the following:

Theorem 9. *Let $\mathcal{X},\mathcal{Y}$ be finite alphabets with $|\mathcal{X}| \geq 2$ and $|\mathcal{Y}| \geq 2$. There does not exist a sequence of Banach–Mazur computable functions $\{F_N\}_{N\in\mathbb{N}}$ with*

1. *$F_N(W) \leq F_{N+1}(W)$ with $W \in \mathcal{CH}_c(\mathcal{X},\mathcal{Y})$ and $N \in \mathbb{N}$;*
2. *$\lim_{N\to\infty} F_N(W) = R_\infty(W)$ for all $W \in \mathcal{CH}(\mathcal{X},\mathcal{Y})$.*

Proof. We assume that such a sequence $\{F_N\}_{N\in\mathbb{N}}$ does exist. Then, from Theorem 7 and the assumptions from this theorem, it can be concluded that R_∞ is a Banach–Mazur computable function. This has created a contradiction. □

With this, we immediately get the following:

Corollary 1. *Consider finite alphabets $\mathcal{X},\mathcal{Y}$ with $|\mathcal{X}| \geq 2, |\mathcal{Y}| \geq 2$, and let $\{F_N\}_{N\in\mathbb{N}}$ be a sequence of Banach–Mazur computable functions that satisfies the following:*

1. *$F_N(W) \leq F_{N+1}(W)$ with $W \in \mathcal{CH}_c(\mathcal{X},\mathcal{Y})$ and $N \in \mathbb{N}$,*
2. *$\lim_{N\to\infty} F_N(W) = R_\infty(W)$ for all $W \in \mathcal{CH}(\mathcal{X},\mathcal{Y})$.*

Then, there exists $\hat{W} \in \mathcal{CH}_c(\mathcal{X},\mathcal{Y})$ such that $\lim_{N\to\infty} F_N(\hat{W}) < R_\infty(\hat{W})$ holds true.

We now want to apply the results for R_∞ to the sphere packing bound as an application. With the results via the rate function, we immediately get

Theorem 10. *Let $\mathcal{X},\mathcal{Y}$ be finite alphabets with $|\mathcal{X}| \geq 2$ and $|\mathcal{Y}| \geq 2$. The sphere packing bound $E_{SP}(\cdot,\cdot)$ is not a Turing computable performance function for $\mathcal{CH}_c(\mathcal{X},\mathcal{Y}) \times \mathbb{R}_c^+$.*

Proof. Assuming that the statement of the theorem is incorrect, then R_∞ is a Turing computable performance function on $\mathcal{CH}_c(\mathcal{X},\mathcal{Y}) \times \mathbb{R}_c^+$. But then the channel functions $\underline{f}(W) = R_\infty(W)$ for $W \in \mathcal{CH}_c(\mathcal{X},\mathcal{Y})$ and $\overline{f}(W) = C(W)$ for $W \in \mathcal{CH}_c(\mathcal{X},\mathcal{Y})$ must be Turing computable channel functions. As was already shown, however, R_∞ is not Banach–Mazur computable. We have thus created a contradiction. □

4. Computability of the Channel Reliability Function and the Sequence of Expurgation Bound Functions

In this section, we consider the reliability function and the expurgation bound and show that these functions are not Turing computable performance functions.

With the help of the results from [35] for C_0 for noisy channels, we immediately get the following theorem:

Theorem 11. *Let $\mathcal{X},\mathcal{Y}$ be finite alphabets with $|\mathcal{X}| \geq 2$ and $|\mathcal{Y}| \geq 2$. The channel reliability function $E(\cdot,\cdot)$ is not a Turing computable performance function for $\mathcal{CH}_c(\mathcal{X},\mathcal{Y}) \times \mathbb{R}_c$.*

Proof. Here, $\underline{f}(W) = C_0(W)$ for $W \in \mathcal{CH}_c(\mathcal{X},\mathcal{Y})$ is a Turing computable function, according to Definition 14. We already know that C_0 is not Banach–Mazur computable on $\mathcal{CH}_c(\mathcal{X},\mathcal{Y})$. This gives the proof in the same way as for the sphere packing bound, i.e., the proof of Theorem 10. □

Now, we consider the rate function for the expurgation bound. The k-letter expurgation bound $E_{ex}(W,R,k)$ as a function of W and R is a lower bound for the channel reliability function. The latter can only be finite for certain intervals $(R_k^{ex}(W), C(W))$. Thus, we want to compute the function in these intervals. In their famous paper [13], Shannon, Gallager, and Berlekamp examined the sequence of functions $\{E_{ex}(\cdot,\cdot,k)\}_{k\in\mathbb{N}}$ and analyzed the relationship to the channel reliability function. They conjectured that for all $W \in \mathcal{CH}(\mathcal{X},\mathcal{Y})$ for all R with $E(W,R) < +\infty$ (one would have convergence and also $E_{ex}(W,R,k) < +\infty$), the relation

$$\lim_{k\to\infty} E_{ex}(W,R,k) = E(W,R)$$

holds. This conjecture was first refuted in [42] and later refuted by a simpler example in [43].

It was already clear with the introduction of the channel reliability function that it had a complicated behavior. A closed-form formula for the channel reliability function is not yet known, and the results of this paper show that such a formula cannot exist. Shannon, Gallager, and Berlekamp tried in [13] in 1967 to find sequences of seemingly simple formulas for the approximation of the channel reliability function. It seems that they considered the sequence of the k-letter expurgation bounds to be very good channel data for its approximation. It was hoped that these sequences could be computed more easily with the use of new powerful digital computers.

Let us now examine the sequence $\{E_{ex}(\cdot,\cdot,k)\}_{k\in\mathbb{N}}$. We have already introduced the concept of computable sequences of computable continuous channel functions. We now introduce the concept of computable sequences of Turing computable performance functions.

Definition 18. *A sequence $\{F_k\}_{k\in\mathbb{N}}$ of Turing computable performance functions is called a computable sequence if there is a Turing machine that generates the description of F_k for input k according to the definition of the function F_k for the values for which the function is defined.*

In the following theorem, we prove that the sequence of the k-letter expurgation bounds is not a computable sequence of computable performance functions. So, the hope mentioned above cannot be fulfilled.

Theorem 12. *Let $\mathcal{X},\mathcal{Y}$ be finite alphabets with $|\mathcal{X}| \geq 2$ and $|\mathcal{Y}| \geq 2$. The sequence of the expurgation lower bounds $\{E_{ex}(\cdot,\cdot,k)\}_{k\in\mathbb{N}}$ is not a computable sequence of Turing computable performance functions.*

Proof. We prove the theorem by contradiction, assuming that there exists a Turing machine TM_* that generates a description of the function $E_{ex}(\cdot,\cdot,k)$ for a given input k, as defined in its formulation. This implies that the sequence $\{R_k^{ex}\}_{k\in\mathbb{N}}$ is computable, since we have an algorithm that can generate each function in the sequence.

Notably, we can express $\underline{f}_k(\cdot)$ as $R_k^{ex}(\cdot)$. Given an input k, the Turing machine TM_* produces the description of $E_{ex}(\cdot,\cdot,k)$, from which R_k^{ex} can be directly obtained via projection (in the sense of primitive recursive functions).

According to Shannon, Gallager, and Berlekamp [13], the following limit holds:

$$\lim_{k\to\infty} R_k^{ex}(W) = C_0(W)$$

for all $W \in \mathcal{CH}(\mathcal{X},\mathcal{Y})$. Furthermore, the sequence $\{R_k^{ex}(W)\}_{k\in\mathbb{N}}$ is monotonically increasing, i.e.,

$$R_k^{ex}(W) \le R_{k+1}^{ex}(W) \quad \text{for all } k \in \mathbb{N} \text{ and } W \in \mathcal{CH}(\mathcal{X},\mathcal{Y}).$$

Let us consider the set

$$\{W \in \mathcal{CH}_c(\mathcal{X},\mathcal{Y}) : C_0(W) > \lambda\}$$

for $\lambda \in \mathbb{R}_c$ with $0 < \lambda < \log_2(\min\{|\mathcal{X}|,|\mathcal{Y}|\})$. We are now constructing a Turing machine TM_* with only one holding state, "stop", which means that it either stops or computes forever. TM_* should stop for input $W \in \mathcal{CH}_c(\mathcal{X},\mathcal{Y})$ if and only if $C_0(W)$ applies, that is, TM_* stops if W is in the above set. According to the assumption, $\{R_k^{ex}(\cdot)\}_{k\in\mathbb{N}}$ is a computable sequence of Turing computable channel functions. For the input W, we can generate the computable sequence $\{R_k^{ex}(W)\}_{k\in\mathbb{N}}$ of computable numbers. We now use the Turing machine TM_λ^1, which receives an arbitrary computable number x as input and stops if and only if $x > \lambda$, i.e., TM_λ^1 has only one hold state and accepts exactly the computable numbers x as input for which $x > \lambda$ holds. We now use this program for the following algorithm.

1. We start with $l = 1$ and let TM_λ^1 compute one step for input $R_1^{ex}(W)$. If $TM_\lambda^1(R_1^{ex}(W))$ stops; then, we stop the algorithm.
2. If $TM_\lambda^1(R_1^{ex}(W))$ does not stop, we set $l = l+1$ and compute $l+1$ steps $TM_\lambda^1(R_r^{ex}(W))$ for $1 \le r \le l+1$. If one of these Turing machines stops, then the algorithm stops; if not, we set $l = l+1$ and repeat the second computation.

The above algorithm stops if and only if there is a $\hat{k} \in \mathbb{N}$ such that $R_{ex}^{\hat{k}}(W) > \lambda$. But this is the case (because of the monotony of the sequence $\{R_k^{ex}(W)\}_{k\in\mathbb{N}}$) if and only if $C_0(W) > \lambda$. But with this, the set

$$\{W \in \mathcal{CH}_c(\mathcal{X},\mathcal{Y}) : C_0(W) > \lambda\}$$

is semi-decidable. So, we have shown that this is not the case. We have thus created a contradiction. □

5. Computability of the Zero-Error Capacity of Noisy Channels with Feedback

In this section, we consider the zero-error capacity for noisy channels with feedback. In our paper [35], we examined the properties of the zero-error capacity without feedback. Let $W \in \mathcal{CH}(\mathcal{X},\mathcal{Y})$. We already noted that Shannon showed in [40] that

$$C_0^{FB} = \begin{cases} 0 & \text{if } C_0(W) = 0 \\ \max_P \min_y \log_2 \frac{1}{\sum_{x:W(y|x)>0} P(x)} & \textit{otherwise.} \end{cases} \tag{21}$$

From (15), recall that

$$\Psi_\infty(W) = \max_{p\in\mathcal{P}(\mathcal{X})} \min_{y\in\mathcal{Y}} \sum_{x:W(y|x)>0} P(x). \tag{22}$$

Then, we have for W with $C_0(W) \neq 0$,

$$C_0^{FB} = \log_2 \frac{1}{\Psi_\infty(W)}.$$

We know that $C_0^{FB}(W) = R_\infty(W)$ if $C_0(W) > 0$. If $C_0(W) = 0$, then there is a channel W with $C_0^{FB}(W) = 0$ and $R_\infty > 0$. Like in Lemma 1, we can show the following:

Lemma 2. *Let $\mathcal{X}, \mathcal{Y}$ be finite non-trivial alphabets. It holds that*

$$C_0^{FB} : \mathcal{CH}_c(\mathcal{X}, \mathcal{Y}) \to \mathbb{R}_c.$$

From Theorem 5 and the relationship between C_0 and C_0^{FB}, we get the following results for C_0^{FB}, which we have already proved for C_0 in [35].

Theorem 13. *Let $\mathcal{X}, \mathcal{Y}$ be finite alphabets with $|\mathcal{X}| \geq 2$ and $|\mathcal{Y}| \geq 2$. For all $\lambda \in \mathbb{R}_c$ with $0 \leq \lambda < \log_2 \min\{|\mathcal{X}|, |\mathcal{Y}|\}$, the sets $\{W \in \mathcal{CH}_c(\mathcal{X}, \mathcal{Y}) : C_0^{FB}(W) > \lambda\}$ are not semi-decidable.*

Theorem 14. *Let $\mathcal{X}, \mathcal{Y}$ be finite alphabets with $|\mathcal{X}| \geq 2$ and $|\mathcal{Y}| \geq 2$. Then, $C_0^{FB} : \mathcal{CH}_c(\mathcal{X}, \mathcal{Y}) \to \mathbb{R}$ is not Banach-Mazur computable.*

Now, we will prove the following:

Theorem 15. *Let $\mathcal{X}, \mathcal{Y}$ be finite alphabets with $|\mathcal{X}| \geq 2$ and $|\mathcal{Y}| \geq 2$. There is a computable sequence of computable continuous functions G with*

1. *$G_N(W) \geq G_{N+1}(W)$ for $W \in \mathcal{CH}(\mathcal{X}, \mathcal{Y})$ and $N \in \mathbb{N}$;*
2. *$\lim_{n\to\infty} G_N(W) = C_0^{FB}(W)$ for $W \in \mathcal{CH}(\mathcal{X}, \mathcal{Y})$.*

Proof. We use for $N \in \mathbb{N}$, $y \in \mathcal{Y}$ and $P \in \mathcal{P}(\mathcal{X})$ the function

$$\sum_{x\in\mathcal{X}} \frac{NW(y|x)}{1 + NW(y|x)} P(x).$$

Then, for

$$\Phi_N(W) = \min_{P\in\mathcal{P}(\mathcal{X})} \max_{y\in\mathcal{Y}} \sum_{x\in\mathcal{X}:W(y|x)>0} P(x),$$

we have the same properties as in Theorem 7 and

$$U_N(W) = \log_2 \frac{1}{\Phi_n(W)}$$

is an upper bound for C_0^{FB}, which is monotonically decreasing. Now, the relation $C_0^{FB}(W) > 0$ holds for $W \in \mathcal{CH}(\mathcal{X}, \mathcal{Y})$ if and only if there are two $x_1, x_2 \in \mathcal{X}$ so that

$$\sum_{y\in\mathcal{Y}} W(y|x_1)W(y|x_2) = 0$$

holds. We now set $g(\hat{x}, x) = \sum_{y\in\mathcal{Y}} W(y|\hat{x})W(y|x) = g(W, \hat{x}, x)$ and have $0 \leq g(\hat{x}, x) \leq 1$ for $x, \hat{x} \in \mathcal{X}$. g is a computable continuous function with respect to $W \in \mathcal{CH}(\mathcal{X}, \mathcal{Y})$. Now, we set

$$V_N(W) = \left(1 - \prod_{x,\hat{x}} g(W, \hat{x}, x)^N\right) U_N(W)$$

for $N \in \mathbb{N}$. $\{V_N\}_{N\in\mathbb{N}}$ is thus a computable sequence of computable continuous functions. Obviously, $V_N(W) \geq V_{N+1}(W)$ for $W \in \mathcal{CH}(\mathcal{X},\mathcal{Y})$ and $N \in \mathbb{N}$ is satisfied.

$$(1 - \prod_{x,\hat{x}} g(W,x,hx))^N = 1$$

if and only if $C_0^{FB} > 0$. So, for $C_0^{FB}(W) = 0$, we always have

$$\lim_{N\to\infty} V_N(W) = 0.$$

For W with $C_0^{FB}(W)$,

$$\lim_{N\to\infty} V_N(W) = \lim_{N\to\infty} U_N(W) = C_0^{FB}(W).$$

This is shown in the proof of Theorem 7. □

This immediately gives us the following theorem.

Theorem 16. *Let $\mathcal{X},\mathcal{Y}$ be finite alphabets with $|\mathcal{X}| \geq 2$ and $|\mathcal{Y}| \geq 2$. For all $\lambda \in \mathbb{R}_c$ with $0 \leq \lambda < \log_2 \min\{|\mathcal{X}|,|\mathcal{Y}|\}$, the sets $\{W \in \mathcal{CH}_c(\mathcal{X},\mathcal{Y}) : C_0^{FB}(W) < \lambda\}$ are semi-decidable.*

Now, we want to look at the consequences of the results above for C_0^{FB}. The same statements apply here as in section 3 for R_∞ with regard to the approximation from below. C_0^{FB} cannot be approximated by monotonically increasing sequences.

There is an elementary relationship between R_∞ and C_0^{FB}, which we use in the following. Again, we assume that $\mathcal{X},\mathcal{Y}$ are finite non-trivial alphabets. We remember the following functions:

$$R_\infty(W) = \log_2 \frac{1}{\Psi_\infty(W)}, \tag{23}$$

where $\Psi_\infty(W) = \max_{Q\in\mathcal{P}(\mathcal{Y})} \min_{x\in\mathcal{X}} \sum_{y:W(y|x)>0} Q(y)$.

$$C_0^{FB} = \begin{cases} 0 & C_0(W) = 0 \\ G(W) & C_0(W) > 0 \end{cases}, \tag{24}$$

where $G(W) = \log_2 \frac{1}{\Psi_\infty(W)}$ and

$$\Psi_\infty(W) = \min_{p\in\mathcal{P}(\mathcal{X})} \min_{y\in\mathcal{Y}} \sum_{x:W(y|x)>0} P(x). \tag{25}$$

Let $A(W)$ be the $|\mathcal{Y}| \times |\mathcal{X}|$ matrix with $(A(W))_{kl} \in \{0,1\}$ for $1 \leq k \leq |\mathcal{Y}|$ and $1 \leq l \leq |\mathcal{X}|$, such that $(A(W))_{kl} = 1$ if and only if $W(k(l)) > 0$. Furthermore, let

$$\mathcal{M}_\mathcal{X} = \left\{ u \in \mathbb{R}^{|\mathcal{X}|} : u = \begin{pmatrix} u_1 \\ \dots \\ u_{|\mathcal{X}|} \end{pmatrix}, u_l \geq 0, \sum_{l=1}^{|\mathcal{X}|} u_l = 1 \right\} \tag{26}$$

and

$$\mathcal{M}_\mathcal{Y} = \left\{ v \in \mathbb{R}^{|\mathcal{Y}|} : v = \begin{pmatrix} v_1 \\ \dots \\ v_{|\mathcal{Y}|} \end{pmatrix}, v_l \geq 0, \sum_{l=1}^{|\mathcal{Y}|} v_l = 1 \right\}. \tag{27}$$

For $v \in \mathbb{R}^{|\mathcal{Y}|}$ and $u \in \mathbb{R}^{|\mathcal{X}|}$, we consider the function $F(v,u) = v^T A(W) u$. The function F is concave in $v \in \mathcal{M}_{\mathcal{Y}}$ and convex in $u \in \mathcal{M}_{\mathcal{X}}$. $\mathcal{M}_{\mathcal{Y}}$ and $\mathcal{M}_{\mathcal{X}}$ are closed convex and compact sets, and $F(v,u)$ is continuous in both variables. So,

$$\max_{v\in\mathcal{M}_{\mathcal{Y}}} \min_{u\in\mathcal{M}_{\mathcal{X}}} F(v,u) = \min_{u\in\mathcal{M}_{\mathcal{X}}} \max_{v\in\mathcal{M}_{\mathcal{Y}}} F(v,u). \tag{28}$$

Let $v \in \mathcal{M}_{\mathcal{Y}}$ be fixed. Then,

$$F(v,u) = \left(\sum_{l=1}^{|\mathcal{X}|} \left(\sum_{k=1}^{|\mathcal{Y}|} v_k A_{kl}(W) \right) u_l \right) \tag{29}$$

$$F(v,u) = \left(\sum_{l=1}^{|\mathcal{X}|} d_l(v) u_l \right), \tag{30}$$

with $d_l(v) = \sum_{k=1}^{|\mathcal{Y}|} v_k A_{kl}(W)$. Now, $d_l(v) \geq 0$ for $1 \leq l \leq |\mathcal{X}|$. Hence,

$$\min_{u\in\mathcal{M}_{\mathcal{X}}} F(v,u) = \min_{1\leq l\leq|\mathcal{X}|} d_l(v) = \min_{1\leq l\leq|\mathcal{X}|} \sum_{k:A_k l(W)>0} v_k = \min_{x\in\mathcal{X}} \sum_{y:W(y|x)>0} Q_v(y),$$

with $Q_v(y) = v_y$ for $y \in \{1,\ldots,|\mathcal{Y}|\}$. So,

$$\max_{v\in\mathcal{M}_{\mathcal{Y}}} \min_{u\in\mathcal{M}_{\mathcal{X}}} F(v,u) = \max_{Q\in\mathcal{P}(\mathcal{Y})} \min_{x\in\mathcal{X}} \sum_{y:W(y|x)>0} Q_v(y) = \Psi_\infty(W).$$

Furthermore, for $u \in \mathcal{M}_{\mathcal{X}}$ fixed,

$$\begin{aligned} F(v,u) &= \left(\sum_{k=1}^{|\mathcal{Y}|} \left(\sum_{l=1}^{|\mathcal{X}|} u_l A_{kl}(W) \right) v_k \right) \\ &= \left(\sum_{k=1}^{|\mathcal{Y}|} \beta_k(u) v_k \right), \end{aligned}$$

with $\beta_k(u) = \sum_{l=1}^{|\mathcal{X}|} u_l A_{kl}(W) \geq 0$ and $1 \leq k \leq |\mathcal{Y}|$. Therefore,

$$\max_{v\in\mathcal{M}_{\mathcal{Y}}} F(v,u) = \max_{1\leq k\leq|\mathcal{Y}|} \beta_k(u) = \max_{1\leq k\leq|\mathcal{Y}|} \sum_{l:A_{kl}(W)>0} u_l = \max_{y\in\mathcal{Y}} \sum_{x:W(Y|x)>0} p_u(x)$$

with $p_u(x) = u_x$ for $1 \leq x \leq |\mathcal{X}|$. It follows that

$$\min_{u\in\mathcal{M}_{\mathcal{X}}} \max_{v\in\mathcal{M}_{\mathcal{Y}}} F(v,u) = \min_{p\in\mathcal{P}(\mathcal{X})} \max_{y\in\mathcal{Y}} \sum_{x:W(y|x)>0} P(x) = \Psi_\infty(W).$$

We get the following lemma.

Lemma 3. *Let $W \in \mathcal{CH}(\mathcal{X},\mathcal{Y})$; then,*

$$R_\infty(W) = G(W).$$

We want to investigate the behavior of $E(\cdot,R)$ for the input $W_1 \otimes W_2$, where $W_1 \otimes W_2$ denotes the Kronecker product of the matrices W_1 and W_2 compared to $E(W_1,R)$ and $E(W_2,R)$. For this purpose, let $\mathcal{X}_1, \mathcal{Y}_1, \mathcal{X}_2, \mathcal{Y}_2$ be arbitrary finite non-trivial alphabets, and we consider $W_l \in \mathcal{CH}(\mathcal{X}_l,\mathcal{Y}_l)$ for $l = 1,2$.

Theorem 17. *Let $\mathcal{X}_1, \mathcal{Y}_1, \mathcal{X}_2, \mathcal{Y}_2$ be arbitrary finite non-trivial alphabets, and $W_l \in CH(\mathcal{X}_l, \mathcal{Y}_l)$ for $l = 1, 2$. Then, we have*

$$R_\infty(W_1 \otimes W_2) = R_\infty(W_1) + R_\infty(W_2).$$

Proof. We use the Ψ_∞ function. It applies to $Q = Q_1 \cdot Q_2$ with $Q_1 \in \mathcal{P}(\mathcal{Y}_1)$ and $Q_2 \in \mathcal{P}(Y_2)$, so that

$$\begin{aligned} &\min_{x_1 \in \mathcal{X}_1, x_2 \in \mathcal{X}_2} \sum_{y_1 : W_1(y_1|x_1) > 0} \sum_{y_2 : W_2(y_2|x_2)} Q_1(y_1) Q_2(y_2) \\ = &\left(\min_{x_1 \in \mathcal{X}_1} \sum_{y_1 : W_1(y_1|x_1) > 0} Q_1(y_1) \right) \left(\min_{x_1 \in \mathcal{X}_1} \sum_{y_2 : W_2(y_2|x_2) > 0} Q_2(y_2) \right). \end{aligned}$$

This applies to all $Q_1 \in \mathcal{P}(\mathcal{Y}_1)$ and $Q_2 \in \mathcal{P}(\mathcal{Y}_2)$ arbitrarily. So,

$$\Psi_\infty(W_1 \otimes W_2) \geq \Psi_\infty(W_1) \cdot \Psi_\infty(W_2).$$

Also, we have

$$\begin{aligned} &\Psi_\infty(W_1 \otimes W_2) \\ = &\min_{P \in \mathcal{P}(\mathcal{X}_1 \times \mathcal{X}_2)} \max_{(y_1, y_2) \in \mathcal{Y}_1 \times \mathcal{Y}_2} \sum_{x_1 : W_1(y_1|x_1) > 0} \sum_{x_2 : W_2(y_2|x_2) > 0} P(x_1, y_2) \\ \leq &\Psi_\infty(W_1) \cdot \Psi_\infty(W_2) \end{aligned}$$

as well. So,

$$\Psi_\infty(W_1 \otimes W_2) = \Psi_\infty(W_1) \cdot \Psi_\infty(W_2)$$

and the theorem is proven. □

We want to investigate the behavior of C_0^{FB} for the input $W_1 \otimes W_2$ compared to $C_0^{FB}(W_1)$ and $C_0^{FB}(W_2)$. For this purpose, let $\mathcal{X}_1, \mathcal{Y}_1, \mathcal{X}_2, \mathcal{Y}_2$ be arbitrary finite non-trivial alphabets and consider $W_l \in CH(\mathcal{X}_l, \mathcal{Y}_l)$ for $l = 1, 2$.

Theorem 18. *Let $\mathcal{X}_1, \mathcal{Y}_1, \mathcal{X}_2, \mathcal{Y}_2$ be arbitrary finite non-trivial alphabets, and $W_l \in CH(\mathcal{X}_l, \mathcal{Y}_l)$ for $l = 1, 2$. Then, we have*

1. $$C_0^{FB}(W_1 \otimes W_2) \geq C_0^{FB}(W_1) + C_0^{FB}(W_2) \tag{31}$$

2. $$C_0^{FB}(W_1 \otimes W_2) > C_0^{FB}(W_1) + C_0^{FB}(W_2) \tag{32}$$

   if and only if

   $$\min_{1 \leq l \leq 2} C_0^{FB}(W_l) = 0 \textit{ and } \max_{1 \leq l \leq 2} C_0^{FB}(W_l) > 0 \textit{ and } \min_{1 \leq l \leq 2} R_\infty(W_l) > 0. \tag{33}$$

Remark 9. *The condition* (33) *is equivalent to*

$$\min_{1 \leq l \leq 2} C_0(W_l) = 0 \textit{ and } \max_{1 \leq l \leq 2} C_0(W_l) > 0 \textit{ and } \min_{1 \leq l \leq 2} R_\infty(W_l) > 0. \tag{34}$$

Proof. (31) follows directly from the operational definition of C. Let (33) now be fulfilled. Then, $C_0^{FB}(W_1 \otimes W_2) > 0$ must be fulfilled. Without loss of generality, we assume $C_0^{FB}(W_1) = 0$, $C_0^{FB}(W_2) > 0$ and $R_\infty(W_1) > 0$, $R_\infty(W_2) > 0$. Since $C_0^{FB}(W_1 \otimes W_2) > 0$,

$$\begin{aligned} C_0^{FB}(W_1 \otimes W_2) &= R_\infty(W_1 \otimes W_2) \\ &= R_\infty(W_1) + R_\infty(W_2) \\ &= R_\infty(W_1) + C_0^{FB}(W_2) \\ &> 0 + C_0^{FB}(W_2) \\ &= C_0^{FB}(W_1) + C_0^{FB}(W_2). \end{aligned}$$

If (32) is fulfilled, then $C_0^{FB}(W_1 \otimes W_2) > 0$. Then, $\max_{1 \le l \le 2} C_0^{FB}(W_l) > 0$ must be, because if $\max_{1 \le l \le 2} C_0^{FB}(W_l) = 0$, then $\max_{1 \le l \le 2} C_0(W_l) = 0$, and thus $C_0(W_1 \otimes W_2) = 0$ also (since the C_0 capacity has no super-activation). This means that $C_0^{FB}(W_1 \otimes W_2) = 0$, which would be a contradiction.

If $\min_{1 \le 2} C_0^{FB}(W_l) > 0$, then

$$\begin{aligned} C_0^{FB}(W_1 \otimes W_2) &= R_\infty(W_1 \otimes W_2) \\ &= R_\infty(W_1) + R_\infty(W_2) \\ &= C_0^{FB}(W_1) + C_0^{FB}(W_2). \end{aligned}$$

This is a contradiction, and thus $\min_{1 \le 2} C_0^{FB}(W_l) = 0$. Furthermore, $\min_{1 \le l \le 2} R_\infty(W_l) > 0$ must apply, because if $\min_{1 \le l \le 2} R_\infty(W_l) = 0$, then $R_\infty(W_1) = 0$ without loss of generality. Then,

$$\begin{aligned} C_0^{FB}(W_1 \otimes W_2) &= R_\infty(W_1 \otimes W_2) \\ &= R_\infty(W_1) + R_\infty(W_2) \\ &= 0 + R_\infty(W_2) \\ &= 0 + C_0^{FB}(W_2) \\ &= C_0^{FB}(W_1) + C_0^{FB}(W_2), \end{aligned}$$

because $C_0^{FB}(W_1) = 0$ when $R_\infty(W_1) = 0$. This is again a contradiction. With this, we have proven the theorem. □

We still want to show for which alphabet sizes the behavior according to Theorem 18 can occur.

Theorem 19. *1. If $|\mathcal{X}_1| = |\mathcal{X}_2| = |Y_1| = |Y_2| = 2$, then for all $W_l \in \mathcal{CH}(\mathcal{X}_l, \mathcal{Y}_l)$ with $l = 1, 2$, we have*

$$C_0^{FB}(W_1 \otimes W_2) = C_0^{FB}(W_1) + C_0^{FB}(W_2). \tag{35}$$

2. *If $\mathcal{X}_1, X_2, \mathcal{Y}_1, \mathcal{Y}_2$ are non-trivial alphabets with*

$$\max\{\min\{|\mathcal{X}_1|, |\mathcal{Y}_1|\}, \min\{|X_2|, |\mathcal{Y}_2|\}\} \ge 3,$$

then there exists $\hat{W}_l \in \mathcal{CH}(\mathcal{X}_l, \mathcal{Y}_l)$ with $l = 1, 2$, such that

$$C_0^{FB}(\hat{W}_1 \otimes \hat{W}_2) > C_0^{FB}(\hat{W}_1) + C_0^{FB}(\hat{W}_2). \tag{36}$$

Proof. 1. If $C_0(W_1) = C_0(W_2)$, then (35) holds, since $C_0(W_1 \otimes W_2) = 0$.

If $\max\{C_0(W_1), C_0(W_2)\} > 0$, we can assume without loss of generality that $C_0(W_1) = 0$. In this case, W_1 must be either

$$W_1 = \begin{pmatrix} 1 & 0 \\ 0 & 1 \end{pmatrix} \quad \text{or} \quad W_1 = \begin{pmatrix} 0 & 1 \\ 1 & 0 \end{pmatrix},$$

which implies that $C_0(W_2) = 1$, and consequently, $C_0^{FB}(W_2) = 1$. Furthermore, if $R_\infty(W_2) > 0$, then W_2 must also be one of the two matrices above, ensuring that (35) holds. If instead $R_\infty(W_2) = 0$, Theorem 17 guarantees that (35) remains valid.

2. We now prove (36) under the assumption that $|\mathcal{X}_1| = |\mathcal{Y}_1| = 2$ and $|\mathcal{X}_2| = |\mathcal{Y}_2| = 3$. If we have found channels $\hat{W}_1, \hat{W}_2$ for this case, such that (36) holds, then it is also clear how general case 2 can be proved. We set $\hat{W}_1 = \begin{pmatrix} 1 & 0 \\ 0 & 1 \end{pmatrix}$, which means $C_0(\hat{W}_1) = C_0^{FB}(\hat{W}_1) = R_\infty(\hat{W}_1) = 1$. For $\hat{W}_2$, we take the three-ary typewriter channel $\hat{W}_2(\epsilon)$ with $\mathcal{X}_2 = \mathcal{Y}_2 = \{0, 1, 2\}$ (see [43]):

$$\hat{W}_2(\epsilon)(y|x) = \begin{cases} 1-\epsilon & y = x, \\ \epsilon & y = x+1 \mod 3. \end{cases}$$

Let $\epsilon \in (0, \frac{1}{2})$ be arbitrary, then $C(\hat{W}_2(\epsilon)) = \log_2(3) - H_2(\epsilon)$. We have $R_\infty(\hat{W}_2(\epsilon)) = \log_2 \frac{3}{2}$ and $C_0(\hat{W}_2(\epsilon)) = 0$. This means that $C_0^{FB}(\hat{W}_2(\epsilon)) = 0$. Thus, because $C_0(\hat{W}_1 \times \hat{W}_2(\epsilon)) \geq C_0(\hat{W}_1) = 1$,

$$\begin{aligned} C_0^{FB}(\hat{W}_1 \otimes \hat{W}_2(\epsilon)) &= R_\infty(\hat{W}_1) = R_\infty(\hat{W}_2(\epsilon)) \\ &= 1 + \log_2(\frac{3}{2}) > C_0^{FB}(\hat{W}_1) + C_0^{FB}(\hat{W}_2(\epsilon)) \end{aligned}$$

and we have proven case 2.

□

6. Behavior of the Expurgation-Bound Rates

In this section, we consider the behavior of the expurgation-bound rate. R_{ex}^k occurs in the expurgation bound as a lower bound for the channel reliability function, where k is the parameter for the k-letter description. Let $\mathcal{X}_1, \mathcal{Y}_1, \mathcal{X}_2, \mathcal{Y}_2$ be arbitrary finite non-trivial alphabets, and $W_l \in CH(\mathcal{X}_l, \mathcal{Y}_l)$ for $l = 1, 2$. We want to examine R_{ex}^k.

Theorem 20. *There exist non-trivial alphabets $\mathcal{X}_1, \mathcal{Y}_1, \mathcal{X}_2, \mathcal{Y}_2$ and channels $W_l \in CH(\mathcal{X}_l, \mathcal{Y}_l)$ for $l = 1, 2$, such that for all $\hat{k}$, there exists $k \geq \hat{k}$ with*

$$R_{ex}^k(W_1 \otimes W_2) \neq R_{ex}^k(W_1) + R_{ex}^k(W_2).$$

Proof. Assume that for all $\mathcal{X}_1, \mathcal{Y}_1, \mathcal{X}_2, \mathcal{Y}_2$ and $W_l \in CH(\mathcal{X}_l, \mathcal{Y}_l)$ with $l = 1, 2$ for all $k \in \mathbb{N}$,

$$R_{ex}^k(W_1 \otimes W_2) = R_{ex}^k(W_1) + R_{ex}^k(W_2).$$

We now take $\mathcal{X}_1', \mathcal{Y}_1', \mathcal{X}_2', \mathcal{Y}_2'$ such that C_0 is superadditive. Then, we have for certain W_1', W_2' with $W_l' \in CH(\mathcal{X}_l', \mathcal{Y}_l')$,

$$C_0(W_1' \otimes W_2') > C_0(W_1') + C_0(W_2'). \tag{37}$$

Then,

$$\begin{aligned} C_0(W_1' \otimes W_2') &= \lim_{k\to\infty} R_{ex}^k(W_1' \otimes W_2') \\ &= \lim_{k\to\infty} R_{ex}^k(W_1') + R_{ex}^k(W_2') \\ &= C_0(W_1') + C_0(W_2'). \end{aligned}$$

This is a contradiction, and thus the theorem is proven. □

We improve the statement of Theorem 20 with the following theorem.

Theorem 21. *There exist non-trivial alphabets $\mathcal{X}_1, \mathcal{Y}_1, \mathcal{X}_2, \mathcal{Y}_2$, channels $W_l \in CH(\mathcal{X}_l, \mathcal{Y}_l)$ for $l = 1,2$ and a $\hat{k}$, such that for all $k \geq \hat{k}$,*

$$R_{ex}^k(W_1 \otimes W_2) > R_{ex}^k(W_1) + R_{ex}^k(W_2)$$

holds true.

Proof. Assume the statement of the theorem is false, which means for all channels $W_l \in CH(\mathcal{X}_l, \mathcal{Y}_l)$ with $l = 1,2$, the following applies: There exists a sequence $\{k_j\}_{j\in\mathbb{N}} \subset \mathbb{N}$ with $\lim_{j\to\infty} k_j = +\infty$, such that

$$R_{ex}^{k_l}(W_1 \otimes W_2) \leq R_{ex}^{k_l}(W_1) + R_{ex}^{k_l}(W_2)$$

for $l \in \mathbb{N}$. We now take $\hat{\mathcal{X}}_1, \hat{\mathcal{Y}}_1, \hat{\mathcal{X}}_2, \hat{\mathcal{Y}}_2$ so that C_0 is superadditive for these alphabets. Then, we have for certain $\hat{W}_1, \hat{W}_2$ with $\hat{W}_l \in CH(\mathcal{X}_l, \mathcal{Y}_l)$ for $l = 1,2$,

$$C_0(\hat{W}_1 \otimes \hat{W}_2) > C_0(\hat{W}_1) + C_0(\hat{W}_2). \tag{38}$$

Then,

$$\begin{aligned} C_0(\hat{W}_1 \otimes \hat{W}_2) = \lim_{j\to\infty} R_{ex}^{k_j}(\hat{W}_1 \otimes \hat{W}_2) &\leq \lim_{j\to\infty} \left(R_{ex}^{k_j}(\hat{W}_1) + R_{ex}^{k_j}(\hat{W}_2) \right) \\ &= C_0(\hat{W}_1) + C_0(\hat{W}_2). \end{aligned}$$

This is a contradiction to (38), and thus the theorem is proven. □

We have already observed that the function $E(W,\cdot)$ exhibits significantly different behavior over certain rate intervals $[R, \hat{R}]$. In particular, we have analyzed the impact of the channel product $W_1 \otimes W_2$ on the intervals $(R_\infty(W_1 \otimes W_2), C(W_1 \otimes W_2))$ and $(E_{ex}^k(W_1 \otimes W_2), C(W_1 \otimes W_2))$ for $k \in \mathbb{N}$.

For the first interval, we established the relation

$$(R_\infty(W_1 \otimes W_2), C(W_1 \otimes W_2)) = (R_\infty(W_1) + R_\infty(W_2), C(W_1) + C(W_2)).$$

However , for the second interval, we have shown that such a simple additive behavior does not hold. Given the proof of Theorem 18, we conclude that there exist channels W_1', W_2' for which

$$R_{ex}^k(W_1' \otimes W_2') > R_{ex}^k(W_1') + R_{ex}^k(W_2')$$

is satisfied for all $k \geq \hat{k}$.

Another important aspect is understanding the conditions under which the interval $[0, \hat{R})$ causes $E(W, r)$ to become infinite. This occurs if and only if $C_0(W) > 0$, in which case, the interval is given by $[0, C_0(W))$. Consequently, there exist channels W_1', W_2' such that for the function $E(W_1' \otimes W_2', \cdot)$, this interval extends beyond $[0, C_0(W_1') + C_0(W_2')]$.

Thus, we conclude that C_0 is generally superadditive.

7. Conclusions

We have shown that the channel reliability function is not a Turing computable performance function. The same conclusion holds for the functions associated with the sphere packing bound and the expurgation bound.

An interesting aspect of our work is that the constraints we impose on Turing computable performance functions are strictly weaker than those typically required for Turing computable functions. Specifically, we do not require that the Turing machine halt for all inputs $(W, R) \in \mathcal{C}_h \times \mathbb{R}_c^+$. This means we allow the Turing machine to compute indefinitely for certain inputs, i.e., it may never halt for some inputs. Consequently, we permit performance functions that are not defined for all $(W, R) \in \mathcal{C}_h \times \mathbb{R}_c^+$. However, we do require the Turing machine to halt for inputs $(W, R) \in \mathcal{C}_h \times \mathbb{R}_c$ whenever the performance function F is defined, and in such cases, the machine must return the computable value $F(W, R)$ as output. This ensures that the algorithm generated corresponds to the number $F(W, R)$ according to Definition 15.

Additionally, we considered the R_∞ function and the zero-error feedback capacity, both of which play a critical role in the context of the channel reliability function. We demonstrated that neither the R_∞ function nor the zero-error feedback capacity is Banach–Mazur computable. Furthermore, we proved that the R_∞ function is additive.

We also established that for all finite alphabets $\mathcal{X}, \mathcal{Y}$ with $|\mathcal{X}| \geq 2$ and $|\mathcal{Y}| \geq 2$, the channel reliability function itself is not a Turing computable performance function. Moreover, we showed that the commonly studied bounds, which have been extensively examined in the literature, are also not Turing computable performance functions. It remains unclear whether non-trivial upper bounds for the channel reliability function that are Turing computable even exist.

In [13], the sequence of k-letter expurgation bounds was considered an effective method for approximating the channel reliability function. It was hoped that these sequences could be computed more efficiently using modern digital computers. However, we have shown that this is not the case. Table 1 gives an overview of the main results of the paper.

As mentioned in the Introduction, future communication systems, such as 6G, will face stringent requirements for trustworthiness. Ultra-reliability, along with the corresponding performance functions, is central to 6G, and this paper addresses that challenge. It is currently unclear how the non-Turing computability of performance functions will impact the system evaluation and certification of future communication systems. A recent study [62] showed that the non-Turing computability of performance functions in artificial intelligence (AI) leads to digital AI algorithms being unable to meet essential legal requirements. It is an intriguing research question whether similar issues might arise in the context of communication systems.

This work does not claim that machine learning or artificial intelligence (AI) approaches are useless for computing capacity functions. Rather, it demonstrates that certain solutions cannot be found by such methods, or that a computer may not be able to assess how close a given result is to the optimum. Nevertheless, employing machine learning tools remains valuable; one must simply be aware that these approaches do not always guarantee optimality. In such cases, alternative theoretical frameworks may be necessary.

Table 1. Overview of results.

Problem	Result
Computability of capacity	R_∞: Yes R_0: Unknown R_0 for alphabet size < 5: Yes
Semi-decidability of capacity $> \lambda$	R_∞: No C_0^{FB}: No
Semi-decidability of capacity $< \lambda$	R_∞: Yes C_0^{FB}: Yes
Computability of capacity function	R_∞: No C_0^{FB}: No
Computability of performance function	$E(W,R)$: No $\{E_{ex}(\cdot,\cdot,k)\}_{k\in\mathbb{N}}$: No
Additivity	R_∞: Yes C_0^{FB}: Unknown C_0^{FB} for alphabet size 2: Yes R_{ex}^k: No

Turing computability and Banach–Mazur computability are two central notions in the theory of computation. Every function that is Turing computable is also Banach–Mazur computable, meaning that Banach–Mazur computability subsumes Turing computability. However, the converse does not hold: not every Banach–Mazur computable function is Turing computable. In fact, if a function is not Banach–Mazur computable, then it cannot be computable under any other standard notion of computability. This underscores the foundational and maximal character of Banach–Mazur computability within the hierarchy of computability concepts. Moreover, as shown in [63], there exist even total functions—functions defined on all computable real numbers—that are Banach–Mazur computable but not Turing computable. For readers interested in a deeper understanding of computability theory—how to determine whether a function is computable, along with illustrative examples and detailed explanations—we recommend the comprehensive work by Soare [64] and Cooper's *New Computational Paradigms* [65]. Practical implications of these theoretical analyses, especially their relevance to real-world applications, are further explored in [66], which may be of particular interest to those seeking connections between theory and practice.

Author Contributions: The contributions of both authors are equal across all categories. All authors have read and agreed to the published version of the manuscript.

Funding: The authors gratefully acknowledge the financial support provided by the Federal Ministry of Education and Research (BMBF) of Germany under the "Souverän. Digital. Vernetzt." program, specifically through the joint project 6G-life, project identification numbers 16KISK002 and 16KISK263. H. Boche and C. Deppe also acknowledge the financial support from the BMBF's quantum program QuaPhySI under grants 16KIS1598K and 16KIS2234, as well as from the QUIET project under grants 16KISQ093 and 16KISQ0170. Additionally, they were supported by the QC-CamNetz project under grants 16KISQ077 and 16KISQ169. Furthermore, they received funding from the DFG through the project "Post Shannon Theorie und Implementierung," under grants BO 1734/38-1 and DE 1915/2-1. Special thanks also go to the BMBF within the national initiative for their support of H. Boche under grant 16KIS1003K and of C. Deppe under grant 16KIS1005.

Data Availability Statement: The original contributions presented in this study are included in the article. Further inquiries can be directed to the corresponding author(s).

Acknowledgments: Holger Boche would like to thank Martin Bossert for insightful discussions and questions regarding the theory of the channel reliability function and the trustworthiness of numerical simulations of this function on digital computers. He also expresses his gratitude to Vince Poor and Martin Bossert for their discussions at ISIT 2019 in Paris, which sparked the research leading to the results presented in this paper. Finally, we express our appreciation to Yannik Böck for his helpful and insightful comments.

Conflicts of Interest: The authors declare no conflicts of interest.

References

1. Shannon, C.E. A mathematical theory of communication. *Bell Syst. Tech. J.* **1948**, *27*, 379–423. 623–656. [CrossRef]
2. Chow, T.Y. What is a Closed-Form Number? *Amer. Math. Mon.* **1999**, *106*, 440–448. [CrossRef]
3. Borwein, J.; Crandall, R. Closed Forms: What They Are and Why We Care. *Not. Am. Math. Soc.* **2013**, *60*, 50–65. [CrossRef]
4. Ahlswede, R. Multi-way communication channels. In Proceedings of the Second International Symposium on Information Theory, Tsahkadsor, Armenia, 2–8 September 1971.
5. Ahlswede, R.; Dueck, G. Identification via channels. *IEEE Trans. Inform. Theory* **1989**, *35*, 15–29. [CrossRef]
6. Sason, I. Observations on graph invariants with the Lovász ϑ-function. *AIMS Math.* **2024**, *9*, 15385–15468. [CrossRef]
7. Sason, I. Observations on the Lovász θ-Function, Graph Capacity, Eigenvalues, and Strong Products. *Entropy* **2023**, *25*, 104. [CrossRef]
8. Gallager, R.G. *Information Theory and Reliable Communication*; John Wiley & Sons, Inc.: Hoboken, NJ, USA, 1968.
9. Haroutunian, E.; Haroutunian, M.; Harutyunyan, A. Reliability Criteria in Information Theory and in Statistical Hypothesis Testing. *Found. Trends Commun. Inf. Theory* **2008**, *4*, 97–263. [CrossRef]
10. Blahut, R.E. *Principles and Practice of Information Theory*; Addison-Wesley Longman Publishing Co., Inc.: Boston, MA, USA , 1987.
11. Elias, P. Coding for noisy channels. *IRE Conv. Rec.* **1955**, *4*, 37–46.
12. Fano, R.M. Transmission of information: A statistical theory of communications. *Am. J. Phys.* **1961**, *29*, 793–794. [CrossRef]
13. Shannon, C.; Gallager, R.; Berlekamp, E. Lower Bounds to Error Probability for Coding in Discrete Memoryless Channels. *Inf. Control* **1967**, *10*, 65–103. [CrossRef]
14. Turing, A. On Computable Numbers, with an Application to the Entscheidungsproblem. *Proc. Lond. Math. Soc.* **1936**, *42*, 230–265.
15. Arimoto, S. An algorithm for computing the capacity of arbitrary discrete memoryless channels. *IEEE Trans. Inf. Theory* **1972**, *18*, 14–20. [CrossRef]
16. Blahut, R. Computation of channel capacity and rate-distortion functions. *IEEE Trans. Inf. Theory* **1972**, *18*, 460–473. [CrossRef]
17. Dueck, G.; Körner, J. Reliability function of a discrete memoryless channel at rates above capacity (corresp.). *IEEE Trans. Inf. Theory* **1979**, *25*, 82–85. [CrossRef]
18. Alajaji, F., Chen, P.; Rached, Z. A note on the Poor-Verdú upper bound for the channel reliability function. *IEEE Trans. Inf. Theory* **2002**, *48*, 309–313. [CrossRef]
19. Ashikhmin, A.; Barg, A.; Litsyn, S. A new upper bound on the reliability function of the Gaussian channel. *IEEE Trans. Inf. Theory* **2000**, *46*, 1945–1961. [CrossRef]
20. Lapidoth, A. On the reliability function of the ideal Poisson channel with noiseless feedback. *IEEE Trans. Inf. Theory* **2002**, *39*, 491–503. [CrossRef]
21. Burnashev, M.; Yamamoto, H. Noisy feedback improves the Gaussian channel reliability function. In Proceedings of the IEEE International Symposium on Information Theory, Honolulu, HI, USA, 29 June–4 July 2014.
22. Hajek, B.; Subramanian, V. Capacity and reliability function for small peak signal constraints. *IEEE Trans. Inf. Theory* **2002**, *48*, 828–839. [CrossRef]
23. Ben-Haim, Y.; Litsyn, S. Improved upper bounds on the reliability function of the Gaussian channel. In Proceedings of the IEEE International Symposium on Information Theory, Seattle, WA, USA, 9–14 July 2006.
24. Endo, H.; Sasaki, M. Reliability and secrecy functions of the wiretap channel under cost constraint. *IEEE Trans. Inf. Theory* **2014**, *60*, 6819–6843.
25. Tyagi, H.; Narayan, P. The Gelfand-Pinsker channel: Strong converse and upper bound for the reliability function. In Proceedings of the IEEE International Symposium on Information Theory, Seoul, Republic of Korea, 28 June–3 July 2009.
26. Somekh-Baruch, A. An upper bound on the reliability function of discrete memoryless channels. *IEEE Trans. Inf. Theory* **2024**, *70*, 3059–3081. [CrossRef]
27. Burnashev, M.; Yamamoto, H. On the reliability function for a BSC with noisy feedback. *Probl. Inf. Transm.* **2010**, *46*, 103–121. [CrossRef]
28. Burnashev, M.; Holevo, A. On the reliability function for a quantum communication channel. *Probl. Peredachi Informatsii* **1998**, *34*, 3–15.

29. Holevo, A. Reliability function of general classical-quantum channel. *IEEE Trans. Inf. Theory* **2002**, *46*, 2256–2261. [CrossRef]
30. Li, K.; Yang, D. Reliability function of classical-quantum channels. *Phys. Rev. Lett.* **2025**, *134*, 010802. [CrossRef]
31. Fettweis, G.P.; Boche, H. 6G: The Personal Tactile Internet—And Open Questions for Information Theory. *IEEE BITS Inf. Theory Mag.* **2021**, *1*, 71–82. [CrossRef]
32. Boche, H.; Schaefer, R.; Poor, H.; Fettweis, G. Trustworthiness Verification and Integrity Testing for Wireless Communication Systems. In Proceedings of the IEEE International Conference on Communications, Seoul, South Korea and Virtual, 16–20 May 2022.
33. Fettweis, G.P.; Boche, H. On 6G and trustworthiness. *Commun. ACM* **2022**, *65*, 48–49. [CrossRef]
34. Alon, N.; Lubetzky, E. The Shannon capacity of a graph and the independence numbers of its powers. *IEEE Trans. Inf. Theory* **2006**, *52*, 2172–2176. [CrossRef]
35. Boche, H.; Deppe, C. Computability of the zero-error capacity of noisy channels. In Proceedings of the 2021 IEEE Information Theory Workshop (ITW), Kanazawa, Japan, 17–21 October 2021; IEEE: Piscataway, NJ, USA, 2021; pp. 1–6.
36. Boche, H.; Deppe, C. Computability of the channel reliability function and related bounds. In Proceedings of the 2022 IEEE International Symposium on Information Theory (ISIT), Espoo, Finland, 26 June–1 July 2022; IEEE: Piscataway, NJ, USA, 2022; pp. 1530–1535.
37. Weihrauch, K. *Computable Analysis: An Introduction*, 1st ed.; Springer Publishing Company, Incorporated: Berlin/Heidelberg, Germany, 2013.
38. Soare, R.I. *Recursively Enumerable Sets and Degrees*, 1st ed.; Springer: Berlin/Heidelberg, Germany, 1987. [CrossRef]
39. Pour-El, M.B.; Richards, J.I. *Computability in Analysis and Physics*; Perspectives in Logic; Cambridge University Press: Cambridge, UK, 2017. [CrossRef]
40. Shannon, C. The zero error capacity of a noisy channel. *IRE Trans. Inf. Theory* **1956**, *2*, 8–19. [CrossRef]
41. Gallager, R. A simple derivation of the coding theorem and some applications. *IEEE Trans. Inf. Theory* **1965**, *11*, 3–18. [CrossRef]
42. Katsman, G.L.; Tsfasman, M.A.; Vladuţ, S.G. Spectra of linear codes and error probability of decoding. In *Coding theory and Algebraic Geometry (Luminy, 1991)*; Lecture Notes in Math; Springer: Berlin/Heidelberg, Germany, 1992; Volume 1518, pp. 82–98.
43. Dalai, M.; Polyanskiy, Y. Bounds on the Reliability Function of Typewriter Channels. *IEEE Trans. Inf. Theory* **2018**, *64*, 6208–6222. [CrossRef]
44. Lovász, L. On the Shannon capacity of a graph. *IEEE Trans. Inf. Theory* **1979**, *25*, 1–7. [CrossRef]
45. Baumert, L.D.; McEliece, R.J.; Rodemich, E.; Rumsey, H.C., Jr.; Stanley, R.; Taylor, H. A combinatorial packing problem. In Proceedings of the Computers in Algebra and Number Theory, New York, NY, USA, 25–26 March 1970; Volume IV, pp. 97–108.
46. Bohman, T. A limit theorem for the Shannon capacities of odd cycles. I. *Proc. Am. Math. Soc.* **2003**, *131*, 3559–3569. [CrossRef]
47. Polak, S.C.; Schrijver, A. New lower bound on the Shannon capacity of C7 from circular graphs. *Inf. Process. Lett.* **2019**, *143*, 37–40. [CrossRef]
48. Delsarte, P. An algebraic approach to the association schemes of coding theory. *Philips Res. Rep. Suppl.* **1973**, *10*, vi+-97.
49. Schrijver, A. A comparison of the Delsarte and Lovász bounds. *IEEE Trans. Inform. Theory* **1979**, *25*, 425–429. [CrossRef]
50. McEliece, R.J.; Rodemich, E.R.; Rumsey, H., Jr.; Welch, L.R. New upper bounds on the rate of a code via the Delsarte-MacWilliams inequalities. *IEEE Trans. Inform. Theory* **1977**, *IT-23*, 157–166.
51. Litsyn, S. New upper bounds on error exponents. *IEEE Trans. Inform. Theory* **1999**, *45*, 385–398. [CrossRef]
52. Barg, A.; McGregor, A. Distance distribution of binary codes and the error probability of decoding. *IEEE Trans. Inform. Theory* **2005**, *51*, 4237–4246. [CrossRef]
53. Kalai, G.; Linial, N. On the distance distribution of codes. *IEEE Trans. Inform. Theory* **1995**, *41*, 1467–1472. [CrossRef]
54. Nötzel, J.; Wiese, M.; Boche, H. The arbitrarily varying wiretap channel—Secret randomness, stability, and super-activation. *IEEE Trans. Inf. Theory* **2016**, *62*, 3504–3531. [CrossRef]
55. Schaefer, R.F.; Boche, H.; Poor, H.V. Secure communication under channel uncertainty and adversarial attacks. *Proc. IEEE* **2015**, *103*, 1796–1813. [CrossRef]
56. Wiese, M.; Nötzel, J.; Boche, H. A channel under simultaneous jamming and eavesdropping attack—Correlated random coding capacities under strong secrecy criteria. *IEEE Trans. Inf. Theory* **2016**, *62*, 3844–3862. [CrossRef]
57. Boche, H.; Deppe, C. Secure identification for wiretap channels; robustness, super-additivity and continuity. *IEEE Trans. Inf. Forensics Secur.* **2018**, *13*, 1641–1655. [CrossRef]
58. Boche, H.; Schaefer, R.F. Capacity results and super-activation for wiretap channels with active wiretappers. *IEEE Trans. Inf. Forensics Secur.* **2013**, *8*, 1482–1496. [CrossRef]
59. Boche, H.; Böck, Y.; Deppe, C. On Effective Convergence in Fekete's Lemma and Related Combinatorial Problems in Information Theory. In *Festschrift in Memory of Ning Cai: Information Theory and Related Fields*; Springer: Cham, Switzerland, 2025; pp. 289–318.
60. Boche, H.; Schaefer, R.F.; Poor, H.V. Algorithmic Computability and Approximability of Capacity-Achieving Input Distributions. *IEEE Trans. Inf. Theory* **2023**, *69*, 5449–5462. [CrossRef]

61. Lee, Y.; Boche, H.; Kutyniok, G. Computability of Optimizers. *IEEE Trans. Inf. Theory* **2024**, *70*, 2967–2983. [CrossRef]
62. Boche, H.; Fono, A.; Kutyniok, G. A Mathematical Framework for Computability Aspects of Algorithmic Transparency. In Proceedings of the IEEE International Symposium on Information Theory, Athens, Greece, 7–12 July 2024; IEEE: Piscataway, NJ, USA, 2024.
63. Hertling, P. A Banach–Mazur computable but not Markov computable function on the computable real numbers. *Ann. Pure Appl. Log.* **2005**, *132*, 227–246. [CrossRef]
64. Soare, R.I. *Turing Computability: Theory and Applications*, 1st ed.; Springer Publishing Company, Incorporated: Berlin/Heidelberg, Germany, 2016.
65. Cooper, S.B.; Löwe, B.; Sorbi, A. *New Computational Paradigms: Changing Conceptions of What Is Computable*; Springer Science & Business Media: Berlin/Heidelberg, Germany, 2007.
66. Boche, H.; Fojtik, V.; Fono, A.; Kutyniok, G. Computability of Classification and Deep Learning: From Theoretical Limits to Practical Feasibility through Quantization. *J. Fourier Anal. Appl.* **2025**, *31*, 35. [CrossRef]

algorithms

MDPI

Article

Structure Approximation-Based Preconditioning for Solving Tempered Fractional Diffusion Equations

Xuan Zhang and Chaojie Wang *

School of Mathematics and Statistics, Beijing Technology and Business University, Beijing 100048, China; 13770615793@163.com
* Correspondence: ikeyan_btbu@163.com

Abstract: Tempered fractional diffusion equations constitute a critical class of partial differential equations with broad applications across multiple physical domains. In this paper, the Crank–Nicolson method and the tempered weighted and shifted Grünwald formula are used to discretize the tempered fractional diffusion equations. The discretized system has the structure of the sum of the identity matrix and a diagonal matrix multiplied by a symmetric positive definite (SPD) Toeplitz matrix. For the discretized system, we propose a structure approximation-based preconditioning method. The structure approximation lies in two aspects: the inverse approximation based on the row-by-row strategy and the SPD Toeplitz approximation by the τ matrix. The proposed preconditioning method can be efficiently implemented using the discrete sine transform (DST). In spectral analysis, it is found that the eigenvalues of the preconditioned coefficient matrix are clustered around 1, ensuring fast convergence of Krylov subspace methods with the new preconditioner. Numerical experiments demonstrate the effectiveness of the proposed preconditioner.

Keywords: tempered fractional diffusion equations; Krylov subspace method; structure approximation; preconditioning

1. Introduction

This paper discusses the numerical solution of variable coefficient tempered fractional diffusion equations (tempered FDEs) with initial boundary value problems

$$\begin{cases} \frac{\partial u(x,t)}{\partial t} = d(x)\left({}_a\boldsymbol{D}_x^{\beta,\lambda} + {}_x\boldsymbol{D}_b^{\beta,\lambda}\right)u(x,t) + f(x,t), \\ u(a,t) = 0,\ u(b,t) = 0,\ t \in [0,T], \\ u(x,0) = u_0(x),\ x \in [a,b], \end{cases} \tag{1}$$

where $f(x,t)$ is the source term, $d(x) \geq 0$ is the diffusion coefficient function, and λ is a non-negative parameter. ${}_a\boldsymbol{D}_x^{\beta,\lambda}$ and ${}_x\boldsymbol{D}_b^{\beta,\lambda}$ denote the left and right Riemann–Liouville tempered fractional derivatives of the function $u(x,t)$ with order $\beta(1 < \beta < 2)$, respectively. They are defined by (see Baeumer and Meerschaert [1])

$${}_a\boldsymbol{D}_x^{\beta,\lambda}u(x) = {}_aD_x^{\beta,\lambda}u(x) - \beta\lambda^{\beta-1}\partial_x u(x) - \lambda^\beta u(x)$$

and

$${}_x\boldsymbol{D}_b^{\beta,\lambda}u(x) = {}_xD_b^{\beta,\lambda}u(x) + \beta\lambda^{\beta-1}\partial_x u(x) - \lambda^\beta u(x)$$

where

$${}_aD_x^{\beta,\lambda}u(x) = \mathrm{e}^{-\lambda x}\,{}_aD_x^{\beta}\left(\mathrm{e}^{\lambda x}u(x)\right) = \frac{\mathrm{e}^{-\lambda x}}{\Gamma(2-\beta)}\frac{\partial^2}{\partial x^2}\int_a^x \frac{\mathrm{e}^{\lambda s}u(s)}{(x-s)^{\beta-1}}ds$$

and
$$ {}_{x}D_{b}^{\beta,\lambda}u(x) = \mathrm{e}^{\lambda x}\, {}_{x}D_{b}^{\beta}\left(\mathrm{e}^{-\lambda x}u(x)\right) = \frac{\mathrm{e}^{\lambda x}}{\Gamma(2-\beta)}\frac{\partial^2}{\partial x^2}\int_x^b \frac{\mathrm{e}^{-\lambda s}u(s)}{(s-x)^{\beta-1}}ds. $$

Tempered FDEs are a crucial class of equations widely applied in fields such as biology, geophysics, and finance [2–4]. These equations are characterized by incorporating tempered fractional derivatives, modifying standard fractional diffusion equations by introducing an exponential tempering factor. This modification allows tempered FDEs to better simulate processes with finite propagation speed, accurately describing actual physical phenomena. However, analytical solutions to tempered FDEs and FDEs are generally difficult to obtain, leading to extensive research on the numerical solutions of FDEs in recent years [5–11].

For tempered fractional derivatives, stability of the resulting finite difference schemes can only be ensured if the spatial step size is sufficiently small when using standard fractional derivative approximations directly [12]. A novel shifted approximation method for tempered fractional derivatives was proposed in [13], successfully developing an unconditionally stable numerical scheme for one-dimensional (1D) tempered fractional diffusion equations with constant coefficients. Additionally, a Crank–Nicolson scheme was proposed [14] for solving initial boundary value problems of a class of variable coefficient tempered fractional diffusion equations, providing the discretization method used in this paper. The inherent non-locality of tempered fractional operators manifests in the algebraic structure of discretized systems, producing coefficient matrices with dense or fully populated configurations. The system's coefficient matrix assumes the configuration $I + DT$, with I denoting the identity matrix, D a diagonal matrix, and T an SPD Toeplitz matrix.

Traditional direct solution methods, such as Gaussian elimination, require large computational cost and storage space. The Krylov subspace methods are typically used to solve these kinds of linear system. Meanwhile, effective preconditioning strategies can significantly accelerate the convergence rate of the Krylov subspace methods [15–18]. For 1D and 2D tempered FDEs, Lei, Fan and Chen [19] proposed a fast-iterative method and a fast-direct method. And they used the circulant preconditioner to accelerate the iteration process. In [20], a robust preconditioner was developed for the discretized scheme of nonlinear tempered FDEs. In [21], a circulant and skew-circulant splitting iteration method was used to solve the discretized system of tempered FDEs. The induced preconditioning form was also investigated. Nevertheless, emerging methodologies demonstrate superior efficacy compared to conventional preconditioning approaches. For 1D tempered FDEs, Tang and Huang [22] approximated the SPD Toeplitz matrix by the τ matrix [15] and proposed a scaled diagonal and Toeplitz approximate splitting (SDTAS) preconditioning method. The equations examined in this study address a notably underexplored class of tempered FDEs in the contemporary literature, characterized by discretization schemes that yield coefficient matrices incorporating SPD Toeplitz structures. This distinctive matrix configuration, possessing both theoretically significant properties and practical computational advantages, constitutes the principal focus of our numerical investigation. Also, some of the latest numerical solution methods for FDEs are described in [23,24]. In addition, it is noticed that a row-by-row inverse approximation strategy has been proposed [25] and applied [26–28]. Inspired by this strategy, we will try to construct an efficient preconditioner for the linear system arising from the numerical solution of tempered FDEs with variable coefficients.

In this paper, we use the second-order finite difference scheme to discretize the tempered FDEs. Specifically, we employ the Crank–Nicolson method for time discretization and the tempered weighted and shifted Grünwald formula for spatial discretization. We observe that the coefficient matrix of the resulting linear system is of the form $I + DT$. We approximate the SPD Toeplitz matrix T by the τ matrix and construct a novel approximate inverse preconditioner inspired by the row-by-row approximation strategy. The preconditioner can be efficiently computed using discrete sine transforms, with each step of the preconditioned Krylov subspace method having a computational complexity of $O(N\log N)$. Spectral analysis establishes eigenvalue clustering near unity for the preconditioned system, which theoretically guarantees the superlinear convergence rate of Krylov subspace iterations—a property rigorously verified through our mathematical proofs. Numerical experiments are carried out to assess the performance of the developed preconditioner.

The remainder of this paper is organized as follows. Section 2 presents the derivation of the discretized system for tempered FDEs. Section 3 details the formulation of an approximate inverse preconditioner. Section 4 performs spectral analysis of the preconditioned matrices. Section 5 validates the computational efficiency of the proposed preconditioner through numerical experiments. Concluding remarks summarizing the key findings are provided in Section 6.

2. Discretization of Tempered FDEs

Let N and M be positive integers, representing the number of spatial and temporal partitions, respectively. We define the spatial step size $h=\frac{a}{N+1}$ and the time step size $\Delta t=\frac{T}{M}$. The spatial and temporal grids are given by $x_i=ih$ for $i=0,1,\ldots,N+1$ and $t_j=j\Delta t$ for $j=0,1,\ldots,M$.

We review that the tempered fractional derivatives in (1) can be approximated using the tempered weighted and shifted Grünwald formula (tempered WSGD) [14]

$$ {}_aD_x^{\beta,\lambda}u(x_i,t_j)-\lambda^\beta u(x_i,t_j)=\frac{1}{h^\beta}\sum_{k=0}^{i+1}g_k^{(\beta)}u(x_{i-k+1},t_j)-\frac{1}{h^\beta}\rho_\beta u(x_i,t_j)+O\left(h^2\right), $$

and

$$ {}_xD_b^{\beta,\lambda}u(x_i,t_j)-\lambda^\beta u(x_i,t_j)=\frac{1}{h^\beta}\sum_{k=0}^{N-i+2}g_k^{(\beta)}u(x_{i+k-1},t_j)-\frac{1}{h^\beta}\rho_\beta u(x_i,t_j)+O\left(h^2\right), $$

where $\rho_\beta=\left(\gamma_1e^{h\lambda}+\gamma_2+\gamma_3e^{-h\lambda}\right)\left(1-e^{-h\lambda}\right)^\beta$; the weights $g_k^{(\beta)}$ are given by

$$ g_k^{(\beta)}=\begin{cases}\gamma_1w_0^{(\beta)}e^{h\lambda}, & k=0,\\ \gamma_1w_1^{(\beta)}+\gamma_2w_0^{(\beta)}, & k=1,\\ \left(\gamma_1w_k^{(\beta)}+\gamma_2w_{k-1}^{(\beta)}+\gamma_3w_{k-2}^{(\beta)}\right)e^{-(k-1)h\lambda}, & k\geq 2,\end{cases} \tag{2} $$

where $w_0^{(\beta)}=1, w_k^{(\beta)}=\left(1-\frac{1+\beta}{k}\right)w_{k-1}^{(\beta)}$, for $k\geq 1$, and $\gamma_1,\gamma_2,\gamma_3$ satisfy the linear system

$$ \begin{cases}\gamma_1+\gamma_2+\gamma_3=1,\\ \gamma_1-\gamma_3=\beta/2.\end{cases} \tag{3} $$

Let $u_i^j\approx u(x_i,t_j), f_i^{j+\frac{1}{2}}=f\left(x_i,t_{j+\frac{1}{2}}\right), t_{j+\frac{1}{2}}=\frac{1}{2}(t_j+t_{j+1})$ and $u_i^{j+\frac{1}{2}}=\frac{1}{2}\left(u_i^j+u_i^{j+1}\right)$ for $i=1,\ldots,N, j=0,1,\ldots,M$. At the mesh point $\left(x_i,t_{j+\frac{1}{2}}\right)$, we consider the Crank–Nicolson technique for time discretization and the tempered WSGD approximation for the tempered fractional derivatives to discretize the tempered FDEs in (1). Under the truncation-error-free assumption [23,24], the second-order finite difference scheme is formulated as follows:

$$\begin{aligned}\frac{u_i^{j+1}-u_i^j}{\Delta t} =& \frac{d_i}{2}\left(\frac{1}{h^\beta}\sum_{k=0}^{i+1} g_k^{(\beta)} u_{i-k+1}^{j+1} - \frac{1}{h^\beta}\rho_\beta u_i^{j+1} + \frac{1}{h^\beta}\sum_{k=0}^{N-i+2} g_k^{(\beta)} u_{i+k-1}^{j+1} - \frac{1}{h^\beta}\rho_\beta u_i^{j+1}\right)\\ &+\frac{d_i}{2}\left(\frac{1}{h^\beta}\sum_{k=0}^{i+1} g_k^{(\beta)} u_{i-k+1}^{j} - \frac{1}{h^\beta}\rho_\beta u_i^{j} + \frac{1}{h^\beta}\sum_{k=0}^{N-i+2} g_k^{(\beta)} u_{i+k-1}^{j} - \frac{1}{h^\beta}\rho_\beta u_i^{j}\right)\\ &+f_i^{j+\frac{1}{2}}.\end{aligned} \tag{4}$$

We define the diagonal matrix as

$$D = \mathrm{diag}(d_1, d_2, \ldots, d_N)$$

and the vectors as

$$u^j = \left[u_1^j, u_2^j, \ldots, u_N^j\right]^T, f^{j+\frac{1}{2}} = \left[f_1^{j+\frac{1}{2}}, f_2^{j+\frac{1}{2}}, \ldots, f_N^{j+\frac{1}{2}}\right]^T.$$

For $j = 0, 1, \ldots, M$ and a given u^0, the differential scheme (4) admits a matrix representation expressed as

$$(I + DG)u^{j+1} = (I - DG)u^j + \Delta t f^{j+\frac{1}{2}}, \tag{5}$$

where I is the identity matrix, and G is an SPD Toeplitz matrix, defined as $G = G_\beta + G_\beta^T$, where G_β^T represents the transpose of G_β. G_β can be represented as

$$G_\beta = -\frac{\Delta t}{2h^\beta}\begin{pmatrix} g_1^{(\beta)}-\rho_\beta & g_0^{(\beta)} & 0 & \cdots & 0 & 0\\ g_2^{(\beta)} & g_1^{(\beta)}-\rho_\beta & g_0^{(\beta)} & 0 & \cdots & 0\\ \vdots & \ddots & \ddots & \ddots & & \vdots\\ g_{N-1}^{(\beta)} & \ddots & \ddots & \ddots & & g_0^{(\beta)}\\ g_N^{(\beta)} & g_{N-1}^{(\beta)} & \cdots & \cdots & g_2^{(\beta)} & g_1^{(\beta)}-\rho_\beta\end{pmatrix}.$$

Consequently, the coefficient matrix A associated with the tempered FDEs (4) is structured as a superposition of the identity matrix and an SPD Toeplitz matrix premultiplying a diagonal matrix, analytically expressed as

$$A = I + DG. \tag{6}$$

Since the system (3) is underdetermined, the following Lemma 1 [14] establishes additional constraints on parameters $\gamma_1, \gamma_2, \gamma_3$ to ensure that the finite difference scheme (4) remains unconditionally stable while attaining second-order accuracy in both spatial and temporal domains.

Lemma 1. *Let S be the solution set of the linear system (3), if $1 < \beta < 2$, $\lambda \geq 0$, $(\gamma_1, \gamma_2, \gamma_3) \in S$, and*

1. $\max\left\{\frac{2(\beta^2+3\beta-4)}{\beta^2+3\beta+2}, \frac{\beta^2+3\beta}{\beta^2+3\beta+4}\right\} < \gamma_1 < \frac{3(\beta^2+3\beta-2)}{2(\beta^2+3\beta+2)}$; *or*
2. $\frac{(\beta-4)(\beta^2+3\beta+2)+24}{2(\beta^2+3\beta+2)} < \gamma_2 < \min\left\{\frac{(\beta-2)(\beta^2+3\beta+4)+16}{2(\beta^2+3\beta+4)}, \frac{(\beta-6)(\beta^2+3\beta+2)+48}{2(\beta^2+3\beta+2)}\right\}$; *or*
3. $\max\left\{\frac{(2-\beta)(\beta^2+\beta-8)}{\beta^2+3\beta+2}, \frac{(1-\beta)(\beta^2+2\beta)}{2(\beta^2+3\beta+4)}\right\} < \gamma_3 < \frac{(2-\beta)(\beta^2+2\beta-3)}{2(\beta^2+3\beta+2)}$

we have

$$g_1^{(\beta)} < 0, \quad g_2^{(\beta)} + g_0^{(\beta)} > 0, \quad g_k^{(\beta)} > 0, \quad \forall k \geq 3, \quad \sum_{k=0}^{\infty} g_k^{(\beta)} = \rho_\beta \geq 0. \tag{7}$$

3. Structure Approximation-Based Preconditioning

In this section, we first construct an inverse approximation for the coefficient matrix based on its structure and the row-by-row strategy. In addition, we approximated the involved SPD Toeplitz matrix by the corresponding τ matrix, thereby introducing a structure approximation-based preconditioner to address the targeted linear system (5).

The row-by-row approximation strategy [25] takes advantage of the fact that $e_i^T A = e_i^T K_i$. Here we take the approximation as $e_i^T A^{-1} \approx e_i^T K_i^{-1}$, where e_i represents the i-th column of the identity matrix, $K_i = I + d_i G, i = 1, 2, \ldots, N$. Based on this, we obtain the approximate inverse preconditioner P_1

$$P_1^{-1} = \sum_{i=1}^{N} e_i e_i^T K_i^{-1}.$$

Recognizing that G exhibits an SPD Toeplitz structure, we employ the τ-based matrix to derive an efficient approximation of G [15]. For convenience, the first column of the G matrix can be expressed as $-\frac{\Delta t}{2h^\beta}\left[2\left(g_1^{(\beta)} - \rho_\alpha\right), g_0^{(\beta)} + g_2^{(\beta)}, g_3^{(\beta)}, \ldots, g_N^{(\beta)}\right]^T$. According to [15], we can compute the τ matrix approximation using Hankel correction

$$\tau(G) = G - HC(G), \tag{8}$$

where $HC(G)$ is a symmetric Hankel matrix, and its anti-diagonal elements can be computed from the corresponding elements in the following first column and last column:

$$-\frac{\Delta t}{2h^\beta}\left(g_3^{(\beta)}, g_4^{(\beta)}, \ldots, g_N^{(\beta)}, 0, 0\right)^T, \quad -\frac{\Delta t}{2h^\beta}\left(0, 0, g_N^{(\beta)}, \ldots, g_4^{(\beta)}, g_3^{(\beta)}\right)^T. \tag{9}$$

It is well-known that $\tau(G)$ defined in (8) admits diagonalization via the discrete sine transform:

$$\tau(G) = S\Lambda S, \quad S = \left(\sqrt{\frac{2}{N+1}} \cdot \sin\frac{\pi i j}{N+1}\right), \quad i, j = 1, 2, \ldots, N, \tag{10}$$

where $\Lambda = \mathrm{diag}(\lambda_1, \lambda_2, \ldots, \lambda_N)$, and S is the discrete sine transform matrix.

Clearly, $G_j = I + d_j \tau(G)$ remains a τ matrix. Using the τ matrix G_j to approximate the SPD Toeplitz matrix K_j, we obtain the τ matrix-based approximate preconditioner

$$P_2^{-1} = \sum_{i=1}^{N} e_i e_i^T G_i^{-1}. \tag{11}$$

With the preconditioner P_2^{-1}, we need to compute $O(N)$ discrete sine transforms for each iteration, which is still computationally intensive. As carried out in [25], we consider using interpolation methods to reduce computational complexity.

Define $\{x_i\}_{i=1}^N$ as the set of all discrete points in the interval $[a, b]$, and the function $q_k(x) = \frac{1}{1+\lambda_k d(x)}$, where $\lambda_k \in sp(\tau(G)) = \{\lambda_1, \lambda_2, \ldots, \lambda_N\}, k = 1, 2, \ldots, N$. Select $l (l \ll N)$

interpolation points $\{(\tilde{x}_j, q_k(\tilde{x}_j))\}_{j=1}^{l}$ in $(x_i, q_k(x_i))\}_{i=1}^{N}$, and then piecewise linear interpolation is applied to construct the interpolating function

$$\begin{aligned} p_k(x) &= \phi_1(x)q_k(\tilde{x}_1) + \phi_2(x)q_k(\tilde{x}_2) + \cdots + \phi_l(x)q_k(\tilde{x}_l) \\ &= \sum_{s=1}^{l} \phi_s(x)q_k(\tilde{x}_s). \end{aligned} \tag{12}$$

By leveraging Equation (10), each G_j is diagonalized into the form $G_j = S\Lambda_j S$ for $j = 1, 2, \ldots, N$ where S denotes the discrete sine transform matrix, and Λ_j represents a diagonal matrix containing the eigenvalues of G_j. Then, applying interpolation (12) to approximate G_j^{-1}, we have

$$G_j^{-1} \approx S\left(\sum_{s=1}^{l} \phi_s(x_j)\Lambda_s^{-1}\right)S. \tag{13}$$

Replacing G_j^{-1} in (11) with approximation values (13), we propose the approximate inverse preconditioner as

$$\begin{aligned} P_3^{-1} &= \sum_{i=1}^{N} e_i e_i^T S\left(\sum_{s=1}^{l} \phi_s(x_i)\Lambda_s^{-1}\right)S \\ &= \sum_{s=1}^{l}\left(\sum_{i=1}^{N} e_i e_i^T \phi_s(x_i)\right)S\left(\Lambda_s^{-1}\right)S \\ &= \sum_{s=1}^{l} \Phi_s S\Lambda_s^{-1}S, \end{aligned} \tag{14}$$

where $\Phi_s = \operatorname{diag}(\varphi_s(x_1), \varphi_s(x_2), \ldots, \varphi_s(x_N))$, $\Lambda_s^{-1} = \operatorname{diag}(q_1(\tilde{x}_s), q_2(\tilde{x}_s), \ldots, q_N(\tilde{x}_s))$, $s = 1, 2, \ldots, l$ are diagonal matrices. For a suitable number of interpolation points l, the computation of the preconditioner (14) requires $O(lN\log N)$ operations. We denote P_3^{-1} as $P_{TAI}^{-1}(l)$, where l represents the number of interpolation points, and have summarized the Algorithm 1 in the table below.

Algorithm 1 Solving system (5) by the PGMRES method with preconditioner $P_{TAI}^{-1}(l)$.

Input: Matrix $A = I + DG$ defined in (6) and the interpolation point l.
Output: The solution $u = [u_1, u_2, \ldots, u_m]$.
Calculate the eigenvalues of G by FFT and calculate the eigenvalues of $\tau(G)$ by DST;
Construct the preconditioner $P_{TAI}^{-1}(l)$ by diagonalizing $\tau(G)$ using Formula (14);
Set the initial vector u^0;
For $k = 1, 2, \ldots, m$ **do**
Use the right-hand term of Formula (5) to calculate b_k by FFT.
Calculate $P_{TAI}^{-1}(l)v$ by DST and calculate Av by FFT.
Obtain u_k by performing MATLAB's gmres.
end for

---

4. Spectral Analysis

In this section, we discuss the spectral properties of the preconditioned matrix $P_3^{-1}A$. First, we review some off-diagonal decay property reasoning.

Lemma 2 ([25]). *Let $\beta \in (1,2)$ and $A = (a_{i,j}) \in \mathcal{L}_{\beta+1}$ be a matrix, which satisfies*

$$|a_{i,j}| \leq \frac{c}{(1+|i-j|)^{\beta+1}}$$

for $\beta > 0$, and some constant $c > 0$. Then $\exists$ a constant ϖ s.t. $\|L\|_\infty \leq \varpi$.

Lemma 3 ([25]). *Let A and P_1 be as defined in Section 3, $d(x) \in C^1[x_L, x_R]$. For any given $\varepsilon > 0$, there exists a constant c_1 and an integer N_1, such that for $l \geq N_1$,*

$$\|P_1^{-1} - A^{-1}\|_\infty \leq c_1 \max_{1\leq i\leq N} \Delta(x_i, l) + \varepsilon,$$

where

$$\Delta(x_i, l) = \max_{i-l\leq k\leq i+l} |x_k - x_i| = (l-1)h.$$

Next, we discuss the spectral properties of $P_3^{-1}A$ by analyzing the approximation $P_3^{-1} - A^{-1}$. Due to

$$P_3^{-1} - A^{-1} = P_3^{-1} - P_2^{-1} + P_2^{-1} - P_1^{-1} + P_1^{-1} - A^{-1},$$

we will respectively analyze the properties of $P_3^{-1} - P_2^{-1}, P_2^{-1} - P_1^{-1}$ and $P_1^{-1} - A^{-1}$. And the approximation property of P_1 and A is given in Lemma 3 above. Then, we give the results of the approximation property of P_2^{-1} and P_1^{-1}.

Theorem 1. *Let P_1 and P_2 be defined as in Section 3. The approximation P_2^{-1} to P_1^{-1} satisfies*

$$P_2^{-1} - P_1^{-1} = E_2 + F_2,$$

where E_2 and F_2 are matrices of small norm and low rank, respectively, i.e., $\|E_2\| < c_2 \cdot \epsilon$ and $rank(F_2) \leq 4\varsigma$ for some positive constant c_2, ϵ and ς.

Proof. We can write $P_2^{-1} - P_1^{-1}$ as

$$\begin{aligned} P_2^{-1} - P_1^{-1} &= \sum_{i=1}^{N} e_i e_i^T \left(G_i^{-1} - K_i^{-1}\right) \\ &= \sum_{i=1}^{N} e_i e_i^T K_i^{-1}(K_i - G_i)G_i^{-1} \\ &= \sum_{i=1}^{N} d_i e_i e_i^T K_i^{-1}(G - \tau(G))G_i^{-1}, \end{aligned}$$

where $\|G_i^{-1}\|_\infty < \eta^{-1}$; for detailed proof, refer to Lemma 4.7 in [25].

As shown in [15], the matrix difference $G - \tau(G)$ admits a decomposition $E_1 + F_1$, where E_1 coincides with $G - \tau(G)$ within the upper-left and lower-right $(N-1) \times (N-1)$ submatrices and vanishes elsewhere, while satisfying $rank(E_1) \leq 2(N-1)$. Further, if we let $\varepsilon > 0$ be fixed, then we have $\|F_1\|_2 < \varepsilon$.

Given that K_i^{-1} exhibits off-diagonal decay, it admits a splitting $\tilde{K}_i + \hat{K}_i$, where

$$\tilde{K}_i = \begin{bmatrix} * & \cdots & * & 0 & \cdots & 0 \\ \vdots & \ddots & & \ddots & \ddots & \vdots \\ * & & \ddots & & \ddots & 0 \\ 0 & \ddots & & \ddots & & * \\ \vdots & \ddots & \ddots & & \ddots & \vdots \\ 0 & \cdots & 0 & * & \cdots & * \end{bmatrix} \quad \text{and} \quad \hat{K}_i = \begin{bmatrix} 0 & \cdots & 0 & * & \cdots & * \\ \vdots & \ddots & & \ddots & \ddots & \vdots \\ 0 & & \ddots & & \ddots & * \\ * & \ddots & & \ddots & & 0 \\ \vdots & \ddots & \ddots & & \ddots & \vdots \\ * & \cdots & * & 0 & \cdots & 0 \end{bmatrix},$$

where '*' denotes the nonzero entries.

Considering

$$\begin{aligned}K_i^{-1}(G-\tau(G))G_i^{-1} &= K_i^{-1}(E_1+F_1)G_i^{-1}\\ &= K_i^{-1}E_1G_i^{-1}+K_i^{-1}F_1G_i^{-1}\\ &= K_i^{-1}E_1G_i^{-1}+(\tilde{K}_i+\hat{K}_i)F_1G_i^{-1}\\ &= (K_i^{-1}E_1+\hat{K}_iF_1)G_i^{-1}+\tilde{K}_iF_1G_i^{-1},\end{aligned}$$

we derive

$$\begin{aligned}\|(K_i^{-1}E_1+\hat{K}_iF_1)G_i^{-1}\|_\infty &\leq (\|K_i^{-1}\|_\infty\cdot\|E_1\|_\infty+\|\hat{K}_i\|_\infty\cdot\|F_1\|_\infty)\cdot\|G_i^{-1}\|_\infty\\ &\leq \varepsilon(\|K_i^{-1}\|_\infty+\|F_1\|_\infty)\cdot\|G_i^{-1}\|_\infty\end{aligned}$$

and

$$\begin{aligned}\| \sum_{i=1}^{N} e_ie_i^T(K_i^{-1}E_1+\hat{K}_iF_1)G_i^{-1} \|_\infty &= \max_{1\leq i\leq N}\|e_i^T(K_i^{-1}E_1+\hat{K}_iF_1)G_i^{-1}\|_1\\ &= \max_{1\leq i\leq N}\|(K_i^{-1}E_1+\hat{K}_iF_1)G_i^{-1}\|_\infty\\ &\leq \varepsilon\cdot\max_{1\leq i\leq N}(\|K_i^{-1}\|_\infty+\|F_1\|_\infty)\cdot\|G_i^{-1}\|_\infty.\end{aligned}$$

Since $\|K_i^{-1}\|_\infty$ and $\|F_1\|_\infty$ are limited due to Lemma 2, it follows that $\|G_i^{-1}\|_\infty$ is also bounded. In other words, there is a constant $c_2 > 0$ such that

$$\left\|\sum_{i=1}^{N} e_ie_i^T(K_i^{-1}E_1+\hat{K}_iF_1)G_i^{-1}\right\|_\infty \leq c_2\cdot\epsilon.$$

Next, we focus on the matrix product $\tilde{K}_iF_1G_i^{-1}$. We assume the block dimensions of $\tilde{K}_i$ align with those of F_1; otherwise, the smaller block is extended accordingly. Through structural analysis of $\tilde{K}_i$ and F_1, the subsequent outcomes are derived:

$$\tilde{K}_iF_1G_i^{-1}=\begin{pmatrix}0&0&\dots&\dots&0&+\\0&0&\dots&\dots&0&+\\0&0&\dots&\dots&0&0\\\vdots&\vdots&&&\vdots&\vdots\\0&0&\dots&\dots&0&0\\+&0&\dots&\dots&0&0\\+&0&\dots&\dots&0&0\end{pmatrix},\quad G_i^{-1}=\begin{pmatrix}+&+&\dots&\dots&+&+\\+&+&\dots&\dots&+&+\\0&0&\dots&\dots&0&0\\\vdots&\vdots&&&\vdots&\vdots\\0&0&\dots&\dots&0&0\\+&+&\dots&\dots&+&+\\+&+&\dots&\dots&+&+\end{pmatrix},$$

where '+' denotes non-negative entries. Therefore, we have

$$\operatorname{rank}\left(\sum_{i=1}^{N} e_ie_i^T\tilde{K}_iF_1G_i^{-1}\right)\leq 4\varsigma,$$

where ς is the dimension of the blocks in $\tilde{K}_iF_1G_i^{-1}$. Consequently,

$$\begin{aligned}\sum_{i=1}^{N} e_ie_i^T\left(K_i^{-1}-K_i^{-1}\right) &= \sum_{i=1}^{N} e_ie_i^T\left(K_i^{-1}E_1+\hat{K}_iF_1\right)G_i^{-1}+\sum_{i=1}^{N} e_ie_i^T\tilde{K}_iF_1G_i^{-1}\\ &= E_2+F_2,\end{aligned}$$

where E_2 and F_2 are matrices of small norm and low rank, respectively. □

Finally, we focus on the approximation property of P_3 and A.

Theorem 2. *Let P_3, P_2, P_1 and A be defined as shown previously. Supposing l is sufficiently smaller than N, there exists N_2 such that for $N > N_2$, it holds that*

$$P_3^{-1} - A^{-1} = E + F,$$

where E and F are of small norm and of low rank, respectively.

Proof. By Theorem 4.2 in [25], we know that $P_3^{-1} - P_2^{-1} = E_3 - F_3$, where E_3 is of small norm, satisfying $\|E_3\|_\infty < c_3$ and F_3 is of small rank. Due to Lemma 3, we know

$$\|P_1^{-1} - A^{-1}\|_\infty \le \max_{1\le i\le N} \Delta(x_i, N_1) + \varepsilon = c_1(N_1 - 1)h + \varepsilon.$$

Let N_2 be an integer such that $(N_1 - 1)h < \varepsilon$, we have

$$\begin{aligned} P_3^{-1} - A^{-1} &= P_3^{-1} - P_2^{-1} + P_2^{-1} - P_1^{-1} + P_1^{-1} - A^{-1} \\ &= E_3 + F_3 + E_2 + F_2 + P_1^{-1} - A^{-1} \\ &= E_3 + E_2 + (P_1^{-1} - A^{-1}) + F_3 + F_2 \\ &\triangleq E + F, \end{aligned}$$

where $E = E_3 + E_2 + (P_1^{-1} - A^{-1})$ and $F = F_3 + F_2$. As

$$\|E\|_\infty = \|E_3\|_\infty + \|E_2\|_\infty + \|P_1^{-1} - A^{-1}\|_\infty < (c_1 + c_2 + c_3 + 1) \cdot \varepsilon,$$

then the conclusion follows. □

5. Numerical Experiments

This section evaluates the computational efficiency of the proposed preconditioning strategy through numerical experiments. All computations were executed in MATLAB (R2022b) on a workstation equipped with a 4.00 GHz AMD Ryzen 9 7940H processor, 16.00 GB RAM, and the Windows 11 OS. We solve the variable-coefficient tempered FDEs:

$$\begin{cases} \frac{\partial u(x,t)}{\partial t} = d(x)\left({}_0\mathbf{D}_x^{\beta,\lambda} + {}_x\mathbf{D}_1^{\beta,\lambda}\right)u(x,t) + f(x,t), \\ u(0,t) = 0, u(1,t) = 0, t \in [0,1], \\ u(x,0) = 0, x \in [0,1]. \end{cases} \tag{15}$$

The source term is given as follows:

$$\begin{aligned} f(x,t) = e^{-\lambda x}x^3(1-x)^3 - td(x)&\left[e^{-\lambda x}\sum_{m=0}^{3}\left((-1)^m\begin{pmatrix}3\\m\end{pmatrix}\frac{\Gamma(4+m)}{\Gamma(4+m-\beta)}x^{3+m-\beta}\right)\right. \\ &\left.+e^{\lambda(x-2)}\sum_{j=0}^{30}\frac{3^j}{j!}\left(\sum_{m=0}^{3}\left((-1)^m\begin{pmatrix}3\\m\end{pmatrix}\frac{\Gamma(4+m+j)}{\Gamma(4+m+j-\beta)}(1-x)^{j+3+m-\beta}\right)\right)\right] \\ &+2td(x)(\lambda^\beta)e^{-\lambda x}x^3(1-x)^3 \end{aligned}$$

and the exact solution is $u(x,t) \simeq te^{-\lambda x}x^3(1-x)^3$.

The resulting linear system of the discretization is solved by the GMRES method with preconditioners. We test P_3^{-1} and denote it as $P_{TAI}^{-1}(l)$, where l represents the number of interpolation points. For comparison, we also test the diagonal and circulant splitting preconditioner [17], the skew-diagonal Toeplitz splitting preconditioner based on τ matrix [22], and the Strang circulant approximate inverse preconditioner [25]. These three preconditioner are denoted as P_{DCS}^{-1}, $P_{SDTAS_\tau}^{-1}$ and $P_{CAI}^{-1}(l)$, respectively.

In all experiments, $\lambda = 1.5$, $\beta = 1.2$. We searched for the optimal number of interpolation points l in the proposed preconditioning matrices $P_{TAI}^{-1}(l)$. For the two experiments, we choose the optimal number of interpolation points l to be 8 and 12, respectively. We specify the same grid density in both space and time $\Delta t = h$, and for a certain initial point u^0. The iterative procedure is initialized with the zero vector and halts once the relative residual error satisfies $\|r_k\|/\|r_0\| < 10^{-7}$, with a cap of 1000 iterations imposed to prevent divergence.

5.1. Test Problem 1

Consider the coefficient

$$d(x) = \frac{e^{5x}}{1+x}.$$

An illustration of the corresponding analytical solution and the numerical solution is shown in Figure 1. We use GMRES with P_{DCS}^{-1}, $P_{SDTAS_\tau}^{-1}$, $P_{CAI}^{-1}(l)$ and $P_{TAI}^{-1}(l)$ preconditioners as well as GMRES without preconditioning to test. The results of the computations at discretization levels $N = 10^8, 10^9, 10^{10}, 10^{11}, 10^{12}$ are shown in Table 1. Here, "IT" denotes the average number of iterations per step, and "CPU" denotes the total computation time(s) of the algorithm. To facilitate the comparison of the performance of different preconditioning matrices, we visualized the results from Table 1, as shown in Figure 2. From Table 1 and Figure 2, we can see that the performance of $P_{TAI}^{-1}(l)$ is significantly better than that of $P_{CAI}^{-1}(l)$, P_{DCS}^{-1} and $P_{SDTAS_\tau}^{-1}$. The number of iterations for each preconditioning method remains relatively stable as the discretization level increases, but the number of iterations for $P_{TAI}^{-1}(l)$ is notably lower than that for the other three. Similarly, in terms of computation time, the computation time for $P_{TAI}^{-1}(l)$ is much lower than that for the other three, and the growth in computation time for $P_{TAI}^{-1}(l)$ is slower as the discretization level increases.

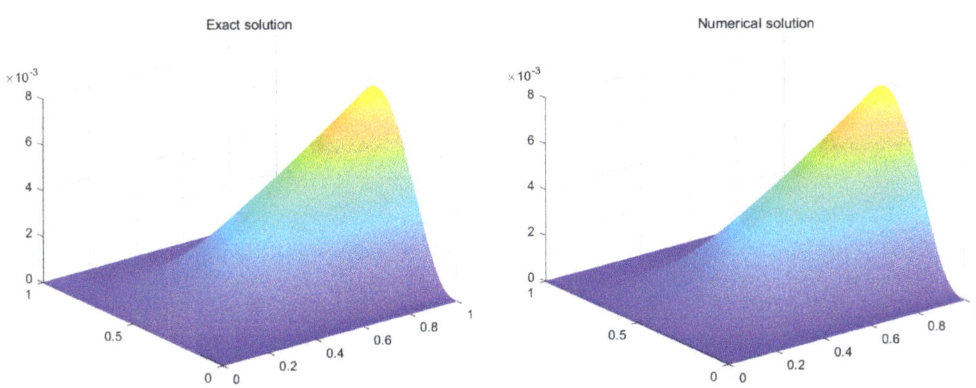

Figure 1. Comparison of the exact solutions and $P_{TAI}^{-1}(10)$ numerical solutions ($d = d_1(x)$, $\lambda = 1.5$, $\beta = 1.2$, $\gamma_1 = 0.75$).

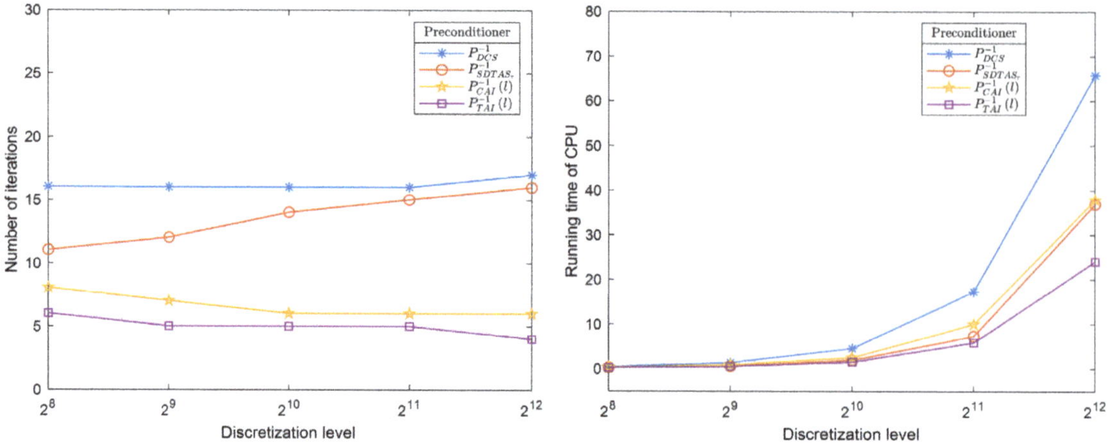

Figure 2. Comparison of average iterations and computation time for P_{DCS}^{-1}, $P_{SDTAS_\tau}^{-1}$, $P_{CAI}^{-1}(l)$ and $P_{TAI}^{-1}(l)$ ($d = d_1(x)$, $\lambda = 1.5$, $\beta = 1.2$, $\gamma_1 = 0.75$).

Table 1. Numerical results of I, P_{DCS}^{-1}, $P_{SDTAS_\tau}^{-1}$, $P_{CAI}^{-1}(l)$ and $P_{TAI}^{-1}(l)$ ($d = d_1(x)$, $\lambda = 1.5$, $\beta = 1.2$, $\gamma_1 = 0.75$).

Method	Index	N				
		2^8	2^9	2^{10}	2^{11}	2^{12}
I	IT	87.34	108.21	123.12	134.07	140.03
	CPU	0.82	3.66	14.33	70.64	555.72
P_{DCS}^{-1} [17]	α	0.1	0.1	0.1	0.1	0.1
	IT	16.06	16.03	16.02	16.01	17.00
	CPU	0.38	1.31	4.53	17.33	65.74
$P_{SDTAS_\tau}^{-1}$ [22]	α	0.1	0.1	0.1	0.1	0.1
	IT	11.04	12.02	14.01	15.01	16.00
	CPU	0.20	0.52	1.91	7.32	36.86
$P_{CAI}^{-1}(l)$ [25]	l	8	8	8	8	8
	IT	8.03	7.01	6.01	6.00	6.00
	CPU	0.25	0.79	2.49	9.99	37.84
$\boldsymbol{P_{TAI}^{-1}(l)}$	l	8	8	8	8	8
	IT	**6.02**	**5.01**	**5.00**	**5.00**	**4.00**
	CPU	**0.19**	**0.46**	**1.49**	**5.87**	**24.03**

The proposed preconditioner and optimal result have been bolded.

To further illustrate the effectiveness of the proposed preconditioning matrices, we plot the eigenvalue distributions of the original coefficient matrix A, the preconditioner P_{DCS}^{-1}, $P_{SDTAS_\tau}^{-1}$, $P_{CAI}^{-1}(l)$ and $P_{TAI}^{-1}(l)$ when $N = 10^8$, as shown in Figure 3. It can be observed that the eigenvalue distribution of the coefficient matrix A without preconditioning is highly dispersed, while the eigenvalue distributions of the preconditioned matrices $AP_{TAI}^{-1}(l)$ are concentrated around 1. Notably, the eigenvalue distribution of $AP_{TAI}^{-1}(l)$ is more concentrated than those of the other preconditioners.

We searched for the optimal number of interpolation points l in the proposed preconditioner $P_{TAI}^{-1}(l)$. As shown in Table 2, we tested GMRES using $P_{TAI}^{-1}(l)$ with the number of interpolation points $l = 4, 6, 8, 10, 12$. To determine the optimal number of interpolation points l, we visualized the number of iterations, as shown in Figure 4. By analyzing Figure 4, we found that when the number of interpolation points $l \geq 8$, the number of iterations tends to stabilize. With this observation, the number of interpolation points $l = 8$ was recommended for test problem 1.

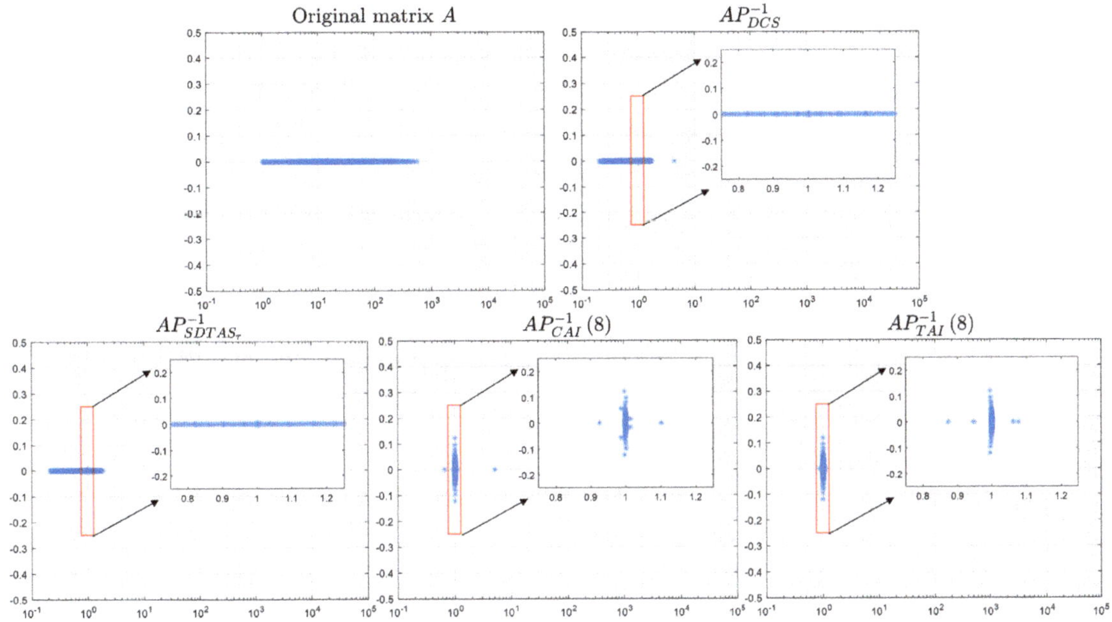

Figure 3. The eigenvalue distributions of the original coefficient matrix A, the preconditioner P_{DCS}^{-1}, $P_{SDTAS_\tau}^{-1}$, $P_{CAI}^{-1}(l)$ and $P_{TAI}^{-1}(l)$ ($d = d_1(x)$, $\lambda = 1.5$, $\beta = 1.2$, $\gamma_1 = 0.75$).

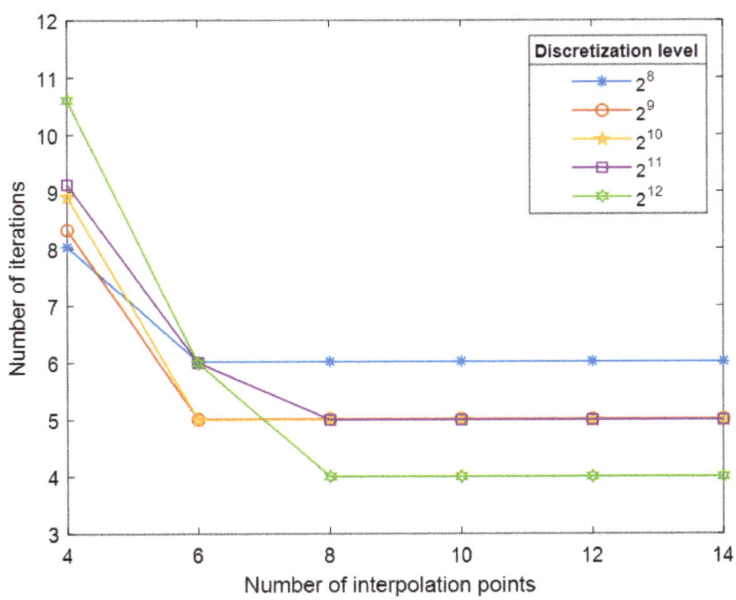

Figure 4. Number of iteration variation curves when $l = 4, 6, 8, 10, 12$ ($d = d_1(x)$, $\lambda = 1.5$, $\beta = 1.2$, $\gamma_1 = 0.75$).

Table 2. Numerical results of $P_{TAI}^{-1}(l)$ at different numbers of interpolation points l ($d = d_1(x)$, $\lambda = 1.5$, $\beta = 1.2$, $\gamma_1 = 0.75$).

N	Index	Number of Interpolation Points l					
		4	6	8	10	12	14
2^8	IT	8.03	6.02	6.02	6.02	6.02	6.02
	CPU	0.17	0.16	0.18	0.22	0.25	0.24
2^9	IT	8.33	5.01	5.01	5.01	5.01	5.01
	CPU	0.49	0.39	0.46	0.47	0.49	0.54
2^{10}	IT	8.90	5.00	5.00	5.00	5.00	5.00
	CPU	1.74	1.45	1.62	1.82	1.80	1.95
2^{11}	IT	9.12	6.00	5.00	5.00	5.00	5.00
	CPU	8.89	6.20	5.70	6.30	6.51	6.79
2^{12}	IT	10.60	5.99	4.00	4.00	4.00	4.00
	CPU	60.43	41.71	42.19	44.64	40.37	50.46

5.2. Test Problem 2

Consider the coefficient

$$d(x) = \frac{e^{3x} + 0.2}{x(1-x)}.$$

An illustration of the corresponding analytical solution and the numerical solution are shown in Figure 5. We compared P_{DCS}^{-1}, $P_{SDTAS_\tau}^{-1}$, $P_{CAI}^{-1}(l)$ and $P_{TAI}^{-1}(l)$. The results of the computations at discretization levels $N = 10^8, 10^9, 10^{10}, 10^{11}, 10^{12}$ are shown in Table 3 and visualized in Figure 6. In terms of the number of iterations, all preconditioning methods show relatively stable iteration numbers as the discretization level increases, but the number of iterations for $P_{TAI}^{-1}(l)$ is notably lower than that for the other three. In terms of computation time, the computation time for $P_{TAI}^{-1}(l)$ is slightly higher than that for $P_{SDTAS_\tau}^{-1}$ at discretization level $N = 10^8, 10^9, 10^{10}$, but the difference is not significant. As the discretization level increases, the computation time for $P_{TAI}^{-1}(l)$ grows more slowly and is significantly lower than that for the other three preconditioners. Additionally, we note that this coefficient is more complex than the last one as it has singularities at point $x = 0$ and $x = 1$. And this is reflected in the higher number of iterations in Table 3 and the more dispersed eigenvalue distribution in Figure 7.

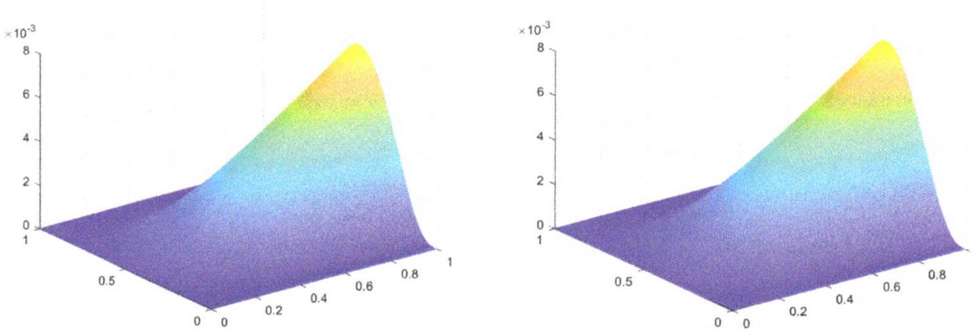

Figure 5. Comparison of the exact solutions and $P_{TAI}^{-1}(l)$ numerical solutions ($d = d_2(x)$, $\lambda = 1.5$, $\beta = 1.2$, $\gamma_1 = 0.75$).

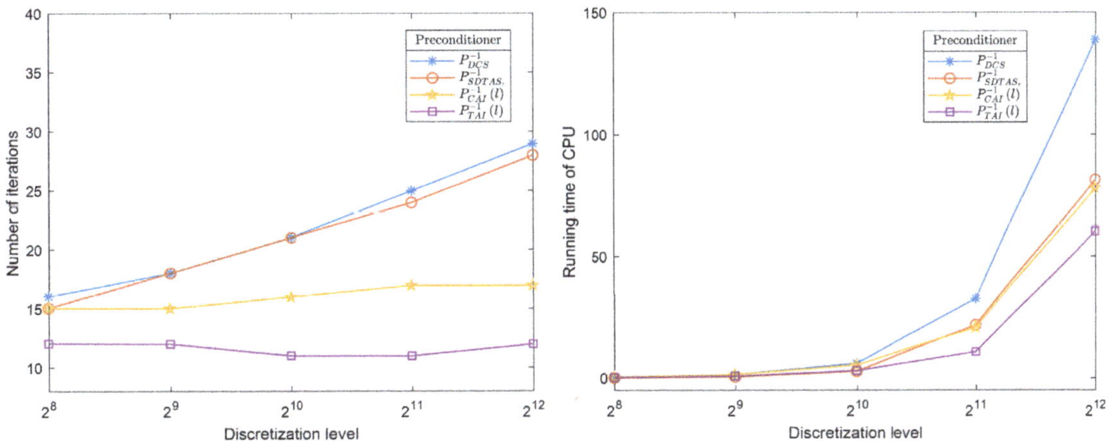

Figure 6. Comparison of average iterations and computation time for P_{DCS}^{-1}, $P_{SDTAS_\tau}^{-1}$, $P_{CAI}^{-1}(l)$ and $P_{TAI}^{-1}(l)$ ($d = d_1(x)$, $\lambda = 1.5$, $\beta = 1.2$, $\gamma_1 = 0.75$).

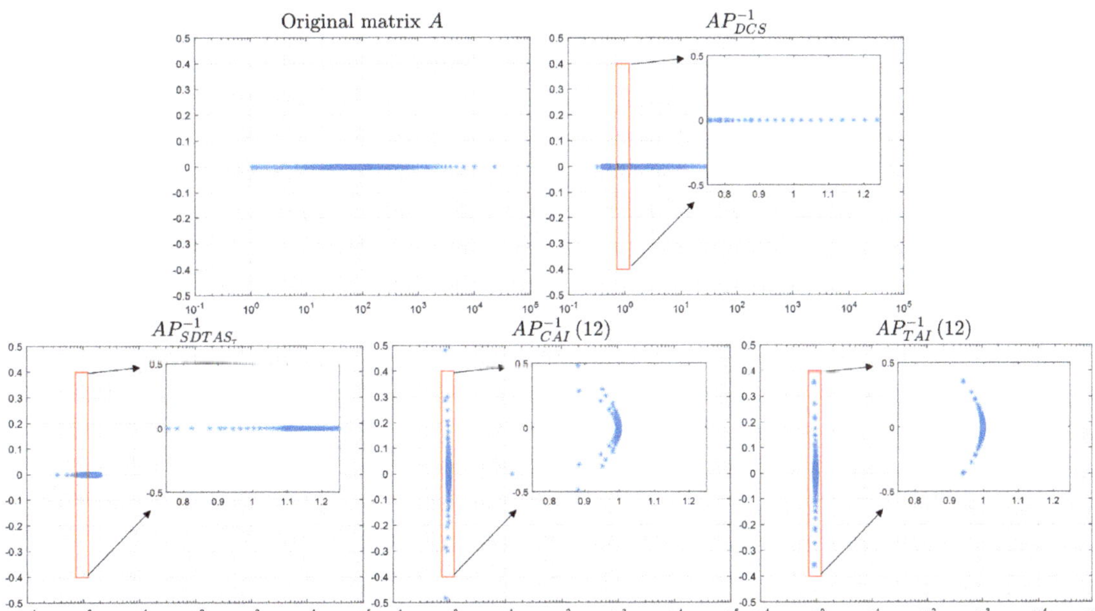

Figure 7. The eigenvalue distributions of the original coefficient matrix A, the preconditioner P_{DCS}^{-1}, $P_{SDTAS_\tau}^{-1}$, $P_{CAI}^{-1}(l)$ and $P_{TAI}^{-1}(l)$ ($d = d_2(x)$, $\lambda = 1.5$, $\beta = 1.2$, $\gamma_1 = 0.75$).

We also plot the eigenvalue distributions of A, the preconditioner P_{DCS}^{-1}, $P_{SDTAS_\tau}^{-1}$, $P_{CAI}^{-1}(l)$ and $P_{TAI}^{-1}(l)$ when $N = 10^8$, as shown in Figure 7. It can be observed that the eigenvalue distribution of the coefficient matrix without preconditioning is highly dispersed, while the eigenvalue distributions of the preconditioned matrices are concentrated around 1. Notably, the eigenvalue distribution of $P_{TAI}^{-1}(l)$ is more concentrated than those of the other preconditioners.

Similarly, we searched for the optimal number of interpolation points l in the proposed preconditioner $P_{TAI}^{-1}(l)$. As shown in Table 4, we tested GMRES using $P_{TAI}^{-1}(l)$ with the number of interpolation points $l = 4, 6, 8, 10, 12$. To determine the optimal number of interpolation points l, we visualized the number of iterations, as shown in Figure 8. By analyzing Figure 8, we found that when the number of interpolation points $l \geq 12$, the number of iterations tends to stabilize. In this view, we selected the optimal number of interpolation points $l = 12$ for the above test.

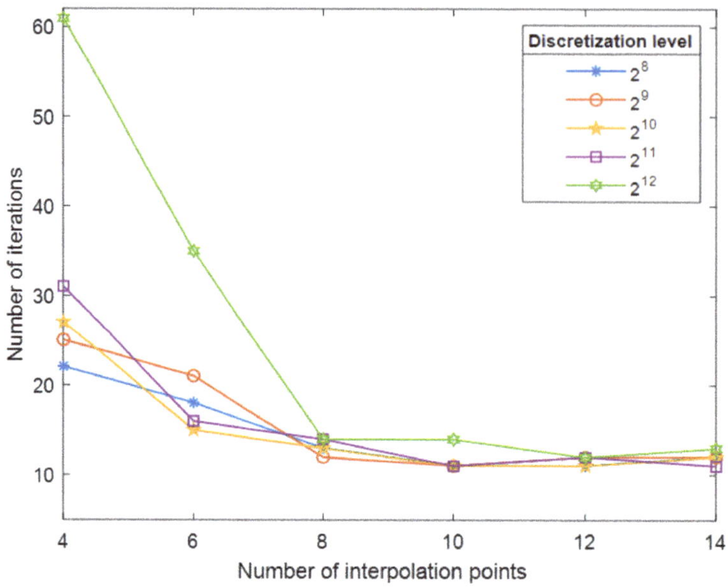

Figure 8. Number of iteration variation curves when $l = 4, 6, 8, 10, 12$ ($d = d_2(x)$, $\lambda = 1.5$, $\beta = 1.2$, $\gamma_1 = 0.75$).

Table 3. Numerical results of I, P_{DCS}^{-1}, $P_{SDTAS_\tau}^{-1}$, $P_{CAI}^{-1}(l)$ and $P_{TAI}^{-1}(l)$ ($d = d_2(x)$, $\lambda = 1.5$, $\beta = 1.2$, $\gamma_1 = 0.75$).

Method	Index	N				
		2^8	2^9	2^{10}	2^{11}	2^{12}
I	IT	125.49	174.34	233.23	300.15	~
	CPU	1.46	7.41	46.45	225.74	~
P_{DCS}^{-1} [17]	α	0.15	0.15	0.15	0.15	0.15
	IT	16.06	18.04	21.02	25.01	29.01
	CPU	0.48	1.52	6.14	32.83	139.03
$P_{SDTAS_\tau}^{-1}$ [22]	α	0.15	0.15	0.15	0.15	0.15
	IT	15.06	18.04	21.02	24.01	28.01
	CPU	0.24	0.65	2.84	22.00	81.56
$P_{CAI}^{-1}(l)$ [25]	l	12	12	12	12	12
	IT	15.06	15.03	16.02	17.01	17.00
	CPU	0.49	1.60	5.42	21.00	78.15
$\boldsymbol{P_{TAI}^{-1}(l)}$	l	12	12	12	12	12
	IT	**12.05**	**12.02**	**11.01**	**11.01**	**12.00**
	CPU	**0.35**	**0.90**	**3.11**	**10.89**	**60.30**

The proposed preconditioner and optimal result have been bolded.

Table 4. Numerical results of $P_{TAI}^{-1}(l)$ at different numbers of interpolation points l ($d = d_2(x)$, $\lambda = 1.5, \beta = 1.2, \gamma_1 = 0.75$).

N	Index	Number of Interpolation Points l					
		4	6	8	10	12	14
2^8	IT	22.09	18.07	13.05	11.04	11.04	12.05
	CPU	0.41	0.40	0.35	0.32	0.36	0.48
2^9	IT	25.05	21.04	12.02	11.02	12.02	12.02
	CPU	1.27	1.29	0.92	0.92	1.00	1.00
2^{10}	IT	27.03	15.01	13.01	11.01	11.01	12.01
	CPU	10.22	3.16	3.10	3.04	3.26	3.53
2^{11}	IT	31.02	16.01	14.01	11.01	12.01	11.01
	CPU	20.98	15.90	12.04	11.23	12.51	11.79
2^{12}	IT	60.93	34.98	14.00	13.99	12.00	13.00
	CPU	626.27	259.42	121.80	112.15	76.09	109.79

6. Concluding Remarks

In this paper, we consider solving the tempered fractional diffusion equations with variable coefficients in a numerical way. The problem is discretized by the Crank–Nicolson method and the tempered weighted and shifted Grünwald formula. For the resulting linear system, we approximate the SPD Toeplitz matrix by the τ matrix and take the advantage of the row-by-row approximation strategy to construct an approximate inverse preconditioner. A spectral analysis reveals that the eigenvalues of the preconditioned system matrix are tightly clustered near unity. Experiments further validate the enhanced convergence enabled by the developed preconditioner.

Author Contributions: Conceptualization, X.Z. and C.W.; methodology, X.Z. and C.W.; software, X.Z. and C.W.; validation, X.Z. and C.W.; formal analysis, X.Z. and C.W.; investigation, X.Z. and C.W.; resources, X.Z. and C.W.; data curation, X.Z. and C.W.; writing—original draft preparation, X.Z.; writing—review and editing, C.W.; visualization, C.W.; supervision, C.W.; funding acquisition, C.W. All authors have read and agreed to the published version of the manuscript.

Funding: This work was supported by the National Natural Science Foundation of China (No. 12001022) and the Disciplinary funding of Beijing Technology and Business University (No. STKY202508).

Data Availability Statement: Data will be made available on request.

Conflicts of Interest: The authors declare no competing interests.

References

1. Baeumer, B.; Meerschaert, M.M. Tempered stable Lévy motion and transient super-diffusion. *J. Comput. Appl. Math.* **2010**, *233*, 2438–2448. [CrossRef]
2. Magin, R.L. Fractional calculus in bioengineering. *Crit. Rev. Biomed. Eng.* **2004**, *32*, 1–104. [CrossRef]
3. Meerschaert, M.M.; Zhang, Y.; Baeumer, B. Tempered anomalous diffusion in heterogeneous systems. *Geophys. Res. Lett.* **2008**, *35*, L17403. [CrossRef]
4. Zhang, H.; Liu, F.; Turner, I.; Chen, S. The numerical simulation of the tempered fractional Black-Scholes equation for European double barrier option. *Appl. Math. Model.* **2016**, *40*, 5819–5834. [CrossRef]
5. Huang, X.; Sun, H.-W. A preconditioner based on sine transform for two-dimensional semi-linear Riesz space fractional diffusion equations in convex domains. *Appl. Numer. Math.* **2021**, *169*, 289–302. [CrossRef]
6. Qin, H.; Pang, H.; Sun, H. Sine transform based preconditioning techniques for space fractional diffusion equations. *Numer. Linear Algebra Appl.* **2023**, *30*, e2474. [CrossRef]
7. Sun, L.-Y.; Lei, S.-L.; Sun, H.-W.; Zhang, J.-L. An α-robust fast algorithm for distributed-order time–space fractional diffusion equation with weakly singular solution. *Math. Comput. Simul.* **2023**, *207*, 437–452. [CrossRef]

8. Zhang, C.-H.; Yu, J.-W.; Wang, X. A fast second-order scheme for nonlinear Riesz space-fractional diffusion equations. *Numer. Algorithms* **2023**, *92*, 1813–1836. [CrossRef]
9. Liu, J.; Fu, H.; Wang, H.; Chai, X. A preconditioned fast quadratic spline collocation method for two-sided space-fractional partial differential equations. *J. Comput. Appl. Math.* **2019**, *360*, 138–156. [CrossRef]
10. Lu, X.; Fang, Z.-W.; Sun, H.-W. Splitting preconditioning based on sine transform for time-dependent Riesz space fractional diffusion equations. *J. Appl. Math. Comput.* **2021**, *66*, 673–700. [CrossRef]
11. Shao, X.-H.; Kang, C.-B. A preconditioner based on sine transform for space fractional diffusion equations. *Appl. Numer. Math.* **2022**, *178*, 248–261. [CrossRef]
12. Qu, W.; Liang, Y. Stability and convergence of the Crank-Nicolson scheme for a class of variable-coefficient tempered fractional diffusion equations. *Adv. Differ. Equ.* **2017**, *2017*, 108. [CrossRef]
13. Wang, W.; Chen, X.; Ding, D.; Lei, S.-L. Circulant preconditioning technique for barrier options pricing under fractional diffusion models. *Int. J. Comput. Math.* **2015**, *92*, 2596–2614. [CrossRef]
14. Li, C.; Deng, W. High order schemes for the tempered fractional diffusion equations. *Adv. Comput. Math.* **2016**, *42*, 543–572. [CrossRef]
15. Serra, S. Superlinear PCG methods for symmetric Toeplitz systems. *Math. Comput.* **1999**, *68*, 793–803. [CrossRef]
16. Wang, C.; Li, H.; Zhao, D. Preconditioning Toeplitz-plus-diagonal linear systems using the Sherman-Morrison-Woodbury formula. *J. Comput. Appl. Math.* **2017**, *309*, 312–319. [CrossRef]
17. Bai, Z.-Z.; Lu, K.-Y.; Pan, J.-Y. Diagonal and Toeplitz splitting iteration methods for diagonal-plus-Toeplitz linear systems from spatial fractional diffusion equations. *Numer. Linear Algebra Appl.* **2017**, *24*, e2093. [CrossRef]
18. Wang, C.; Li, H.; Zhao, D. Improved block preconditioners for linear systems arising from half-quadratic image restoration. *Appl. Math. Comput.* **2019**, *363*, e124614. [CrossRef]
19. Lei, S.; Fan, D.; Chen, X. Fast solution algorithms for exponentially tempered fractional diffusion equations. *Numer. Methods Partial Differ. Equ.* **2018**, *34*, 1301–1323. [CrossRef]
20. Zhao, Y.-L.; Zhu, P.-Y.; Gu, X.-M.; Zhao, X.-L.; Jian, H.-Y.A preconditioning technique for all-at-once system from the nonlinear tempered fractional diffusion equation. *J. Sci. Comput.* **2020**, *83*, 10. [CrossRef]
21. Qu, W.; Lei, S.-L. On CSCS-based iteration method for tempered fractional diffusion equations. *Jpn. J. Ind. Appl. Math.* **2016**, *33*, 583–597. [CrossRef]
22. Tang, S.-P.; Huang, Y.-M. A matrix splitting preconditioning method for solving the discretized tempered fractional diffusion equations. *Numer. Algorithms* **2023**, *92*, 1311–1333. [CrossRef]
23. Feng, Y.; Zhang, X.; Chen, Y.; Wei, L. A compact finite difference scheme for solving fractional Black-Scholes option pricing model. *J. Inequal. Appl.* **2025**, *2025*, 36. [CrossRef]
24. Zhang, X.; Wei, L.; Liu, J. Application of the LDG method using generalized alternating numerical flux to the fourth-order time-fractional sub-diffusion model. *Appl. Math. Lett.* **2025**, *168*, 109580. [CrossRef]
25. Pan, J.; Ke, R.; Ng, M.K.; Sun, H.-W. Preconditioning techniques for diagonal-times-Toeplitz matrices in fractional diffusion equations. *SIAM J. Sci. Comput.* **2014**, *36*, A2698–A2719. [CrossRef]
26. Chou, L.-K.; Lei, S.-L. Fast ADI method for high dimensional fractional diffusion equations in conservative form with preconditioned strategy. *Comput. Math. Appl.* **2017**, *73*, 385–403. [CrossRef]
27. Du, N.; Sun, H.-W.; Wang, H. A preconditioned fast finite difference scheme for space-fractional diffusion equations in convex domains. *Comput. Appl. Math.* **2019**, *38*, 14. [CrossRef]
28. Gan, D.; Zhang, G.-F. Efficient ADI schemes and preconditioning for a class of high-dimensional spatial fractional diffusion equations with variable diffusion coefficients. *J. Comput. Appl. Math.* **2023**, *423*, 114938. [CrossRef]

algorithms

MDPI

Article

Computational Aspects of L_0 Linking in the Rasch Model

Alexander Robitzsch [1,2]

[1] IPN—Leibniz Institute for Science and Mathematics Education, Olshausenstraße 62, 24118 Kiel, Germany; robitzsch@leibniz-ipn.de

[2] Centre for International Student Assessment (ZIB), Olshausenstraße 62, 24118 Kiel, Germany

Abstract: The L_0 linking approach replaces the L_2 loss function in mean–mean linking under the Rasch model with the L_0 loss function. Using the L_0 loss function offers the advantage of potential robustness against fixed differential item functioning effects. However, its nondifferentiability necessitates differentiable approximations to ensure feasible and computationally stable estimation. This article examines alternative specifications of two approximations, each controlled by a tuning parameter ε that determines the approximation error. Results demonstrate that the optimal ε value minimizing the RMSE of the linking parameter estimate depends on the magnitude of DIF effects, the number of items, and the sample size. A data-driven selection of ε outperformed a fixed ε across all conditions in both a numerical illustration and a simulation study.

Keywords: L_0 loss function; mean–mean linking; Rasch model; differential item functioning; differentiable approximation

1. Introduction

Item response theory (IRT) models [1–3] are statistical models for multivariate discrete random variables. This article focuses on dichotomous (i.e., binary) random variables and the comparison of two groups through a linking method.

Let $\boldsymbol{X} = (X_1, \ldots, X_I)$ denote a vector of $I \in \mathbb{N}$ random variables $X_i \in \{0,1\}$, commonly referred to as items or (scored) item responses. A unidimensional IRT model [4] represents the probability distribution $\mathsf{P}(\boldsymbol{X} = \boldsymbol{x})$ for $\boldsymbol{x} = (x_1, \ldots, x_I) \in \{0,1\}^I$,

$$\mathsf{P}(\boldsymbol{X} = \boldsymbol{x}; \boldsymbol{\delta}, \boldsymbol{\gamma}) = \int \prod_{i=1}^{I} \Big[P_i(\theta; \gamma_i)^{x_i} (1 - P_i(\theta; \gamma_i))^{1-x_i} \Big] \phi(\theta; \mu, \sigma) \, \mathrm{d}\theta, \quad (1)$$

where ϕ denotes the density of the normal distribution with mean μ and standard deviation (SD) σ. The distribution parameters of the latent variable θ, often labeled as a trait or ability variable, are collected in the vector $\boldsymbol{\delta} = (\mu, \sigma)$. The vector $\boldsymbol{\gamma} = (\gamma_1, \ldots, \gamma_I)$ contains the item parameters associated with the item response functions (IRFs) $P_i(\theta; \gamma_i) = \mathsf{P}(X_i = 1 | \theta)$ for $i = 1, \ldots, I$. The IRF of the Rasch model [5–7] is defined as

$$P_i(\theta; \gamma_i) = \Psi(\theta - b_i), \quad (2)$$

where b_i denotes the item difficulty b_i, and $\Psi(x) = (1 + \exp(-x))^{-1}$ is the logistic distribution function. In this formulation, the item parameter vector is given as $\gamma_i = (b_i)$.

For a sample of N individuals with independently and identically distributed observations $\boldsymbol{x}_1, \ldots, \boldsymbol{x}_N$ from the distribution of the random variable $\boldsymbol{X}$, the unknown parameters of the IRT model in (1) can be consistently estimated using maximum likelihood estimation (ML; [8–10]).

IRT models are commonly used to compare the performance of two groups on a test by examining differences in the latent variable θ within the framework of the IRT model in (1). This article focuses on a generalization of the mean–mean linking method [11] based on the Rasch model. The purpose of a linking method is to estimate the difference between the distributions of θ in the two groups. This difference serves as a summary measure of group performance on the multivariate vector of dichotomous items $\boldsymbol{X}$.

The linking approach consists of two steps. First, the Rasch model is estimated separately for each group, allowing for potential differential item functioning (DIF), where items may function differently across groups [12–14]. Second, differences in item parameters are used to estimate group differences in the θ variable through a linking method [11,15,16].

This article investigates the performance of a generalization of mean–mean (MM; [11]) linking in the presence of fixed uniform DIF [14] in item difficulties. The traditional MM method relies on mean differences in item difficulties, which corresponds to using an L_2 loss function. MM linking is a widely used linking or equating method, as discussed in popular textbooks on Rasch modeling [6,7,17,18]. In this study, we investigate a generalization of the MM linking method in the Rasch model using the L_0 loss function [19]. Using this robust loss function can essentially remove items with DIF effects from the group comparison directly in the linking method (see also [20–27]). DIF effects can also be treated through the application of robust procedures in MM linking [19,28–31].

The L_0 loss function, being nondifferentiable, requires differentiable approximations to ensure feasible and computationally stable estimation. This article explores alternative specifications of these approximations, which depend on a tuning parameter ε that controls the approximation error. Previous research relied on fixed ε values based on prior knowledge or simulation studies. Here, the choice of a fixed ε parameter is examined and compared with a data-driven approach for determining ε.

The rest of this article is structured as follows. Section 2 introduces L_0 linking in the Rasch model. Section 3 presents a numerical illustration of alternative specifications of L_0 linking in a simplified setting. In Section 4, findings from a simulation study are reported. An empirical example is provided in Section 5. This article closes with a discussion in Section 6 and a conclusion in Section 7.

2. L_0 Linking in the Rasch Model

This section discusses the L_0 linking approach in the Rasch model. Section 2.1 covers item parameter identification and the ordinary MM linking method. Section 2.2 introduces the L_0 loss function and presents two differentiable approximations. Section 2.3 applies these approximations to define the L_0 linking approach in the Rasch model. Finally, Section 2.4 examines its statistical properties.

2.1. Identified Item Parameters and Mean–Mean Linking

To introduce the L_0 linking method as a replacement for ordinary mean–mean linking in the Rasch model, we first outline the identification of item parameters in a group-specific estimation of the Rasch model when no DIF effects are present. In this case, the identified item parameters in the first group are $\widehat{b}_{i1} = b_i$, where b_i represents the invariant item parameters across both groups. For identification, the mean of θ in the first group is fixed at 0, while the standard deviation σ remains identifiable within this group.

In the second group, the mean μ and the SD σ can be identified when invariant item difficulties are assumed. Thus, μ and σ represent group differences in θ. The identified item parameters in this group, estimated separately under the assumption of a θ mean of 0 and an estimated SD σ, are given by

$$\widehat{b}_{i2} = b_i - \mu. \tag{3}$$

Linking methods aim to recover the group parameter μ using the group-specific item parameters obtained from separate Rasch model estimations.

The MM linking method estimates the group mean $\hat{\mu}$ for the second group as

$$\hat{\mu} = -\frac{1}{I}\sum_{i=1}^{I}\left(\widehat{b}_{i2} - \widehat{b}_{i1}\right). \tag{4}$$

The linking parameter $\hat{\mu}$ in MM linking is obtained as the minimizer of the squared loss function (i.e., the L_2 loss function; [19])

$$\hat{\mu} = \arg\min_{\mu} H(\mu), \text{ with } H(\mu) = \frac{1}{I}\sum_{i=1}^{I}\rho\left(\widehat{b}_{i2} - \widehat{b}_{i1} + \mu\right), \text{ where } \rho(x) = \frac{1}{2}x^2. \tag{5}$$

Thus, the estimate $\hat{\mu}$ satisfies the estimating equation

$$\frac{1}{I}\sum_{i=1}^{I}\rho'\left(\widehat{b}_{i2} - \widehat{b}_{i1} + \hat{\mu}\right) = 0, \text{ where } \rho'(x) = x \tag{6}$$

and ρ' denotes the derivative of ρ with respect to x. Clearly, (6) is equivalent to (4).

This paper investigates the computational aspects of MM linking in (5) when the squared L_2 loss function is replaced with the L_0 loss function, which aims to robustify the linking method in the presence of fixed DIF effects.

2.2. L_0 Loss Function and Differentiable Approximations

In this section, we introduce the L_0 loss function [32,33], which is defined as

$$\rho(x) = \mathbf{1}(x \neq 0). \tag{7}$$

This loss function equals 0 for $x = 0$ and 1 for $x \neq 0$. The L_0 loss function has been widely applied in statistical modeling, particularly for obtaining sparse solutions (see, e.g., [34–39]).

The exact L_0 loss function in (7) has the disadvantage of being nondifferentiable at $x = 0$, making it difficult to use in numerical optimization. To address this, differentiable approximations of the L_0 loss function have been proposed.

The ratio loss function, as an approximation of the L_0 loss function, is defined as (see [40–43])

$$\rho_\varepsilon(x) = \frac{x^2}{x^2 + \varepsilon}, \tag{8}$$

where $\varepsilon > 0$ is a tuning parameter. We have found that $\varepsilon = 0.01$ performs satisfactorily in applications [19,44].

The linking parameter estimate based on the L_2 loss function can be obtained using the L_0 approximation (8) with a sufficiently large ε value, such as $\varepsilon = 1000$. In this case, $\rho_\varepsilon(x) \approx x^2/\varepsilon$, and the resulting estimate closely matches the L_2 estimate, which is the ordinary MM parameter estimate.

An alternative differentiable approximation of the L_0 loss function is based on the Gaussian density function, denoted as the Gaussian function hereafter, and is given by (see [45–47])

$$\rho_\varepsilon(x) = 1 - \exp\left(-\frac{x^2}{\varepsilon}\right), \tag{9}$$

where $\varepsilon > 0$ is again a tuning parameter.

Figure 1 displays the ratio and the Gaussian loss functions for $\varepsilon = 0.001$ and $\varepsilon = 0.01$. It can be seen that the two loss functions exhibit similar behavior around $x = 0$, which can be explained by the fact that their first two derivatives coincide, with $\rho_\varepsilon'(0) = 0$ and $\rho_\varepsilon''(0) = 2/\varepsilon$. For larger $|x|$ values, the Gaussian loss function grows faster toward the upper asymptote of 1 compared to the ratio loss function.

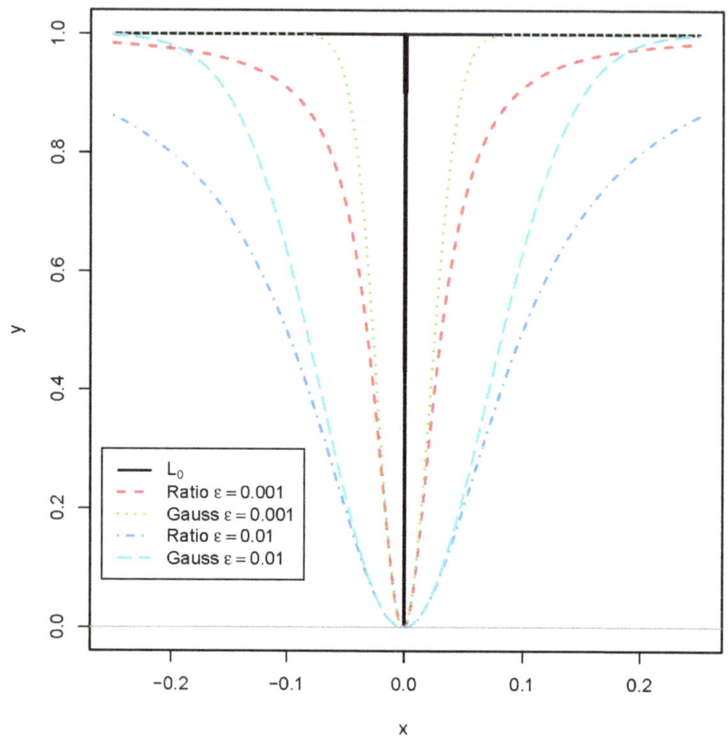

Figure 1. Ratio loss function and Gaussian loss function ρ_ε for $\varepsilon = 0.001$ and $\varepsilon = 0.01$ as differentiable approximations of the L_0 loss function.

The ordinary MM parameter estimate can be obtained using the Gaussian L_0 loss function approximation, similar to the ratio function, by selecting a sufficiently large ε value.

2.3. L_0 Linking as a Robust Mean–Mean Linking in the Rasch Model

MM linking can be modified by using the L_0 loss function instead of the L_2 loss function. In the former case, the loss is defined by counting the number of non-vanishing deviations $\widehat{b}_{i2}$ from $\widehat{b}_{i1} + \mu$, which corresponds to the number of non-vanishing DIF effects. To obtain a stable linking parameter estimate in the presence of sampling errors, the L_0 loss function is replaced by the differentiable approximation ρ_ε, and the estimated mean $\hat{\mu}$ is obtained as

$$\hat{\mu} = \arg\min_{\mu} H(\mu) \text{ with } H(\mu) = \frac{1}{I}\sum_{i=1}^{I} \rho_\varepsilon\Big(\widehat{b}_{i2} - \widehat{b}_{i1} + \mu\Big). \tag{10}$$

This approach can also be referred to as robust MM linking or L_0 linking in the Rasch model, where "robust" refers to the linking parameter estimate being resilient to the presence of fixed DIF effects.

Equivalently to (10), the linking parameter estimate $\hat{\mu}$ solves the estimating equation

$$\frac{\partial H}{\partial \mu} = \frac{1}{I}\sum_{i=1}^{I} \rho'_\varepsilon\left(\widehat{b}_{i2} - \widehat{b}_{i1} + \hat{\mu}\right) = 0. \tag{11}$$

Equation (10) represents a one-dimensional optimization problem that can be numerically solved using standard optimizers implemented in statistical software.

2.4. Statistical Properties of the Estimated Linking Parameter in L_0 Linking

We now investigate the statistical properties of the linking parameter estimate $\hat{\mu}$ obtained from (10). The difference in estimated item difficulties required in the L_0 linking approach can be written as

$$\widehat{b}_{i2} - \widehat{b}_{i1} = -\mu + \kappa_i + u_i \tag{12}$$

with fixed DIF effects κ_i and sampling errors u_i, where $\mathsf{E}(u_i) = 0$ and $\mathsf{Var}(u_i) = V_i$. Asymptotic unbiasedness follows from the general properties of ML estimation.

The L_0 linking approach is analyzed by starting from the estimating equation

$$\frac{1}{I}\sum_{i=1}^{I} \rho'_\varepsilon\left(\widehat{b}_{i2} - \widehat{b}_{i1} + \hat{\mu}\right) = \frac{1}{I}\sum_{i=1}^{I} \rho'_\varepsilon(\hat{\mu} - \mu + \kappa_i + u_i) = 0. \tag{13}$$

Now, we apply a Taylor expansion with respect to μ, as in standard M-estimation theory ([48]; see also [25,49]), and obtain

$$0 = \frac{1}{I}\sum_{i=1}^{I} \rho'_\varepsilon(\hat{\mu} - \mu + \kappa_i + u_i) \simeq \frac{1}{I}\sum_{i=1}^{I} \rho'_\varepsilon(\kappa_i + u_i) + \frac{1}{I}\sum_{i=1}^{I} \rho''_\varepsilon(\kappa_i + u_i)(\hat{\mu} - \mu) = 0. \tag{14}$$

The bias and variance of $\hat{\mu}$ can be derived from (14) and are given by

$$\mathsf{Bias}(\hat{\mu}) = -\frac{\sum_{i=1}^{I} \mathsf{E}\left[\rho'_\varepsilon(\kappa_i + u_i)\right]}{\sum_{i=1}^{I} \mathsf{E}\left[\rho''_\varepsilon(\kappa_i + u_i)\right]} \text{ and} \tag{15}$$

$$\mathsf{Var}(\hat{\mu}) = \frac{\sum_{i=1}^{I} \mathsf{Var}\left[\rho'_\varepsilon(\kappa_i + u_i)\right]}{\left\{\sum_{i=1}^{I} \mathsf{E}\left[\rho''_\varepsilon(\kappa_i + u_i)\right]\right\}^2}, \tag{16}$$

where approximate independence of item parameters across items is assumed in (16). As a summary precision measure of the linking parameter estimate, the mean squared error (MSE) can be determined as

$$\mathsf{MSE}(\hat{\mu}) = \mathsf{E}(\hat{\mu} - \mu)^2 = \mathsf{Bias}(\hat{\mu})^2 + \mathsf{Var}(\hat{\mu}) = \frac{\sum_{i=1}^{I} \left\{ \left(\mathsf{E}\left[\rho'_\varepsilon(\kappa_i + u_i)\right]\right)^2 + \mathsf{Var}\left[\rho'_\varepsilon(\kappa_i + u_i)\right] \right\}}{\left\{\sum_{i=1}^{I} \mathsf{E}\left[\rho''_\varepsilon(\kappa_i + u_i)\right]\right\}^2}. \tag{17}$$

Although it might not be immediately evident from Equations (15)–(17), the bias, variance, and MSE depend on the choice of the tuning parameter ε in the L_0 approximation ρ_ε.

In the next two sections, we compare the two differentiable approximations—the ratio and Gaussian loss functions—regarding their statistical properties in a numerical illustration and a simulation study. In particular, we focus on the choice of the tuning parameter ε.

3. Numerical Illustration

3.1. Method

In this Numerical Illustration, the properties of the estimated linking parameter $\hat{\mu}$ were studied in a simplified setting in which no item responses were simulated. It was assumed that the difference $\widehat{b}_{i2} - \widehat{b}_{i1}$ had a variance of V/N, where N denotes the sample size. Hence, this illustration assumed equal sampling variances of item parameter differences, which might be violated in practice. However, this assumption eases the statistical treatment and aims at yielding clearly interpretable results. Furthermore, we assumed that we had I items, and a proportion π of the items had an unbalanced DIF effect κ, while a proportion $1-\pi$ of the items did not show DIF.

From Section 2.4, we know that the linking parameter satisfies the estimating equation

$$\frac{1}{I}\sum_{i=1}^{I}\rho'_\varepsilon\left(\widehat{b}_{i2} - \widehat{b}_{i1} + \hat{\mu}\right) = \frac{1}{I}\sum_{i=1}^{I}\rho'_\varepsilon(\hat{\mu} - \mu + \kappa_i + u_i) = 0, \tag{18}$$

where $\mathsf{Var}(u_i) = V/N$. Because all item parameter differences have equal sampling variances, (18) can be simplified to

$$\sum_{i=1}^{I\pi}\rho'_\varepsilon(\hat{\mu} - \mu + \kappa + u_i) + \sum_{I\pi+1}^{I}\rho'_\varepsilon(\hat{\mu} - \mu + u_i) = 0, \tag{19}$$

assuming that $I\pi$ is an integer. By using the bias Formula (15), we obtain

$$\mathsf{Bias}(\hat{\mu}) = -\frac{\pi\mathsf{E}[\rho'_\varepsilon(\kappa + u_i)]}{\pi\mathsf{E}[\rho''_\varepsilon(\kappa + u_i)] + (1-\pi)\mathsf{E}[\rho''_\varepsilon(u_i)]}, \tag{20}$$

where we use $\mathsf{E}[\rho'_\varepsilon(u_i)] = 0$ because u_i has a symmetric distribution. The variance can be computed as (see (16))

$$\mathsf{Var}(\hat{\mu}) = \frac{\pi\mathsf{Var}[\rho'_\varepsilon(\kappa + u_i)] + (1-\pi)\mathsf{Var}[\rho'_\varepsilon(u_i)]}{\left\{\pi\mathsf{E}\left[\rho''_\varepsilon(\kappa + u_i)\right] + (1-\pi)\mathsf{E}\left[\rho''_\varepsilon(u_i)\right]\right\}^2}, \tag{21}$$

The root mean square error (RMSE) as the square root of the MSE can be obtained as

$$\mathsf{RMSE}(\hat{\mu}) = \sqrt{\mathsf{MSE}(\hat{\mu})} = \sqrt{\mathsf{Bias}(\hat{\mu})^2 + \mathsf{Var}(\hat{\mu})}. \tag{22}$$

The expected values and variances in (20) and (21) can be numerically evaluated.

The bias, SD, and RMSE are evaluated for $\hat{\mu}$ for sample sizes N of 250, 500, and 1000, as well as the number of items I as 10, 20, and 40. We simulated fixed DIF effects $\kappa = 0.4$ and $\kappa = 0.8$, representing small and large DIF. The tuning parameter ε in the ratio loss function and Gaussian loss function ρ_ε was chosen as 1, 0.95, 0.9, 0.85, 0.8, 0.75, 0.7, 0.65, 0.6, 0.55, 0.5, 0.45, 0.4, 0.35, 0.3, 0.25, 0.2, 0.15, 0.1, 0.095, 0.09, 0.085, 0.08, 0.075, 0.07, 0.065, 0.06, 0.055, 0.05, 0.045, 0.04, 0.035, 0.03, 0.025, 0.02, 0.015, 0.01, 0.009, 0.008, 0.007, 0.006, 0.005, 0.004, 0.003, 0.002, and 0.001. In total, 46 ε values were evaluated in this Numerical Illustration. We only report results for the ratio loss function because the findings for the Gaussian loss function were very similar. The statistical software R (Version 4.4.1; [50]) was used for the analysis in this study. Symbolic derivatives of the two loss functions were computed with the R package Deriv (Version: 4.1.6; [51]). Replication material for this illustration can be retrieved from https://osf.io/un6q4 (accessed on 20 February 2025).

3.2. Results

Figure 2 displays the absolute bias, the SD, and the RMSE of the estimated mean $\hat{\mu}$ for $I = 20$ items as a function of the DIF effect κ and the sample size N. The tuning parameter ε is displayed on a logarithmic scale on the x-axis. The bias increased with increasing values of ε in the loss function ρ_ε. In contrast, the SD decreased with increasing values of ε. The RMSE reflects the bias–variance trade-off of the linking parameter estimate. There was an optimal ε parameter that minimizes the RMSE. This optimal ε parameter decreased with increasing sample size N. Moreover, the optimal ε parameter was larger for $\kappa = 0.8$ than for $\kappa = 0.4$.

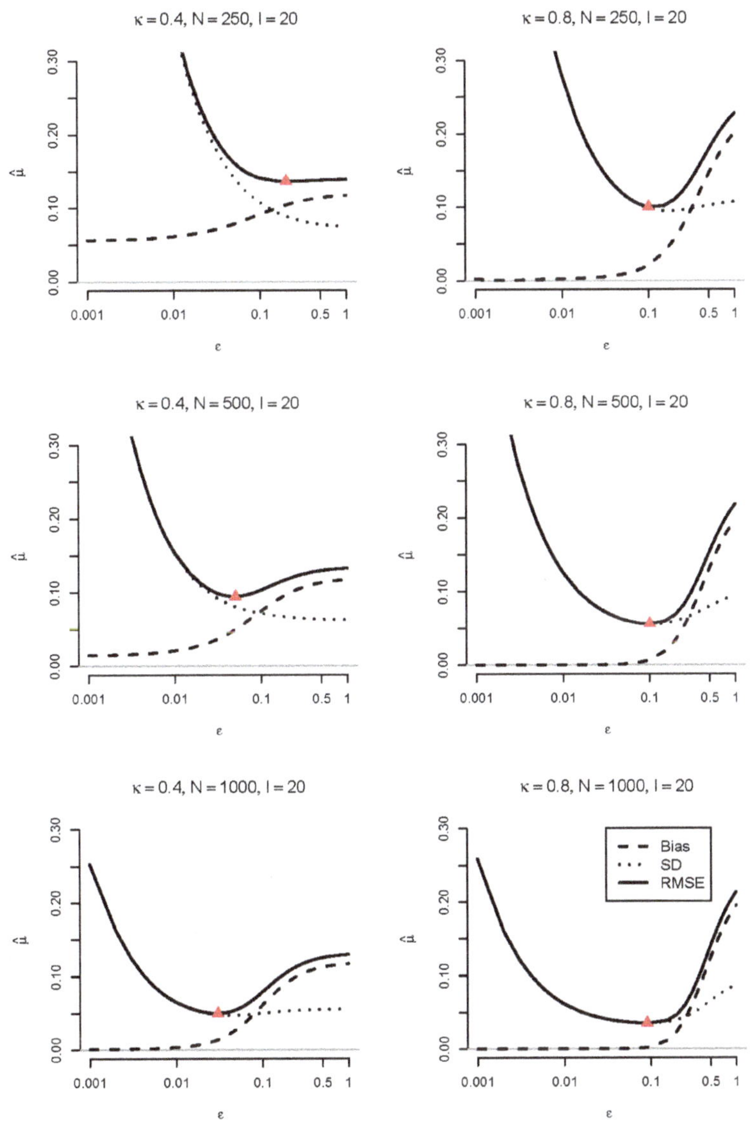

Figure 2. Numerical Illustration: Absolute bias, standard deviation (SD), and root mean square error (RMSE) of the estimated mean $\hat{\mu}$ using the ratio loss function for $I = 20$ items as a function of sample size N and DIF effect size κ. The minimum RMSE values are depicted with a triangle. The ε parameter on the x-axis is displayed on a logarithmic scale.

Table 1 presents the optimal ε values that minimize the RMSE of the estimated mean $\hat{\mu}$ under a ratio loss function. These values are reported for different DIF effect sizes κ, numbers of items I, and sample sizes N. As the sample size N increased, the optimal ε generally decreased. This pattern was more pronounced for small item numbers (e.g., $I = 10$), where ε dropped sharply with increasing N. Larger item numbers I were associated with smaller optimal ε values, suggesting that when more items were available, the best trade-off under the ratio loss function occurred at a lower ε value. This effect was particularly evident for $\varepsilon = 0.4$, where ε decreased substantially as I increased from 10 to 40. When the DIF effect size κ increased from 0.4 to 0.8, the optimal ε values tended to be slightly higher for the same I and N. This suggests that stronger DIF effects required a higher ε to achieve the lowest RMSE, likely due to greater bias introduced by DIF at the smaller effect size $\kappa = 0.4$.

Overall, the results highlight a trade-off between sample size, the number of items, and DIF effect size in determining the optimal correction for minimizing the RMSE.

Table 1. Numerical Illustration: optimal ε value yielding the minimum root mean square error (RMSE) of the estimated mean $\hat{\mu}$ using the ratio loss function as a function of the DIF effect size κ, number of items I, and sample size N.

I	$\kappa = 0.4, N =$			$\kappa = 0.8, N =$		
	250	**500**	**1000**	**250**	**500**	**1000**
10	0.900	0.065	0.030	0.150	0.100	0.090
20	0.200	0.050	0.030	0.100	0.100	0.090
40	0.100	0.035	0.025	0.100	0.095	0.085

4. Simulation Study

4.1. Method

The Rasch model was used as the IRF in the data-generating model for two groups. For identification purposes, the mean of the latent variable θ in the first group was fixed at 0, with an SD σ of 1. In the second group, the mean μ was set to 0.3 to represent the difference in θ between the groups, while the SD σ was set to 1.2.

The simulation study was conducted for $I = 10$, 20, and 40 items. In the $I = 10$ condition, base item difficulty values b_i were set to −0.314, 0.411, −1.097, −0.542, −1.854, −0.403, −0.895, 0.715, 0.841, and 0.139, resulting in a mean of $M = -0.300$ and an SD of 0.850. These item difficulties were used in the data generation for the first group. In the second group, the same values were applied, except for the first three items, where item difficulties were adjusted to $b_{i2} = b_i + \kappa$. This introduced fixed DIF in 30% of the items. The DIF effect size κ was set to 0.4 and 0.8, representing small and large DIF conditions, respectively. For item sets larger than 10, the same 10-item parameter set was repeated accordingly. The item parameters are also available at https://osf.io/un6q4 (accessed on 20 February 2025). Note that item parameters remained fixed across all replications within each condition.

Sample sizes of $N = 125$, 250, 500, and 1000 per group were selected to reflect small- to large-scale applications of the Rasch model.

A total of 5000 replications were conducted for each of the 24 conditions, corresponding to the combinations of 4 sample sizes (N) $\times$ 3 item numbers (I) $\times$ 2 DIF effect sizes (κ). For each simulated dataset, L_0 linking was performed using various specifications. Both the ratio and Gaussian loss functions ρ_ε (see Section 2.2) were applied. The ρ_ε loss functions were evaluated for a sequence of 11 ε values: 1, 0.75, 0.50, 0.25, 0.10, 0.075, 0.05, 0.025, 0.01, 0.005, and 0.001.

Additionally, as demonstrated in Section 3, the optimal ε value corresponding to the minimal RMSE is dependent on the sample size N. To account for this, a data-driven approach for selecting the ε value was explored. Let $\overline{V}$ denote the average variance of the estimated item difficulty differences $\widehat{b}_{i2} - \widehat{b}_{i1}$. For a fixed $y \in (0,1)$, ε_y is chosen such that

$$\rho_{\varepsilon_y}\left(\sqrt{\overline{V}}\right) = y. \tag{23}$$

In the simulation, the following y values were chosen: 0.1, 0.2, 0.3, 0.4, 0.5, 0.6, 0.7, 0.8, and 0.9.

The bias, standard deviation (SD), and root mean square error (RMSE) of the estimated mean, $\hat{\mu}$, were calculated for all specifications of the L_0 linking approach. The relative RMSE of $\hat{\mu}$ was defined as the ratio of the RMSE for a given specification to the RMSE of a reference method, multiplied by 100. Across all conditions, the reference method was the ratio loss function with a fixed ε value of 0.01.

All analyses for this simulation study were conducted using the statistical software R (Version 4.4.1; [50]). The Rasch model was fitted with the `sirt::xxirt()` function from the R package sirt (Version 4.2-106; [52]). The optimization of L_0 linking was performed with the `stats::nlminb()` function. Replication materials for this simulation study can be assessed at https://osf.io/un6q4 (accessed on 20 February 2025).

4.2. Results

Table 2 presents the absolute bias as a function of the DIF effect size κ, the number of items I, and the sample size N. Overall, the absolute bias generally decreased as κ increased from 0.4 to 0.8. The bias in the estimated $\hat{\mu}$ was highest for the smallest number of items ($I = 10$) and slightly decreased as the number of items increased. This reduction in bias was more pronounced for smaller sample sizes. As the sample size N increased, the bias systematically decreased, with the lowest bias observed for the largest sample size ($N = 1000$). For the data-driven ε choices $\varepsilon_{0.2}$ and $\varepsilon_{0.4}$, the bias also decreased as the sample size increased.

The biases for the ratio and Gaussian loss functions were relatively similar, although the bias was slightly smaller under conditions with a larger DIF effect size ($\kappa = 0.8$) compared to a smaller DIF effect size ($\kappa = 0.4$). Additionally, the bias decreased as ε values in the ρ_ε function were reduced. Specifically, the bias was slightly higher for $\varepsilon = 0.2$ compared to $\varepsilon = 0.4$, particularly at smaller N. These findings suggest that while the choice of the loss function influenced estimation accuracy, its effect diminished as I and N increased.

Table 3 presents the relative RMSE of the estimated mean $\hat{\mu}$ as a function of the DIF effect size κ, the number of items I, and the sample size N. In general, larger ε values performed better in smaller samples and with fewer items. Thus, the optimal ε for minimizing the RMSE depends on κ, I, and N. The data-driven estimates $\varepsilon_{0.2}$ and $\varepsilon_{0.4}$ generally outperformed the fixed choice $\varepsilon = 0.01$ based on the loss function ρ_ε. Overall, it can be concluded that $\varepsilon_{0.4}$ was superior to $\varepsilon_{0.2}$. Although $\varepsilon_{0.2}$ produced a lower RMSE than $\varepsilon_{0.4}$ in many simulation conditions, the differences were typically small. However, in scenarios where $\varepsilon_{0.2}$ performed worse than $\varepsilon_{0.4}$, its RMSE exceeded the reference value of 100 and was substantially higher than that of $\varepsilon_{0.4}$. This supports the use of $\varepsilon_{0.4}$ as a conservative default choice. In most conditions, the Gaussian loss function slightly outperformed the ratio loss function. In large samples ($N = 1000$), smaller ε values, such as $\varepsilon = 0.05$ or $\varepsilon = 0.01$, proved effective.

Table 2. Simulation Study: Absolute bias of estimated mean $\hat{\mu}$ as a function of the DIF effect size κ, number of items I, and sample size N.

κ	I	N	Ratio Function, $\varepsilon =$						Gaussian Function, $\varepsilon =$					
			0.25	**0.10**	**0.05**	**0.01**	$\varepsilon_{0.2}$	$\varepsilon_{0.4}$	**0.25**	**0.10**	**0.05**	**0.01**	$\varepsilon_{0.2}$	$\varepsilon_{0.4}$
0.4	10	125	**0.107**	**0.103**	**0.102**	**0.102**	**0.110**	**0.105**	**0.107**	**0.101**	**0.100**	**0.101**	**0.112**	**0.106**
		250	**0.098**	**0.087**	**0.082**	**0.079**	**0.096**	**0.085**	**0.101**	**0.086**	**0.080**	**0.078**	**0.101**	**0.087**
		500	**0.088**	**0.066**	**0.052**	**0.041**	**0.068**	**0.049**	**0.097**	**0.067**	**0.046**	**0.033**	**0.075**	**0.048**
		1000	**0.082**	**0.050**	**0.031**	0.015	**0.034**	0.019	**0.096**	**0.057**	0.026	0.010	**0.035**	0.013
	20	125	**0.104**	**0.100**	**0.099**	**0.099**	**0.107**	**0.102**	**0.104**	**0.099**	**0.096**	**0.096**	**0.109**	**0.103**
		250	**0.098**	**0.086**	**0.080**	**0.075**	**0.097**	**0.084**	**0.102**	**0.084**	**0.075**	**0.069**	**0.102**	**0.086**
		500	**0.089**	**0.066**	**0.051**	**0.036**	**0.069**	**0.048**	**0.097**	**0.068**	**0.044**	0.028	**0.076**	**0.046**
		1000	**0.081**	**0.049**	0.028	0.009	**0.031**	0.014	**0.095**	**0.056**	0.023	0.003	**0.032**	0.008
	40	125	**0.105**	**0.101**	**0.098**	**0.096**	**0.108**	**0.103**	**0.106**	**0.099**	**0.096**	**0.096**	**0.110**	**0.105**
		250	**0.098**	**0.086**	**0.077**	**0.070**	**0.097**	**0.083**	**0.101**	**0.084**	**0.071**	**0.063**	**0.101**	**0.086**
		500	**0.099**	**0.076**	**0.059**	**0.039**	**0.079**	**0.055**	**0.107**	**0.078**	**0.051**	0.029	**0.087**	**0.054**
		1000	**0.087**	**0.054**	**0.033**	0.012	**0.036**	0.018	**0.100**	**0.062**	0.027	0.006	**0.036**	0.012
0.8	10	125	**0.114**	**0.093**	**0.087**	**0.084**	**0.138**	**0.102**	**0.105**	**0.078**	**0.074**	**0.074**	**0.152**	**0.099**
		250	**0.069**	**0.037**	0.027	0.023	**0.064**	**0.033**	**0.066**	0.021	0.015	0.015	**0.067**	0.023
		500	**0.048**	0.017	0.008	0.003	0.019	0.006	**0.047**	0.004	0.000	0.001	0.009	0.000
		1000	**0.039**	0.011	0.004	0.001	0.005	0.001	**0.040**	0.002	0.000	0.000	0.000	0.000
	20	125	**0.112**	**0.082**	**0.073**	**0.069**	**0.140**	**0.096**	**0.103**	**0.063**	**0.055**	**0.054**	**0.155**	**0.095**
		250	**0.069**	**0.033**	0.020	0.014	**0.063**	0.029	**0.065**	0.015	0.007	0.005	**0.065**	0.017
		500	**0.047**	0.015	0.006	0.000	0.017	0.004	**0.046**	0.003	0.002	0.003	0.007	0.001
		1000	**0.038**	0.011	0.004	0.000	0.005	0.001	**0.039**	0.002	0.000	0.000	0.000	0.000
	40	125	**0.109**	**0.075**	**0.061**	**0.054**	**0.140**	**0.092**	**0.099**	**0.052**	**0.041**	**0.036**	**0.156**	**0.090**
		250	**0.071**	**0.033**	0.020	0.011	**0.065**	0.029	**0.067**	0.015	0.006	0.005	**0.067**	0.018
		500	**0.051**	0.020	0.011	0.005	0.022	0.009	**0.050**	0.007	0.003	0.003	0.011	0.003
		1000	**0.039**	0.012	0.005	0.001	0.006	0.002	**0.040**	0.002	0.001	0.001	0.001	0.001

Note. $\varepsilon_{0.2}, \varepsilon_{0.4}$ = computed ε values in loss function ρ_ε such that $\rho_{\varepsilon_y}(\sqrt{V}) = y$ for $y = 0.2$ and $y = 0.4$, where $\sqrt{V}$ is the square root of the average variance of the item difficulty difference $\widehat{b}_{i2} - \widehat{b}_{i1}$; absolute biases larger than 0.03 are printed in bold.

Table 3. Simulation Study: Relative root mean square error (RMSE) of estimated mean $\hat{\mu}$ as a function of the DIF effect size κ, number of items I, and sample size N.

κ	I	N	Ratio Function, $\varepsilon =$						Gaussian Function, $\varepsilon =$					
			0.25	**0.10**	**0.05**	**0.01**	$\varepsilon_{0.2}$	$\varepsilon_{0.4}$	**0.25**	**0.10**	**0.05**	**0.01**	$\varepsilon_{0.2}$	$\varepsilon_{0.4}$
0.4	10	125	83.5	90.5	95.0	100	80.2	86.3	83.0	92.9	99.0	105.2	79.1	84.0
		250	83.4	88.1	93.3	100	83.7	89.4	83.2	89.1	96.6	105.8	83.2	88.1
		500	92.6	89.0	91.0	100	89.1	92.0	95.6	89.8	92.3	103.8	90.5	91.6
		1000	123.1	102.5	94.8	100	95.5	96.2	134.4	108.1	94.6	102.4	97.5	94.0
	20	125	83.2	88.6	93.8	100	81.8	85.1	83.0	90.9	98.1	105.6	81.4	83.6
		250	85.9	86.9	91.3	100	85.7	87.8	86.4	87.0	93.7	104.5	86.4	86.5
		500	101.9	93.4	91.7	100	94.0	92.1	106.3	94.1	91.0	103.2	96.8	90.7
		1000	141.1	111.1	97.7	100	99.2	95.7	155.9	118.4	95.8	100.4	100.7	91.7
	40	125	85.6	88.9	93.5	100	85.2	86.5	85.4	89.8	97.1	105.9	85.2	85.6
		250	91.5	89.7	91.6	100	91.1	89.9	92.4	89.3	92.5	104.4	92.4	89.3
		500	120.2	105.7	97.9	100	107.2	96.8	126.2	107.1	94.9	101.5	112.2	95.7
		1000	169.0	127.9	106.9	100	109.1	98.3	187.6	137.6	103.0	99.7	110.8	94.2

Table 3. *Cont.*

κ	I	N	Ratio Function, $\varepsilon =$						Gaussian Function, $\varepsilon =$					
			0.25	**0.10**	**0.05**	**0.01**	$\varepsilon_{0.2}$	$\varepsilon_{0.4}$	**0.25**	**0.10**	**0.05**	**0.01**	$\varepsilon_{0.2}$	$\varepsilon_{0.4}$
0.8	10	125	87.2	92.6	96.0	100	85.6	89.3	87.9	95.9	100.5	106.1	86.8	88.7
		250	90.3	89.4	92.8	100	89.6	90.2	91.4	89.1	94.6	106.2	91.4	89.0
		500	94.8	87.2	89.8	100	87.1	90.7	97.7	84.0	87.5	105.3	84.6	86.6
		1000	101.5	87.9	88.4	100	88.0	93.7	106.2	85.6	86.5	102.4	87.2	91.9
	20	125	88.7	90.9	95.0	100	91.6	88.7	88.5	92.2	97.6	104.7	94.4	88.2
		250	94.6	88.3	90.9	100	92.9	88.5	94.8	85.6	90.8	104.9	94.7	85.2
		500	97.2	86.3	87.6	100	86.6	88.6	99.0	83.7	86.1	104.1	84.2	85.5
		1000	106.8	90.5	90.2	100	90.0	94.0	109.8	88.1	88.7	102.4	88.3	91.4
	40	125	92.1	90.7	94.0	100	98.3	90.2	90.2	89.4	95.3	103.8	102.7	88.8
		250	101.0	90.8	91.2	100	98.6	90.4	100.3	87.5	90.1	104.0	100.1	87.6
		500	105.4	90.3	89.7	100	90.8	90.2	106.1	87.0	87.9	104.9	87.7	87.6
		1000	116.4	94.8	93.3	100	93.3	95.4	118.6	92.0	92.2	101.8	91.9	93.7

Note. $\varepsilon_{0.2}, \varepsilon_{0.4}$ = computed ε values in loss function ρ_ε such that $\rho_{\varepsilon_y}(\sqrt{V}) = y$ for $y = 0.2$ and $y = 0.4$, where $\sqrt{V}$ is the square root of the average variance of the item difficulty difference $\widehat{b}_{i2} - \widehat{b}_{i1}$. The ratio loss function with $\varepsilon = 0.01$ was chosen as the reference method when computing the relative RMSE. Cells with the smallest RMSE values are printed with a gray background color.

To provide further insight into the absolute bias and relative RMSE, two additional figures are presented below.

Figure 3 presents the absolute bias, SD, and RMSE of the estimated mean $\hat{\mu}$ using the ratio loss function for $I = 20$ items as a function of the DIF effect size κ and sample size N. The absolute bias increased with larger ε, while the SD decreased, illustrating a bias–variance trade-off in the RMSE. This trade-off results in an optimal ε value that minimizes the RMSE. As shown in Figure 3, the optimal ε was smaller for a larger DIF effect size (i.e., $\kappa = 0.8$) than for $\kappa = 0.4$. Additionally, the optimal ε decreased with increasing sample size N. As expected, the RMSE was lower for larger sample sizes.

Figure 4 presents the relative RMSE of the estimated mean based on data driven ε_y values for the ratio loss function ρ_ε with $\varepsilon = \varepsilon_y$. The results indicate that an optimal RMSE was achieved for a specific y value, depending on the DIF effect size κ, the number of items I, and the sample size N. Overall, the findings in Figure 4 support the selection of $\varepsilon_{0.2}$ and $\varepsilon_{0.4}$, as presented in Tables 2 and 3.

Following the suggestion of a reviewer, bias and RMSE were regressed onto the simulation factors using a two-way analysis of variance (ANOVA). The factors included sample size N, number of items I, the size of the DIF effect κ, the type of loss function (i.e., ratio vs. Gaussian function), and the chosen ε value in the loss function ρ_ε. All simulation factors were treated as categorical factors in the ANOVA. The same item numbers I (e.g., $I = 10, 20, 40$) and ε values (i.e., $\varepsilon = 0.01, 0.05, 0.10, 0.25$) as reported in Tables 2 and 3 were used. The main focus of the analysis was the proportion of variance explained by the main effects and two-way interactions of the factors in the ANOVA.

In the two-way ANOVA with bias as the dependent variable, 96.0% of the variance was explained by the main factors and their two-way interactions. The largest proportion was attributed to sample size N (39.8%), followed by κ (24.8%) and ε (24.8%). The number of items I (0.1%) and the type of loss function (0.2%) contributed minimally to the variability in bias. Among the two-way interactions, only the interaction between N and κ ($N \times \kappa$, 2.3%) and $N \times \varepsilon$ (1.7%) accounted for non-negligible proportions of variance.

In the two-way ANOVA with RMSE as the dependent variable, 99.3% of the variance was explained by the simulation factors and their two-way interactions. As expected, sample size N accounted for the largest proportion of explained variance (89.9%), followed by number of items I (3.2%), κ (1.0%), ε (0.5%), and the type of loss function (0.0%). Among the two-way interactions, $N \times I$ (1.3%), $N \times \kappa$ (1.0%), and $N \times \varepsilon$ (2.1%) contributed with non-negligible amounts to the variance.

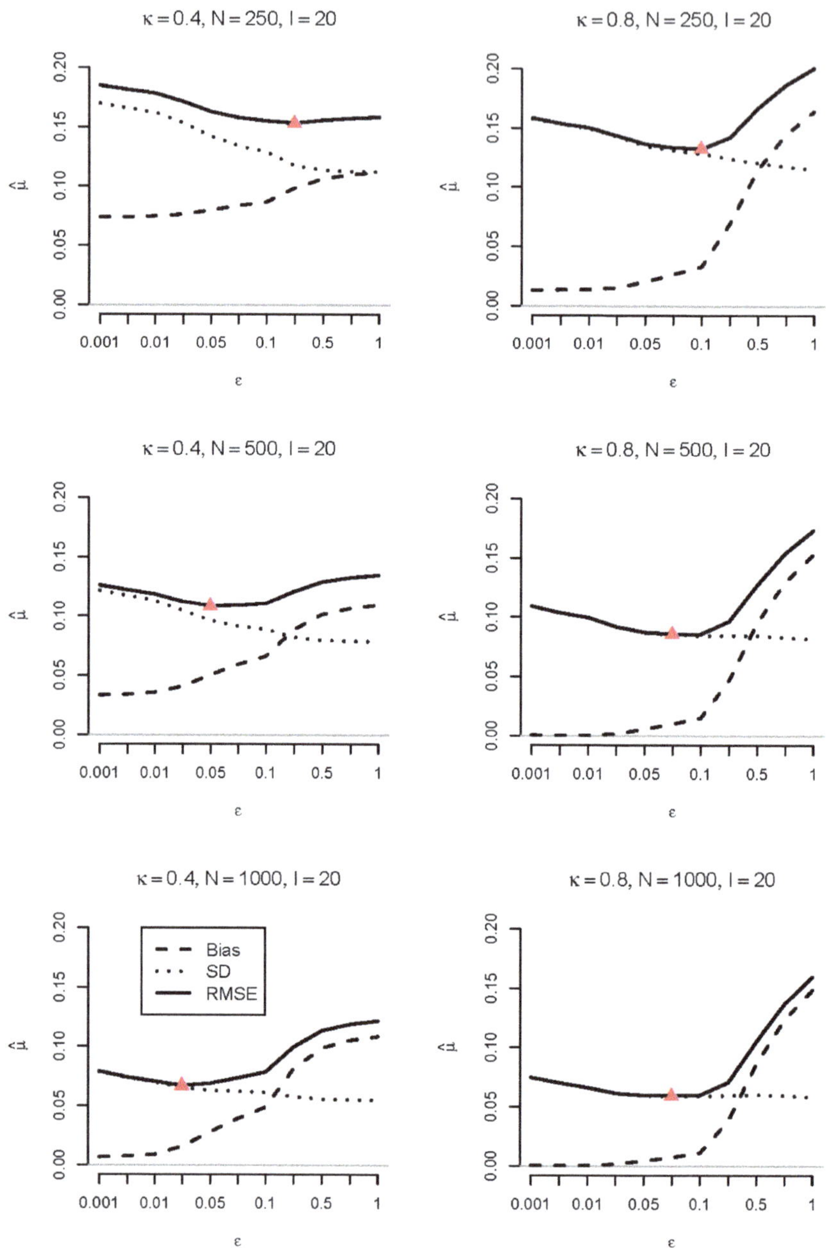

Figure 3. Simulation Study: Absolute bias, standard deviation (SD), and root mean square error (RMSE) of the estimated mean $\hat{\mu}$ using the ratio loss function for $I = 20$ items as a function of sample size N and DIF effect size κ. The minimum RMSE values are depicted with a triangle.

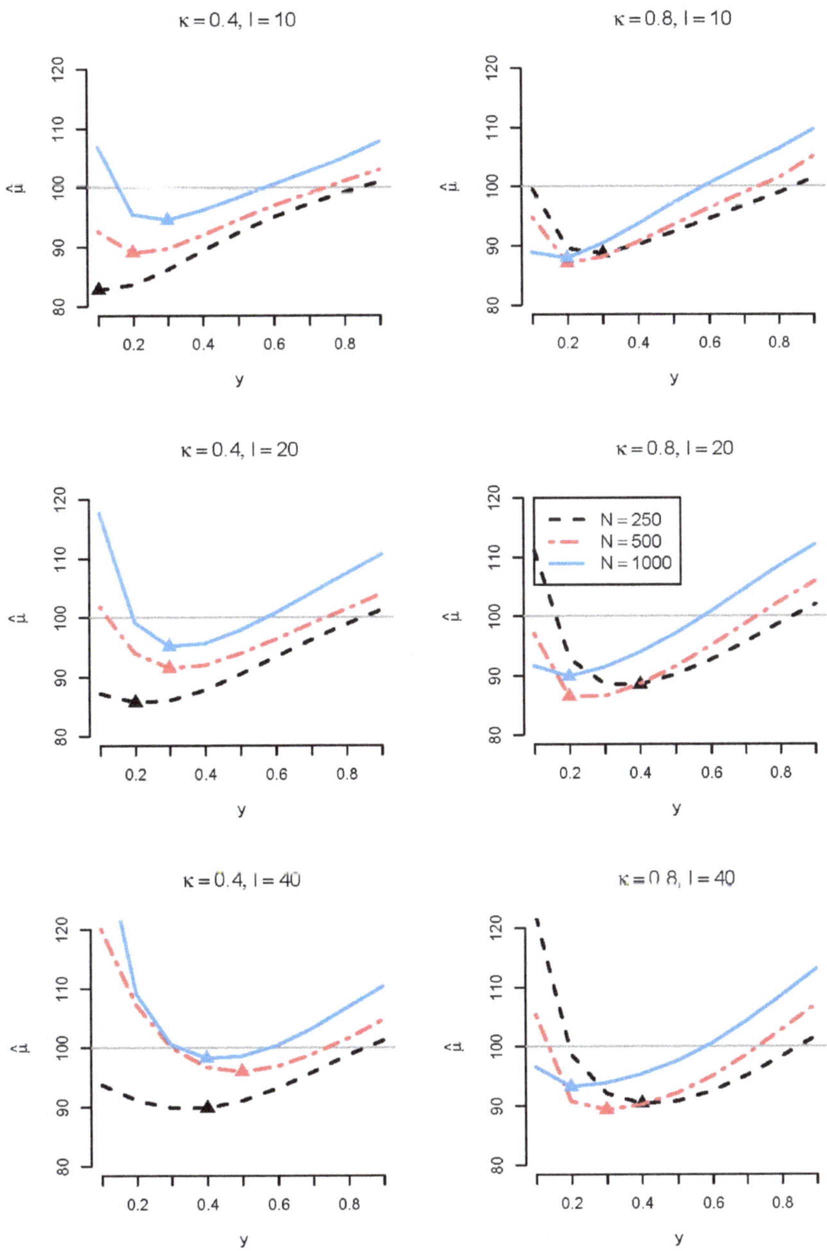

Figure 4. Simulation Study: Relative root mean square error (RMSE) of the estimated mean $\hat{\mu}$ using the ratio loss function based on $\varepsilon = \varepsilon_y$ determined through $\rho_{\varepsilon_y}(\sqrt{V}) = y$ as a function of sample size N, the number of items I, and DIF effect size κ. The minimum relative RMSE values are depicted with a triangle. The ratio loss function with $\varepsilon = 0.01$ was chosen as the reference method when computing the relative RMSE.

5. Empirical Example

We now illustrate L_0 linking in the Rasch model using an empirical dataset. The `dataDIF` dataset from the R package equateIRT (Version 1.0.0; [53,54]) was selected for this purpose. The dataset contains 20 dichotomous items and three groups, each with 1000 subjects. For illustration, only Groups 1 and 2 were linked using the Rasch model.

As in the Simulation Study (see Section 4), the Rasch model was fitted using the `sirt::xxirt()` function from the R package sirt (Version 4.2-106; [52]). The optimization of L_0 linking was performed using the `stats::nlminb()` function, with R code specifically written for this paper, available at https://osf.io/un6q4 (accessed on 20 February 2025).

The average standard error of item difficulty differences was 0.126. The mean ability difference between Group 1 and Group 2, obtained from MM linking based on the L_2 loss function, was 0.482. Slight deviations from this estimate were observed with different specifications of the L_0 linking function. For the ratio loss function, the mean estimate based on $\varepsilon = 0.01$ was 0.535. Empirical choices of the ε parameter, specifically $\varepsilon_{0.2}$ and $\varepsilon_{0.4}$, were also explored. For the ratio loss function, the estimates for $\varepsilon_{0.2} = 0.064$ and $\varepsilon_{0.4} = 0.024$ yielded mean differences of 0.518 and 0.520, respectively. The mean estimate based on the Gaussian loss function was 0.537, with estimates for $\varepsilon_{0.2} = 0.072$ and $\varepsilon_{0.4} = 0.031$ yielding 0.519 and 0.517, respectively.

DIF effects for the 20 items were also computed based on the estimated mean difference of 0.520, obtained with $\varepsilon_{0.4}$ and the ratio loss function. Figure 5 displays the DIF effects along with their 95% confidence intervals. Item 1 exhibited a significantly positive DIF effect (0.798, with a standard error of 0.112), while DIF effects for the remaining 19 items did not significantly differ from 0.

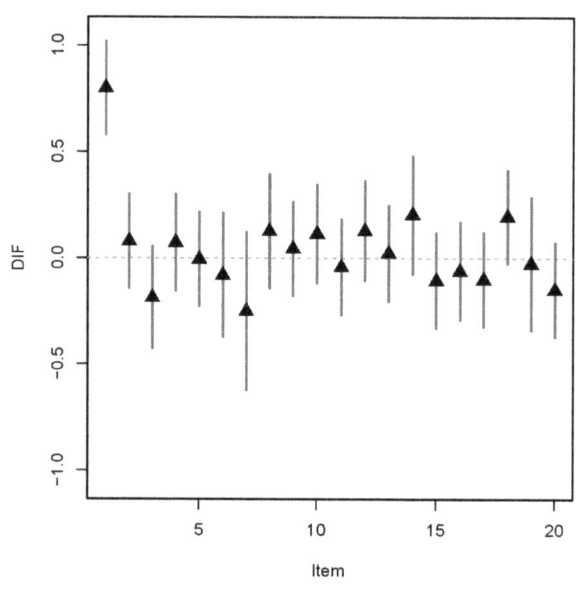

Figure 5. Empirical example: DIF parameter estimates (displayed with a black triangle) along with their 95% confidence intervals.

6. Discussion

This article examined the computational aspects of L_0 linking in the Rasch model. L_0 linking serves as a robust alternative to MM linking when fixed DIF effects are present. Since the L_0 loss function is not differentiable at $x = 0$, the ratio loss function and the Gaussian loss function were used as differentiable approximations. Both approximations rely on a tuning parameter ε, which controls the approximation error. A numerical illustration and a simulation study demonstrated that the optimal ε value minimizing the RMSE of the linking parameter estimate $\hat{\mu}$ depends on the magnitude of DIF effects, the number of items, and the sample size. A data-driven selection of ε provided better performance than a fixed ε across all conditions. Additionally, the Gaussian loss function showed a slight advantage over the ratio loss function, though the differences are likely negligible in practice.

This study aimed to determine group differences in a robust manner, ensuring insensitivity to DIF effects. Detecting DIF items was treated as a nuisance, as the goal was not to identify deviating items but rather to obtain a consistent estimate of the mean difference in ability between the two groups. In contrast, much of the psychometric literature focuses on detecting DIF items [22,27,55–57], with group difference estimation being, at best, a by-product of the procedure.

Using the L_0 loss function effectively removes items with large DIF effects from the linking process. As a result, the estimated group difference is based solely on items with little to no DIF. This approach may pose a threat to validity, as it alters the construct being measured by treating items with DIF effects as construct-irrelevant [58,59]. Restricting the item set in this way can change the interpretation of the ability variable [60–64].

7. Conclusions

The L_0 loss function proved effective in linking two groups based on the Rasch model in the presence of differential item functioning. Two differentiable approximations (i.e., the ratio and Gaussian loss functions) of the nondifferentiable L_0 loss function have been proposed. The smoothness of the approximation depends on the tuning parameter ε. A simulation study demonstrated that a data-driven choice of ε, based on the average standard error of item difficulty differences, produced estimates with a lower RMSE compared to estimates based on a fixed ε value, such as $\varepsilon = 0.01$.

Funding: This research received no external funding.

Data Availability Statement: This article only uses simulated datasets. Replication material for Sections 3 and 4 can be found at https://osf.io/un6q4 (accessed on 20 February 2025). The dataset `dataDIF` used in the empirical example in Section 5 is available from the equateIRT package (https://doi.org/10.32614/CRAN.package.equateIRT; accessed on 20 February 2025).

Conflicts of Interest: The author declares no conflict of interest.

Abbreviations

The following abbreviations are used in this manuscript:

ANOVA	analysis of variance
DIF	differential item functioning
IRF	item response function
IRT	item response theory
ML	maximum likelihood
MM	mean–mean
MSE	mean square error
RMSE	root mean square error
SD	standard deviation

References

1. Bock, R.D.; Gibbons, R.D. *Item Response Theory*; Wiley: Hoboken, NJ, USA, 2021. [CrossRef]
2. Chen, Y.; Li, X.; Liu, J.; Ying, Z. Item response theory—A statistical framework for educational and psychological measurement. *arXiv* **2021**, arXiv:2108.08604. [CrossRef]
3. Yen, W.M.; Fitzpatrick, A.R. Item response theory. In *Educational Measurement*; Brennan, R.L., Ed.; Praeger Publishers: Westport, CT, USA, 2006; pp. 111–154.
4. Van der Linden, W.J. Unidimensional logistic response models. In *Handbook of Item Response Theory, Volume 1: Models*; van der Linden, W.J., Ed.; CRC Press: Boca Raton, FL, USA, 2016; pp. 11–30. [CrossRef]
5. Rasch, G. *Probabilistic Models for Some Intelligence and Attainment Tests*; Danish Institute for Educational Research: Copenhagen, Denmark, 1960.
6. Bond, T.; Yan, Z.; Heene, M. *Applying the Rasch Model*; Routledge: New York, NY, USA, 2020. [CrossRef]
7. Debelak, R.; Strobl, C.; Zeigenfuse, M.D. *An Introduction to the Rasch Model with Examples in R*; CRC Press: Boca Raton, FL, USA, 2022. [CrossRef]
8. Bock, R.D.; Aitkin, M. Marginal maximum likelihood estimation of item parameters: Application of an EM algorithm. *Psychometrika* **1981**, *46*, 443–459. [CrossRef]
9. Glas, C.A.W. Maximum-likelihood estimation. In *Handbook of Item Response Theory, Volume 2: Statistical Tools*; van der Linden, W.J., Ed.; CRC Press: Boca Raton, FL, USA, 2016; pp. 197–216. [CrossRef]
10. Robitzsch, A. A comprehensive simulation study of estimation methods for the Rasch model. *Stats* **2021**, *4*, 814–836. [CrossRef]
11. Kolen, M.J.; Brennan, R.L. *Test Equating, Scaling, and Linking*; Springer: New York, NY, USA, 2014. [CrossRef]
12. Holland, P.W.; Wainer, H. (Eds.) *Differential Item Functioning: Theory and Practice*; Lawrence Erlbaum: Hillsdale, NJ, USA, 1993. [CrossRef]
13. Millsap, R.E. *Statistical Approaches to Measurement Invariance*; Routledge: New York, NY, USA, 2011. [CrossRef]
14. Penfield, R.D.; Camilli, G. Differential item functioning and item bias. In *Handbook of Statistics, Volume 26: Psychometrics*; Rao, C.R., Sinharay, S., Eds.; Elsevier: Amsterdam, The Netherlands, 2007; pp. 125–167. [CrossRef]
15. Lee, W.C.; Lee, G. IRT linking and equating. In *The Wiley Handbook of Psychometric Testing: A Multidisciplinary Reference on Survey, Scale and Test*; Irwing, P., Booth, T., Hughes, D.J., Eds.; Wiley: New York, NY, USA, 2018; pp. 639–673. [CrossRef]
16. Sansivieri, V.; Wiberg, M.; Matteucci, M. A review of test equating methods with a special focus on IRT-based approaches. *Statistica* **2017**, *77*, 329–352. [CrossRef]
17. Andrich, D.; Marais, I. *A Course in Rasch Measurement Theory*; Springer: New York, NY, USA, 2019. [CrossRef]
18. Lamprianou, I. *Applying the Rasch Model in Social Sciences Using R and BlueSky Statistics*; Routledge: New York, NY, USA, 2019. [CrossRef]
19. Robitzsch, A. Extensions to mean–geometric mean linking. *Mathematics* **2025**, *13*, 35. [CrossRef]
20. Von Davier, M.; Bezirhan, U. A robust method for detecting item misfit in large scale assessments. *Educ. Psychol. Meas.* **2023**, *83*, 740–765. [CrossRef]
21. De Boeck, P. Random item IRT models. *Psychometrika* **2008**, *73*, 533–559. [CrossRef]
22. Halpin, P.F. Differential item functioning via robust scaling. *Psychometrika* **2024**, *89*, 796–821. [CrossRef]
23. He, Y.; Cui, Z.; Fang, Y.; Chen, H. Using a linear regression method to detect outliers in IRT common item equating. *Appl. Psychol. Meas.* **2013**, *37*, 522–540. [CrossRef]
24. Magis, D.; De Boeck, P. Identification of differential item functioning in multiple-group settings: A multivariate outlier detection approach. *Multivar. Behav. Res.* **2011**, *46*, 733–755. [CrossRef]
25. Robitzsch, A. Robust and nonrobust linking of two groups for the Rasch model with balanced and unbalanced random DIF: A comparative simulation study and the simultaneous assessment of standard errors and linking errors with resampling techniques. *Symmetry* **2021**, *13*, 2198. [CrossRef]
26. Robitzsch, A. A comparison of linking methods for two groups for the two-parameter logistic item response model in the presence and absence of random differential item functioning. *Foundations* **2021**, *1*, 116–144. [CrossRef]
27. Wang, W.; Liu, Y.; Liu, H. Testing differential item functioning without predefined anchor items using robust regression. *J. Educ. Behav. Stat.* **2022**, *47*, 666–692. [CrossRef]
28. Hu, H.; Rogers, W.T.; Vukmirovic, Z. Investigation of IRT-based equating methods in the presence of outlier common items. *Appl. Psychol. Meas.* **2008**, *32*, 311–333. [CrossRef]
29. Jurich, D.; Liu, C. Detecting item parameter drift in small sample Rasch equating. *Appl. Meas. Educ.* **2023**, *36*, 326–339. [CrossRef]
30. Liu, C.; Jurich, D. Outlier detection using t-test in Rasch IRT equating under NEAT design. *Appl. Psychol. Meas.* **2023**, *47*, 34–47. [CrossRef] [PubMed]
31. Manna, V.F.; Gu, L. *Different Methods of Adjusting for Form Difficulty Under the Rasch Model: Impact on Consistency of Assessment Results*; (Research Report No. RR-19-08); Educational Testing Service: Princeton, NJ, USA, 2019. [CrossRef]

32. Oelker, M.R.; Pößnecker, W.; Tutz, G. Selection and fusion of categorical predictors with L_0-type penalties. *Stat. Model.* **2015**, *15*, 389–410. [CrossRef]
33. Oelker, M.R.; Tutz, G. A uniform framework for the combination of penalties in generalized structured models. *Adv. Data Anal. Classif.* **2017**, *11*, 97–120. [CrossRef]
34. Atamturk, A.; Gómez, A.; Han, S. Sparse and smooth signal estimation: Convexification of l_0-formulations. *J. Mach. Learn. Res.* **2021**, *22*, 1–43.
35. Dai, S. Variable selection in convex quantile regression: L_1-norm or L_0-norm regularization? *Eur. J. Oper. Res.* **2023**, *305*, 338–355. [CrossRef]
36. Huang, J.; Jiao, Y.; Liu, Y.; Lu, X. A constructive approach to L_0 penalized regression. *J. Mach. Learn. Res.* **2018**, *19*, 1–37.
37. Panokin, N.V.; Kostin, I.A.; Karlovskiy, A.V.; Nalivaiko, A.Y. Comparison of sparse representation methods for complex data based on the smoothed L_0 norm and modified minimum fuel neural network. *Appl. Sci.* **2025**, *15*, 1038. [CrossRef]
38. Soubies, E.; Blanc-Féraud, L.; Aubert, G. A continuous exact l_0 penalty (CEL0) for least squares regularized problem. *SIAM J. Imaging Sci.* **2015**, *8*, 1607–1639. [CrossRef]
39. Yang, Y.; McMahan, C.S.; Wang, Y.B.; Ouyang, Y. Estimation of l_0 norm penalized models: A statistical treatment. *Comp. Stat. Data Anal.* **2024**, *192*, 107902. [CrossRef]
40. Liu, W.; Li, Z.; Chen, W. Evaluating model robustness using adaptive sparse L_0 regularization. *arXiv* **2024**, arXiv:2408.15702. [CrossRef]
41. O'Neill, M.; Burke, K. Variable selection using a smooth information criterion for distributional regression models. *Stat. Comput.* **2023**, *33*, 71. [CrossRef]
42. Wang, B.; Wang, L.; Yu, H.; Xin, F. A new regularized reconstruction algorithm based on compressed sensing for the sparse underdetermined problem and applications of one-dimensional and two-dimensional signal recovery. *Algorithms* **2019**, *12*, 126. [CrossRef]
43. Xiang, J.; Yue, H.; Yin, X.; Wang, L. A new smoothed l_0 regularization approach for sparse signal recovery. *Math. Probl. Eng.* **2019**, *2019*, 1978154. [CrossRef]
44. Robitzsch, A. L_0 and L_p loss functions in model-robust estimation of structural equation models. *Psych* **2023**, *5*, 1122–1139. [CrossRef]
45. Paik, J.W.; Lee, J.H.; Hong, W. An enhanced smoothed L_0-norm direction of arrival estimation method using covariance matrix. *Sensors* **2021**, *21*, 4403. [CrossRef]
46. Wang, L.; Yin, X.; Yue, H.; Xiang, J. A regularized weighted smoothed L_0 norm minimization method for underdetermined blind source separation. *Sensors* **2018**, *18*, 4260. [CrossRef]
47. Zhu, J.; Li, X. A smoothed l_0-norm and l_1-norm regularization algorithm for computed tomography. *J. Appl. Math.* **2019**, *2019*, 8398035. [CrossRef]
48. Boos, D.D.; Stefanski, L.A. *Essential Statistical Inference*; Springer: New York, NY, USA, 2013. [CrossRef]
49. Simakhin, V.A.; Shamanaeva, L.G.; Avdyushina, A.E. Robust parametric estimates of heterogeneous experimental data. *Russ. Phys. J.* **2021**, *63*, 1510–1518. [CrossRef]
50. R Core Team. *R: A Language and Environment for Statistical Computing*; R Core Team: Vienna, Austria, 2024. Available online: https://www.R-project.org (accessed on 15 June 2024).
51. Clausen, A.; Sokol, S. Deriv: Symbolic Differentiation, 2024. R Package Version 4.1.6. Available online: https://cran.r-project.org/web/packages/Deriv/ (accessed on 13 September 2024).
52. Robitzsch, A. sirt: Supplementary Item Response Theory Models, 2024. R Package Version 4.2-106. Available online: https://github.com/alexanderrobitzsch/sirt (accessed on 31 December 2024).
53. Battauz, M. equateIRT: An R package for IRT test equating. *J. Stat. Softw.* **2015**, *68*, 1–22. [CrossRef]
54. Battauz, M. equateMultiple: Equating of Multiple Forms, 2024. R Package Version 1.0.0. Available online: https://cran.r-project.org/web/packages/equateMultiple/index.html (accessed on 13 September 2024).
55. Chen, Y.; Li, C.; Ouyang, J.; Xu, G. DIF statistical inference without knowing anchoring items. *Psychometrika* **2023**, *88*, 1097–1122. [CrossRef] [PubMed]
56. Halpin, P.F.; Gilbert, J. Testing whether reported treatment effects are unduly dependent on the specific outcome measure used. *arXiv* **2024**, arXiv:2409.03502. [CrossRef]
57. Strobl, C.; Kopf, J.; Kohler, L.; von Oertzen, T.; Zeileis, A. Anchor point selection: Scale alignment based on an inequality criterion. *Appl. Psychol. Meas.* **2021**, *45*, 214–230. [CrossRef]
58. Camilli, G. The case against item bias detection techniques based on internal criteria: Do item bias procedures obscure test fairness issues? In *Differential Item Functioning: Theory and Practice*; Holland, P.W., Wainer, H., Eds.; Erlbaum: Hillsdale, NJ, USA, 1993; pp. 397–417.
59. Shealy, R.; Stout, W. A model-based standardization approach that separates true bias/DIF from group ability differences and detects test bias/DTF as well as item bias/DIF. *Psychometrika* **1993**, *58*, 159–194. [CrossRef]

60. De Los Reyes, A.; Tyrell, F.A.; Watts, A.L.; Asmundson, G.J.G. Conceptual, methodological, and measurement factors that disqualify use of measurement invariance techniques to detect informant discrepancies in youth mental health assessments. *Front. Psychol.* **2022**, *13*, 931296. [CrossRef]
61. El Masri, Y.H.; Andrich, D. The trade-off between model fit, invariance, and validity: The case of PISA science assessments. *Appl. Meas. Educ.* **2020**, *33*, 174–188. [CrossRef]
62. Funder, D.C.; Gardiner, G. MIsgivings about measurement invariance. *Eur. J. Pers.* **2024**, *38*, 889–895. [CrossRef]
63. Welzel, C.; Inglehart, R.F. Misconceptions of measurement equivalence: Time for a paradigm shift. *Comp. Political Stud.* **2016**, *49*, 1068–1094. [CrossRef]
64. Zwitser, R.J.; Glaser, S.S.F.; Maris, G. Monitoring countries in a changing world: A new look at DIF in international surveys. *Psychometrika* **2017**, *82*, 210–232. [CrossRef] [PubMed]

algorithms

MDPI

Article

An Automated Framework for Streamlined CFD-Based Design and Optimization of Fixed-Wing UAV Wings

Chris Pliakos [1,2], Giorgos Efrem [1,2], Dimitrios Terzis [1,2] and Pericles Panagiotou [1,2,*]

1 Laboratory of Fluid Mechanics and Turbomachinery, Department of Mechanical Engineering, Aristotle University of Thessaloniki, 54124 Thessaloniki, Greece; pliakosc@auth.gr (C.P.); egiorgosm@auth.gr (G.E.); diterzis@auth.gr (D.T.)

2 UAV Integrated Research Center (UAV-iRC), Center for Interdisciplinary Research and Innovation (CIRI), Aristotle University of Thessaloniki, 57001 Thessaloniki, Greece

* Correspondence: peripan@auth.gr

Abstract: The increasing complexity of the UAV aerodynamic design, imposed by novel configurations and requirements, has highlighted the need for efficient tools for high-fidelity simulation, especially for optimization purposes. The current work presents an automated CFD framework, tailored for fixed-wing UAVs, designed to streamline the geometry generation of wings, mesh creation, and simulation execution into a Python-based pipeline. The framework employs a parameterized meshing module capable of handling a broad range of wing geometries within an extensive design space, thereby reducing manual effort and achieving pre-processing times in the order of five minutes. Incorporating GPU-enabled solvers and high-performance computing environments allows for rapid and scalable aerodynamic evaluations. An automated methodology for assessing the CFD results is presented, addressing the discretization and iterative errors, as well as grid resolution, especially near wall surfaces. Comparisons with the results produced by a specialized mechanical engineer with over five years of experience in aircraft-related CFD indicate high accuracy, with deviations below 3% for key aerodynamic metrics. A large-scale deployment further demonstrates consistency across diverse wing samples. A Bayesian Optimization case study then illustrates the framework's utility, identifying a wing design with an 8% improvement in the lift-to-drag ratio, while maintaining an average y^+ value below 1 along the surface. Overall, the proposed approach streamlines fixed-wing UAV design processes and supports advanced aerodynamic optimization and data generation.

Keywords: CFD automation; fixed-wing UAV; wing design; uncertainty; optimization

1. Introduction

In recent decades, fixed-wing UAVs have found an increasingly diverse range of applications, including precision agriculture [1], cargo transport [2], and environmental monitoring [3]. UAVs can also be used for beach monitoring [4] and search and rescue situations in various environments [5] (i.e., forests and mountains, as well as highly densely populated areas). This growth is guided by advancements in autonomy, propulsion systems, and materials, enabling UAVs to meet evolving operational demands while maintaining adaptability for a broad spectrum of missions.

Despite these advancements, the design methodologies for fixed-wing UAVs largely resemble the "traditional" design methods employed for manned aircrafts [6,7]. The latter have evolved through a systematic, iterative, human intensive approach segmented into three primary stages: conceptual, preliminary, and detailed design. The conceptual phase lays the groundwork by defining high-level system requirements and exploring multiple configurations to address mission-specific criteria. At this phase, which is marked by significant uncertainty, rapid prototyping and multiple testing of various configurations are key to advances in the next stages. The need for the exploration of the design space before progressing requires the utilization of low-fidelity and semi-empirical methods to assess the impact of alterations, typically in geometry. The preliminary phase refines these configurations through focused analyses of key components, ensuring alignment with performance, stability, and manufacturability goals. Computational Fluid Dynamics (CFD) analyses are fundamental for assessing aerodynamic performance and optimizing UAV designs, especially in this stage. High-fidelity methods, such as Reynolds-Averaged Navier–Stokes (RANS) simulations, require detailed meshes that can be laborious to generate and validate, adding significant overhead to the design process. It is acknowledged that experimental testing, particularly with rapid prototyping (RP), remains fundamental in fixed-wing UAV development. However, conducting wind tunnel tests often requires significant infrastructure, including specialized facilities, calibration procedures, and trained personnel, making it resource-intensive—especially for large-scale UAVs in the tactical, MALE, and HALE categories [8]. In contrast, CFD provides a standardized and reproducible method for systematically analyzing multiple design variations in design offices, acting as a third way of analyzing engineering problems, in addition to theoretical relations and experiments [9]. Consequently, CFD is often the primary tool for aerodynamic assessment, while experimental testing serves as a crucial validation step where resources permit.

Finally, the detail design phase involves the details of the selected configuration, including the construction drawings, resolving all remaining uncertainties to deliver a prototype. This structured, iterative process, while effective, underscores the resource-intensive nature of fixed-wing UAV development.

This is even more evident when addressing specialized applications or unconventional configurations. Especially concerning the latter, and following the design trends of modern aviation, novel configurations are investigated [2,10,11] and new lift and drag estimation methods are introduced to assist in the early stages of development [12]. Among these novel configurations, Blended Wing Body (BWB) designs are gaining significant attention due to their potential to improve aerodynamic efficiency, increase payload capacity, and reduce fuel consumption. Unlike conventional UAV designs, BWBs integrate the fuselage and wings into a unified aerodynamic shape, which presents unique advantages and challenges in aerodynamic analysis. These designs are particularly relevant for missions demanding long endurance and high efficiency, such as surveillance or cargo delivery, making them a prime focus for modern research frameworks [13]. The framework presented in this study addresses these challenges directly by automating the generation and analysis of both conventional and BWB UAV meshes, emphasizing their potential importance in future UAV developments.

Several studies have explored the potential for fully automating the time-intensive phase of aerodynamic evaluation [14–16]. These works highlight specific algorithmic strategies to accelerate aspects of the design process, such as focusing on the solution phase alone, automating calculations (e.g., decomposing forces into lift and drag), or employing high-performance computing. Other research efforts have adopted a more holistic approach to address the problem comprehensively.

Specifically, in [17], the authors developed a framework to automatically handle mesh generation and CFD analysis. However, their analysis is limited to simple trapezoidal subsonic UAV wing planforms. Additionally, the study in [18] examined the efficiency of multi-fidelity algorithms that combine low-fidelity panel methods with CFD for Blended

Wing Body (BWB) UAVs. Their approach began with a baseline geometry, which was deformed using Free-Form Deformation (FFD). This study, though, offers constrained degrees of freedom within the design space, as the configuration cannot deviate from a given baseline, e.g., providing no degrees of freedom in terms of wingspan. Furthermore, in [19], the authors applied FFD to locally morph computational grids and perform optimization studies using RANS CFD simulations. Similarly, in [20], researchers focused on validating an automated CFD chain, creating a Python-based framework that integrated multiple software tools for geometry manipulation. Both the above works, however, are limited to a specific baseline configuration, e.g., the Common Research Model in [19]. Moreover, studies [21,22] introduced machine learning methodologies for optimizing UAVs, including wings, fuselage, and engine configurations, by using high-level parameters (e.g., aspect ratio, wingspan, taper ratio, or thrust for engines) and targeting specific Unmanned Combat Aerial Vehicle (UCAV) designs. These works employed neural networks trained on low-fidelity panel data generated from frameworks capable of sampling design spaces, creating geometry models, and conducting analyses. Although these studies present a promising foundation that could potentially integrate CFD data, they do not eventually involve CFD results, which limits the fidelity and applicability of their optimization frameworks.

To cover the aforementioned research gaps, this study aims to develop an innovative, robust, and streamlined framework employing high-end commercial software to enable fully automated, high-fidelity CFD analyses of UAV wings. More specifically, the key objectives of this work are as follows:

- Provide a general algorithm for automation of CFD-based investigations. All aspects are based on an extensive literature survey at every part of the study, combining well-established common practices with proposed novel algorithms that unify all the components. Due to budget constraints, the authors could not develop the framework to work with all possible software alternatives. However, in case other research groups want to employ a different software, they will only have to emphasize specific parameters, and the overall architecture will remain as suggested.
- In contrast to existing frameworks that focus on given platforms or narrow design spaces, examine an extensive design space, allowing its application to the vast majority of UAV configurations [8].
- Accommodate wings for both conventional and tailless configurations (flying wings, BWBs), while incorporating a set of 35 design parameters that can completely control the wing planform and its airfoils.
- Apart from presenting the pipeline, suggest robust evaluation criteria and metrics in an automated format.

It must be noted at this point that, based on these objectives, this work aims to present and demonstrate a comprehensive algorithm and its corresponding framework, transitioning from geometry to simulation. The validation against experimental or flight-testing data is beyond the scope of this study, as the individual methods have already been validated in prior non-automated studies.

This paper proceeds as follows: Section 2 provides a detailed overview of the design space, focusing on UAV types and wing geometry parameterization. Section 3 outlines the framework's components, including its integration of OpenVSP (v3.40.1), BETA CAE ANSA (v24.2.1, Root, Switzerland), and ANSYS Fluent [v2023 R2], with detailed sub-algorithms for each module. Section 4 discusses the evaluation metrics used to quantify errors from mesh generation and introduces a novel rapid assessment method for CFD results. In Section 5, the computational grid is validated against common geometries and expert benchmarks, supplemented by a large-scale deployment to assess result quality. Finally, the adaptability of the framework is demonstrated through an optimization case study, which highlights its capability to automate CFD pre-processing and analysis within constrained design spaces.

2. Design Space

This study organizes the design space into two components: geometric design space and flow conditions design space.

- The geometric design space defines the shape of the wing, including planform parameters and airfoil shapes, which dictate the aerodynamic performance of UAVs.
- The flow conditions design space considers environmental and operational parameters such as velocity and altitude, which influence aerodynamic performance under different mission scenarios.

Specifically, the wing geometries and flow conditions incorporated into the framework are derived from a diverse set of UAVs and their respective operational conditions. The design space includes UAVs ranging from the Micro class (<2 kg MTOW) to MALE and HALE-Strike categories (>600 kg MTOW), as classified by NATO and detailed in [8]. Table 1 summarizes these UAV categories along with their associated operating conditions.

Table 1. Design space regarding the UAV types that this framework can handle.

Class	Category	GTOW [kg]	Altitude [ft]	Cruise Speed Range [km/h]	Reynolds Number Range	Flow Regime
Class I	Micro Mini Small	<2 2–15 15–150	<200 <3000 <5000	30–100 30–100 50–150	10^4–10^6	Laminar to Transitional
Class II	Tactical	150–600	<18,000	100–400	10^6–10^7	Predominantly turbulent
Class III	MALE HALE Strike	>600 >600 >600	<45,000 <65,000 <65,000	200–300 400–800 400–800	$> 10^7$	Fully turbulent

The following sections elaborate on the geometric and flow conditions design space, detailing how they are parametrized and integrated into the framework to accommodate this wide range of UAV designs. Although this framework also covers conventional planforms, particular attention is given to tailless and Blended Wing Body (BWB) configurations, which, despite not being universally optimal for all missions, remain an important research focus in modern aviation. This is evidenced by multiple global initiatives—such as NASA's X-48 and X-56 prototypes [23,24]—and the recent EU-funded EXAELIA project [25], whose flight demonstrators prominently feature BWB architectures. Moreover, BWBs pose complex challenges in simultaneously achieving lift generation and flight stability, making them valuable for testing and refining the framework's capabilities. Thus, they serve as exemplary case studies even if they are not invariably the most efficient choice for every UAV application.

2.1. Geometric Design Space and Parametrization Techniques

To enable fully autonomous geometry generation without human intervention, the wing planform must be parameterized in such way as to account for the degrees of freedom necessary for a designer during the conceptual and preliminary stages of UAV design. For the wing parametrization, the current study employes "low-level" variables, such as wing chords (c_r, c_t) and wingspan (b), which offer a clearer and more practical representation of geometry.

The design space accommodates both conventional and BWB UAVs. Conventional UAV wings are typically defined with one or two sections (i.e., the distinct trapezoidal planform surfaces that constitute the wing, are referred to as wing sections), as seen in

Figure 1, and are differentiated from the rest of the aircraft. In contrast, BWB UAVs have a more integrated structure, where the "fuselage-body" and wings blend into a continuous aerodynamic shape, as seen in Figure 1.

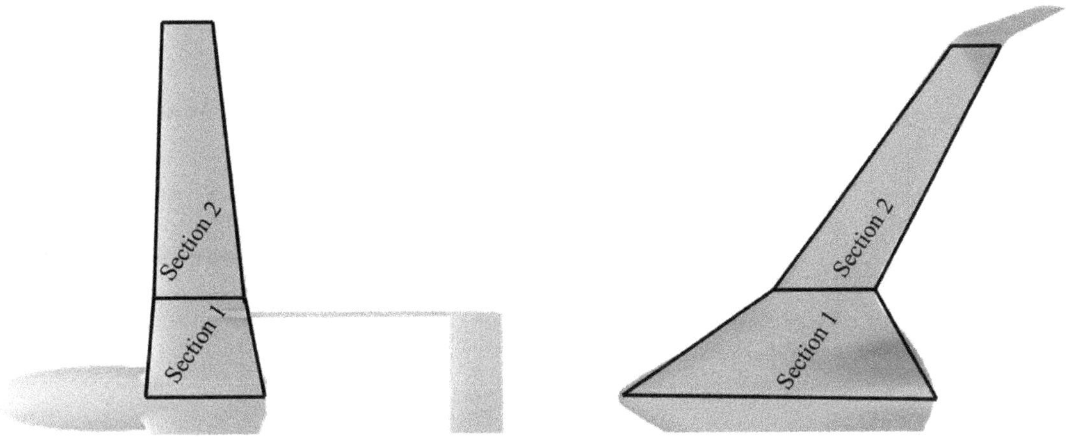

Figure 1. The two distinct sections used to generate a conventional and a BWB wing.

In most cases, and especially for BWB configurations, accurately capturing the complexity of the geometry requires multiple sections [26]. However, each additional section increases the number of design variables, leading to higher dimensionality in the design space. While greater dimensionality allows for detailed representations and subtle geometric variations, it also significantly increases computational costs during optimization. This framework restricts the design space for both conventional and BWB UAVs to two distinct trapezoidal sections which are smoothly blended to avoid sharp transitions, as explained in Section 3.1. While this parameterization includes non-planar features (dihedral), it does not currently incorporate additional non-planar elements like winglets, flaps, or slats. This limitation simplifies the geometry and meshing processes at this stage, providing a stable basis that can be extended to more complex design spaces in the future.

The necessary parameters and their respective range that define the planform of a wing instance for both configurations are tabulated in Table 2 and are also depicted in Figure 2.

Table 2. Design variables used to parameterize the wing planform and their respectable range.

Planform Parameter	Description	Units	Limits
c_1	Centerline chord length	m	$c_1 \in [0.2,\ 10]$
c_2	Root chord length	m	$c_2 \in [0.3 \times c_1,\ c_1]$
c_3	Tip chord length	m	$c_3 \in [0.3 \times c_2,\ c_2]$
b_1	c_2 spanwise location	m	$b_1 \in [0.2 \times b_2,\ 0.7 \times b_2]$
b_2	c_3 spanwise location (semispan)	m	$b_2 \in [1,\ 10]$
Λ_1	Sweep angle of section 1@$c/4$	deg	$\Lambda_1 \in [0,\ 60]$
Λ_2	Sweep angle of section 2@$c/4$	deg	$\Lambda_2 \in [0,\ 60]$
i_1	Twist angle of c_2@$c/4$	deg	$i_1 \in [-5,\ 5]$
i_2	Twist angle of c_3@$c/4$	deg	$i_2 \in [-7,\ 7]$
γ_1	Dihedral angle of section 1	deg	$\gamma_1 \in [-10,\ 10]$
γ_2	Dihedral angle of section 2	deg	$\gamma_2 \in [-10,\ 10]$

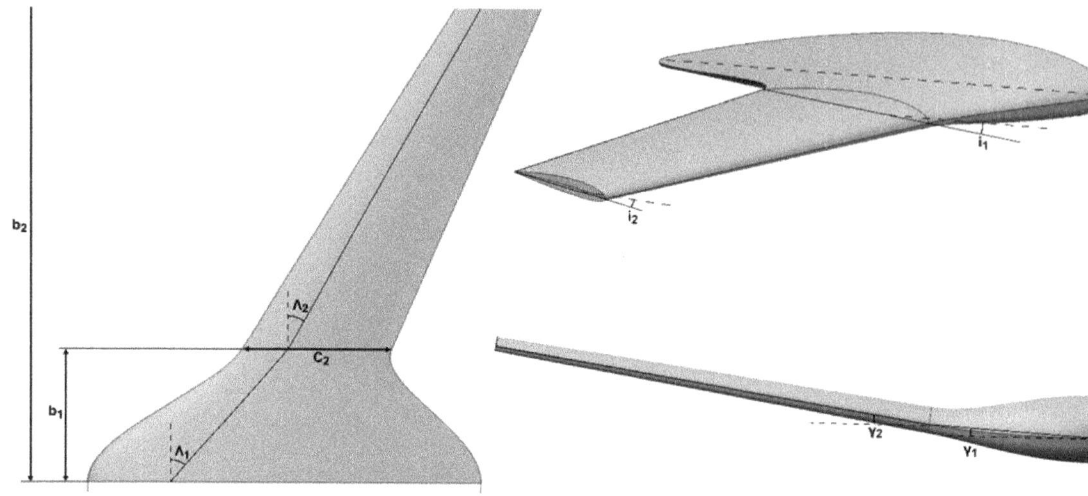

Figure 2. Design variables used to parameterize the wing planform.

A total of 11 low-level parameters are required to fully define the planform of a two-section wing, without including any details about the airfoil shape. It should be noted that all parameters are referenced from the coordinate system with an origin on the leading edge of the centerline chord. The x-axis spans along the chordwise direction and the y-axis spans along the spanwise direction of the wing.

Design variable constraints have been defined to exclude unrealistic wing geometries such as having taper ratio values larger than 1, wings with very thin sections that would be impossible to manufacture, or wings with excessive aft and forward sweep angles (Figure 3). These parameters, combined with constraints, ensure that the design space remains realistic and aligned with established aerodynamic standards.

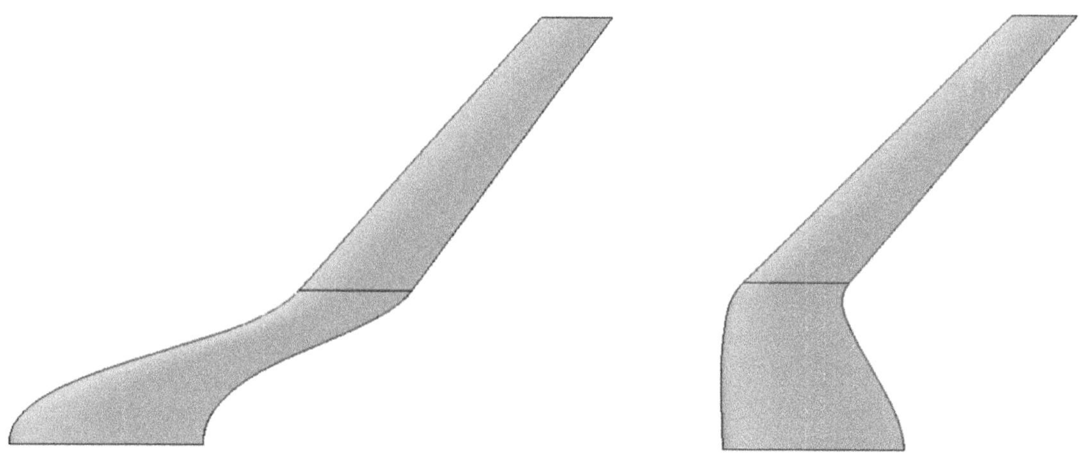

Figure 3. Unrealistic wing designs produced when the design space is not being constrained. The planform surfaces are displayed with the leading edge being on the left.

The wing's cross-section is defined by three distinct airfoils: one at the root, one at the kink (midsection break), and one at the tip. Airfoil profiles are assigned to these spanwise locations, with interpolation between them. The airfoil shape greatly affects the aerodynamic characteristics of wing geometry. The precise shape of an airfoil can vary greatly depending on its intended use, flight conditions, and performance requirements. One of the most common airfoil databases is the one from UIUC [27], which contains more than 1500 airfoil shapes from real cases. Selecting airfoils based on their unique categorical identifiers transforms the design space into a high-dimensional, discrete domain. This discrete nature lacks the continuity required for efficient aerodynamic shape optimization, where smooth transitions between design variables are essential. To address this, parameterization techniques that represent airfoil shapes through continuous variables are employed.

Common parametrization techniques include the Bézier–PARSEC method, Class Function/Shape Function Transformations (CST), B-Splines combined with dimensionality reduction techniques such as Principal Component Analysis (PCA), and others [28]. However, the main drawbacks of those methods are the generation of non-smooth trailing edges with the frequent crossing of the lower pressure surface and the upper suction one and the demand of a large amount of design to accurately represent the airfoil in terms of geometric similarity and aerodynamic performance. Given these challenges, a novel approach to airfoil parameterization was required—one that could achieve high shape diversity while maintaining a low dimensionality for efficient optimization. The method adopted in this study is based on the Bézier–GAN (BGAN) parameterization technique, developed by Chen, Chiu, and Fuge from the University of Maryland [29]. This deep learning model, based on Info-GAN structures, specifically designed for aerodynamic shape generation, leverages the smooth, continuous properties of Bézier curves within a GAN framework to produce realistic airfoil shapes.

These networks utilize latent codes and noise variables as inputs to the network, to effectively capture both major and minor shape variations in airfoils, enabling the synthesis of smooth, aerodynamic designs. The latent codes form a low-dimensional representation that serves as the primary mechanism for representing major shape features, such as thickness, camber, reflex, and overall curvature. Alongside the latent codes, noise variables can be introduced to handle finer, more detailed aspects of the airfoil shape. These noise variables provide an additional level of granularity, allowing for subtle adjustments that add diversity to the generated shapes. Following the training methodologies proposed by Chen et al., the parameters depicted in Table 3 are selected to train the airfoil generator.

Table 3. Training parameters for the BGAN model.

Training Parameter	Value	Description
Bézier degree	32	The number of Bézier control points
Latent codes dimension	8	Number of latent codes
Noise dimension	0	Number of components in noise vector
Train steps/epochs	150,000	-
Batch size	32	Number of samples per network pass
Bounds	[0, 1]	Bounds of latent codes and noise components
Latent code sampling PDF	Uniform	Probability distribution

Thus, with only eight design variables, it is possible to accurately represent an airfoil that belongs in the original UIUC database (training dataset), as well as to generate new novel configurations that enhance the exploration of the design space. It is important to note that while the UIUC database primarily contains airfoils analyzed at low Reynolds numbers, the BGAN training dataset utilizes only the geometry of the airfoils and not the results of the corresponding analyses. Moreover, many of the airfoils in the database are widely used in operating aircrafts, where they perform effectively at significantly higher Reynolds numbers.

2.2. Operating Conditions

The design space for this framework is confined to the subsonic regime, where flow velocities remain below Mach 0.3. This range is representative of typical UAV operational conditions according to [8,30,31] and ensures that compressibility effects can be neglected. Within this regime, velocities primarily influence computational mesh and turbulence modeling strategies. Table 1 highlights that each UAV class operates under different conditions without a uniform trend applying to all classifications. The selected operational design space is dependent on the wing geometry, which is sampled from the geometric design space. The altitude was kept constant (at sea level) for all wings, while the cruise speed was sampled within the range defined individually for each UAV class [8,32].

3. Framework Breakdown

The proposed framework automates the CFD workflow for UAV wings, integrating geometry generation, meshing, and simulation execution into a Python-based pipeline, as illustrated in Figure 4. It eliminates manual intervention, promotes consistency across a large design space, and significantly accelerates the aerodynamic evaluation process for both individual case studies and optimization-driven analyses.

The three modules are as follows:

- Geometry Modeling: Utilizes OpenVSP's Python API [33] for generating 3D UAV wing models. Implemented using an object-oriented programming (OOP) approach, the geometry module employs a *Wing* class that encapsulates design parameters, flight conditions, and methods for geometry generation and blending.
- Meshing: Utilizes BETA CAE's ANSA pre-processor [34] to transform geometries into solver-ready grids, adhering to stringent quality standards for subsonic flows.
- Simulation Execution: Employs ANSYS Fluent via the appropriate API—PyFluent (v0.21) [35], a module for automating simulation setup, execution, and result post-processing.

The framework relies on XML files for data exchange between modules, allowing for consistent information flow. As presented in Section 5, high-performance computing (HPC) with the GPU-native Fluent solver significantly enhances computational efficiency, reducing processing times and enabling rapid CFD analysis execution.

An important comment must be made regarding the turbulence modeling approach, since it affects two latter key modules (meshing and solution). Several main approaches are encountered in the CFD literature, balancing accuracy and computational cost. Direct Numerical Simulation (DNS) resolves all turbulence scales but is computationally impractical for most applications, due to its high computational cost. Large Eddy Simulation (LES) resolves larger turbulent structures while modeling smaller eddies, requiring significant resources, especially for optimization purposes when the number of required solutions is in the hundreds or thousands, depending on the optimization study [17]. However, Reynolds-Averaged Navier–Stokes (RANS) models offer computational efficiency suitable for steady-state aerodynamic analyses, making them the industry standard [36,37].

In this study, the RANS approach with Menter's k-omega SST [38] turbulence modeling is adopted, validated through prior work against both in-house test flight data and assessed against experimental results [39]. While this validation confirms its suitability within the design space intended, it is important to note that the model has not been explicitly validated for every possible wing configuration that may arise from the sampling of this space. However, its extensive use in similar studies further supports its applicability to this framework [40]. This choice is made to align with the computational tools available, specifically the GPU-native solvers in the utilized version of ANSYS Fluent 2023R2 [41,42].

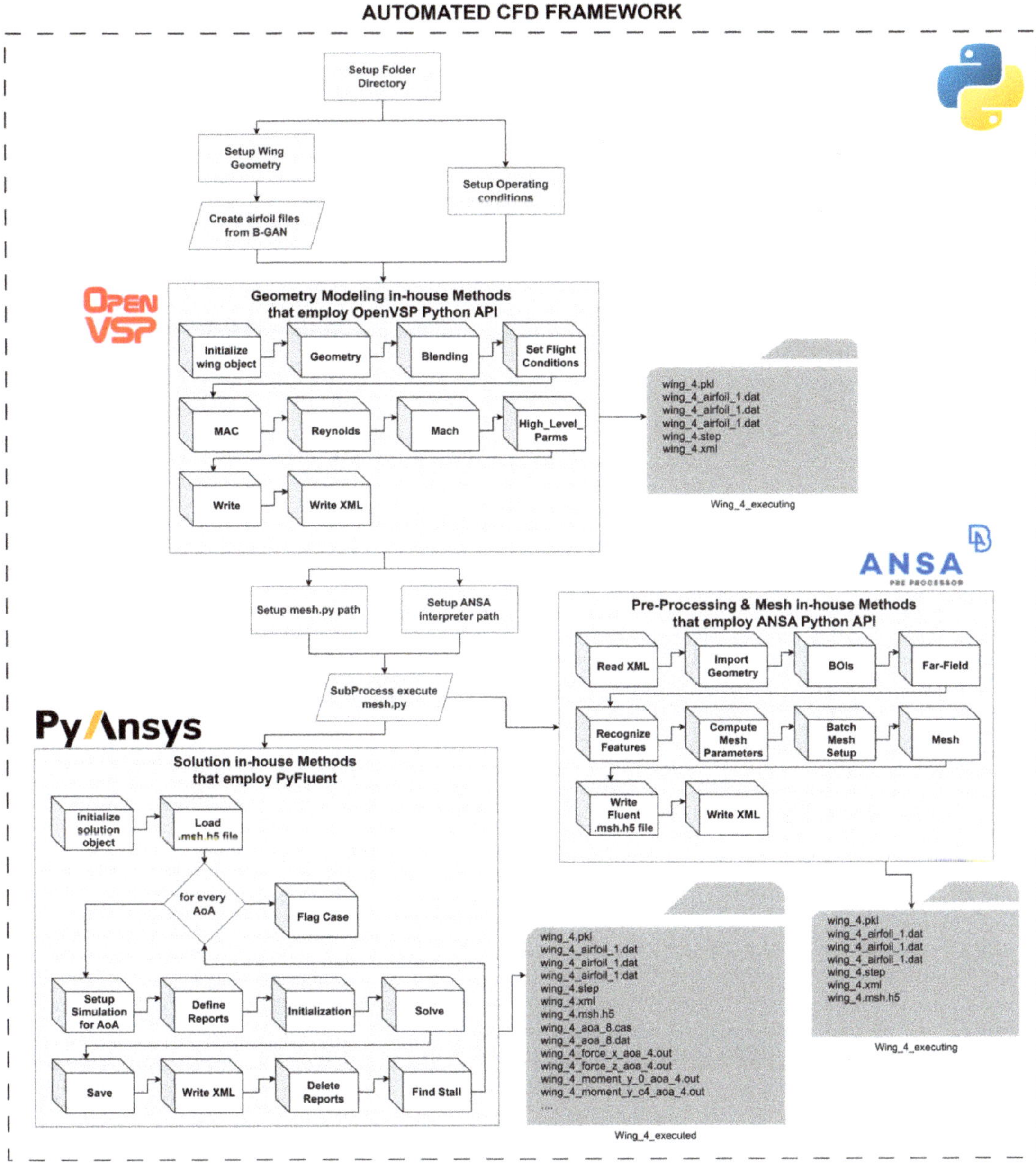

Figure 4. Framework pipeline. More than 35 custom functions have been developed to facilitate the framework.

3.1. Geometry Module

The geometry module is critical for generating CFD-ready wing geometries, ensuring compatibility with the following meshing and simulation processes. According to [41], a "good" geometric model tailored to the requirements of CFD not only enhances workflow efficiency but also ensures reliable and reproducible results—an essential objective of this framework, where robustness is paramount. Using an object-oriented programming approach, the module features a dedicated *Wing* class, as shown in Figure 5.

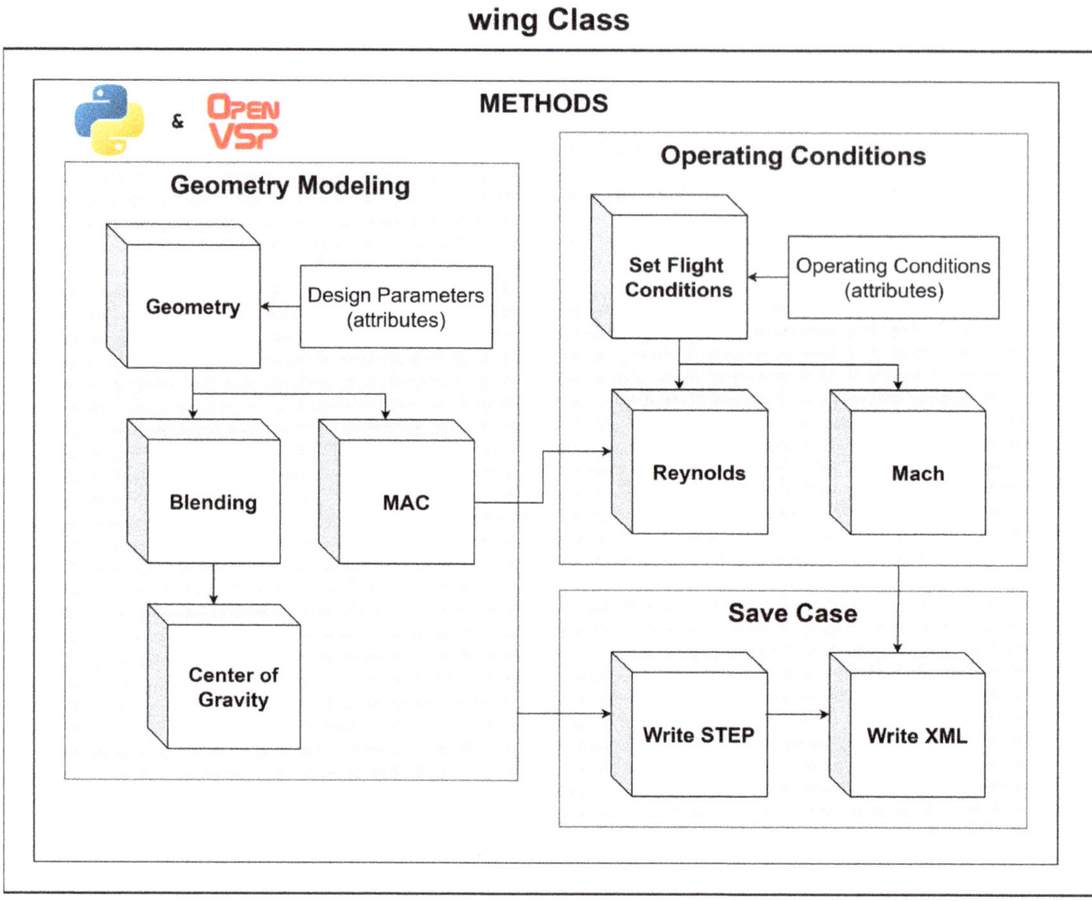

Figure 5. Wing class developed for the geometry module along with its sub-methods.

The *Wing* class methods can be distinguished into three categories:

- Geometry Modeling: involves defining design parameters and producing the core geometry, automating blending between sections, calculating the Mean Aerodynamic Chord (MAC), and determining the center of gravity.
- Operating Conditions: definition of flight conditions and computation of key metrics.
- Case Management: exports geometry in STEP format and records attributes in an XML file for case tracking.

Trailing edge (TE) treatment, section blending, and Mean Aerodynamic Chord (MAC) calculation are integral to ensure that the generated wing geometries are appropriate for CFD meshing. The trailing edge cut is applied to improve mesh quality and numerical stability, as sharp TEs often lead to a high aspect ratio or skewed cells, affecting solver convergence [42]. To maintain consistency, the TE thickness is set to 1% of the chord length, a commonly recommended guideline for subsonic applications [41]. Blending between wing sections is fully automated to eliminate abrupt transitions, ensuring geometric continuity across all generated designs. The framework prioritizes the second section as the primary lifting surface, with the first section adjusted to enforce tangency at the leading and trailing edges, preventing discontinuities at the symmetry plane.

Additionally, the MAC is computed using a weighted averaging approach, serving as the reference chord length for moment coefficient (Cm) calculations, which define the pitching moment characteristics of the wing about its aerodynamic center [7]. Moreover, MAC serves as the characteristic length for the calculation of the Reynolds number. These treatments eliminate human intervention and are executed in the background, minimizing the workload needed for geometry preparation. Further details on TE treatment methodology, blending algorithms, and MAC computation are provided in Appendix A.1.

The right-hand side of Figure 5 highlights additional capabilities of the geometry module. While these functions, such as the calculation of Reynolds and Mach numbers, do not directly contribute to geometry generation, they provide essential metrics for flow characterization and categorization. Finally, through case management methods, the generated wing geometry can be exported in STEP file format, while the design parameters of the wing along with the calculated metrics can be recorded in an XML file for case tracking.

3.2. Mesh Module

The mesh module bridges the gap between raw geometry and solver-ready computational meshes. This module is tasked with two primary objectives: geometry pre-processing and mesh generation. The first objective builds upon the modeled wing generated by the geometry module, performing geometric manipulations to prepare a watertight control volume for mesh generation. This includes steps such as feature recognition, body of influence (BOI) definition, and far-field boundary creation. These steps are further analyzed and discussed in Appendices A.2 and A.3.

The second objective (mesh generation) involves discretizing the computational domain into smaller cells or elements, which act as control volumes for solving the governing equations of fluid flow. The quality of the mesh directly impacts numerical accuracy, numerical stability, and computational efficiency, as it determines the resolution of key physical phenomena such as boundary layers, wake regions, and separation zones.

Implemented via the ANSA Python API, the module uses an object-oriented *pre_processor* class with four method categories, as illustrated in Figure 6. The process begins with import methods, which handle the data transfer from the geometry module, importing STEP files and extracting attributes from the XML file for a case-specific setup. Next, feature recognition is performed to identify critical regions such as leading edges, trailing edges, and sharp perimeters. Bodies of Influence (BOIs) are then defined, along with the far-field boundaries of the computational domain. Following these geometric pre-processing steps, the meshing operations take place. Mesh parameters are dynamically adjusted using the custom *Compute_Mesh_Parameters* method and the geometric attributes of the given wing. The custom *Batch_Mesh_Setup* method then updates the meshing sessions/scenarios before generating the mesh in the following sequence: (1) surface meshing for both the wing wall and the far-field boundaries, (2) inflation layer mesh, and finally (3) volume meshing. Finally, the Export Mesh and Save Case methods save the mesh in Fluent-compatible *.msh.h5* format and generate XML files for case tracking and attribute documentation.

At this stage, one notable feature of the XML file becomes evident: it serves as a bridge between the modules by enabling the transfer of all attributes and data from the *Wing* class to the *pre_processor* class. This eliminates the need for direct serialization, streamlining data handling within the framework. Once the geometry generation step is complete, the XML file ensures that the meshing module can independently proceed at a later time without requiring direct interaction with the geometry module.

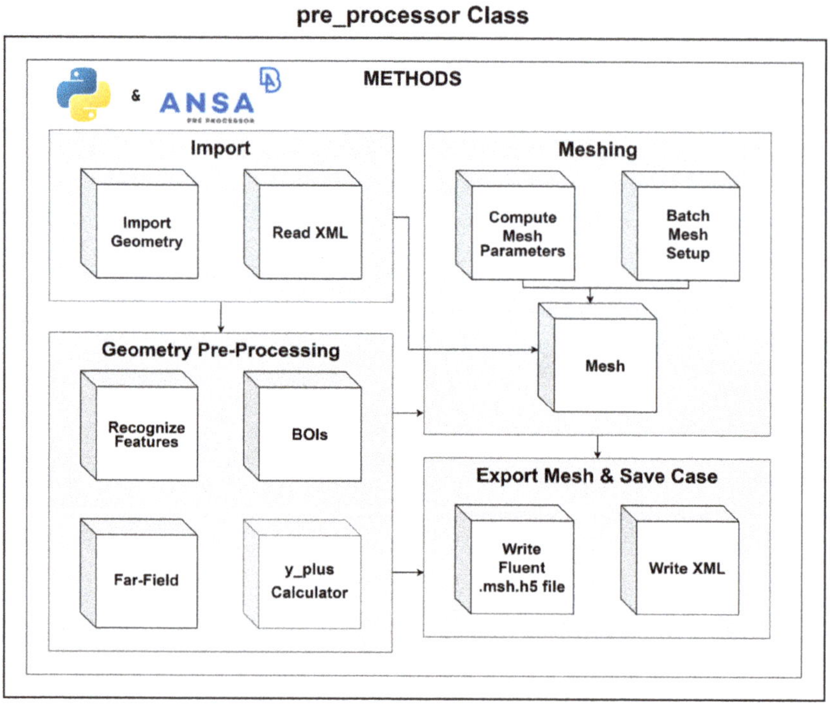

Figure 6. *Pre_Processor* class developed for the meshing module along with its sub-methods.

3.2.1. Meshing for CFD

Selecting the appropriate meshing criteria depends on the geometric complexity, flow conditions, and the desired level of simulation fidelity. Different mesh types—categorized as structured, unstructured, or hybrid—each offer distinct benefits and challenges. Structured grids, characterized by their uniform and ordered connectivity, are highly efficient and accurate for simple geometries and flow-aligned features [43]. However, their rigid structure makes them challenging to apply to complex or multi-element configurations. Unstructured grids, on the other hand, provide flexibility to adapt to highly irregular geometries, covering intricate features like sharp edges or highly curved surfaces. Hybrid grids combine the advantages of both, employing structured grids in regions where precision is important, and unstructured grids in less critical areas.

In this work, the hybrid mesh approach is selected. A structured curvilinear mesh (inflation layer) is employed over the boundary layer region to capture critical near-wall phenomena, while for the remainder of the domain, an unstructured grid is chosen to flexibly adapt to the overall geometry. As for discretization elements, hexahedrals are predominantly used for both boundary layers and far-field regions, as they offer superior numerical accuracy and alignment with flow gradients [41].

Considering the practical implementation, the mesh of any arbitrary wing within the framework is generated via custom meshing scenarios which are passed through the ANSA *batch mesh* tool. These scenarios are tailored by parametrizing meshing options with the wing's geometric characteristics, as observed in Table 4. The meshing module operates autonomously, requiring no additional user inputs. The *batch mesh* tool for CFD applications usually requires a surface meshing scenario, an inflation layer scenario, and a volume-meshing scenario. Each meshing scenario consists of multiple meshing sessions, addressing different aspects of the geometry. Specifics considering the meshing scenarios, the meshing parameters, and special treatments are discussed in Appendix A.3.

Table 4. Parameters that control surface mesh.

		Wing-Wall Session	Wingtip Session	Far-Field Session
Mesh type	**Algorithm**	CFD	CFD	CFD
	Element Type	Quads and Trias	Quads and Trias	Quads and Trias
	Order	1st	1st	1st
Mesh Sizing	**Growth Rate**	1.2	1.2	1.2
	Max Length	$f(MAC)$	$f(c_3)$	$f(c_1)$
Curvature Refinement	**Distortion Angle**	0	0	15
	Min length	$f(c_3)$	$f(c_3)$	-
Leading Edge Treatment	**Distribution**	Anisotropic	-	-
	Min first height	$f(c_3)$		
	Growth Factor	1.15		
	Max Aspect	1		
Trailing Edge Treatment	**Distribution**	Anisotropic	-	-
	Min Aspect	0.05		
	Growth Factor	1.15		
	Max Aspect	0.7		
Sharp Edge Treatment	**Max Length**	-	$f(c_3)$	-

3.2.2. Surface Mesh

The shaded fields in Table 4 represent meshing parameters that are directly parametrized using geometric inputs specific to the wing's design. These parametrizations are chosen with guidance from the established literature and reflect best practices to ensure computational accuracy and efficiency. For instance, the "minimum length" under "curvature refinement" and the "minimum first height" in "leading edge treatment" share a value of approximately 0.1% of the tip chord. Consistent with guidelines from the literature, refining key areas, such as leading and trailing edges to approximately 0.1% of the chord length and ensuring 80–100 cells along the chordwise direction, enhances the resolution required for capturing curvature effects and boundary layer dynamics [41]. Additionally, anisotropic distribution and gradual growth factors in mesh elements are recommended for resolving high-gradient regions near walls [43]. Other mesh parametrizations are derived by trial and error while testing the limits of the design space and grid independence studies that are mentioned in Section 5.1.

The automatic control over mesh sizing is achieved through *.ansa_mpar* files, which are edited automatically and passed to the ANSA pre-processing software. The *.ansa_mpar* files are configuration files that specify mesh parameters for different regions of a geometry. Each meshing session corresponds to an ansa parameter file. The modification of the *.ansa_mpar* files is achieved via the *ansa_mpar_file_editor* module, a custom utility developed to automate the process of editing these files. This module enables dynamic adjustments to mesh parameters by leveraging Python's file-handling capabilities and regular expressions to target specific configuration settings within *.ansa_mpar* files. The modification of *.ansa_mpar* files is performed during the call of the *compute_mesh_parameters*, a custom method included in the *pre_processing* class.

3.2.3. Inflation Layer Mesh

This study employs a wall-resolving approach to accurately capture near-wall phenomena, which are critical for predicting aerodynamic characteristics. The near-wall region is dominated by the boundary layer, transitioning from the viscous sublayer dominated by laminar flow, where fluid particles move in orderly layers, to turbulent flow, characterized by chaotic fluctuations. These transitions significantly affect performance metrics such as skin friction and separation zones, making precise boundary layer modeling a necessity [44,45].

To address these challenges, the near-wall treatment focuses on resolving flow structures adjacent to the wall, guided by the non-dimensional wall distance y^+ [46]. Depending on the turbulence modeling approach, the meshing strategy ensures the first cell lies at a specific y^+, which in CFD applications is called first-layer y^+, or simply y^+. As mentioned at the beginning of Section 3, this study employs the k-omega SST turbulence model [38]. Considering the latter, grid refinements target average y^+ values less than one ($y^+ < 1$), which is essential for resolving the viscous sublayer.

The ANSA software allows us to have more control over specific features of the inflation layer; these features are listed below.

- The first two layers are of the same height, equal to the first layer height calculation discussed in Appendix A.3.
- A growth factor is applied for a specific number of layers that are calculated according to the total boundary layer height (see Appendix A.3).
- To ensure the full coverage of the physical boundary layer and a smooth transition from the inflation layer to the volume mesh, additional layers are added on top for redundancy.

The inflation layer height is calculated iteratively, starting with an initial thickness of twice the first layer height. Successive layers are generated using a growth factor, typically set to 1.2 for smooth transitions. The iterative process continues until the total inflation thickness equals or exceeds the estimated boundary layer thickness (δ). When the total inflation thickness exceeds the flat plate boundary layer height, the number of layers is returned and adjusted by a safety factor (1.1) to ensure adequate coverage, according to suggested practices [41]. Finally, additional layers are placed on top for redundancy. The following inflation layer (Figure 7) is produced automatically using the proposed framework.

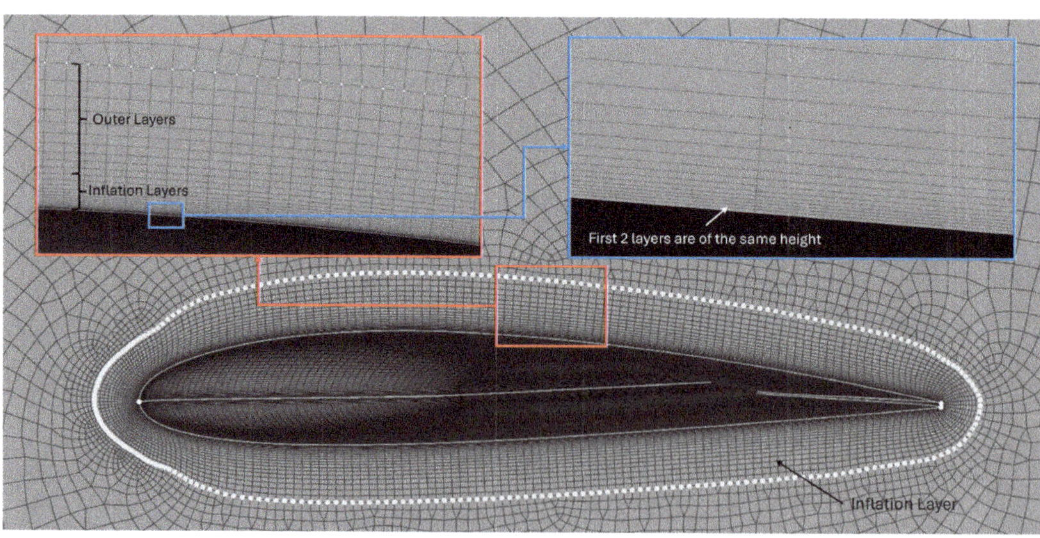

Figure 7. An example of the inflation layer that resulted from the automatic algorithm.

The zoomed-in views in Figure 7 highlight critical aspects of the grid structure at the symmetry plane. The right view focuses on the inflation layers, showing finely spaced layers adjacent to the body, with the first two layers being the same height. The left view shows the transition from the inflation layers to the additional layers and then the outer grid, where 10 coarser layers extend to the outer domain. Note that the inflation layer growth factor also applies to the outer layers, which are added as a safety cushion. This ensures that the region of the actual boundary layer will always fall in this curvilinear structured grid.

3.2.4. Volume Mesh

Volume meshing is the final step during the mesh generation process, generating elements in the space between the inflation layer top cap and the far-field boundaries. The utilized volume-meshing algorithm produces an unstructured grid of hexahedrals wherever possible, and tetrahedrals (pyramids) in places where hexas are not allowed. For consistency, the meshing algorithm is called "HexaPoly".

3.3. *Solver Module*

The solver module integrates ANSYS Fluent 2023R2 via PyFluent to automate simulation setup, execution, and post-processing. Utilizing Fluent's GPU-native solver, calculations achieve up to 7$\times$ faster computational times compared to parallel CPU solvers, significantly reducing simulation duration [47]. A dedicated *solution* class, illustrated in Figure 8, manages input and output files, simulation setup, and execution. It also supports stall detection and convergence monitoring methods, ensuring high-fidelity results with minimal manual effort.

To initiate this process, instantiating the solution class also launches Fluent automatically according to the specified launcher settings. Whether running in GPU or CPU mode, with or without GUI, and using a predefined number of processors, the solver is initialized with the appropriate computational resources before proceeding with the case setup and execution.

Once Fluent is up and running, the module proceeds with loading the computational mesh from a *.msh.h5* file. It then parses the XML file, extracting previously calculated attributes, including the MAC, reference surface area, Reynolds number, velocity, and altitude. These values are utilized in defining the simulation's boundary conditions and reference parameters for later force and moment calculations.

The simulation setup is then performed iteratively over a predefined range of angles of attack. For each AoA in the range, the class executes all setup procedures detailed in Appendix A.4. Monitoring report files for lift, drag, and moments are also generated during the simulation, providing real-time feedback on solution convergence and stability. After initializing the solution, the simulation then enters an iterative solution phase, where Fluent runs for a predefined number of iterations while continuously checking for convergence, as described in Algorithm for Convergence Detection section. Once the solver detects convergence, the aerodynamic coefficients C_L, C_D, and C_M are computed using the final force and moment values. Post-processing includes extracting maximum and mean y^+ values to evaluate the quality of the boundary layer resolution. The final results are stored in the XML file, and Fluent's output files (*.cas.h5*, *.dat.h5*, *.out*) are also saved.

Throughout this process, robust error handling mechanisms ensure that Fluent automatically retries execution or logs issues if it encounters errors such as failed launches or missing files. The class is designed to efficiently manage multiple cases, automating the CFD workflow.

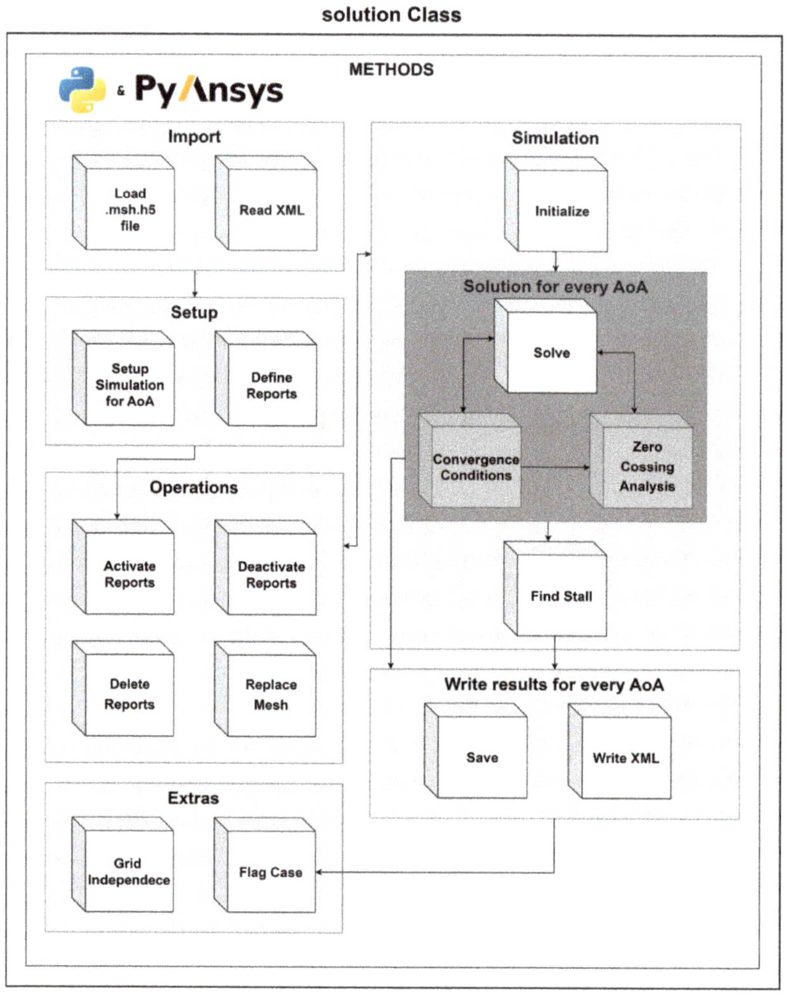

Figure 8. Solution class responsible for solution setup and execution.

Algorithm for Convergence Detection

In CFD, convergence refers to the stabilization of iterative calculations of flow variables, indicating that the numerical solution is approaching a state that sufficiently satisfies the governing equations and boundary conditions. Typically, convergence is judged by a three-order-of-magnitude drop in residuals of continuity, momentum, and turbulence equations, alongside the stabilization of forces such as lift and drag [48]. Achieving convergence to machine precision is realistically impossible, and practical thresholds must balance accuracy and computational cost.

In this framework, a custom convergence detection algorithm is implemented due to the limitations of Fluent's built-in methods for GPU-native solvers (Fluent v2023R2—v2024R2). This algorithm is incorporated as a hidden method within the *solution* class and called by the *solve* method while a simulation is running. This dependency can be observed in Figures 4 and 8. The method incorporates residual monitoring, periodicity checks, and termination criteria, focusing specifically on the aerodynamic quantities of interest: the forces acting along the x and z axes. The residual of these forces is calculated iteratively as the maximum relative change in force values over a specified window of past iterations (N), using the formula of Equation (1).

$$R^{(i)}_{F_{x,z}} = \max_{N} \left(\frac{\left| F^{(i)}{}_{x,\, z} - F^{(i-j)}{}_{x,\, z} \right|}{\left| F^{(i)}{}_{x,\, z} \right|} \right) \tag{1}$$

Note the following:
$R^{(i)}_{F_{x,\, z}}$: Maximum residual force in the x or z direction at iteration i;
$F^{(i)}_{x,z}$: Current force in the x or z direction at iteration i;
$F^{(i-j)}_{x,z}$: Force value in the x or z direction from j-th previous iteration.

Residual convergence is flagged when both forces drop below a predefined residual flag for three consecutive checks, performed at specified iteration check interval. Periodicity detection, initiated after a defined iteration threshold and a defined level of convergence (residual flag should be at least as low as one order of magnitude larger than the threshold), uses zero-crossing analysis to identify stable oscillatory behavior [49]. If periodicity is confirmed, the solution is conditionally converged. Additionally, a maximum iteration cap of 2000 iterations is imposed to prevent excessive computational costs in scenarios where convergence or periodicity detection cannot be achieved. In those cases, the evaluation metrics described in Section 4 can assist in investigating the convergence issue.

Based on the findings of a sensitivity study, combining a 10^{-3} residual flag, 100-iteration checking window, and 10-iteration check interval is suggested as a balanced trade-off between computational cost and convergence robustness. The approach ensures high reliability and robustness in detecting convergence, accommodating the complexities of GPU-native solvers and aerodynamic flows.

4. Evaluation Metrics

The reliability of CFD results must consider the quantification of numerical errors, especially in an automated framework where human intervention is minimized. Thus, it is essential to ensure that the solutions generated are accurate, especially when considering critical aerodynamic quantities like lift and drag. The error in CFD modeling can be categorized into round-off errors, discretization errors, and iterative errors [50–52].

- Round-off errors arise from the finite precision of numerical calculations performed by computers, particularly in large-scale simulations with many iterations, where the accumulation of small errors can impact the solution.
- Discretization errors, on the other hand, result from the approximation of continuous governing equations using numerical schemes and finite spatial or temporal resolution. They encompass truncation errors, which arise from the omission of higher-order terms in the numerical approximation, and additional artifacts introduced by grid quality, boundary condition definition, and numerical schemes. Discretization errors are often treated as an epistemic uncertainty [53], reflecting incomplete knowledge of the true solution due to mesh and scheme limitations.
- Iterative errors stem from the incomplete convergence of the solver to a stable solution, either due to insufficient iterations or suboptimal solver settings, and are similarly treated as an epistemic uncertainty [54].

While these errors cannot be entirely eliminated, estimating their impact is essential for assessing the numerical fidelity of CFD results. Such error estimation safeguards against misinterpreting numerical artifacts as physical phenomena and helps ensure that the automated workflow produces robust and reliable outputs.

To complement the error estimation process, this study also introduces a rapid reliability assessment methodology for evaluating the overall quality of CFD results. This assessment uses established best practices and guidelines for CFD simulations in the subsonic regime [41,48]. By systematically evaluating critical parameters—such as boundary layer resolution, the number of discretized cells within the boundary layer, and the convergence behavior of key forces—the methodology identifies unreliable simulations and highlights potential sources of inaccuracy. These quality checks act as a double-layer safeguard, ensuring that the solutions meet predefined standards of fidelity before progressing further in the design process.

Together, error estimation and rapid reliability assessment form a comprehensive framework for validating CFD outputs. The framework not only quantifies numerical uncertainties but also ensures solution quality through practical and experience-based reliability checks. This dual approach provides designers with robust and reliable outputs, enabling informed decision-making during the design and optimization process.

4.1. Discretization Error Quantification

This subsection focuses on two primary error sources: the Grid Convergence Index (GCI), which quantifies discretization errors, and iterative errors, which arise from incomplete solver convergence. These methods allow for the estimation of numerical uncertainties, enhancing confidence in the CFD solutions.

The Grid Convergence Index (GCI), rooted in Richardson extrapolation, is a well-established method for estimating discretization error in CFD simulations, while it has been validated against experimental data across diverse aerodynamic applications [55]. The GCI evaluates the convergence of key aerodynamic quantities, such as lift and drag, across systematically refined grids. The procedure is as follows:

1. **Define a Representative Grid Size**: for three-dimensional grids, Equation (2) is used.

$$h = \left[\frac{1}{N}\sum_{i=1}^{N} \mathrm{V_i}\right]^{\frac{1}{3}} \tag{2}$$

   Note that V_i is the volume of the i_{th} cell and N is the total number of cells.

2. **Grid Refinement:** perform analyses on three grids (coarse, medium, and fine), characterized by grid sizes $h_1 < h_2 < h_3$, with a refinement ratio r (Equation (3)).

$$r = \frac{h_{coarse}}{h_{fine}} > 1.3 \tag{3}$$

3. **Apparent Order of Accuracy p:** Calculate p using Equations (4)–(6).

$$p = \frac{1}{\ln(r_{21})}\left|\ln\left(\frac{\varphi_3 - \varphi_2}{\varphi_2 - \varphi_1}\right) + q(p)\right| \tag{4}$$

$$q(p) = ln\left(\frac{r_{21}^p - s}{r_{32}^p - s}\right) \tag{5}$$

$$s = 1 \times sgn\left(\frac{\varphi_3 - \varphi_2}{\varphi_2 - \varphi_1}\right) \tag{6}$$

In these equations, φ is the aerodynamic quantity of interest. The equations for p can be solved using fixed-point iteration.

4. **Extrapolated Solution:** Use Richardson extrapolation (Equation (7)) to approximate the solution at an infinitely fine grid.

$$\varphi_{ext}^{21} = \frac{r_{21}^{p}\varphi_1 - \varphi_2}{r_{21}^{p} - 1} \tag{7}$$

5. **Discretization Error (GCI):** The error estimates are reported (Equations (8) and (9)).

$$\begin{aligned} \varepsilon_{31} &= \left|\frac{\varphi_3-\varphi_1}{\varphi_1}\right| \\ \varepsilon_{3,ext} &= \left|\frac{\varphi_3-\varphi_{ext}^{21}}{\varphi_{ext}^{21}}\right| \end{aligned} \tag{8}$$

$$GCI_{fine,31} = 1.25\frac{\varepsilon_{a,31}}{r_{31}^{p} - 1} \tag{9}$$

4.2. Iterative Error Quantification

Iterative errors arise due to the non-linearity inherent in the governing equations, such as the Reynolds-Averaged Navier–Stokes (RANS) equations, and the iterative nature of numerical solvers [52,56]. Non-linearities from convective terms, turbulence closure models, and deferred corrections in discretization contribute significantly to iterative errors. Additionally, the solution of linearized algebraic systems through iterative methods introduces convergence-related discrepancies. While iterative errors can be reduced with additional iterations, achieving complete convergence is often computationally prohibitive, particularly in complex turbulent flows. This necessitates the adoption of reliable methods to quantify and manage iterative errors within acceptable limits to ensure the fidelity of CFD simulations.

Despite significant advancements in CFD, iterative errors remain an open problem, with numerous studies endeavoring to address their impact and quantification [50–52,55,56]. The approach to iterative error estimation employed in this study aligns with the same study utilized for the discretization error, thereby ensuring consistency and credibility within the numerical uncertainty framework. In this context, iterative error fulfills a dual role. It serves as a practical indicator of convergence, enabling engineers to assess whether a solution has stabilized by closely monitoring the error as the solution progresses. Furthermore, it provides an approximation of uncertainty, allowing for the estimation of numerical error should the simulation be terminated prematurely.

To quantify the iterative error, the methodology proposed by Ferziger [57] is employed. The iterative error, denoted as ε_{iter}, is estimated using the formula of Equation (10).

$$\varepsilon_{iter,i}^{n} \cong \frac{\left(\varphi_i^{n+1} - \varphi_i^{n}\right)}{\lambda_i - 1} \tag{10}$$

Note that n is the iteration number, φ_i is the solution variable, and λ_i is the principal eigenvalue of the solution matrix, approximated using Equation (11).

$$\lambda_i = \frac{\left\|\varphi_i^{n+1} - \varphi_i^{n}\right\|}{\left\|\varphi_i^{n} - \varphi_i^{n-1}\right\|} \tag{11}$$

The uncertainty in iteration convergence, δ_{iter}, is then calculated as shown in Equation (12).

$$\delta_{iter} = \frac{\left\|\varepsilon_{iter,i}^{n}\right\|}{\lambda_{ave} - 1} \tag{12}$$

In this equation, λ_{ave} is the average value of λ_i over a reasonable number of iterations. Following recommendations in prior studies, λ_{ave} is calculated using 1% of the total iterations [51].

4.3. Solution Confidence

Unlike global error estimates, key simulation quality indicators provide a practical and immediate assessment of grid and solution reliability. The confidence metrics utilized in this study are systematically implemented as part of the automated process, providing a quick and actionable diagnostic tool to assess simulation quality. By flagging runs that deviate from established thresholds, this method empowers engineers to either proceed with confidence or refine their setup, thus safeguarding the integrity of the design process.

According to widely accepted guidelines for the subsonic regime, as well as experimental validations [58], proper resolution of turbulence effects—particularly when using the low-Reynolds variant of the k-omega SST turbulence model adopted in this study—requires careful treatment of the boundary layer grid. For accurate turbulence modeling and wall shear stress prediction, an average y^+ value of less than 1 and a maximum y^+ value of 2 should be enforced across the wing surface. While a maximum y^+ value strictly below 1 is suggested by some researchers (see Table 5) as an ideal target, it is often unrealistic to achieve this consistently in automated frameworks, especially when considering the broad design space and flow conditions investigated in this work.

Table 5. Proposed y^+ values and prism layers in boundary layers in different studies.

Study	Proposed y^+	Proposed Prism Layers
Menter et al., 1994 [38]	3	N/A
Georgiadis et al., 1995 [58]	2	N/A
Menter et al., 2015 [59]	1	30
Goetten et al., 2019 [41]	N/A	20–40
Menter et al., 2003 [60]	2	N/A
ANSYS–Menter 2021 [48]	1	30–40

Nevertheless, it should be noted that this practical guideline is applied to ensure that the low-Reynolds modeling will consider the phenomena encountered within the viscous sublayer, which appears at a y^+ smaller than 5 [46].

Several studies have attempted to quantify the sensitivity of aerodynamic quantities to variations in y^+ values across a range of geometries and flow conditions [58,59]. However, these efforts remain limited, both in scope and applicability, as they do not comprehensively cover the design space or operational conditions explored in this study. As such, relying solely on y^+ values for a quantified grid-resolution error remains impractical and, in many cases, misleading.

In addition to satisfying the first layer height requirements near wall boundaries, an accurate boundary layer resolution also demands a sufficient number of prism layers within the boundary layer to properly capture the flow phenomena starting from the near-wall region of the viscous sublayer and moving on to the buffer zone and logarithmic region. Existing studies have established that 20 to 40 prism layers are typically required to discretize the boundary layer accurately and ensure numerical fidelity (see Table 5). This ensures that steep gradients, particularly in the near-wall regions, are resolved with an adequate grid density.

By combining the guidelines for y^+ and the boundary layer discretization, a systematic confidence assessment system is suggested in the current study, indicatively using color coding to flag deviations from established thresholds. This system allows for a rapid visual evaluation of simulation reliability, as illustrated in Figure 9.

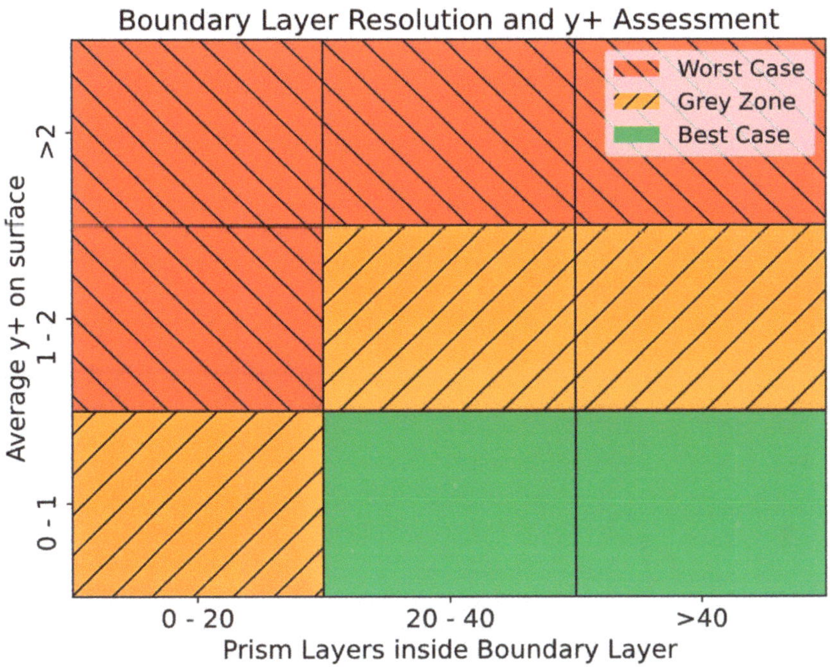

Figure 9. Qualitative metric of the grid resolution based on the y^+ and the amount of prism layers inside the boundary layer.

The green color represents the best-case scenario according to most guidelines, the orange color (left cross pattern) represents a type of grey zone where some studies agree, and the red color (right cross pattern) indicates poor confidence about the results of the analysis. In this framework, the y^+ values (both average and maximum) are extracted using the solver module and the functionality provided by PyFluent, utilizing built-in methods.

A critical factor contributing to the confidence in the results is the convergence behavior of each case. As described in Section 3, a substantial computational budget is allocated to the solution, and an automated algorithm continuously monitors the quantities of interest (forces generated on the wings) until they stabilize within a predefined tolerance level. Cases that fail to converge may indicate oscillatory or divergent behavior, or, in rare instances, a very slow rate of convergence, as observed in the authors' experience. For every CFD result, the convergence condition is reported alongside the residuals for each force, providing designers with valuable insights into the simulation setup.

Inflation Layer Exploration

This section and Figure 10, describes the approach adopted to generate a structured inflation layer mesh from unstructured CFD simulation data with the scope of accurately defining the grid elements inside the boundary layer (Figure 11). The development of a structured inflation layer mesh, while complex, enables the detailed post-processing of these regions.

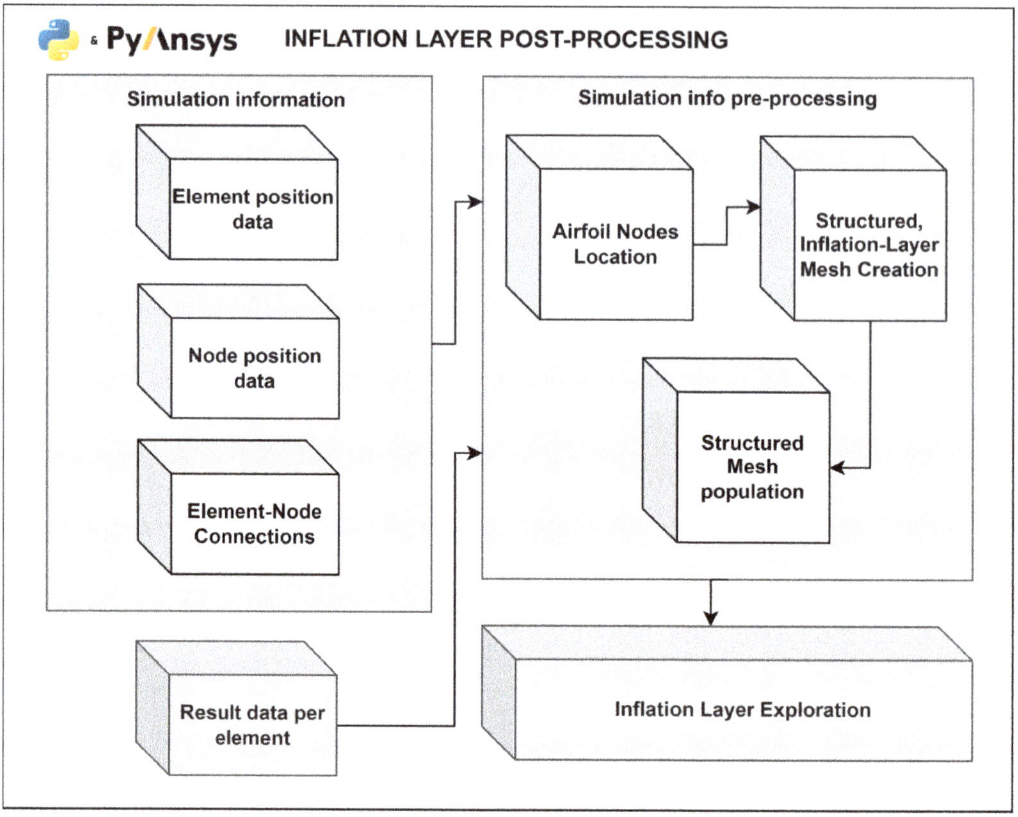

Figure 10. Structured inflation layer flowchart.

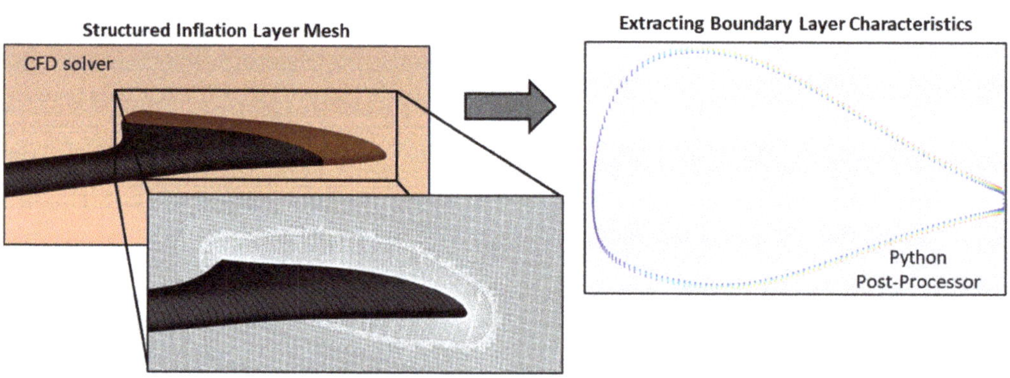

Figure 11. Boundary layer recognition.

The initial step involves extracting the simulation data, including element positions, node positions, and element–node connectivity. This information is gathered via PyFluent and forms the foundation for mapping relationships between nodes and elements, which is necessary for reconstructing structured layers. The data structure allows for the efficient traversal and identification of edges shared between elements, enabling the formation of a coherent network around the airfoil. The airfoil boundary is located by identifying nodes lying along its surface. These nodes are determined based on their spatial arrangement (their proximity to the plane of interest), their velocity magnitude (which should be zero according to the no-slip boundary condition imposed), and distinct geometric features, such as proximity to the airfoil shape and minimal deviation in the tangential direction. Once identified, the airfoil nodes are chained into a continuous sequence, representing the airfoil surface from the leading edge to the trailing edge. This chaining process preserved the geometric coherence of the airfoil outline.

Subsequently, elements connected to the airfoil nodes are isolated, using the connection information from the solver, forming the first inflation layer directly adjacent to the airfoil. The elements are ranked based on their proximity and connectivity to ensure an unambiguous representation of the layer.

Using the elements of the first layer as a foundation, additional inflation layers are constructed incrementally. For each layer, the following process is applied:

1. **Element Connectivity Traversal**: The neighboring elements of the current layer are identified through their shared edges.
2. **Velocity and Y-Coordinate Filtering**: Candidate elements for the next layer are filtered based on predefined constraints on x-velocity component and vertical (z-axis) alignment, ensuring physical relevance.
3. **One-to-One Mapping**: A one-to-one mapping is enforced between elements of consecutive layers to maintain coherence. This ensured that each element in a new layer corresponded to exactly one element in the previous layer, preserving the structured arrangement.
4. **Continuity Validation**: Additional continuity checks ensured the spatial arrangement of elements remained consistent. A maximum allowable distance criterion was applied between consecutive elements to detect and resolve discontinuities.

With the structured data array, including computed variables such as the fluid velocity and turbulent viscosity ratio, the boundary layer height can be determined at any position along the airfoil [48,61]. This enables a direct comparison with theoretical boundary layer heights and allows for the counting of prism cells within the boundary layer. While this proposed methodology shows promise for automatically extracting boundary layer information, its application is limited by the strong three-dimensional effects arising from varying boundary layer development rates along the wing. Consequently, constructing concise metrics to inform designers is beyond the scope of this study. However, the method can still be applied manually by selecting specific points of interest on the wing surface.

5. Framework Performance

The performance evaluation of the proposed framework is conducted through a combination of validation studies and a large-scale development in order to acquire statistical insights across a large sample of the design space. Firstly, in Section 5.1, a grid independence study is conducted alongside the quantification of discretization errors in the generated grids. It must be noted at this point that the main goal of this work is to present and demonstrate the entire pipeline of a framework that leads from geometry to simulation. Validating the framework against experimental or flight-testing data is beyond the scope of this work, especially given the fact that the methods have been validated in previous studies in their non-automated form. Additionally, in Section 5.2, a validation case is selected to benchmark the framework's performance against the expertise of a highly skilled mechanical engineer specializing in CFD. This comparison focused on both time efficiency and the accuracy of the results.

Following this, in Section 5.3, an extensive series of analyses were conducted, sampling 1165 wings from the predefined design space (Section 2). The purpose of these analyses is to assess the framework's performance across four primary aspects:

(1) sampling a range of wing configurations;
(2) meeting boundary-layer resolution and mesh-quality thresholds (Section 4);
(3) ensuring solver convergence and minimal iterative error;
(4) achieving computational efficiency for large-scale design exploration.

The findings indicate that the framework can handle a wide range of wing configurations without user intervention, while also providing detailed information on computational durations for geometry generation, mesh generation, solution setup, and solution execution. Additionally, the grids generated were evaluated using the quality metrics described in Section 4.

All the analyses presented in this section for the framework's performance are conducted at the Aristotle University of Thessaloniki (AUTh) High Performance Computing (HPC) cluster, leveraging its advanced computational capabilities. This state-of-the-art system facilitated the efficient execution of the large-scale simulations required for validating the framework and analyzing the sampled wings. The HPC cluster specifications are detailed in Table 6.

Table 6. AUTh's system cluster specifications.

Component	Quantity	Specification
CPU Cores	16	AMD EPYC 7742
GPU	1	NVIDIA A100 40 GB
RAM	128	Gb of DDR4

It should be noted that the definition of a "highly skilled Mechanical Engineer specializing in CFD" is inherently subjective. In this case, the expert is an engineer with over five years of experience in CFD, specifically for aircraft and UAV applications [39,62–64]. The expert has served as the lead CFD engineer on multiple research and industrial projects, developing expertise in aerodynamic analysis, mesh optimization, and simulation validation. While this level of expertise provides a solid benchmark for comparison, it is acknowledged that individual skill sets and methodologies can vary significantly across practitioners, which may influence the comparison outcomes.

5.1. Grid Independence Studies and Error Quantification

This section focuses on performing grid independence studies within the framework, ensuring that the solution converges under mesh refinement using previously established practices [39]. Because these studies are performed by the framework automatically, the simulation setup, including model and solution scheme selection, matches the setup detailed in Algorithm for Convergence Detection section.

The ONERA M6 wing is selected for the grid independence studies due to its simplicity, public availability, and frequent use in benchmarking studies [65]. This well-documented geometry, depicted in Figure 12 is a staple in aerodynamic validation, offering established reference data for comparison. Although the ONERA M6 wing is commonly validated in high-speed subsonic and transonic flow regimes, this study is focused on subsonic incompressible flow conditions. Transonic regimes demand more intricate grid setups and solver configurations, which are outside the framework's intended operational domain [66]. The ONERA M6 model, along with the corresponding design space parametrization, is illustrated in Figure 12 and Table 7.

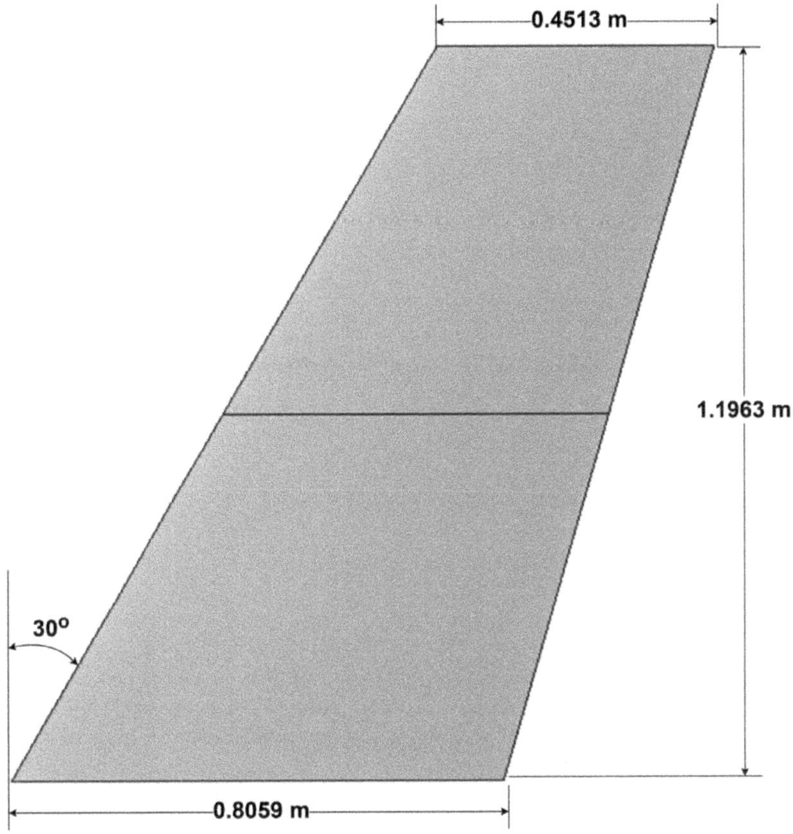

Figure 12. ONERA M6 wing planform.

Table 7. Parametrization of the ONERA M6 wing.

Parameter	ONERA M6
c_1	805.9 mm
c_2	629.5 mm
c_3	451.3 mm
b_1	598.2 mm
b_2	1196.3 mm
Λ_1	26.7°
Λ_2	26.7°
i_1	0°
i_2	0°
γ_1	0°
γ_2	0°

The studies are conducted under sea-level atmospheric properties, with a freestream velocity of 25 m/s. Two angles of attack (AoAs) are selected: a moderate 4° and a higher 12°. The latter is commonly more demanding in terms of convergence, requiring more iterations due to the possible flow separation on the suction surface.

The study is executed by progressively increasing the number of grid elements using a scale factor that affects the hyper-parameters of the meshing algorithm. In Figure 13, the lift and drag forces on the ONERA M6 wing are illustrated for both AoAs.

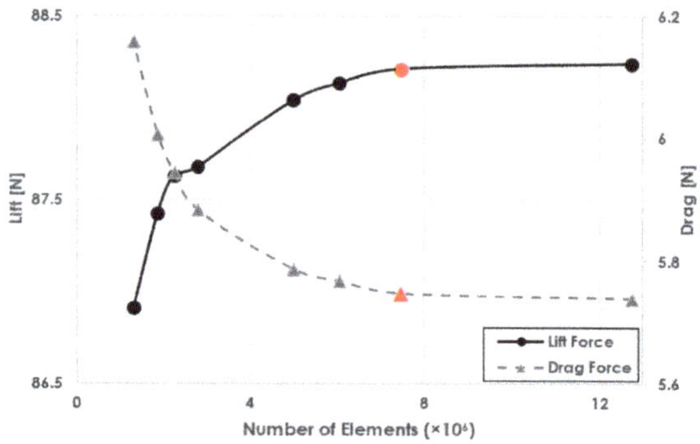

(a)

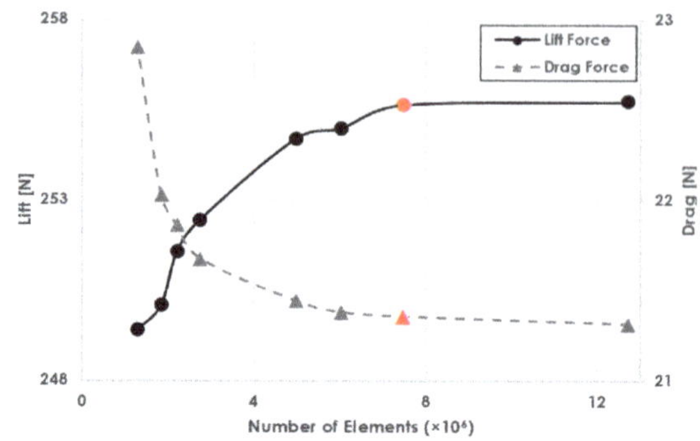

(b)

Figure 13. Grid independence study for ONERA M6 wing. (**a**) Lift and drag at 4° AoA for a varying number of grid elements; (**b**) lift and drag at 12° AoA for a varying number of grid elements. Red points indicates the selected refinement that satisfies the study.

The results highlight that for both cases, the lift and drag forces converge to stable values as the mesh density increases. This also validates the usage of a universal grid per wing and the importance of the BOIs in the proposed framework. Beyond a certain number, which in this case is for approximately 7.5 million grid elements, further refinement provides diminishing returns in accuracy. Thus, the appropriate parameters are being fine-tuned for the meshing module in order to reliably provide computational grids with this refinement. Using these parameters as the baseline, further investigation is being conducted into the determination of the discretization error as per the methodology described in Section 4.1. Three wings are chosen for this phase: the ONERA M6 wing, the RADAERO conventional wing (details are present in Section 6), and a wing belonging to the EURRICA BWB UAV [62]. The planform of the EURRICA wing is illustrated in Figure 14, along with the parametrization in Table 8.

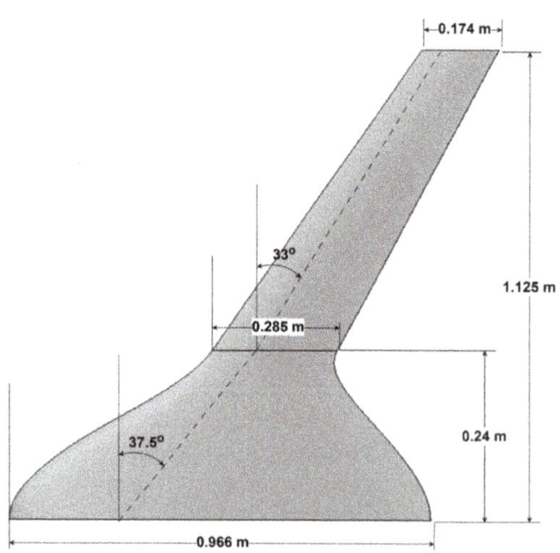

Figure 14. EURRICA wing planform.

Table 8. Parametrization of the EURRICA wing.

Parameter	EURRICA *
c_1	0.966 m
c_2	0.285 m
c_3	0.174 m
b_1	0.3765 m
b_2	1.0433 m
Λ_1	37.5°
Λ_2	33.0°
i_1	-
i_2	-
γ_1	-
γ_2	-

* data restrictions apply.

By following this systematic approach, the GCI provides a quantified measure of the discretization error, yielding a transparent assessment of grid-resolution effects. Although GCI is traditionally applied to single-case simulations, this study extends its methodology to the broader design space by evaluating representative samples. The three sampled wings represent the design space of the framework as the most interesting cases. The mean GCI error is used as an aggregated estimate of the discretization error over the design space. In the absence of experimental validation in this study, the GCI remains a credible indicator of numerical errors.

The evaluation metrics for the following grid independence studies are the lift and drag forces. As illustrated in Figure 15, for each case, the least refined computational grid is the one generated using the hyper-parameters selected from the previous grid dependency study. Then, following the GCI approach, systematically more refined grids are created. The final errors calculated are shown in Table 9.

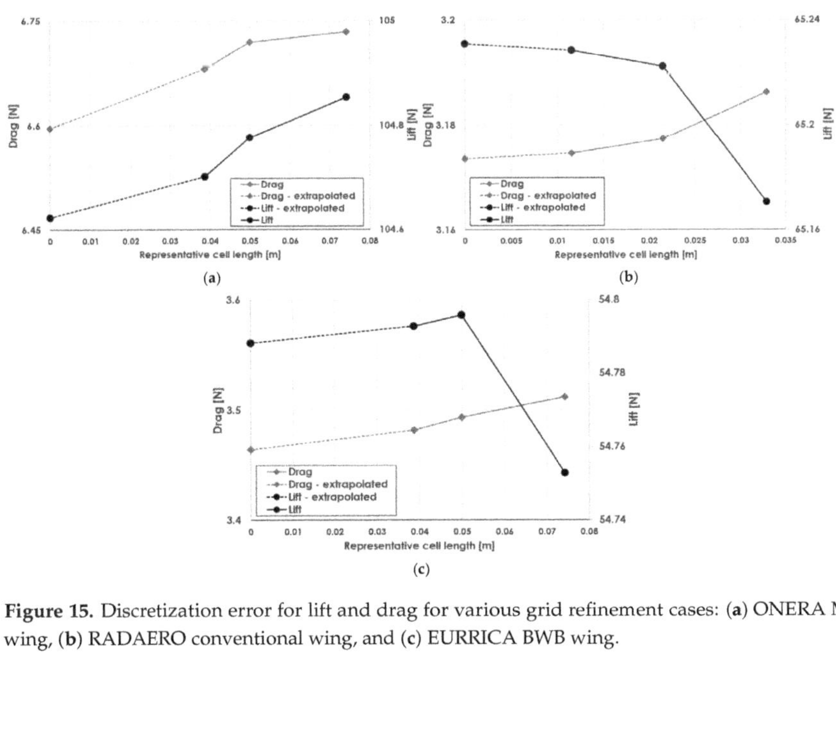

Figure 15. Discretization error for lift and drag for various grid refinement cases: (**a**) ONERA M6 wing, (**b**) RADAERO conventional wing, and (**c**) EURRICA BWB wing.

Table 9. Grid discretization errors.

	Drag			Lift		
Platform	Relative Error $(\varepsilon_{31})_{Drag}$	Extrapolated Relative Error $(\varepsilon_{3,ext})_{Drag}$	Drag GCI$_{31}$	Relative Error $(\varepsilon_{31})_{Lift}$	Extrapolated Relative Error $(\varepsilon_{3,ext})_{Lift}$	Lift GCI$_{31}$
ONERA M6	0.80%	2.10%	1.21%	0.15%	0.22%	0.09%
RADDAERO	0.37%	0.40%	0.06%	0.09%	0.09%	0.02%
EURRICA	0.86%	1.37%	0.40%	0.07%	0.06%	0.03%

It is evident that the discretization error for the three cases between the least-fine grid and the extrapolated one, is in the order of 1%. The drag for all cases seems to be more sensitive regarding the grid resolution. This error can be reported as a safe estimate for the grid of this framework.

5.2. Solver Compared with Expert-Grade Results

To evaluate the efficiency and accuracy of the proposed framework, a comparison was conducted against a manually prepared simulation, performed by an experienced CFD mechanical engineer. To ensure consistent and comparable results, the ONERA M6 wing geometry (Figure 12, Table 7) generated by the framework was also provided to the expert. The engineer manually meshed the geometry while preserving the features of the wing. The simulation parameters, including models, solution schemes, and boundary conditions, are appropriately configured to match the setup performed automatically by the framework, as detailed in Algorithm for Convergence Detection section. The validation focuses on key aerodynamic quantities, including the lift coefficient C_L, drag coefficient C_D, and residual convergence trends. The framework is assessed for its ability to replicate these results while reducing the time and effort required for pre-processing and simulation setup.

The automated framework demonstrates high reliability, with the drag polar predictions deviating by less than 3% from the manually obtained results. This agreement highlights the framework's capability to deliver high-level accuracy for subsonic aerodynamic evaluations. As illustrated in Figure 16, the framework successfully captured the lift and drag characteristics across the drag polar of the ONERA M6 wing.

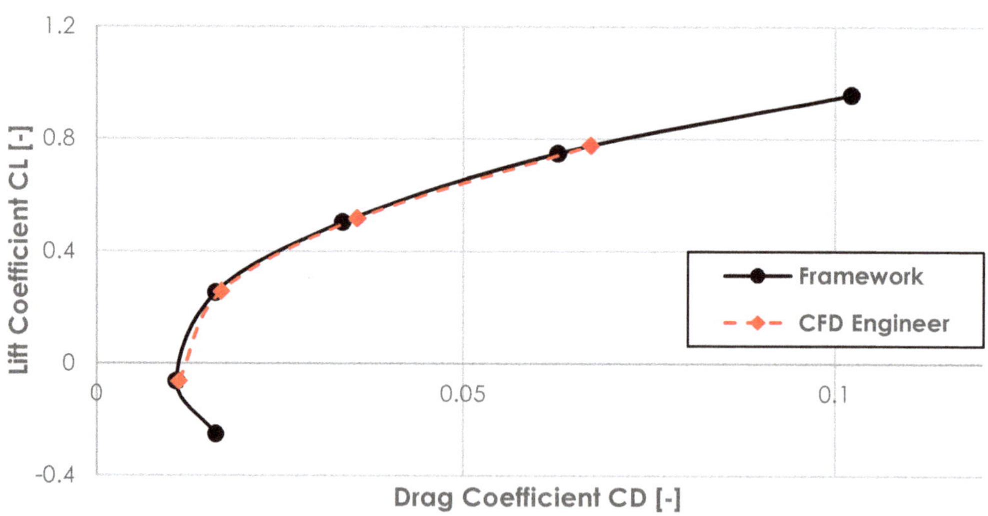

Figure 16. Drag polar comparison of ONERA M6 between the framework and a CFD engineer.

One of the key strengths of the framework lies in its ability to significantly reduce the time required for geometry pre-processing, meshing, and simulation setup. The CFD engineer took approximately 40 min to manually generate the mesh and configure the solver for the ONERA M6 case. In contrast, the automated framework completed these tasks in under 5 min, achieving an 88% reduction in lead time. In this lead time, only the mesh generation and the solution setup are taken into consideration, since the solution execution time is the same for both cases (given that the grid resolution is similar).

5.3. Large Scale Deployment

To evaluate the scalability and robustness of the proposed framework, 1165 wing geometries are sampled from the design space outlined in Section 2. The sampling process employs a Latin Hypercube Sampling (LHS) technique to ensure a uniform distribution of design variables across the multidimensional design space [67]. These sampled wings represent a diverse range of conventional and unconventional configurations, including both conventional wings and more complex blended geometries typically found in tailless, flying wing, or BWB UAVs. Figure 17 provides a visual depiction of the distributions for the high-level planform parameters, illustrating the diversity and coverage achieved in the sampling process.

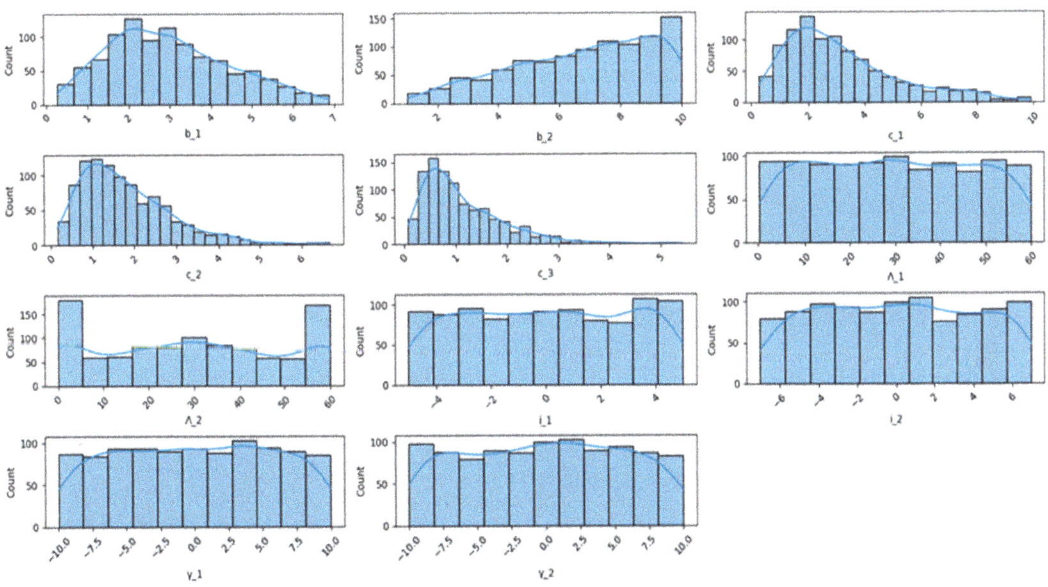

Figure 17. Distribution of the sampled planform high-level parameters. Each subfigure corresponds directly to a specific design variable from Table 2 (e.g., chord lengths c_i, spanwise positions b_i, sweep angles Λ_i, twist angles i_i, and dihedral angles γ_i).

For each wing configuration, the corresponding flow velocity is sampled according to the methodology described in Section 2. The angle of attack range spans from -4° to $+16^{\circ}$, with an additional 4° added in cases where stall has not yet occurred. This approach ensures a comprehensive aerodynamic characterization for each wing. The final dataset comprises 12,858 computational analyses, with an average of 11 simulation runs per configuration. This extensive dataset provides a robust foundation for evaluating the framework's performance in terms of computational time, robustness, and mesh quality. From the total number of analyses, 96.75% were successfully completed, while the remaining

3.25% encountered issues related to mesh resolution (e.g., y^+ values) or convergence failure across the majority of runs. Such outcomes offer valuable insights into areas requiring improvement in mesh generation and solver setup for specific configurations.

Table 10 summarizes execution time statistics across the framework's main phases, excluding geometry generation, which is negligible in comparison to other modules. From these data, it can be concluded that the median execution time for the pipeline from mesh generation to solution execution is approximately 539 s (9 min), with a standard deviation of 150 s. These results emphasize the framework's capability to deliver high-fidelity aerodynamic results within a short timeframe, significantly enhancing the efficiency of the design process.

Table 10. Summary statistics of required execution time for 1165 wings (rounded).

Type of Value	Mesh Generation [s]	Writing Mesh to Disk [s]	Loading Mesh in FLUENT [s]	Initializing Solution in FLUENT [s]	Analysis Execution in FLUENT [s]
Minimum Value	54	0.5	1	8	38
Maximum Value	3385	89	115	56	1150
Mean Value	255	36	50	19	259
Median Value	232	33	45	17	212

Figure 18 depicts the distribution of the two most time-consuming phases—mesh generation and simulation execution. The distribution plots reveal that mesh generation exhibits less variability compared to simulation execution, which is influenced by the complexity of each configuration.

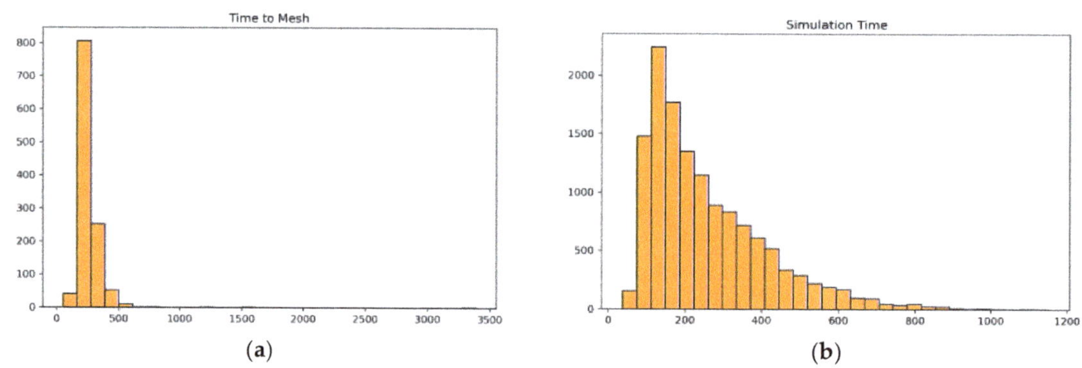

Figure 18. Distribution of the two most time-consuming phases of the framework for 1165 wings. (**a**) Mesh generation time, which is mostly centered around 250–300 s. (**b**) Simulation execution time, which is mostly centered around 150 s.

While as described, y^+ is not an absolute measure of grid fidelity, it serves as a practical first step in assessing the quality of boundary layer resolution. In contrast, metrics such as the number of prism layers within the boundary layer provide a more comprehensive but inherently complex three-dimensional evaluation, which should be examined as a secondary step by the designer at critical spanwise locations on the wing surface. Equation (13) shows the criteria used to define a high-quality mesh.

$$y^+_{avg@wing\_surface} < 1 \text{ and } y^+_{max@wing\_surface} < 2 \quad (13)$$

Among the 12,858 cases, 93.2% met these quality constraints, indicating a robust and consistent mesh generation process. Outliers, representing 0.5% of cases with abnormal y^+

values exceeding two orders of magnitude above the quality threshold, are excluded from the analysis. Table 11 provides summary statistics for the y^+ values of the valid cases.

Table 11. Summary statistics of the results for grid resolution.

Type of Value	$y^+_{average}$	$y^+_{maximum}$
Minimum	0.32	0.79
Maximum	9.18	29.53
Mean	0.48	1.55
Median	0.46	1.40

To further analyze the distribution of y^+ values, Figure 19 provides scatter plots of the average and maximum y^+ values for all cases. Figure 19a presents the full dataset, excluding the extreme outliers, and highlights the strong clustering of cases that meet the quality criteria, shown by the green diamond points. The presence of a small subset of extreme values, where y^+_{max} exceeds 10, indicates specific challenges in grid resolution for certain geometries or flow conditions. These cases, although rare, suggest areas for localized adjustments to boundary layer refinement settings.

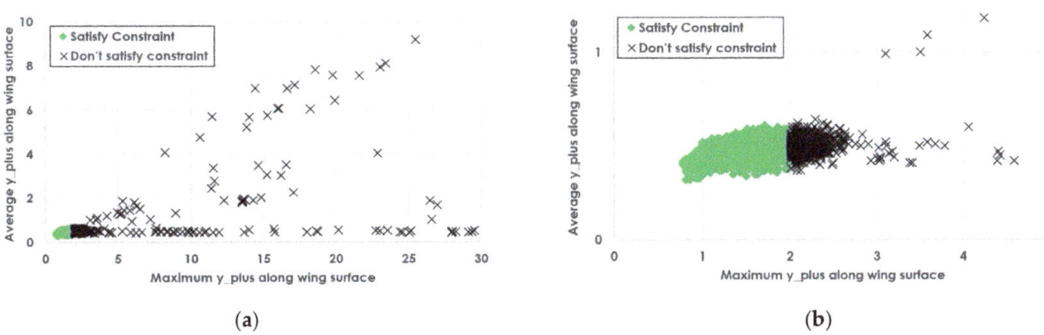

Figure 19. Scatter plot of the average and maximum y^+ values for all the cases. (**a**) All cases without the extreme outliers. (**b**) Focused scatter plot around $y^+_{mean} < 1$ and $y^+_{max} < 5$.

Figure 19b focuses on cases that satisfy or marginally exceed the quality thresholds, offering a clearer view of the robust performance achieved by the framework. The tightly clustered data points illustrate the consistency of the automated meshing process, particularly for the majority of sampled wings. Overall, these visualizations confirm that the framework maintains a high degree of mesh quality across a diverse range of wing configurations, with only minor deviations requiring further attention.

Regarding the iterative error, the same batch of wings is used to investigate the total uncertainty from either non-converged or prematurely converged cases. Solutions are either converged fully or stopped at 2000 iterations (maximum iterations) to assess the impact of incomplete convergence.

Figure 20 illustrates the average iterative error (for both forces in X and Z axis) for converged and non-converged wings across the sampled angles of attack. Non-converged wings exhibit significantly higher iterative errors, particularly at low angles of attack, where the error reaches its peak. In contrast, converged wings demonstrate negligible iterative errors across the entire range, underscoring the importance of convergence in achieving reliable results. This comparison emphasizes the role of iterative errors as a diagnostic tool for assessing the solution quality and the reliability of early terminated simulations.

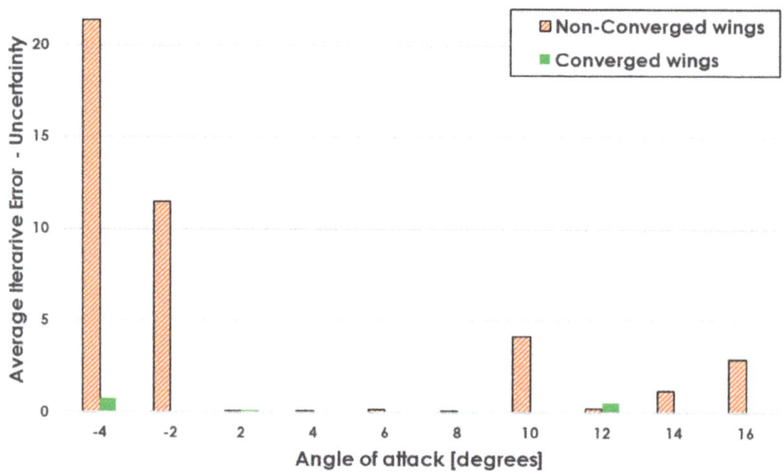

Figure 20. Average iterative error for every angle of attack, for converged and non-converged wings.

6. Optimization Case Study

To demonstrate the power of the automated CFD framework, one aerodynamic shape optimization case study is conducted. This includes a conventional UAV wing with the goal of showcasing the adaptability and robustness of the algorithm. The objective of optimization is to maximize the lift-to-drag (L/D) while also satisfying the sensitive stability constraints. All the design variables described in Section 2 are selected, except for the dihedral angle, since it plays a minor role in the aerodynamic performance and the longitudinal stability of the UAV [6,7].

Bayesian Optimization (BO) was chosen for these cases, as it is a method well-suited for high-cost optimization problems [68]. BO utilizes a surrogate model, typically a Gaussian Process (GP), to map the aerodynamic behavior to inputs (i.e., the design variables). The Expected Improvement (EI) criterion drives the algorithm in balancing exploration (unseen design areas) and exploitation (refining promising regions), enabling efficient exploration of high-dimensional design spaces while minimizing the number of analyses required. Classic BO does not offer a straightforward way of incorporating constraints into the optimization formulation. To tackle this, Ref. [69] introduces Constrained Bayesian Optimization (cBO), which incorporates inequality constraints by placing Gaussian Process priors on both the objective and constraint functions. This approach allows for the optimization of an expensive objective function while simultaneously considering feasibility constraints. For the CFD analyses, the AUTh HPC infrastructure was utilized, using the specifications described in Table 6.

Conventional UAV Wing—RADAERO

The RADAERO platform (Figure 21), a conventional fixed-wing UAV with an inverted V-tail configuration, is selected as the reference configuration. The RADAERO platform is a platform that has been 100% designed and built by the Laboratory of Fluid Mechanics and Turbomachinery [70] and has successfully completed several hours of flight testing.

The initial design variables for this case are given in Table 12. The wing's airfoil—NACA 2414—and dihedral angle are kept constant along the wing sections. The upper and lower bound of the design variables are constrained to a $\pm$ 20% from the baseline configuration, ensuring a resemblance to the already designed aircraft. This minimizes the impact of the new wing on the overall performance of the UAV. Flight conditions are fixed at a cruising speed of 25 m/s at sea level, with a reference Reynolds number of 200.000 and an angle of attack of 4°. Since RADAERO already features a horizontal and vertical stabilizer, and in a hypothetical scenario of later-stage optimization it imposes a stability constraint on the wing, in order to ensure that the tail remains the same.

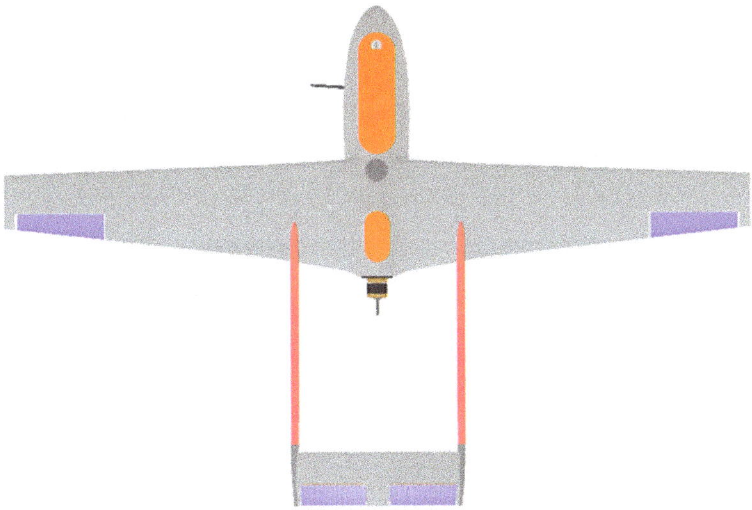

Figure 21. Top view of the RADAERO platform.

Table 12. RADAERO wing planform design space.

Design Variable	Baseline *	Lower Bound	Upper Bound
c_1	-	0.10–0.50 m	
c_2	-		
c_3	-		
b_1	0.24 m	0.19 m	0.29 m
b_2	1.125 m	0.9 m	1.35 m
Λ_1	0°	0°	20°
Λ_2	0°	0°	20°
i_1	-	−2.0–0.0	
i_2	-		

* Data restrictions apply.

The optimization problem formulation is displayed in Equation (14).

$$\begin{gathered} maximize \frac{L}{D} \\ \text{subject to} \begin{cases} C_L \geq 0.414 \\ 0 \leq \left| C_{M\frac{c}{4}} \right| \leq |-0.0781| \end{cases} \end{gathered} \tag{14}$$

An initial DoE stage (Exploration) is performed, so as to explore the design space. In this phase, using LHS, random configurations are analyzed, thus providing information to the GPs, mapping the inputs to the outputs, and constructing the foundation of feasible and infeasible regions. According to [71,72], the majority of the computational budget should be distributed to the exploitation stage i.e., the infill stage. Guided by the EI acquisition function, the optimizer specifically selects points in the design space that offer a high probability of improving the current best score of the quantity of interest. A total of 30 wing designs are evaluated with a ratio of exploration-to-exploitation equal to 1:2. As illustrated in Figure 22, circles denote valid solutions that satisfy constraints, while crosses represent invalid solutions.

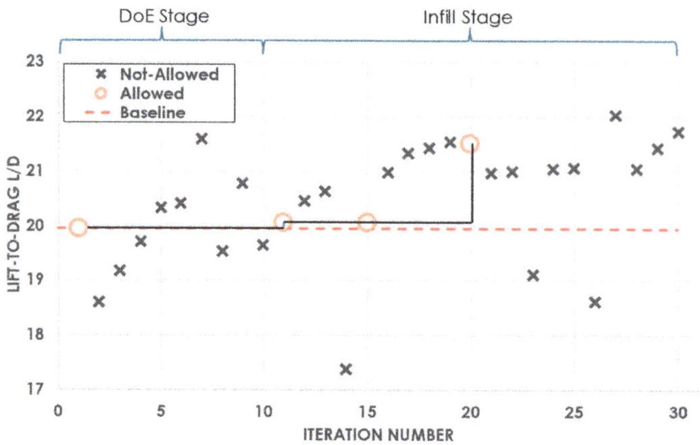

Figure 22. Optimization history of RADAERO wing planform.

The framework successfully identified a final optimal wing design with an 8% increase in L/D, a 2% improvement in C_L, and a modest reduction in $C_{M_{c/4}}$, aligning with the constraint (Table 13). On the optimized wing, the average y^+ value along the wing was kept below 1. This highlights the framework's effectiveness in navigating a constrained design space, as evidenced by the progressive improvements across iterations and the ability to maintain stability and aerodynamic performance, while also providing reliable and fully automated CFD results.

Table 13. Initial and optimized aerodynamic performance of RADAERO wing.

Variable	Initial Value	After Optimization	Change	$y^+_{avg}opt.$	$y^+_{max}opt.$	*Iter.Error*
L/D	19.96	21.52	8%			
C_L	0.4143	0.4225	2%	0.42	1.09	6.85×10^{-4}
C_M	−0.0781	−0.076	−2.7%			

The optimized wing planform is compared to the baseline in Figure 23. It is evident that the span of the wing increased leading along with its aspect ratio, which has an explicit effect on the reduction in induced drag [7].

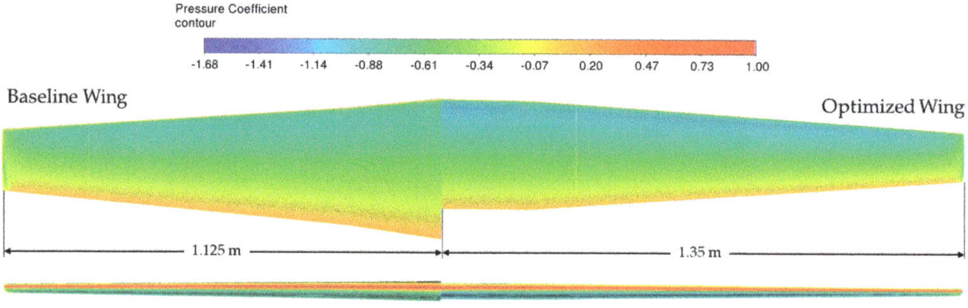

Figure 23. Pressure coefficient contours of baseline and optimized wing, including a top and front view.

7. Conclusions

This study presents the development and validation of an automated CFD pre-processing framework designed to streamline high-fidelity aerodynamic simulations tailored for fixed-wing UAV applications. By integrating the geometric modeling, mesh generation, and simulation setup into a cohesive workflow, this framework significantly reduces manual effort and computational inefficiencies. By leveraging Python APIs and a combination of open-source and commercial tools, tshe framework achieves a fully parameterized and automated pipeline, reducing pre-processing times to mere minutes and making it suitable for rapid iterations in design workflows. Moreover, a methodology for estimating the reliability of the framework's results is proposed, incorporating considerations for discretization error, potential early solution termination, non-dimensional y^+ values on the wing's surface, and grid resolution within the boundary layer.

Adhering to best practices and guidelines established by CFD experts and practitioners, the framework demonstrated high accuracy compared to expert-generated results, as well as high consistency across a large number of sampled wings. Additionally, various grid independence studies have been performed, covering a wide range of the design space.

The framework's integration with high-performance computing (HPC) environments featuring GPU solvers minimizes the labor-intensive work needed to prepare a geometry for CFD simulation. This results in pre-processing durations in the order of 5–7 min and the complete execution of the framework in less than 10–15 min for a single wing at a given angle of attack.

Moreover, the framework is integrated with an off-the-shelf optimizer, functioning as a robust black-box function. Using Bayesian Optimization, the framework identified an optimal wing configuration that achieved an 8% improvement in L/D, along with a 2% increase in C_L, and a modest reduction in C_M. These improvements, while incremental, highlight the framework's adaptability and demonstrate the advantages of encapsulating all modules within a unified Python pipeline. The framework's reliable mesh generation ensures seamless execution of cases without computational issues, even under varying conditions.

In summary, the framework represents a significant step forward in streamlining the pre-processing and analysis phases of UAV design. It provides a scalable, efficient, and accurate solution for high-fidelity aerodynamic evaluations, while establishing a robust foundation for future advancements in optimization.

Future work could address the following areas to enhance the framework's capabilities and expand its scope of use. The framework can be extended to accommodate more complex non-planar features, such as wings with winglets, fins, fences, and tail configurations. Incorporating these components can potentially enable the analysis of complete fixed-wing UAV and aircraft configurations. Moreover, the framework provides a great opportunity to generate large-scale datasets suitable for machine learning applications of aerodynamic shape optimization for UAVs.

Author Contributions: Conceptualization, C.P. and P.P.; methodology, C.P. and G.E.; software, C.P., G.E. and D.T.; validation, C.P. and P.P.; investigation, C.P. and G.E.; resources, P.P. and C.P.; data curation, C.P., G.E. and D.T.; writing—original draft preparation, C.P., G.E. and D.T.; writing—review and editing, C.P. and P.P.; visualization, C.P., G.E. and D.T.; supervision, P.P.; funding acquisition, P.P. All authors have read and agreed to the published version of the manuscript.

Funding: The research work was supported by the Hellenic Foundation for Research and Innovation (HFRI) under the Basic Research Financing (Horizontal support for all Sciences), National Recovery and Resilience Plan (Project Number: 016429, Project Acronym: INDIANA).

Data Availability Statement: Data available on request due to restrictions related to the details of the baseline platform. The data presented in this study are available on request from the corresponding author.

Acknowledgments: Results presented in this work have been produced using the Aristotle University of Thessaloniki (AUTh) High Performance Computing Infrastructure and Resources.

Conflicts of Interest: The authors declare no conflicts of interest.

Appendix A.

Appendix A.1. Geometry Module Features

The following paragraphs dive into the geometry pre-processing methods and treatments.

Appendix A.1.1. Trailing Edge Treatment

Trailing edge (TE) treatments are essential in CFD modeling, as they influence the progression of the inflation layer and ensures stability in numerical solutions. For subsonic wing simulations, two common TE treatments—rounded and straight cut—are considered (Figure A1), each with unique implications for modeling and meshing.

The straight cut design is chosen for this framework due to its compatibility with meshing automation, ensuring robust feature recognition by the meshing software. This decision prioritizes automation reliability over marginal quality improvements offered by rounded edges [41]. OpenVSP facilitates the parameterized control of TE thickness via the input of the chord lengths (c_1, c_2, c_3), automatically trimming the trailing edge for each airfoil to 1% of the chord length, which adheres to the common guidelines.

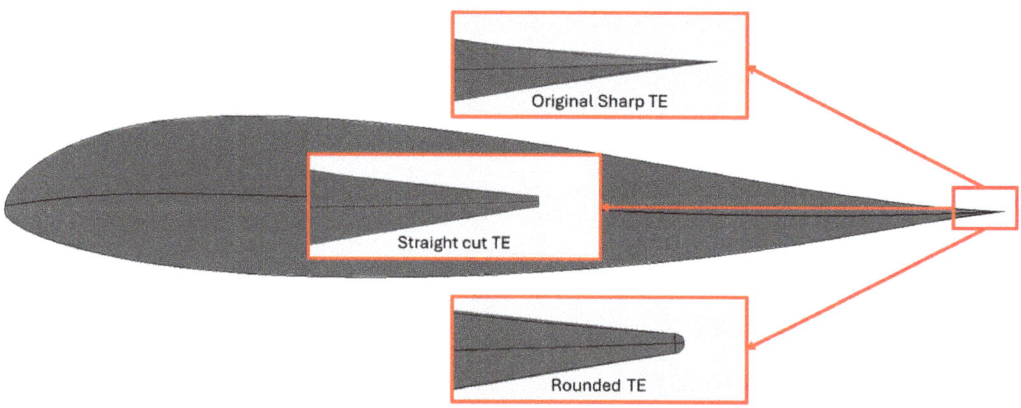

Figure A1. Trailing edge treatment.

Appendix A.1.2. Blending Between Sections

Blending between the two wing sections is essential to eliminate sharp transitions, ensuring aerodynamic continuity and structural smoothness. OpenVSP (v3.40.1) automates this process, effectively reducing manual effort. Universal rules are applied consistently across all wing geometries, regardless of whether they are conventional or BWB designs (Figure A2). These rules prioritize Section 2, preserving its role as the primary lifting surface, while adjustments to Section 1 ensure tangency with the second, at critical points such as the leading and trailing edges.

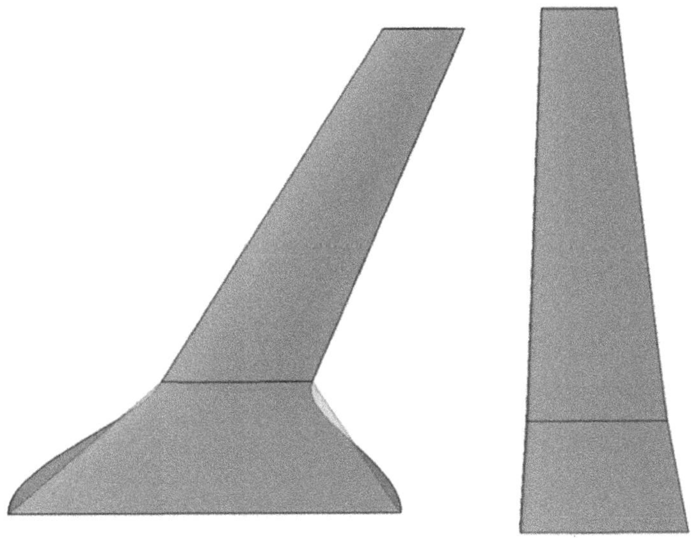

Figure A2. Blending between the 2 wing sections (faded region is the pre-blended one).

Symmetry along the centerline is preserved by carefully aligning the leading and trailing edge vertices, preventing the formation of sharp features at the root airfoil. A parameter known as "blending strength" is consistently applied to control the curvature and ensures uniformity across the design space. The blending effect is particularly evident in configurations with significant angle differences between sections, such as variations in sweep or dihedral angles.

Appendix A.1.3. Mean Aerodynamic Chord Calculation

Taking the example of a cranked wing (two-sectioned wing) from [7], the definition of MAC can be generalized for wings with multiple sections. Each wing section can be treated as an "independent" wing, allowing its MAC to be calculated separately. To determine the overall MAC for the entire wing, a weighted average of these individual MACs is calculated, factoring in the contribution of each section to the total planform surface area of the wing (Equation (A1)). Although the blending features are not accounted for in the approximation of the MAC, this does not pose any issues due to the fact that it is consistent between all generated wings.

$$\bar{c} = \sum \overline{c_i}\, w_i \quad where,\ \overline{c_i} = \frac{2}{3} c_{root} \left(\frac{1 + \lambda_i + \lambda_i^2}{1 + \lambda_i} \right) \quad and,\ w_i = \frac{S_i}{S_{tot}} \tag{A1}$$

Appendix A.2. Meshing Module–Geometry Pre-Processing Features

The following paragraphs dive into the mesh pre-processing methods, emphasizing their contribution to creating a watertight control volume with additional features for mesh refinement.

Appendix A.2.1. Control Volume Boundaries/Far-Field

Wing aerodynamic simulations focus on analyzing the aerodynamic performance of a wing under free atmospheric conditions. To accurately represent these conditions, the control volume (far-field) should be large enough so that the flow field at its boundaries remain unaffected by disturbances caused by the wing "wall". However, the size of the control volume should also be carefully managed to avoid exceeding computational capacity.

Control volumes can take on various shapes, such as rectangular parallelepipeds, bullet-shaped geometries, or semi-spheres. To the best of the authors' knowledge, there is no universally established standard regarding the optimal shape of the control volume, as the choice often depends on the specific simulation requirements. Based on previous, in-house experience, and in order to facilitate automation, the rectangular parallelepiped shape was selected to represent the far-field bounds.

The parametrized dimensions that define the artificial far-field boundaries adhere to common practices [41,43,48] and are illustrated in Figure A3. The origin of reference is located at the leading edge of the root airfoil. According to best practices, the distance between the upstream and downstream boundaries is set to 25 chord lengths, with the root chord leading edge is positioned at 25% of this distance. Vertically, the far-field boundaries extend 10 chord lengths above and below the origin. For the lateral extent, the boundary is defined by the semispan of the wing (b_2), which has been specified as five semispan lengths.

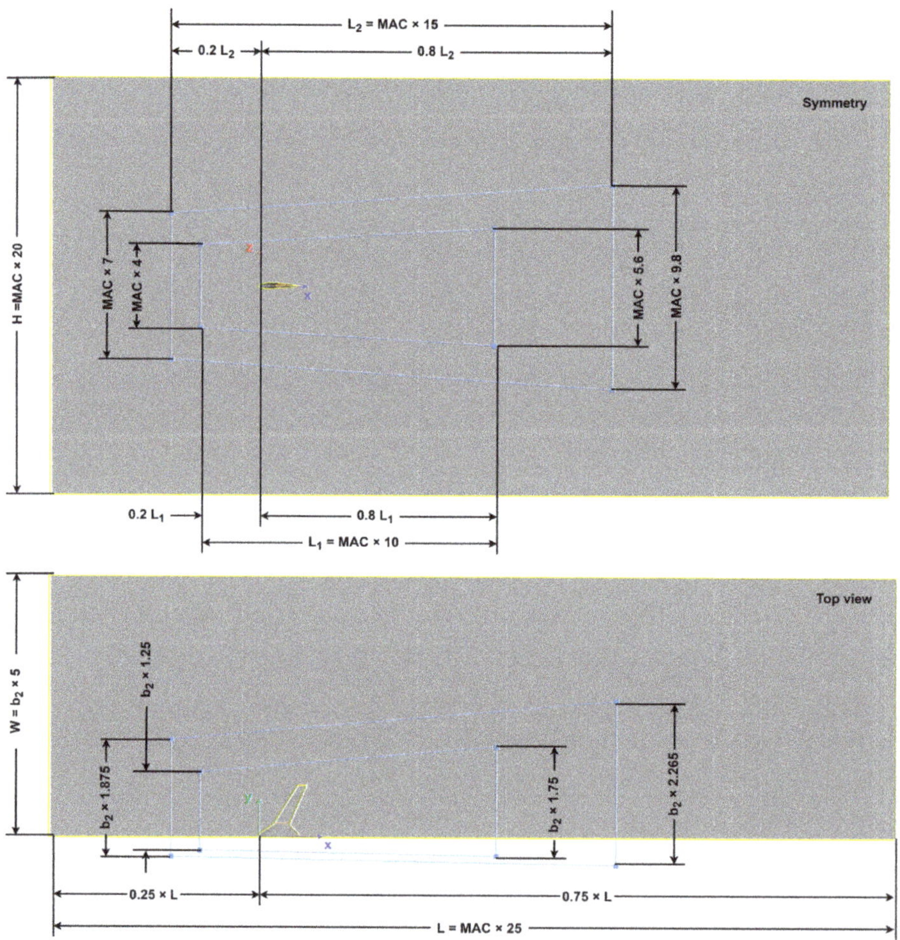

Figure A3. Control volume dimensions and layout. The yellow outline denotes the outer boundary of the computational domain, while the blue lines represent internal sizing boxes used to define mesh refinement regions around the geometry of interest.

Appendix A.2.2. Bodies of Influence (BOIs)

Bodies of Influence (BOIs) are auxiliary geometries defined around the wing wall that enhance mesh control and improve cell quality within the volume surrounding the wing. To align with the objectives of this framework, every generated geometry must be meshed, ensuring that the mesh design accommodates simulations across various angles of attack. By strategically defining BOIs around the wing wall, the mesh can be refined in critical regions, such as the wake and upstream flow areas, thereby enabling the use of a "universal mesh per geometry", which improves efficiency.

Considering the shape of the far-field defined in the previous subsection, the *BOIs* method generates two trapezoidal frustums, as auxiliary geometries for mesh refinement. As shown in Figure A3, the frustums are strategically oriented with their larger bases positioned towards the wing's wake, where greater refinement is essential, particularly at higher angles of attack. The dimensions of each frustum are also parametrized with the MAC and the wing's semispan (b_2).

Appendix A.2.3. Part Identifiers (PIDs)

To improve robustness, the framework assigns unique part identifiers (PIDs) to key geometric features, enabling precise referencing for meshing and analysis setup. The identified features include the "wing wall", "wingtip cap", "symmetry face", "opposite symmetry face", "inlet", "outlet", "upper far-field", and "lower far-field". The wing is segmented into the "wing wall" and "wingtip cap" PIDs to streamline meshing, while far-field boundary differentiation aids in defining boundary conditions for analysis setup.

Appendix A.2.4. Feature Recognition

Traditional approaches to pre-processing often rely on extensive manual interventions, including the creation of multiple custom PIDs to apply localized meshing parameters. While this approach allows for fine control over mesh refinement, it introduces significant challenges:

- Time-Intensive Processes: Manual custom PID creation demands meticulous geometry manipulation, which is labor-intensive and prone to errors.
- Lack of Robustness: The process is highly dependent on the operator's expertise, reducing the ability to automate and standardize the meshing for diverse geometries.
- Automation Limitations: Manual adjustments are difficult to replicate in Python-based environments, limiting the scalability and efficiency of the pre-processing module.

To overcome these challenges, the pre-processing module leverages the feature-recognition capabilities provided by ANSA. The custom *feature-recognition* method automates the identification and tagging of critical geometric elements on the wing, such as the leading edge, trailing edge, and wingtip sharp features. This automated approach ensures that appropriate meshing parameters will be later applied to the relevant recognized regions without the need for excessive custom PID definitions, thereby streamlining the workflow and enhancing the framework's ability to mesh arbitrary wing geometries consistently.

Appendix A.3. Meshing Module–Meshing Features

Appendix A.3.1. Surface Mesh Details

The surface meshing scenario not only refers to the wing wall but also to the far-field artificial boundaries that together with the wing comprise the watertight volume called domain. This scenario includes three sessions: the wing wall, the wingtip and the far-field meshing sessions, executed in order from the smallest to the largest cell size. As defined earlier in the *feature-recognition* method, three key aspects of the wing geometry are identified: the leading edge (LE), trailing edge (TE), and wingtip. The wing-wall session not only includes the meshing parameters for the wing surface but also applies specialized treatments for the leading and trailing edges. Similarly, the wingtip session incorporates specific adaptations to handle the meshing process of the sharp edges around the wingtip airfoil. Finally, the far-field session generates the surface mesh on the far-field boundaries. All parameters considering the surface mesh sessions are summarized in Table 4.

The first three mesh parameter categories—namely "Mesh type," "Mesh Sizing," and "Curvature Refinement"—are shared across all sessions and define the fundamental or global parameters needed for surface grid creation. The mesh type specifies the type of algorithm and elements used for meshing. In this case, the ANSA CFD meshing algorithm is employed, generating first-order quad elements where possible and first-order trias in regions where quads cannot be formed. This algorithm generates unstructured curvilinear grids with first-order quadrangle elements on the specified PIDs. The mesh sizing parameters dictate the growth rate of surface elements and impose a constraint on the maximum element length.

The leading and trailing edges of the wing are meshed using an anisotropic distribution of quad elements, which ensures a finer resolution near the sharp or highly curved features. To ensure smooth transitions and controlled spacing, constant-height zones are defined both above and below the leading edge. This region of elements forms a fine structured mesh near the stagnation point, where large gradients are expected. Moving further away from this constant-height zone, the element height increases according to the specified growth rate, ensuring a gradual transition to coarser elements. Finally, a maximum element aspect ratio is enforced to prevent the excessive stretching of elements, maintaining high-quality discretization. The result of this treatment can be observed in Figure A4. Similarly, the meshing treatment for the trailing edge ensures that the trimmed surface is discretized with four rows of elements, forming an anisotropic structured mesh. Moving away from the trimmed surface on the upper and lower wing surfaces, the element height increases in accordance with the specified growth factor, while the generated elements form a structured grid. The height of the initial elements immediately adjacent to the trimmed surface is set to one-quarter of the thickness of the trimmed surface, ensuring a smooth transition from face to face. The result of this trailing edge treatment is illustrated in Figure A4.

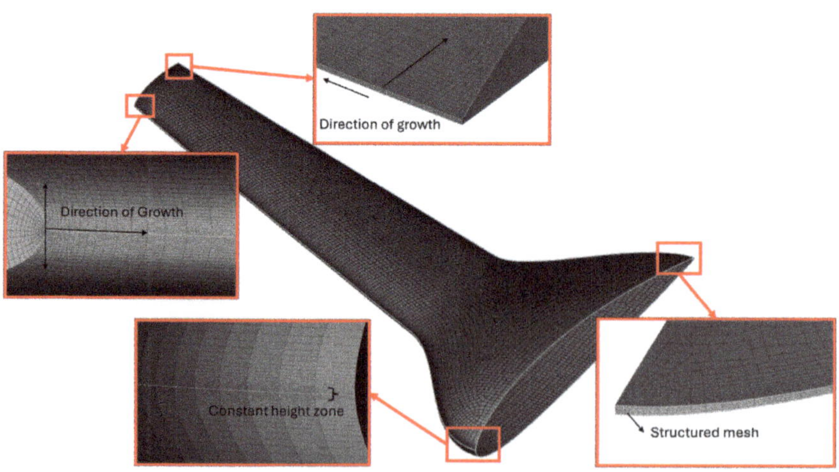

Figure A4. Specific mesh treatment along the wing surface.

As shown in Table 4, the approach for handling sharp features—whether convex or concave—is straightforward and governed by a single meshing parameter: the maximum element length. Simply put, along the sharp features, a maximum element length is enforced to achieve the desired level of discretization. Beyond the sharp edge, the element length increases progressively in accordance with the global growth factor.

Appendix A.3.2. Inflation Layer Details

The first layer height (h_1) is calculated to position the first cell within the viscous sublayer, ensuring precise wall shear stress and velocity gradient calculations. The height of the viscous sublayer is approximated for a flat plate using the Schlichting skin-friction correlation (Equation (A2)) for wall shear stress τ_w, which is valid for Reynolds numbers $Re < 10^9$, according to Schlichting and Gersten [44].

$$h_1 = \frac{y^+ \mu_\infty}{\rho_\infty u_*}, \quad where \quad u_* = \sqrt{\frac{C_f \frac{1}{2} \rho_\infty u_\infty^2}{\rho}} \tag{A2}$$

Note that, given the fact that flows over airfoils and wings encounter pressure gradients, the boundary layer thickness will vary in regard to the theoretical flat plate (zero pressure gradient) value. Therefore, the real height of the viscous sublayer can only be determined after the execution of a simulation. Thus, it can be used to check the validity of a given simulation, as discussed in more detail in Section 4.

Another important aspect for the inflation layer is that its total height was designed to be larger than the total height of the boundary layer. This choice is guided by a well-established rationale [44,48], ensuring a sufficient number of cells within this critical region for accurate simulation. The total boundary layer height (δ) can be approximated using Equation (A3) according to [37]. This relationship applies only for a fully turbulent flow over a flat plate. However, it can serve as a reliable indication, given that a turbulent boundary layer is thicker than its laminar counterpart (e.g., provided that the pressure gradients are identical).

$$\delta = 0.37 \cdot Re^{-1/5} \cdot \bar{c} \tag{A3}$$

Appendix A.3.3. Volume Mesh Details

Figure A5 illustrates the meshing algorithm's result on the symmetry plane. Two meshing parameters are needed to fully define the volume-meshing scenario, including a global growth rate, which is set to 1.2, and a maximum element length, which is equal to the parametrized value ($0.65 \times c_1$), similar to the surface meshing scenario.

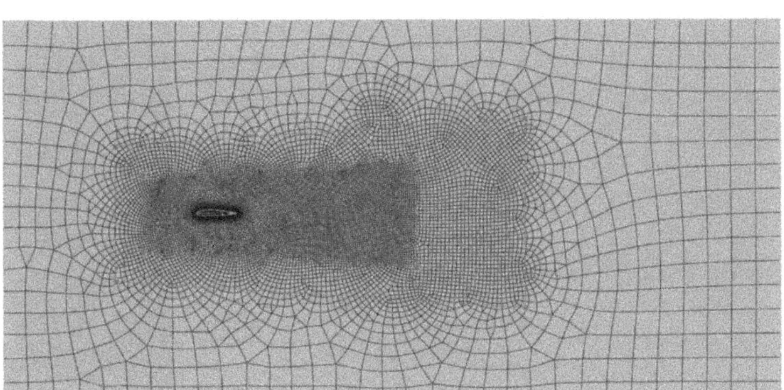

Figure A5. An illustration of the HexaPoly algorithm used for the discretization of the volume.

Appendix A.4. Solution Module–Solution Setup

At the core of CFD lie the Navier–Stokes equations (momentum conservation), the continuity equation (mass conservation), and the energy equation, which govern the behavior of the fluid flow. For the incompressible low-Mach number flows over wings considered in this work, the energy equation is omitted due to the absence of significant compressibility effects and heat transfer [41]. As previously mentioned in Section 3, the k-omega SST is selected as the turbulence model, with its parameters kept to the default values recommended by Menter. Regarding more specific solver settings, the framework incorporates the following key aspects:

- **Gradient Correction:** According to Menter et al. in [48], the *"fast-mode warped face gradient correction"* option supported by Fluent is enabled due to the unstructured hexahedral type of mesh generated by the mesh module. This option improves the accuracy of gradient calculations on unstructured or highly distorted meshes.
- **Solution Scheme:** The SIMPLE (Semi-Implicit Method for Pressure Linked Equations) solution scheme is utilized within this computational framework. The SIMPLE scheme strikes a balance between computational efficiency and numerical stability, making it well-suited for steady-state external aerodynamic simulations. Compared to other algorithms, the SIMPLE scheme's less stringent requirements on relaxation and computational resources align with the focus on automating simulations within a broad design space.
- **Initialization:** In this work, hybrid initialization is employed as the default approach due to its robustness and efficiency in complex aerodynamic problems. Hybrid initialization combines elements of potential flow solutions and mass-weighted averages to provide a physically realistic starting point for the flow field, minimizing the computational effort required for convergence.
- **Materials:** The state of the material (air) specified for the simulation is determined based on the atmospheric model *"U.S. Standard Atmosphere 1976"* [73]. In this model, air properties are defined as functions of altitude. These relationships have been implemented within a Python class called *atmosphere*, enabling direct access to or the calculation of air properties based solely on the specified altitude.
- **Boundary Conditions (BC):** Inlet and outlet BCs are dependent on the angle of attack of the wing. Simulations are performed across a wide range of AoAs to capture the complete drag polar. To account for the changes in the flow field due to varying AoAs, the *"Upper Far-Field"* and *"Lower Far-Field"* PIDs are adjusted accordingly.

At a *"Velocity-Inlet"* boundary, the freestream parameters must be specified, including the freestream velocity, pressure, and the freestream turbulent characteristics. The freestream velocity is defined component-wise, taking into consideration the angle of attack (α). According to Rumsey and Spalart in [74], while using the k-omega SST model, the turbulence intensity (Tu) and turbulence viscosity ratio (β) are calculated from Equation (A4).

$$Tu = 0.0008165 \text{ and } \beta = 2 \times 10^{-7}\, Re \tag{A4}$$

Similarly, the *"Pressure-Outlet"* BC requires specifying the turbulence characteristics of the outflow, as defined above, along with a gauge pressure set to zero to represent atmospheric conditions at the outlet.

References

1. Velusamy, P.; Rajendran, S.; Mahendran, R.K.; Naseer, S.; Shafiq, M.; Choi, J.G. Unmanned Aerial Vehicles (UAV) in Precision Agriculture: Applications and Challenges. *Energies* **2021**, *15*, 217. [CrossRef]
2. Panagiotou, P.; Mitridis, D.; Dimopoulos, T.; Kapsalis, S.; Dimitriou, S.; Yakinthos, K. Aerodynamic Design of a Tactical Blended-Wing-Body UAV for the Aerial Delivery of Cargo and Lifesaving Supplies. In Proceedings of the AIAA Scitech 2020 Forum, Orlando, FL, USA, 6–10 January 2020; American Institute of Aeronautics and Astronautics: Reston, VA, USA, 2020.
3. Green, D.R.; Hagon, J.J.; Gómez, C.; Gregory, B.J. Using Low-Cost UAVs for Environmental Monitoring, Mapping, and Modelling: Examples From the Coastal Zone. *Coast. Manag. Glob. Chall. Innov.* **2019**, 465–501. [CrossRef]
4. Queralta, J.P.; Raitoharju, J.; Gia, T.N.; Passalis, N.; Westerlund, T. AutoSOS: Towards Multi-UAV Systems Supporting Maritime Search and Rescue with Lightweight AI and Edge Computing. *arXiv* **2020**, arXiv:2005.03409.
5. Martinez-Alpiste, I.; Golcarenarenji, G.; Wang, Q.; Alcaraz-Calero, J.M. Search and Rescue Operation Using UAVs: A Case Study. *Expert Syst. Appl.* **2021**, *178*, 114937. [CrossRef]
6. Raymer, D. *Aircraft Design: A Conceptual Approach*, 6th ed.; American Institute of Aeronautics and Astronautics, Inc.: Washington, DC, USA, 2018; ISBN 978-1-62410-490-9.
7. Gudmundsson, S. *General Aviation Aircraft Design: Applied Methods and Procedures*; Butterworth-Heinemann: Oxford, UK, 2022.
8. Mitridis, D.; Kapsalis, S.; Terzis, D.; Panagiotou, P. An Evaluation of Fixed-Wing Unmanned Aerial Vehicle Trends and Correlations with Respect to NATO Classification, Region, EIS Date and Operational Specifications. *Aerospace* **2023**, *10*, 382. [CrossRef]
9. Anderson, J. *Computational Fluid Dynamics*; Wendt, J.F., Ed.; Springer: Berlin/Heidelberg, Germany, 2009; ISBN 978-3-540-85055-7.
10. Psarros, A.; Kapsalis, S.; Dimopoulos, T.; Mitridis, D.; Terzis, D.; Giannakis, E.; Panagiotou, P.; Savaidis, G.; Yakinthos, K. Detail and Structural Design of a Fixed-Wing BWB UAV. *J. Phys. Conf. Ser.* **2024**, *2716*, 012069.
11. Lehmkuehler, K.; Wong, K.; Verstraete, D. Design and Test of a UAV Blended Wing Body Configuration. In Proceedings of the ICAS 2012, Brisbane, Australia, 23–28 September 2012.
12. Götten, F.; Havermann, M.; Braun, C.; Marino, M.; Bil, C. Wind-Tunnel and CFD Investigations of UAV Landing Gears and Turrets—Improvements in Empirical Drag Estimation. *Aerosp. Sci. Technol.* **2020**, *107*, 106306. [CrossRef]
13. Torenbeek, E. Blended Wing Body Aircraft: A Historical Perspective. *Encycl. Aerosp. Eng.* **2016**. [CrossRef]
14. Zhang, M.; Gong, J.; Axner, L.; Barth, M. Automation of High-Fidelity CFD Analysis for Aircraft Design and Optimization Aided by HPC. In Proceedings of the 28th Euromicro International Conference on Parallel, Distributed and Network-Based Processing (PDP), Västerås, Sweden, 11–13 March 2020.
15. Papkov, V.; Shadymov, N.; Pashchenko, D. CFD-Modeling of Fluid Flow in Ansys Fluent Using Python-Based Code for Automation of Repeating Calculations. *Int. J. Mod. Phys. C* **2023**, *34*, 2350114. [CrossRef]
16. Salmon, F.; Chatellier, L. PyMeshFOAM: Automated Meshing for CFD and Fluid–Structure Simulations. *SoftwareX* **2023**, *23*, 101431. [CrossRef]
17. Benaouali, A.; Kachel, S. A Surrogate-Based Integrated Framework for the Aerodynamic Design Optimization of a Subsonic Wing Planform Shape. *Proc. Inst. Mech. Eng. G J. Aerosp. Eng.* **2018**, *232*, 872–883. [CrossRef]
18. Mohammad Zadeh, P.; Sayadi, M. An Efficient Aerodynamic Shape Optimization of Blended Wing Body UAV Using Multi-Fidelity Models. *Chin. J. Aeronaut.* **2018**, *31*, 1165–1180. [CrossRef]
19. Lyu, Z.; Kenway, G.K.W.; Martins, J.R.R.A. Aerodynamic Shape Optimization Investigations of the Common Research Model Wing Benchmark. *AIAA J.* **2015**, *53*, 968–985.
20. Gu, X.; Ciampa, P.D.; Nagel, B. An Automated CFD Analysis Workflow in Overall Aircraft Design Applications. *CEAS Aeronaut. J.* **2018**, *9*, 3–13. [CrossRef]
21. Karali, H.; Inalhan, G.; Tsourdos, A. AI-Driven Multidisciplinary Conceptual Design of Unmanned Aerial Vehicles. In Proceedings of the AIAA SciTech Forum and Exposition, Orlando, FL, USA, 8–12 January 2024; American Institute of Aeronautics and Astronautics Inc.: Reston, VA, USA, 2024.
22. Karali, H.; Inalhan, G.; Tsourdos, A. Advanced UAV Design Optimization Through Deep Learning-Based Surrogate Models. *Aerospace* **2024**, *11*, 669. [CrossRef]
23. Liebeck, R.H. The X-48B and X-48C Take to the Air. In *Beyond Tube and Wing*; NASA: Washington, DC, USA, 2020; p. 163.
24. Grauer, J.A.; Boucher, M.J. System Identification of Flexible Aircraft: Lessons Learned from the x-56a Phase 1 Flight Tests. In Proceedings of the AIAA Scitech 2020 Forum, Orlando, FL, USA, 6–10 January 2020; pp. 1–26. [CrossRef]
25. EXperimental Aircraft for European Leadership in Aviation. Available online: https://exaelia.eu/ (accessed on 15 February 2025).
26. Panagiotou, P.; Fotiadis-Karras, S.; Yakinthos, K. Conceptual Design of a Blended Wing Body MALE UAV. *Aerosp. Sci. Technol.* **2018**, *73*, 32–47. [CrossRef]
27. Selig, M.S. UIUC Airfoil Coordinates Database. Available online: https://m-selig.ae.illinois.edu/ads/coord_database.html (accessed on 15 February 2025).
28. Masters, D.A.; Taylor, N.J.; Rendall, T.C.S.; Allen, C.B.; Poole, D.J. Geometric Comparison of Aerofoil Shape Parameterization Methods. *AIAA J.* **2017**, *55*, 1575–1589. [CrossRef]

29. Chen, W.; Chiu, K.; Fuge, M. Airfoil Design Parameterization and Optimization Using Bezier Generative Adversarial Networks. *AIAA J.* **2020**, *58*, 4723–4735.
30. Agez, B. Preliminary Design Correlations and Cost Estimation for Fixed-Wing Military Unmanned Aerial Vehicles. In Proceedings of the IEEE Aerospace Conference Proceedings; IEEE Computer Society, Big Sky, MT, USA, 2–9 March 2024.
31. Cotting, M.C. An Initial Study to Categorize Unmanned Aerial Vehicles for Flying Qualities Evaluation. In Proceedings of the 47th AIAA Aerospace Sciences Meeting including The New Horizons Forum and Aerospace Exposition, Orlando, FL, USA, 5–8 January 2009.
32. Verstraete, D.; Palmer, J.L.; Hornung, M. Preliminary Sizing Correlations for Fixed-Wing Unmanned Aerial Vehicle Characteristics. *J. Aircr.* **2017**, *55*, 715–726. [CrossRef]
33. McDonald, R.A. Advanced Modeling in Open VSP. In Proceedings of the 16th AIAA Aviation Technology, Integration, and Operations Conference, Washington, DC, USA, 13–17 June 2016; American Institute of Aeronautics and Astronautics Inc.: Reston, VA, USA, 2016.
34. ANSA Pre-Processor—BETA CAE Systems. Available online: https://www.beta-cae.com/ansa.htm (accessed on 30 December 2024).
35. PyFluent Documentation 0.21.0—PyFluent. Available online: https://fluent.docs.pyansys.com/version/0.21/ (accessed on 30 December 2024).
36. Spalart, P. Reflections on RANS Modelling. *Notes Numer. Fluid Mech. Multidiscip. Des.* **2010**, *111*, 7–24. [CrossRef]
37. Menter, F.; Hüppe, A.; Matyushenko, A.; Kolmogorov, D. An Overview of Hybrid RANS–LES Models Developed for Industrial CFD. *Appl. Sci.* **2021**, *11*, 2459. [CrossRef]
38. Menter, F.R. Two-Equation Eddy-Viscosity Turbulence Models for Engineering Applications. *AIAA J.* **1994**, *32*, 1598–1605. [CrossRef]
39. Dimopoulos, T.; Paliaikos, D.; Christou, V.; Kaparos-Tsafos, P.; Panagiotou, P. Experimental and Computational Investigation of the Vortical Structures Generated from a Blended-Wing-Body UAV Model. *Aerosp. Sci. Technol.* **2023**, *139*, 108377. [CrossRef]
40. Kontogiannis, S.G.; Ekaterinaris, J.A. Design, Performance Evaluation and Optimization of a UAV. *Aerosp. Sci. Technol.* **2013**, *29*, 339–350. [CrossRef]
41. Goetten, F.; Finger, D.F.; Marino, M.; Bil, C. A Review of Guidelines and Best Practices for Subsonic Aerodynamic Simulations Using RANS CFD. In *APISAT 2019: Asia Pacific International Symposium on Aerospace Technology*; Engineers Australia: Gold Coast, Australia, 2019.
42. Veríssimo, R. Best Practice Guidelines in External Aerodynamics CFD: Applied to Unmanned Aerial Vehicles at Cruise Conditions. Doctoral dissertation, Academia da Força Aérea, São Paulo, Brazil, 2016.
43. Hirsch, C. *Numerical Computation of Internal and External Flows: The Fundamentals of Computational Fluid Dynamics*; Elsevier: Amsterdam, The Netherlands, 2007.
44. Schlichting, H.; Gersten, K. Boundary-Layer Theory. *Bound.-Layer Theory* **2016**, 1–799. Available online: https://books.google.co.jp/books/about/Boundary_Layer_Theory.html?id=bOUyDQAAQBAJ&redir_esc=y (accessed on 15 February 2025).
45. Pope, S.B. Turbulent Flows. *Meas. Sci. Technol.* **2001**, *12*, 2020–2021. [CrossRef]
46. Wilcox, D.C. *Turbulence Modeling for CFD*; DCW Industries: La Canada, CA, USA, 1998.
47. ANSYS. *ANSYS Unleashing the Full Power of GPUs for Ansys Fluent, Part 2*; ANSYS: Canonsburg, PA, USA, 2022.
48. Menter, F.; Sechner, R.; Germany GmbH; Matyushenko, A.A.; Petersburg, S. *Best Practice: RANS Turbulence Modeling in Ansys CFD*; ANSYS: Canonsburg, PA, USA, 2021.
49. Sreenivasan, K.R.; Prabhu, A.; Narasimha, R. *Zero-Crossings in Turbulent Signals*; ICTP: Trieste, Italy, 1983; Volume 137.
50. Celik, I.; Karaismail, E.; Parsons, D. *A Reliable Error Estimation Technique for CFD Applications*; NATO: Brussels, Belgium, 2007.
51. Ferziger, J.H.; Perić, M. Further Discussion of Numerical Errors in CFD. *Int. J. Numer. Methods Fluids* **1996**, *23*, 1263–1274. [CrossRef]
52. Eça, L.; Eça, L.; Hoekstra, M. On the Influence of the Iterative Error in the Numerical Uncertainty of Ship Viscous Flow Calculations. In Proceedings of the 26th Symposium on Naval Hydrodynamics, Rome, Italy, 17–22 September 2006.
53. Cary, A.W.; Schaefer, J.A.; Duque, E.P.N.; Lawrence, S.S. Application of a Cfd Uncertainty Quantification Framework for Industrial-Scale Aerodynamic Analysis. In Proceedings of the AIAA Scitech 2019 Forum, San Diego, CA, USA, 7–11 January 2019; American Institute of Aeronautics and Astronautics Inc.: Reston, VA, USA, 2019.
54. Schaefer, J.; Romerot, V.; Schafert, S.; Denham11, C. Approaches for Quantifying Uncertainties in Computational Modeling for Aerospace Applications. In Proceedings of the AIAA Scitech 2020 Forum, Orlando, FL, USA, 6–10 January 2020.
55. Celik, I.B.; Ghia, U.; Roache, P.J.; Freitas, C.J.; Coleman, H.; Raad, P.E. Procedure for Estimation and Reporting of Uncertainty Due to Discretization in CFD Applications. *J. Fluids Eng. Trans. ASME* **2008**, *130*, 0780011–0780014. [CrossRef]
56. Mártins, M.A.; Marchi, C.H. Estimate of Iteration Errors in Computational Fluid Dynamics. *Numer. Heat Transf. Part B Fundam.* **2008**, *53*, 234–245. [CrossRef]
57. Ferziger, J.H. Estimation and Reduction of Numerical Error. *ASME-Publ.-Fed* **1993**, *158*, 1.

58. Georgiadis, N.J.; Dudek, J.C.; Tierney, T.P. AIAA-95-2613 Grid Resolution and Turbulent Inflow Boundary Condition Recommendations for NPARC Calculations. In Proceedings of the 31st Joint Propulsion Conference and Exhibit, San Diego, CA, USA, 10–12 July 1995.
59. Menter, F.R.; Smirnov, P.E.; Liu, T.; Avancha, R. A One-Equation Local Correlation-Based Transition Model. *Flow Turbul. Combust.* **2015**, *95*, 583–619. [CrossRef]
60. Menter, F.R.; Kuntz, M.; Langtry, R. Ten Years of Industrial Experience with the SST Turbulence Model. *Turbul. Heat Mass Transf.* **2003**, *4*, 625–632.
61. Anderson, J.D. *Fundamentals of Aerodynamics*; McGraw Hill: New York, NY, USA, 1984; ISBN 0070016569.
62. Panagiotou, P.; Dimopoulos, T.; Dimitriou, S.; Yakinthos, K. Quasi-3D Aerodynamic Analysis Method for Blended-Wing-Body UAV Configurations. *Aerospace* **2021**, *8*, 13. [CrossRef]
63. Antoniou, S.; Kapsalis, S.; Panagiotou, P.; Yakinthos, K. Parametric Investigation of Leading-Edge Slats on a Blended-Wing-Body UAV Using the Taguchi Method. *Aerospace* **2023**, *10*, 720. [CrossRef]
64. Dimitriadis, G.; Panagiotou, P.; Dimopoulos, T.; Yakinthos, K. Aerodynamic Stability Derivative Calculations Using the Compressible Source and Doublet Panel Method. *J. Aircr.* **2024**, *61*, 1034–1046. [CrossRef]
65. Mayeur, J.; Dumont, A.; Destarac, D.; Gleize, V. RANS Simulations on TMR Test Cases and M6 Wing with the Onera ElsA Flow Solver. In Proceedings of the 53rd AIAA Aerospace Sciences Meeting, Kissimmee, FL, USA, 5–9 January 2015; American Institute of Aeronautics and Astronautics Inc.: Reston, VA, USA, 2015.
66. Tinoco, E.N.; Brodersen, O.P.; Keye, S.; Laflin, K.R.; Feltrop, E.; Vassberg, J.C.; Mani, M.; Rider, B.; Wahls, R.A.; Morrison, J.H.; et al. Summary Data from the Sixth AIAA CFD Drag Prediction Workshop: CRM Cases. *J. Aircr.* **2017**, *55*, 1352–1379. [CrossRef]
67. Helton, J.C.; Davis, F.J. Latin Hypercube Sampling and the Propagation of Uncertainty in Analyses of Complex Systems. *Reliab. Eng. Syst. Saf.* **2003**, *81*, 23–69. [CrossRef]
68. Snoek, J.; Larochelle, H.; Adams, R.P. Practical Bayesian Optimization of Machine Learning Algorithms. *arXiv* **2012**, arXiv:1206.2944.
69. Gardner, J.R.; Kusner, M.J.; Xu, Z.; Weinberger, K.Q.; Cunningham, J.P. Bayesian Optimization with Inequality Constraints. In Proceedings of the 31st International Conference on International Conference on Machine Learning, Beijing, China, 21–26 June 2014.
70. Bliamis, C.; Vlahostergios, Z.; Misirlis, D.; Yakinthos, K. Numerical Evaluation of Riblet Drag Reduction on a MALE UAV. *Aerospace* **2022**, *9*, 218. [CrossRef]
71. Parekh, J.; Bekemeyer, P.; Helm, S.; François, D.G.; Grabe, C. Surrogate Based Design Space Exploration and Exploitation for an Efficient Airfoil Optimization under Uncertainties Using Transition Models. *Aerosp. Sci. Technol.* **2024**, *154*, 109532. [CrossRef]
72. Martins, J.R.; Ning, A. *Engineering Design Optimization*; Cambridge University Press: Cambridge, UK, 2021. [CrossRef]
73. NASA. *U.S. Standard Atmosphere*; NASA: Washington, DC, USA, 1976.
74. Spalart, P.R.; Rumsey, C.L. Effective Inflow Conditions for Turbulence Models in Aerodynamic Calculations. *AIAA J.* **2007**, *45*, 2544–2553. [CrossRef]

algorithms

MDPI

Article

The Euler-Type Universal Numerical Integrator (E-TUNI) with Backward Integration

Paulo M. Tasinaffo *, Gildárcio S. Gonçalves, Johnny C. Marques, Luiz A. V. Dias and Adilson M. da Cunha

Instituto Tecnológico de Aeronáutica (ITA), São José dos Campos 12228-900, SP, Brazil; gildarcio@ita.br (G.S.G.); johnny@ita.br (J.C.M.); vdias@ita.br (L.A.V.D.); cunha@ita.br (A.M.d.C.)

* Correspondence: tasinaffo@ita.br

Abstract: The Euler-Type Universal Numerical Integrator (E-TUNI) is a discrete numerical structure that couples a first-order Euler-type numerical integrator with some feed-forward neural network architecture. Thus, E-TUNI can be used to model non-linear dynamic systems when the real-world plant's analytical model is unknown. From the discrete solution provided by E-TUNI, the integration process can be either forward or backward. Thus, in this article, we intend to use E-TUNI in a backward integration framework to model autonomous non-linear dynamic systems. Three case studies, including the dynamics of the non-linear inverted pendulum, were developed to verify the computational and numerical validation of the proposed model.

Keywords: Euler-Type Universal Numerical Integrator; neural differential equations; non-linear auto regressive moving average with exogenous inputs; Runge–Kutta neural network; universal numerical integrator

1. Introduction

The Euler-Type Universal Numerical Integrator (E-TUNI) is a particular case of a Universal Numerical Integrator (UNI). In turn, the UNI is the coupling of a conventional numerical integrator (e.g., Euler, Runge–Kutta, Adams-Bashforth, Predictive-Corrector, among others) with some kind of universal approximator of functions (e.g., MLP neural networks, SVM, RBF, wavelets, fuzzy inference systems, among others). Furthermore, UNIs generally work exclusively with neural networks with feed-forward architecture through supervised learning with input/output patterns.

In [1], the first work involving the mathematical modelling of an artificial neuron is presented. In [2,3], it is mathematically demonstrated, independently, that feed-forward neural networks with Multi-Layer Perceptron (MLP) architecture are universal approximators of functions. For the mathematical demonstration of the universality of feed-forward networks, a crucial starting point is the Stone-Weierstrass theorem [4]. An interesting work on the universality of neural networks involving the ReLU neuron can be found in [5]. In summary, many neural architectures were developed in the last half of the twentieth century, involving shallow neural networks [6]. On the other hand, in this century, many architectures of deep neural networks demonstrated the great power of neural networks [7].

So, artificial neural networks solve an extensive range of computational problems. However, in this article, we limit the application of artificial neural networks with feed-forward architecture in the resolution of mathematical problems involving modelling autonomous non-linear dynamic systems governed by a system of ordinary differential equations. With the neural networks, it is possible to solve the inverse problem of modelling dynamical systems, i.e., given the solution of the dynamical system, then obtain the instantaneous derivative functions or the mean derivative functions of the system.

The starting point for the proper design of a Universal Numerical Integrator (UNI) is the conventional numerical integrators [8–15]. In [16], a qualitative and very detailed description of the design of a UNI is presented. Also, in [16], an appropriate classification is given for the various types of Universal Numerical Integrators (UNIs) found in the literature.

According to these authors, the UNIs can be divided into three large groups, giving rise to three different methodologies, namely: (i) the NARMAX methodology (Nonlinear Auto Regressive Moving Average with Exogenous input); (ii) the instantaneous derivatives methodology (e.g., Runge–Kutta neural network, Adams-Bashforth neural network, Predictive-Corrector neural network, among others), and (iii) mean derivatives methodologies or E-TUNI. For a detailed understanding of the similarities and differences between the existing UNIS types, see again [16].

In practice, the leading scientific works involving the proper design of a UNI are: (i) the NARMAX methodology in [17–21]; (ii) the Runge–Kutta neural network in [22–25]; (iii) the Adams-Bashforth neural network in [26]; and (iv) the E-TUNI in [27,28]. For this article, it should be noted that E-TUNI works exclusively with mean derivative functions instead of instantaneous derivative functions. Furthermore, the NARMAX and mean derivative methodologies are of fixed steps in the simulation phase, while the instantaneous derivative methodologies are of varied integration steps in the simulation phase [16]. However, all of them are fixed steps in the training phase.

In this paragraph, we briefly describe existing work on E-TUNI. In [27], it is a technological application of E-TUNI using neural networks with MLP architecture. In [28], it is a technological application of E-TUNI using fuzzy logic and genetic algorithms. Still in [28], the fuzzy membership functions are adjusted automatically, using genetic algorithms through supervised learning using input/output patterns.

However, none of the previous works used E-TUNI with backward integration. Therefore, this article's originality lies in using E-TUNI in a backward integration process coupled with a shallow neural network with MLP architecture. As far as we know, this has not yet been done.

This article is divided as follows: Section 2 briefly describes the symbology and notation adopted in this paper. Section 3 describes the context in which this work can be applied to real-world problems. Section 4 briefly describes the basic structure of a Universal Numerical Integrator (UNI). Section 5 describes the detailed mathematical development of E-TUNI, designed with backward integration. Section 6 analyzes the numerical accuracy of E-TUNI using Landau symbols. Section 7 presents the numerical and computational results validating the proposed model. Section 8 presents the main conclusions of this work.

2. Symbols and Notations Adopted

For a more detailed understanding of the theoretical development presented in this paper, we define all the symbols and variables used in this work. The proposed method is called Euler-Type Universal Numerical Integrator (E-TUNI) and uses backward integration. This method is discrete. Thus, we propose a discrete method to approximate a continuous system of autonomous ordinary differential equations. Therefore, below, we present all the symbologies and variables used here. They are divided into two groups: (i) continuous variables and (ii) discrete variables.

(i) Continuous Variables

$\dot{y} = f(y)$—System of continuous differential equations.
$y = [y_1 \quad y_2 \ldots y_n]^T$—State Variables.
$f(y) = [f_1(y) \quad f_2(y) \ldots f_n(y)]^T$—Instantaneous derivative functions.
d—Plant noise.
d'—Measuring instrument noise.
$y_j^i(t) = g_j^i(t)$—Particular continuous and differentiable curve of a family of solution curves of the dynamical system $\dot{y} = f(y)$.
$\dot{y}_j^i(t) = \dot{g}_j^i(t)$—First derivative of $y_j^i(t)$.

(ii) Discrete Variables

${}^k y^i = y^i(t_0 + k \cdot \Delta t)$—Vector of state variables at time t_k.
${}^k y_j^i$—Scalar state variable for $j = 1, 2, \ldots, n$ at time t_k. It is a generic discretization point of the state variables generated by the integers i, j, and k.
n—Total number of state variables.
${}^k u = u(t_0 + k \cdot \Delta t)$—Vector of control variables at time t_k.
${}^k u_j$—Scalar control variable for $j = 1, 2, \ldots, m$ at time t_k.
m—Total number of control variables.
${}^{k+1} y^i = y^i[t_0 + (k+1) \cdot \Delta t]$—Exact vector of state variables at time t_{k+1}.
${}^{k+1} y_j^i$—Exact scalar state variable for $j = 1, 2, \ldots, n$ at time t_{k+1}.
${}^{k+1} \hat{y}^i = \hat{y}^i[t_0 + (k+1) \cdot \Delta t]$—Estimated Vector of state variables by UNI or E-TUNI at time t_{k+1}.
${}^{k+1} \hat{y}_j^i$—Scalar state variable estimated by UNI or E-TUNI for $j = 1, 2, \ldots, n$ at time t_{k+1}.
${}^{k+1} \bar{y}^i$—Estimated Vector of state variables when using only the integrator and without using the neural network at time t_{k+1}.
$tan_{\Delta t} {}^k \alpha^i = tan^+_{\Delta t} {}^k \alpha^i = [tan^+_{\Delta t} {}^k \alpha_1^i \quad tan^+_{\Delta t} {}^k \alpha_2^i \ldots tan^+_{\Delta t} {}^k \alpha_n^i]^T$—Exact vector of positive mean derivative functions at time t_k.
$tan_{\Delta t} {}^k \alpha_j^i = tan^+_{\Delta t} {}^k \alpha_j^i = \frac{{}^{k+1} y_j^i - {}^k y_j^i}{\Delta t}$—Scalar positive mean derivative functions for $j = 1, 2, \ldots, n$ at time t_k.
$tan_{\Delta t} {}^k \hat{\alpha}^i = tan^+_{\Delta t} {}^k \hat{\alpha}^i = [tan^+_{\Delta t} {}^k \hat{\alpha}_1^i \quad tan^+_{\Delta t} {}^k \hat{\alpha}_2^i \ldots tan^+_{\Delta t} {}^k \hat{\alpha}_n^i]^T$—Estimated vector of positive mean derivative functions by the E-TUNI at time t_k.
$tan^-_{\Delta t} {}^k \alpha^i = [tan^-_{\Delta t} {}^k \alpha_1^i \quad tan^-_{\Delta t} {}^k \alpha_2^i \ldots tan^-_{\Delta t} {}^k \alpha_n^i]^T$—Exact vector of negative mean derivative functions at time t_k.
$tan^-_{\Delta t} {}^k \alpha_j^i = \frac{{}^k y_j^i - {}^{k-1} y_j^i}{\Delta t}$—Scalar negative mean derivative functions for $j = 1, 2, \ldots, n$ at time t_k.
$tan^-_{\Delta t} {}^k \hat{\alpha}^i = [tan^-_{\Delta t} {}^k \hat{\alpha}_1^i \quad tan^-_{\Delta t} {}^k \hat{\alpha}_2^i \ldots tan^-_{\Delta t} {}^k \hat{\alpha}_n^i]^T$—Estimated vector of negative mean derivative functions by the E-TUNI at time t_k.
$tan^k \theta^i = tan^{+k} \theta^i = [tan^k \theta_1^i \quad tan^k \theta_2^i \ldots tan^k \theta_n^i]^T$—Vector of positive instantaneous derivatives at time t_k.
$tan^k \theta_j^i = tan^{+\,k} \theta_j^i = \lim_{\Delta t \to 0} \frac{{}^{k+1} y_j^i - {}^k y_j^i}{\Delta t}$—Scalar positive instantaneous derivative for $j = 1, 2, \ldots, n$ at instant t_k.
$tan^{-k} \theta^i = [tan^{-k} \theta_1^i \quad tan^{-k} \theta_2^i \ldots tan^{-k} \theta_n^i]^T$—Vector of negative instantaneous derivatives at instant t_k.
$tan^{-\,k} \theta_j^i = \lim_{\Delta t \to 0} \frac{{}^k y_j^i - {}^{k-1} y_j^i}{\Delta t}$—Scalar negative instantaneous derivative for $j = 1, 2, \ldots, n$ at time t_k.
t_k—Time instant $t_k = t_0 + k \cdot \Delta t$.
t_{k+1}—Time instant $t_{k+1} = t_0 + (k+1) \cdot \Delta t$.
Δt—Integration step.

i—Over-index that enumerates a particular curve from the family of curves of the dynamical system to be modelled ($i = 1, 2, \ldots, q$).
j—Under-index that enumerates the state and control variables.
k—Over-index that enumerates the discrete time instants ($k = 1, 2, \ldots, r$).
r—Total number of horizons of the time variable.
q—Total number of curves from the family of curves curves of the dynamic system to be modelled.
t_k^*—Instant of time within the interval $[t_k, t_{k+1}]$ as a result of the Differential Mean Value Theorem (see Theorem 2).
t_k^x—Instant of time within the interval $[t_k, t_{k+1}]$ as a result of the Integral Mean Value Theorem (see Theorem 3).

To understand this symbology, the first step is to understand the difference between ${}^{k+1}y^i$, ${}^{k+1}\tilde{y}^i$, and ${}^{k+1}\hat{y}^i$. The vector variable ${}^{k+1}y^i$ is the exact value of the state variables at time $t_{k+1} = t_0 + (k+1) \cdot \Delta t$. The vector variable ${}^{k+1}\tilde{y}^i$ is the estimated value of the state variables using only the numerical integrator. Finally, the vector variable ${}^{k+1}\hat{y}^i$ is the estimated value of the state variables using the numerical integrator coupled with an artificial neural network. Figures 1–4 follow this convention for a better understanding of the model proposed in this work. Additionally, it is important to understand the meaning of the auxiliary variables i, j, and k. This is described in the next paragraph.

Here, an important issue is to elucidate the use of the over-indexes k and i and the sub-index j in the variables ${}^ky_j^i$ and $tan_{\Delta t}{}^k\alpha_j^i$. Figure 1 will help in this explanation. When the auxiliary variables i, j, and k are used simultaneously, they uniquely identify the secant ($tan_{\Delta t}{}^k\alpha_j^i$) at the point ${}^ky_j^i$. Notice that the over-index k indicates the time instant $t_k = t_0 + k \cdot \Delta t$ of the secant, the sub-index j indicates the state variable in question, where $j = 1, 2, \ldots, n$, and the over-index i ($i = 1, 2, \ldots, q$) indicates the particular curve, where the respective secant is located, of the family of possible curves of the system of differential equations considered. The value of q can be as large as one wants. The larger the value of q the more different curves will be trained by the neural network, and the better its generalization will be.

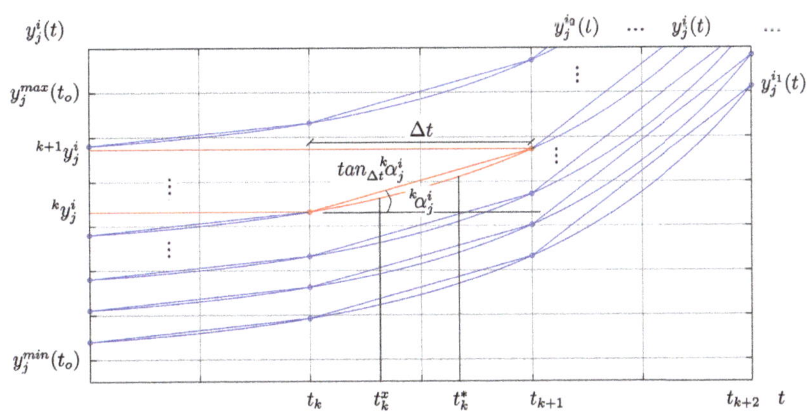

Figure 1. Symbology and notation used in this article.

This unique mapping of the secant $tan_{\Delta t}{}^k\alpha_j^i$ will be of fundamental importance for the demonstration of Theorem 4 that will be presented and demonstrated in Section 5. This theorem establishes that if the Euler integrator uses the secant instead of the instantaneous derivatives, it will be a discrete and exact solution for a system of ordinary and autonomous differential equations. Furthermore, the mapping mentioned above is unique because of the uniqueness theorem for systems of ordinary differential equations. Finally, an artificial neural network will be used to learn the secants of the considered dynamic system through supervised learning using input/output training patterns.

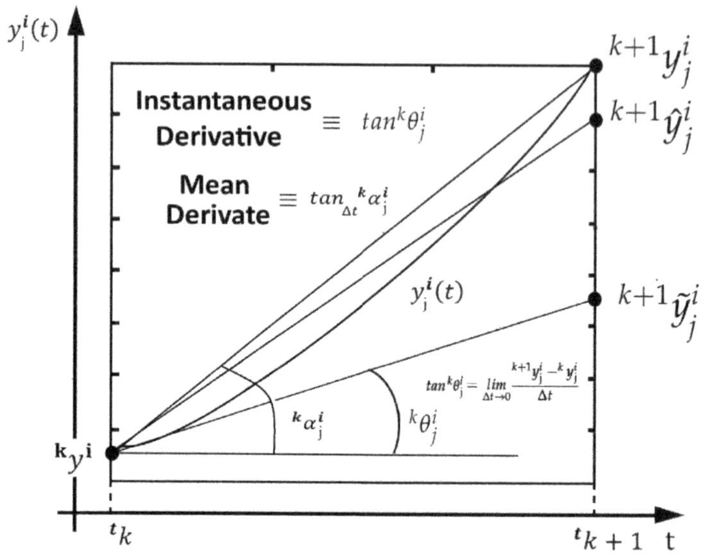

Figure 2. Basic difference between the instantaneous derivative and the mean derivative (Source: [16]).

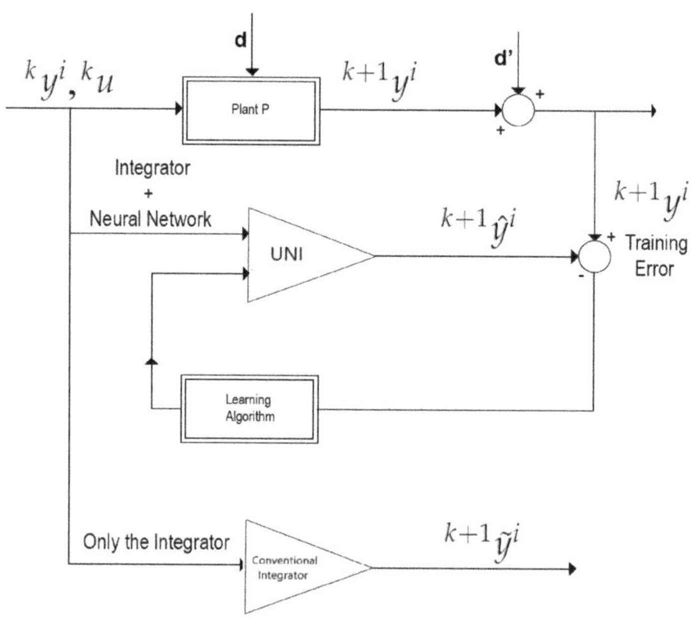

Figure 3. General graphic diagram of the operation of a Universal Numerical Integrator (UNI) (Source: [16]).

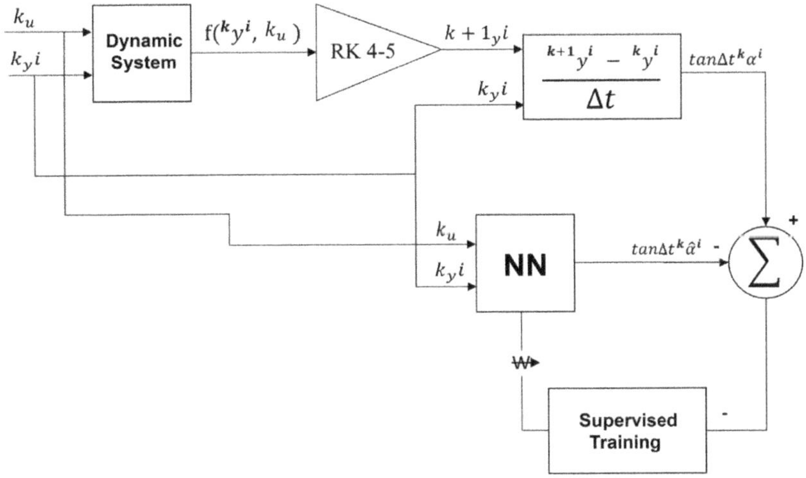

Figure 4. The E-TUNI designed according to the direct approach (Source: [16,27]).

3. Contextualization

This section clarifies some critical issues regarding using the E-TUNI in mathematics, physics, and engineering problems. These issues will help provide a better theoretical and practical understanding of the method proposed in this article. To this end, in the following, we formulate five essential questions regarding the proper design of E-TUNI and give succinct and objective answers to all of them.

What is the difference between E-TUNI and the Conventional Euler method? The traditional Euler method works with instantaneous derivative functions, and the E-TUNI works with mean derivative functions. Although this difference may seem insignificant, in reality, it is not. We also can refer to Figure 2 to answer this question. In this figure, ${}^{k+1}\tilde{y}^i_j$, ${}^{k+1}\hat{y}^i_j$, and ${}^{k+1}y^i_j$ are, respectively, the solution obtained by conventional Euler, the solution obtained by E-TUNI, and the exact solution of the dynamical system at time t_{k+1}. As can be seen, the mean derivative gives a more accurate solution than the instantaneous derivative. Another advantage of E-TUNI is that it can be designed using real-world training patterns through supervised learning. To this end, E-TUNI uses an artificial neural network to learn the mean derivative functions with high precision. Notice also a difference between the values ${}^{k+1}\hat{y}^i_j$ and ${}^{k+1}y^i$. This difference is caused by the training of the neural network since the error generated by this same neural network is non-zero.

What are the advantages of E-TUNI with backward integration compared to other conventional numerical integration methods? Since E-TUNI uses a neural network, its accuracy is equivalent to any other higher-order numerical integrator. This property is because artificial neural networks are universal approximators of functions [2–5]; that is, the training error of the neural network can be as small as desired. The other advantage of E-TUNI is that it has a mathematical structure only of the first-order, which means it is much simpler than higher-order integrators. The disadvantage of E-TUNI, concerning higher-order integrators, is that the former has a fixed step, and the latter has a variable step. This difference means that if it is desired to vary the integration step of E-TUNI, a new neural training will be necessary. Furthermore, as previously mentioned, E-TUNI can work with real-world data and not only with theoretical models.

How does the algorithm guarantee accuracy and stability when finding the endpoints of the integration interval during the backward integration process? In this paper, we only empirically verify that this is possible through the practical examples presented in the numerical results section at the end of this paper. However, a convergence proof of the numerical stability of the proposed model is left for future work. However, here, we prove that the general expression of E-TUNI (which works with mean derivative functions) is an exact solution for a system of Ordinary Differential Equations (ODEs) and as demonstrated by Theorem 4.

Is this valuable method for dynamical systems of nonlinear differential equations of any dimension n? As exemplified by Equations (1)–(3), E-TUNI is capable of solving a non-linear dynamic modelling problem of any order. However, it seems reasonable to assume that the larger the dimension n of the proposed problem, the greater the computational effort required to train the neural network used. This article exemplifies its technological application with physics problems of up to four state variables.

Does the E-TUNI model have application value for new problems in a specific discipline such as Physics or Engineering? Yes, this method can be applied to any physical problem governed by an autonomous non-linear ordinary differential equation with n state variables and m control variables. However, its use in partial differential equations requires further studies. A good application of the proposed method would be, for example, forecasting the stock market, forecasting river flows in hydro-graphic basins, control problems applied to aerospace engineering, among others. The E-TUNI models for forward and backward integration can also be used in optimal control to solve problems involving Pontryagin's principle. Additionally, the E-TUNI can be an alternative to the traditional NARMAX model and Recurrent Neural Networks (RNNs). Finally, Figure 3 graphically schematizes the coupling of an E-TUNI model to any real-world plant, which can be learned through supervised learning with input/output training patterns.

4. Universal Numerical Integrator (UNI)

Figure 3 illustrates a general scheme for adequately designing a Universal Numerical Integrator (UNI). Notice that in Figure 3, when one couples a conventional numerical integrator (e.g., Euler, Runge–Kutta, Adams-Bashforth, predictive-corrector, among others) to some kind of universal approximators of functions (e.g., MLP neural networks, RBF, SVM, fuzzy inference systems, among others), the UNI design can be achieved high numerical accuracy through supervised learning using input/output training patterns. This allows for solving real-world problems involving the modeling of non-linear dynamic systems.

Still, regarding Figure 3, note that ${}^{k+1}\hat{y}_j^i$ is the prediction made at instant t_{k+1} by the UNI used and ${}^{k+1}y_j^i$ is the real value generated by the plant at the same instant. Note that these two values are compared in the "Training Error" block, and the weights present in the UNI are updated through supervised learning with input/output training patterns. Since artificial neural networks are considered universal approximators of functions, the neural training error can be as small as desired. Notice that ${}^{k+1}\bar{y}_j^i$ is the output generated if only the conventional numerical integrator is used. However, in the latter case, training it with real-world training patterns is impossible.

As previously mentioned, a Universal Numerical Integrator (UNI) can be of three types, thus giving rise to three distinct methodologies, namely: (i) NARMAX model, (ii) instantaneous derivatives methodology (e.g., Runge–Kutta neural network, Adams-Bashforth neural network, predicted-corrector neural network, among others), and (iii) mean derivatives methodology or E-TUNI. The three types of universal numerical integrators are equally precise, as the Artificial Neural Network (ANN) is a universal approximator of functions [2–5], every UNI can have its approximation error as close to zero, as much as one likes.

To fully understand the difference between the instantaneous and mean derivative methodologies, see Figure 2 again. This figure presents the geometric difference between the instantaneous and mean derivative functions. It is well-known that the mean derivative ($tan_{\Delta t}{}^{k}\alpha^{i}$) is the tangent of the angle of the secant line connecting two distinct points of a mathematical function. On the other hand, the instantaneous derivative ($tan^{k}\theta^{i}$) is the tangent of the angle of the tangent line to any given point of a mathematical function.

The mean derivatives methodology occurs when a universal approximator of functions is coupled to the Euler-type first-order integrator. In this case, the first-order integrator would have a substantial error if instantaneous derivative functions were used. However, when the mean derivative functions replace the instantaneous derivative functions, the integrator error is reduced to zero [16,27]. In this way, it is possible to train an artificial neural network to learn the mean derivative functions through two possible approaches [16]: (i) the direct approach and (ii) the indirect or empirical approach.

Figure 4 schematically represents the direct approach. Figure 5 schematically represents the indirect or empirical approach. In the direct approach, the artificial neural network is trained separately from the first-order integrator. The artificial neural network is trained and coupled to the first-order integrator in the indirect or empirical approach. Both approaches are equivalent to each other. However, the back-propagation algorithm must be recalculated using the indirect or empirical approach. In the direct approach, this is unnecessary [16].

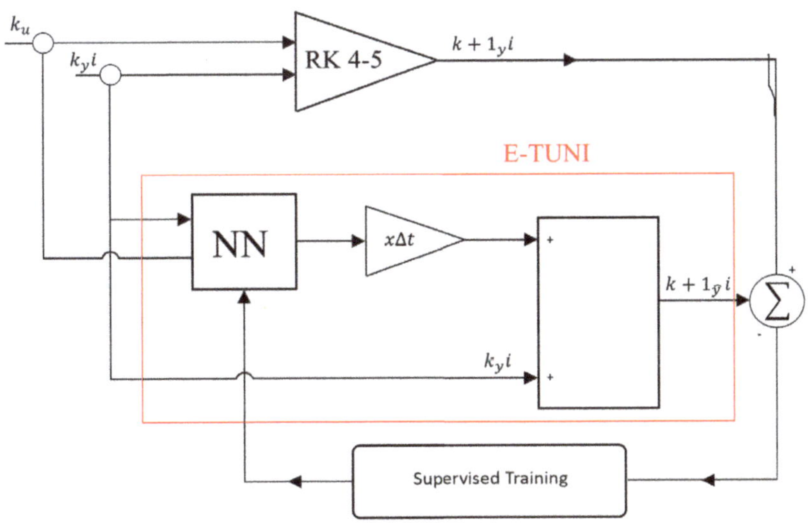

Figure 5. The E-TUNI designed according to the indirect or empirical approach (Source: [16]).

However, in this article, only the direct approach will be used to train the neural network with the mean derivative functions. In this sense, giving a more detailed explanation of Figure 4 is useful. The "Dynamic System" block is the state equations of the dynamic system that we want to reproduce through E-TUNI. A higher-order numerical integrator solves the theoretical dynamical system (e.g., Runge–Kutta 4-5, among others). After this, the values ${}^{k}y^{i}$ and ${}^{k+1}y^{i}$ are used to calculate the mean derivative of this theoretical system, i.e., $tan_{\Delta t}{}^{k}\alpha^{i}$. In parallel, the "NN" block contains the neural network. The neural network inputs will be ${}^{k}y^{i}$ (state variable) and ${}^{k}u$ (control variable), calculated at time t_k. The output of the neural network will be the mean derivative $tan_{\Delta t}{}^{k}\hat{\alpha}^{i}$. Notice that the same inputs ${}^{k}y^{i}$ and ${}^{k}u$ are simultaneously stimulated in the original theoretical dynamical system and the neural network. Thus, after the dynamical system is adequately trained, the output variable of the neural network ($tan_{\Delta t}{}^{k}\hat{\alpha}^{i}$) should be the same as the output variable of the original dynamical system ($tan_{\Delta t}{}^{k}\alpha^{i}$), at least for a small residual error. Furthermore, if we want to learn a real-world plant, we must only replace the theoretical model with a computational data acquisition system.

The same explanation applies to Figure 5. However, since the integrator is trained with the neural network in this case, the reference value in training will not be the mean derivative functions but an instant future ahead of state variables, i.e., ${}^{k+1}y^{i}$.

Additionally, in the remainder of this article, although the dynamical system can be used with both state variables and control variables, we will consider dynamical systems with only state variables. It is also essential to note that in the E-TUNI, the integration step (Δt) can be any (it does not need to be infinitesimal). It should be small only in the case where control variables are used.

This difference between the direct and indirect approach also applies to the instantaneous derivatives methodology. However, in this case, the direct approach only applies to theoretical models, as instantaneous derivative functions cannot be determined directly in real-world problems [16]. Furthermore, this difference between the direct and indirect approach does not apply to the NARMAX model. However, the NARMAX model is also a particular case of UNI. This is because, although a conventional integrator is not coupled to the NARMAX model, the universal approximator of functions behaves as if it were a numerical integrator [16].

5. The Euler-Type Universal Numerical Integrator (E-TUNI)

Firstly, in this section, we briefly introduce the Euler-Type Universal Numerical Integrator (E-TUNI) and present the general expression of this unique type of Universal Numerical Integrator (UNI). Next, we present the mathematical foundations of E-TUNI with forward and backward integrations. It is also important to highlight that this integrator is inherently of first-order.

As a result, Equation (1) mathematically represents a system of n autonomous non-linear ordinary differential equations with dependent variables $y_1, y_2, \ldots, y_n$. Based on this, it is possible to establish an initial value problem for a first-order system, also described by (1):

$$\begin{cases} \dot{y}_1 = f_1(y_1, y_2, \ldots y_n), & y_1(t_0) = \eta_1 \\ \dot{y}_2 = f_2(y_1, y_2, \ldots y_n), & y_2(t_0) = \eta_2 \\ \quad\vdots & \quad\vdots \\ \dot{y}_n = f_n(y_1, y_2, \ldots y_n), & y_n(t_0) = \eta_n \end{cases} \quad (1)$$

The system represented by Equation (1) is a non-linear and autonomous (time-invariant) system of ordinary differential equations. It is important to notice that the method presented here will be limited to this type of equation. Thus, neither non-autonomous systems nor Partial Differential Equations (PDEs) will be considered here.

Additionally, the solution of the differential Equation (1) can be obtained through a first-order approximation. Such a solution was obtained by the mathematician Leonard Euler in 1768. This solution, keeping the convention described by Figure 2, is given by Equation (2):

$$\begin{cases} {}^{k+1}y_1^i \cong tan^k\theta_1^i \cdot \Delta t + {}^{k}y_1^i, & {}^{0}y_1^i = \eta_1 \\ {}^{k+1}y_2^i \cong tan^k\theta_2^i \cdot \Delta t + {}^{k}y_2^i, & {}^{0}y_2^i = \eta_2 \\ \quad\vdots & \quad\vdots \\ {}^{k+1}y_n^i \cong tan^k\theta_n^i \cdot \Delta t + {}^{k}y_n^i, & {}^{0}y_n^i = \eta_n \end{cases} \quad (2)$$

However, it is essential to notice that the accuracy of Equation (2) is awful. Because of this, if the mean derivative functions replace the instantaneous derivative functions, then the Euler-type first-order integrator becomes precise (see demonstration of Theorem 4). This new solution is given by Equation (3):

$$\begin{cases} {}^{k+1}y_1^i = tan_{\Delta t}{}^k\alpha_1^i \cdot \Delta t + {}^k y_1^i, & {}^0 y_1^i = \eta_1 \\ {}^{k+1}y_2^i = tan_{\Delta t}{}^k\alpha_2^i \cdot \Delta t + {}^k y_2^i, & {}^0 y_2^i = \eta_2 \\ \vdots & \vdots \\ {}^{k+1}y_n^i = tan_{\Delta t}{}^k\alpha_n^i \cdot \Delta t + {}^k y_n^i, & {}^0 y_n^i = \eta_n \end{cases} \tag{3}$$

for

$$tan_{\Delta t}{}^k\alpha_j^i = \frac{{}^{k+1}y_j^i - {}^k y_j^i}{\Delta t} \tag{4}$$

Note that Equation (3) is straightforward to obtain, as the mean derivative functions sound easily computable, for real-world problems, via Equation (4), for $j = 1, 2, \ldots, n$. Here, the variable n is the total number of state variables of the dynamical system given by (1).

Before we proceed with the rest of this article, we will give an intuitive justification for the passage from Equation (2) to Equation (3), with the help of Figure 2. If an artificial neural network is trained to learn the instantaneous derivative function ($tan^k\theta^i$) of any non-linear dynamical system and this neural network is subsequently coupled to the first-order Euler integrator, then the output of this model will be ${}^{k+1}\tilde{y}_j^i$ (see Figure 2 again). Therefore, this value is very different from the real value ${}^{k+1}y_j^i$. However, if the neural training on the Euler integrator, mentioned above, is continued through the indirect approach, its training error will be reduced to almost zero, since the neural network is a universal approximator of functions. Therefore, the new output will be ${}^{k+1}\hat{y}_j^i$. Notice that graphically, the instantaneous derivative function has been forced to converge to the mean derivative function to reduce the integrator error to almost zero. Additionally, by the uniqueness theorem (Theorem 1 which will be presented later) there is no other way for this problem to converge.

Finally, it is crucial to notice that a neural network can compute the mean derivative functions, as schematized by Figure 6. In this way, the E-TUNI works with a first-order numerical integrator coupled to a neural network with any feed-forward architecture (e.g., MLP neural network, RBF, SVM, wavelets, fuzzy inference systems, Convolutional Neural Network (CNN), among others).

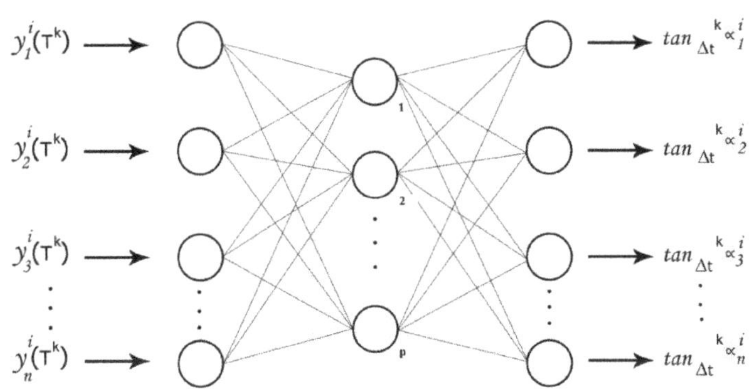

Figure 6. A MLP neural network designed with the concept of mean derivative functions.

5.1. Fundamental Theorem

In this section, the general expression of E-TUNI is demonstrated. For this purpose, let the system of non-linear differential Equations (5) be:

$$\dot{y} = f(y) \tag{5}$$

where, $y = [y_1 \quad y_2 \quad \ldots \quad y_n]^T$ and $f(y) = [f_1(y) \quad f_2(y) \quad \ldots \quad f_n(y)]^T$. The uniqueness theorem is a fundamental theorem about Equation (5).

Theorem 1 (T1). *Assume that each of the functions $f_1(y_1, y_2, \ldots, y_n), \ldots, f_n(y_1, y_2, \ldots, y_n)$ has continuous partial derivatives with respect to $y_1, y_2, \ldots, y_n$. So the known initial value problem $\dot{y} = f(y)$ for $y(t_0)$ has one and only one solution $y = y(t)$ in $\mathbb{R}$, starting from each $y(t_0)$. If two solutions $y = \phi(t)$ have a common point, they must be identical.*

For the formal demonstration of the general expression of E-TUNI, which will numerically and discretely solve Equation (5), two hypotheses will be assumed: (i) a set of points that is an exact solution of the dynamical system (5) is known and which we will call ${}^k y_j^i$ and (ii) the existence of two sets of continuous and differentiable functions that pass through these points is assumed, namely, $y_j^i(t)$ and $\dot{y}_j^i(t)$. Figure 7 mathematically illustrates these two hypotheses when $i = 1,2,3,4$, $j = 1,2$, and $k = 0,1,2,3,4$. The meanings of the auxiliary variables i, j, and k are the same as those described in Figure 1. Furthermore, only the points ${}^k y_j^i$ must be known. The functions $y_j^i(t)$ and $\dot{y}_j^i(t)$ just need to exist; that is, it is not necessary to know them.

$$\begin{bmatrix} y_1^1(t) \\ y_1^2(t) \\ y_1^3(t) \\ y_1^4(t) \end{bmatrix} \equiv \begin{bmatrix} {}^0y_1^1 & {}^1y_1^1 & {}^2y_1^1 & {}^3y_1^1 & {}^4y_1^1 \\ {}^0y_1^2 & {}^1y_1^2 & {}^2y_1^2 & {}^3y_1^2 & {}^4y_1^2 \\ {}^0y_1^3 & {}^1y_1^3 & {}^2y_1^3 & {}^3y_1^3 & {}^4y_1^3 \\ {}^0y_1^4 & {}^1y_1^4 & {}^2y_1^4 & {}^3y_1^4 & {}^4y_1^4 \end{bmatrix} \qquad \begin{bmatrix} y_2^1(t) \\ y_2^2(t) \\ y_2^3(t) \\ y_2^4(t) \end{bmatrix} \equiv \begin{bmatrix} {}^0y_2^1 & {}^1y_2^1 & {}^2y_2^1 & {}^3y_2^1 & {}^4y_2^1 \\ {}^0y_2^2 & {}^1y_2^2 & {}^2y_2^2 & {}^3y_2^2 & {}^4y_2^2 \\ {}^0y_2^3 & {}^1y_2^3 & {}^2y_2^3 & {}^3y_2^3 & {}^4y_2^3 \\ {}^0y_2^4 & {}^1y_2^4 & {}^2y_2^4 & {}^3y_2^4 & {}^4y_2^4 \end{bmatrix}$$

$$[t_0 \quad t_1 \quad t_2 \quad t_3 \quad t_4] \qquad\qquad [t_0 \quad t_1 \quad t_2 \quad t_3 \quad t_4]$$

j=1
i=1, 2, 3, 4
k=0, 1, 2, 3, 4

j=2
i=1, 2, 3, 4
k=0, 1, 2, 3, 4

Figure 7. Example of numerical discretization of the solution of the differential Equation (5).

What do the matrices mean in Figure 7? The first line of these point matrices represents a set of exact points belonging to the first curve of the family of solution curves of the considered system, and so on. For example, all points ${}^0y_1^1$, ${}^1y_1^1$, ${}^2y_1^1$, ${}^3y_1^1$, and ${}^4y_1^1$ pass through the continuous and differentiable function $y_1^1(t)$, and so on. Since $i = 4$, the family of curves, in this case, is composed of four curves. Based on the continuous hypothesis, i can be as large as one wants. Since the neural network, responsible for modelling the system (5), will be designed with the supervised learning approach through input/output training patterns, knowing in advance the discrete solution of the system (5), is not absurd. Thus, the system (5) can be replaced by the following set of solutions (6):

$$\begin{cases} \dot{y}_j^i(t) = \dot{g}_j^i(t) \\ y_j^i(t) = g_j^i(t) \end{cases} \tag{6}$$

where $i = 1,2,\ldots,q$; $j = 1,2,\ldots,n$; $k = 0,1,2,\ldots,r$. It is essential to note that changing the values of q, n, r, and Δt can obtain any finite density of discrete point solutions of (5) over a finite domain. Thus, the great advantage of Equation (6) concerning Equation (5) is that the former is an explicit function only of the variable t. Thus, the differential and integral mean value theorems can be applied in (6) to arrive at the general expression of E-TUNI, which uses the functions of mean derivatives. The differential and integral mean value theorems cannot be applied in (5) because, in this case, the system in question is an explicit function of y and not of t.

Theorem 2 (The Differential Mean Value Theorem). *If a function $g_j^i(t)$ for $j = 1,2,\ldots,n$ is a continuous function and defined over the closed interval $[t_k, t_{k+1}]$ is differentiable over the open interval (t_k, t_{k+1}), then there exists at least one number t_k^* with $t_k < t_k^* < t_k + \Delta t = t_{k+1}$ such that, $\dot{g}_j^i(t_k^*) = \frac{{}^{k+1}g_j^i - {}^{k}g_j^i}{\Delta t}$.*

Theorem 3 (The Integral Mean Value Theorem). *If a function $\dot{g}_j^i(t)$ for $j = 1,2,\ldots,n$ is a continuous function and defined over the closed interval $[t_k, t_{k+1}]$, then there exists at least one internal point t_k^x in $[t_k, t_{k+1}]$ such that, $\dot{g}_j^i(t_k^x) \cdot \Delta t = \int_{t_k}^{t_{k+1}} \dot{g}_j^i(t)dt$.*

The notation used to represent ${}^{k}y_j^i$ is sufficient to map it uniquely to its respective region of interest, where its associated characteristic secant $tan_{\Delta t}{}^{k}\alpha_j^i$ is confined. Thus, it can be stated that for the state ${}^{k}y_j^i = y_j^i(t_0 + k \cdot \Delta t)$, we have a single characteristic secant associated with it and given by $tan_{\Delta t}{}^{k}\alpha_j^i$. The existence of a unique secant associated with each point ${}^{k}y_j^i$ is an immediate consequence of the uniqueness theorem (Theorem 1).

Consider also $y_j^i = y_j^i(t)$ for $j = 1,2,\ldots,n$ a particular trajectory of a family of solutions of the system of differential equations $\dot{y} = f(y)$ passing through $y_j^i(t_0)$ at time t_0, i.e., initializing within a finite domain of interest $[y_j^{min}(t_0), y_j^{max}(t_0)]^n$.

In [29,30], by definition, the secant curve between two points ${}^{k}y_j^i$ and ${}^{k+1}y_j^i$, belonging to the curve $y_j^i(t)$ for $j = 1,2,\ldots,n$ is the straight line segment that joins these two points. Thus, the tangents of the secants between the points ${}^{k}y_1^i$ and ${}^{k+1}y_1^i$, ${}^{k}y_2^i$ and ${}^{k+1}y_2^i$, …, ${}^{k}y_n^i$ and ${}^{k+1}y_n^i$ are defined as:

$$tan_{\Delta t}\alpha^i(t + k \cdot \Delta t) = tan_{\Delta t}{}^{k}\alpha^i = \begin{bmatrix} tan_{\Delta t}{}^{k}\alpha_1^i & tan_{\Delta t}{}^{k}\alpha_2^i & \ldots & tan_{\Delta t}{}^{k}\alpha_n^i \end{bmatrix}^T \quad (7)$$

where $tan_{\Delta t}{}^{k}\alpha_j^i = \frac{{}^{k+1}y_j^i - {}^{k}y_j^i}{\Delta t}$ for $j = 1,2,\cdot,n$.

Property 1. *Applying Theorem 2 on the curve $\dot{g}_j^i(t)$ is equivalent to applying Theorem 1 on the curve $g_j^i(t)$ both on the same interval closed $[t_k, t_{k+1}]$, i.e., $\dot{g}_j^i(t_k^x) = \dot{g}_j^i(t_k^*)$.*

Proof. If one applies Theorem 2 to the continuous curve $\dot{g}_j^i(t)$, this results in a $\dot{g}_j^i(t_k^x)$ for $t_k < t_k^x < t_{k+1}$ such that $\dot{g}_j^i(t_k^x) \cdot \Delta t = \int_{t_k}^{t_{k+1}} \dot{g}_j^i(t)dt = {}^{k+1}g_j^i - {}^{k}g_j^i$ as a result of the fundamental theorem of calculus. This way, $\dot{g}_j^i(t_k^x) = \frac{{}^{k+1}g_j^i - {}^{k}g_j^i}{\Delta t} \stackrel{\text{def}}{=} tan_{\Delta t}{}^{k}\alpha_j^i$. On the other hand, the application of Theorem 1 on the continuous and differentiable curve $g_j^i(t)$ implies the existence of a $\dot{g}_j^i(t_k^*)$ for $t_k < t_k^* < t_{k+1}$, such that $\dot{g}_j^i(t_k^*) = \frac{{}^{k+1}g_j^i - {}^{k}g_j^i}{\Delta t} \stackrel{\text{def}}{=} tan_{\Delta t}{}^{k}\alpha_j^i$. This way, $\dot{g}_j^i(t_k^x) = \dot{g}_j^i(t_k^*)$. However, this demonstration does not prove that $t_k^x = t_k^*$. □

Theorem 4. *The general discrete and exact solution ${}^{k+1}y_j^i$ for $j = 1,2,\ldots,n$ of the autonomous system of nonlinear differential equations of the type $\dot{y}^i = f(y^i)$ can be established through the first-order Euler relation of the type ${}^{k+1}y_j^i = tan_{\Delta t}{}^{k}\alpha_j^i \cdot \Delta t + {}^{k}y_j^i$ for a given ${}^{k}y_j^i$ and Δt fixed, since* *the general solution of this dynamical system, given by,* $y_j^i(t) = g_j^i(t)$ *and* $\dot{y}_j^i(t) = \dot{g}_j^i(t)$ *are previously known for* $j = 1, 2, \ldots, n$; $i = 1, 2, \ldots, \infty$ *and* $t \in [t_o, t_f]$.

Proof. Let the first-order non-linear and autonomous dynamical system be given by $\dot{y}_j^i(t) = f_j(y_1^i, y_2^i, \ldots, y_n^i) = f_j(y^i)$ for $j = 1, 2, \ldots, n$ and $i = 1, 2, \ldots, \infty$. If the solution of the dynamical system is known and equal to $y_j^i(t) = g_j^i(t)$, then the function $f_j(y^i)$ can be replaced by $\dot{g}_j^i(t) = h_j^i(t)$, i.e., $\dot{y}_j^i(t) = h_j^i(t)$. In this way, we can write that $\int_{^k y_j^i}^{^{k+1} y_j^i} dy_j^i(t) = \int_{t_k}^{t_{k+1}} h_j^i(t)dt$. Note that the indices i, j, and k uniquely map the secant we are interested in and in accordance with Figure 1. This last integral can still be simplified as ${}^{k+1}y_j^i - {}^k y_j^i = \int_{t_k}^{t_{k+1}} h_j^i(t)dt$. Thus, applying the mean integral value theorem, in this last expression, we obtain ${}^{k+1}y_j^i - {}^k y_i^j = h_j^i(t_k^x) \cdot \Delta t = \dot{g}_j^i(t_k^x) \cdot \Delta t$ where $t_k^x \in [t_k, t_{k+1}]$ and for $h_j^i(t) = \dot{g}_j^i(t)$. On the other hand, applying the differential mean value theorem on the function $y_j^i(t) = g_j^i(t)$ for $j = 1, 2, \ldots, n$ in the interval $[t_k, t_{k+1}]$ we obtain that $\dot{g}_j^i(t_k^*) = \frac{^{k+1}g_j^i - ^k g_j^i}{\Delta t} \stackrel{\text{def}}{=} tan_{\Delta t}{}^k\alpha_j^i$. Thus, by Property 1 we have that $\dot{g}_j^i(t_k^*) = \dot{g}_j^i(t_k^x) = tan_{\Delta t}{}^k\alpha_j^i$ for $j = 1, 2, \ldots, n$. Therefore, ${}^{k+1}y_j^i = tan_{\Delta t}{}^k\alpha_i^j \cdot \Delta t + {}^k y_j^i$ for $j = 1, 2, \ldots, n$ or, in vector form, it turns out that ${}^{k+1}y^i = tan_{\Delta t}{}^k\alpha^i \cdot \Delta t + {}^k y^i$. □

Note that the functions $\dot{y}_j^i(t)$ and $y_j^i(t)$, used in the previous demonstration, need to be continuous and differentiable because of Theorems 2 and 3, but they do not need to be known. Their existence is enough. What needs to be known are the points ${}^k y_j^i$. Finally, through a mathematical demonstration, very similar to Theorem 4, one can demonstrate the general expression of E-TUNI with backward integration, i.e., ${}^{k-1}y_j^i = -tan_{\Delta t}^{-}{}^k\alpha_j^i . \Delta t + {}^k y_j^i$ for $tan_{\Delta t}^{-}{}^k\alpha_j^i = \frac{^k y_j^i - ^{k-1} y_j^i}{\Delta t}$ and $j = 1, 2, \ldots, n$. For more details on E-TUNI and its relationship with other types of UNIs, see [16,31].

5.2. General E-TUNI Algorithm with Forward and Backward Integrations

This section describes first-order Euler integrators with forward and backward integration. They are divided into two classes: (i) the conventional Euler integrator, which works with instantaneous derivative functions (low numerical precision and variable step), and (ii) the E-TUNI type integrator, which works with mean derivative functions (high numerical precision and fixed step).

Therefore, it is important to mathematically relate the mean derivatives functions with the instantaneous derivatives functions (see again Figure 2). Thus, it is easily seen that if $\dot{y} = f(y)$ then,

$$
\begin{gathered}
{}^k\dot{y}_i^i = f({}^k y^i) = \lim_{\Delta t \to 0} tan_{\Delta t}{}^k y_j^i = \lim_{\Delta t \to 0} \frac{^{k+1}y_j^i - ^k y_j^i}{\Delta t} \\
for \quad j = 1, 2, \ldots, n
\end{gathered} \tag{8}
$$

or

$$
\begin{gathered}
\lim_{\Delta t \to 0} tan_{\Delta t}{}^k y_j^i = tan^k \Theta_j^i \\
for \quad j = 1, 2, \ldots, n
\end{gathered} \tag{9}
$$

Figure 2 graphically illustrates the convergence of mean derivatives functions to instantaneous derivatives functions when Δt tends to zero. Based on this, it is possible to enunciate two basic types of first-order numerical integrators or Euler integrators. An Euler integrator that uses instantaneous derivatives functions, given by $tan^k \Theta_j^i = f_j({}^k y^i)$ for $j = 1, 2, \ldots, n$ and an Euler integrator that uses mean derivatives functions, given by $tan_{\Delta t}^k y_j^i = \frac{^{k+1}y_j^i - ^k y_j^i}{\Delta t} = g_j[{}^k y^i, {}^{k+1} y^i, \Delta t]$.

A significant difference between the mean derivatives functions and the instantaneous derivatives functions is that the instantaneous derivatives functions $f_j({}^k y^i)$ for $j = 1, 2, \ldots, n$ is only dependent on ${}^k y^i$, but the mean derivatives functions $g_j[{}^k y^i, {}^{k+1} y^i, \Delta t]$ for $j = 1, 2, \ldots, n$ is dependent on ${}^k y^i$, ${}^{k+1} y^i$ and Δt at the point ${}^k y^i$. As will be seen later, this difference is significant.

The first important point to be considered here is the possibility of carrying out both forward and backward integration of the Euler Integrator with instantaneous derivatives. So, the instantaneous derivative functions at the points $y^i_j(t)$ for $j = 1, 2, \ldots, n$ can be defined in two different ways:

$$ {}^k\dot{y}^i_j = f^+_j({}^k y^i) = \lim_{\Delta t \to 0} \frac{{}^{k+1}y^i_j - {}^k y^i_j}{\Delta t} = tan^{+\,k}\theta^i_j \tag{10} $$

or

$$ {}^k\dot{y}^i_j = f^-_j({}^k y^i) = \lim_{\Delta t \to 0} \frac{{}^{k}y^i_j - {}^{k-1} y^i_j}{\Delta t} = tan^{-\,k}\theta^i_j \tag{11} $$

However, if the instantaneous derivatives functions $f_j(.)$ exist at the point ${}^k y^i$, then necessarily $f^+_j({}^k y^i) = f^-_j({}^k y^i) = f_j({}^k y^i)$ or $tan^{+\,k}\theta^i_j = tan^{-\,k}\theta^i_j = tan^k\theta^i_j$ (see Figure 8). In this way, the expressions of forward and backward propagating Euler integrators, necessarily designed with the instantaneous derivative functions, are given, respectively, by (i.e., with low numerical precision):

$$ \begin{aligned} {}^{k+1}y^i_j &\approx f_j({}^k y^i) \cdot \Delta t +{}^k y^i_j = \\ {}^{k+1}y^i_j &\approx tan\,{}^k\theta^i_j \cdot \Delta t +{}^k y^i_j = \end{aligned} \tag{12} $$

$$ \begin{aligned} {}^{k-1}y^i_j &\approx -f_j({}^k y^i) \cdot \Delta t +{}^k y^i_j = \\ {}^{k-1}y^i_j &\approx -tan\,{}^k\theta^i_j \cdot \Delta t +{}^k y^i_j = \end{aligned} \tag{13} $$

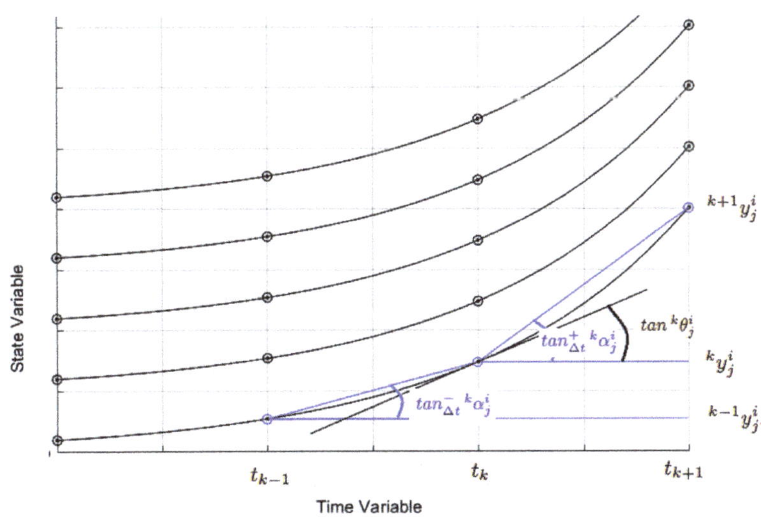

Figure 8. Geometric finding that instantaneous derivative functions are symmetric, but mean derivative functions are not.

Note that Equation (13) can also be obtained directly from Equation (12) by making the substitution of the variable $\Delta t = -\Delta t$.

Additionally, like $f_j^+({}^ky^i) = f_j^-({}^ky^i) = f_j({}^ky^i)$, the Euler integrator with instantaneous derivatives functions has a symmetric solution between intervals $[t_{k-1}, t_k]$ and $[t_k, t_{k+1}]$, thus implying low numerical precision, for the outputs ${}^{k-1}y_j^i$ and ${}^{k+1}y_j^i$ for $j = 1, 2, \ldots, n$. To say that a solution is symmetric at the point k means to say that $|{}^ky_j^i - {}^{k-1}y_j^i| = |{}^{k+1}y_j^i - {}^ky_j^i|$ to $j = 1, 2, \ldots, n$.

This Euler integrator symmetry property only occurs when instantaneous derivative functions are used. However, in Euler's integrator, designed with the mean derivatives functions, this symmetry of the solution around the point t_k is not verified (see Figure 8 again). This is important because in Euler's integrator, designed with mean derivatives functions, the backward solution does not necessarily decrease when the forward solution grows.

In [32], several difference operators can be applied to a function ${}^ky_j^I$ for $j = 1, 2, \ldots, n$. However, the two operators that interest us are the forward difference and the backward difference, given below, respectively:

$$\Delta^k y_j^i = {}^{k+1}y_j^i - {}^ky_j^i \quad for \quad j = 1, 2, \ldots, n \tag{14}$$

$$\nabla^k y_j^i = {}^ky_j^i - {}^{k-1}y_j^i \quad for \quad j = 1, 2, \ldots, n \tag{15}$$

Thus, using the finite difference operators, there are two different ways to represent the secant at the point ${}^ky_j^i$ and with integration step Δt:

$$tan_{\Delta t}^{+}\,{}^k\alpha_j^i = \frac{\Delta^k y_j^i}{\Delta t} = \frac{{}^{k+1}y_j^i - {}^ky_j^i}{\Delta t} \quad for \quad j = 1, 2, \ldots, n \tag{16}$$

$$tan_{\Delta t}^{-}\,{}^k\alpha_j^i = \frac{\nabla^k y_j^i}{\Delta t} = \frac{{}^ky_j^i - {}^{k-1}y_j^i}{\Delta t} \quad for \quad j = 1, 2, \ldots, n \tag{17}$$

Comparing Equation (16) with the result of Theorem T4, one can obtain the following recursive and exact equation to represent the solution of autonomous non-linear ordinary differential equations system for a forward integration process (i.e., with high numerical accuracy):

$${}^{k+1}y_j^i = tan_{\Delta t}^{+}\,{}^k\alpha_j^i \cdot \Delta t + {}^ky_j^i \quad for \quad j = 1, 2, \ldots, n \tag{18}$$

or

$${}^{k+1}y_j^i = \frac{\Delta^k y_j^i}{\Delta t} \cdot \Delta t + {}^ky_j^i \quad for \quad j = 1, 2, \ldots, n \tag{19}$$

Equations (18) and (19) represent an Euler-type integrator, which uses mean derivatives functions and forward integration. However, to obtain the Euler integrator with backward recursion, it is enough to analyze the asymmetry of the mean derivative functions at the point ${}^ky_j^i$ and as is illustrated in Figure 8. In this way, we can obtain the following equation to perform the backward integration of E-TUNI (i.e., with high numerical precision):

$${}^{k-1}y_j^i = -tan_{\Delta t}^{-}\,{}^k\alpha_j^i \cdot \Delta t + {}^ky_j^i \quad for \quad j = 1, 2, \ldots, n \tag{20}$$

or

$$^{k-1}y_j^i = -\frac{\nabla^k y_j^i}{\Delta t} \cdot \Delta t + ^k y_j^i \qquad (21)$$
$$for \quad j = 1, 2, \ldots, n$$

Thus, the iterative equations of the first-order Euler integrator, using mean derivatives, which perform forward and backward recursions, are, respectively, Equations (18) and (20). The negative sign that appears in Equation (20) means, not necessarily, that when $^{k+1}y_j^i$ increases, then $^{k-1}y_j^i$ decreases, because they are two neural networks independent of each other. Therefore, it is observed that, in general, $|tan_{\Delta t}^{+}\,{}^k\alpha_j^i| \neq |tan_{\Delta t}^{-}\,{}^k\alpha_j^i|$, and therefore Euler integrators with mean derivatives functions do not have a symmetric solution, i.e., in general, $|^{k+1}y_j^i -^k y_j^i| \neq |^k y_j^i -^{k-1} y_j^i|$ for $j = 1, 2, \ldots, n$. As can be easily seen in Figure 8, the negative mean derivative has a different slope than the positive mean derivative for the same point in t_k.

It is interesting to note that the negative sign that appears in Equations (13), (20) and (21) is because of the inverted direction of the flow of time (from present to past) in backward integration.

Additionally, the following algorithm is proposed to determine the mean derivatives through the direct methodology involving both forward and backward integrations in the Universal Numerical Integrator (UNI) of the E-TUNI type. This approach requires five steps.

1. Given a finite domain of interest $[^k y_j^{min}, {}^k y_j^{max}]^n$ computed at time t_k for $j = 1, 2, \ldots, n$ state variables, generate, according to a uniform probability distribution, q initial conditions such that,

$$p^i = \begin{bmatrix} ^k y_1^i & ^k y_2^i & ^k y_3^i & \ldots & ^k y_n^i \end{bmatrix}^T$$

and

$$P = \begin{bmatrix} p^1 : & p^2 : & p^3 : & \cdots : & p^q \end{bmatrix}_{nxq}$$

which are the E-TUNI's input training patterns at time t_k for both the forward and backward integrators. The number q of training patterns should be large enough to ensure adequate supervised training. To this end, the training patterns should be appropriately divided, with one portion for training and another for testing.

2. Using a high-order integrator, propagate all initial conditions p^i to obtain the corresponding states at time t_{k+1} and at time t_{k-1}. Thus, assemble the output patterns $^+T^i$ and $^-T^i$ to train the positive and negative mean derivatives.

$$^+T^i = \begin{bmatrix} tan_{\Delta t}^{+}\,{}^k\alpha_1^i & tan_{\Delta t}^{+}\,{}^k\alpha_2^i & tan_{\Delta t}^{+}\,{}^k\alpha_3^i & \ldots & tan_{\Delta t}^{+}\,{}^k\alpha_n^i \end{bmatrix}^T$$

$$^+T = \begin{bmatrix} ^+T^1 : & ^+T^2 : & ^+T^3 : & \cdots : & ^+T^q \end{bmatrix}_{nxq}$$

and

$$^-T^i = \begin{bmatrix} tan_{\Delta t}^{-}\,{}^k\alpha_1^i & tan_{\Delta t}^{-}\,{}^k\alpha_2^i & tan_{\Delta t}^{-}\,{}^k\alpha_3^i & \ldots & tan_{\Delta t}^{-}\,{}^k\alpha_n^i \end{bmatrix}^T$$

$$^-T = \begin{bmatrix} ^-T^1 : & ^-T^2 : & ^-T^3 : & \cdots : & ^-T^q \end{bmatrix}_{nxq}$$

Note: Alternatively, in this step, a data acquisition system could capture real-world dynamic systems' behavior.

3. Once input vectors P and output vectors ^+T and ^-T are required by the universal approximator of functions, train two neural networks through supervised learning. One training pair $[P, ^+T]$ to learn the positive mean derivative function and one training pair

$[P, ^{-}T]$ to learn the negative mean derivative function. These two neural networks will look similar to the one in Figure 6.

4. When the two supervised trainings are consolidated, it is possible to simulate the dynamics of the system through the following discrete recursive expressions:

$$^{k+1}\hat{y}^i = tan^{+}_{\Delta t}{}^{k}\hat{\alpha}^i \cdot \Delta t +^k y^i$$

and

$$^{k-1}\hat{y}^i = -tan^{-}_{\Delta t}{}^{k}\hat{\alpha}^i \cdot \Delta t +^k y^i$$

5. Using the E-TUNI expression to propagate the positive mean derivative, integrate the dynamical system from the initial instant t_o to the final instant t_f. Then, integrate the E-TUNI expression from t_f to t_o using the negative mean derivative. By the uniqueness theorem, the initial starting point of the first integration must coincide with the final arrival point of the second integration.

6. Analysis of the Numerical Accuracy of E-TUNI Using Landau Symbols

In this section, an analysis of the accuracy of the E-TUNI solution is performed. For this purpose, the numerical accuracy of the conventional Euler method, which works with instantaneous derivative functions, is initially analyzed. Next, an analysis of the accuracy of the E-TUNI solution, i.e., the Euler method that works with mean derivative functions, is performed. It is essential to note that the mean derivative functions will be obtained through an artificial neural network.

6.1. Numerical Accuracy of the Conventional Euler Method

The explicit Euler method is a numerical integration technique for solving ordinary differential equations of the form:

$$\frac{dy}{dt} = f(t, y), \quad y(t_0) = y_0. \tag{22}$$

The formula for the method is:

$$y_{n+1} = y_n + hf(t_n, y_n), \tag{23}$$

where h is the integration step; y_n is the approximation of the exact solution $y(t_n)$; $f(t_n, y_n)$ is the instantaneous derivative of the solution at the point (t_n, y_n). Therefore, it is a well-known result that the difference between the exact solution and the Euler approximation is given by:

$$y(t_{n+1}) - y_{n+1} = \frac{h^2}{2} y''(t_n) + O(h^3). \tag{24}$$

Therefore, the accuracy of the method is evaluated by two errors: (i) The local truncation error $E_{\text{local}} = O(h^2)$ and (ii) the global truncation error $E_{\text{global}} = O(h)$. Understanding the global error is quite simple; since the Euler method performs $N = \frac{T}{h}$ steps to integrate up to a time T, the global error is obtained by adding the local errors over this interval. Finally, the accuracy of the Euler method is first order since the global error is $O(h)$. This result shows that the Euler method is accurate only for small steps, and higher-order methods such as Runge–Kutta are preferable to obtain greater accuracy.

6.2. The E-TUNI Numerical Accuracy

In the modified Euler method, i.e., in E-TUNI, we employ the mean derivative functions $\bar{f}_n$, which can be obtained by an Artificial Neural Network (ANN):

$$y_{n+1} = y_n + h\bar{f}_n, \tag{25}$$

where the mean derivative is defined as:

$$\bar{f}_n = \frac{1}{h}\int_{t_n}^{t_{n+1}} f(t, y(t))dt. \tag{26}$$

If the mean derivative is estimated by an Artificial Neural Network (ANN), we will have:

$$\bar{f}_n^{\text{ANN}} \approx \bar{f}_n + \varepsilon_{\text{ANN}}, \tag{27}$$

where ε_{ANN} represents the error of the neural network. Expanding the exact solution $y(t)$ around t_n, we have that:

$$y(t_{n+1}) = y(t_n + h) = y(t_n) + hy'(t_n) + \frac{h^2}{2}y''(t_n) + O(h^3). \tag{28}$$

The mean derivative can be approximated by expanding $y'(t)$:

$$y'(t) = y'(t_n) + (t - t_n)y''(t_n) + O(h^2). \tag{29}$$

Thus, substituting Equation (29) into the integral (26) and integrating over the interval $[t_n, t_{n+1}]$, we have:

$$\bar{f}_n = y'(t_n) + \frac{h}{2}y''(t_n) + O(h^2). \tag{30}$$

Thus, substituting the mean derivative Equation (30) into the modified Euler method, we finally have:

$$y_{n+1} = y_n + hy'(t_n) + \frac{h^2}{2}y''(t_n) + O(h^3). \tag{31}$$

Equation (31) shows that the local error of the method has increased to $O(h^3)$, improving accuracy. On the other hand, if the mean derivative is approximated by an Artificial Neural Network (ANN):

$$\bar{f}_n^{\text{ANN}} = \bar{f}_n + \varepsilon_{\text{ANN}}. \tag{32}$$

So, the modified method becomes:

$$y_{n+1} = y_n + h(\bar{f}_n + \varepsilon_{\text{ANN}}). \tag{33}$$

So, the total error will be:

$$y(t_{n+1}) - y_{n+1} = O(h^3) + O(h\varepsilon_{\text{ANN}}). \tag{34}$$

Thus, if the artificial neural network is accurate enough, we can make $\varepsilon_{\text{ANN}} \to 0$, making the integration error close to $O(h^3)$. Thus, the local error being equal to $O(h^3) + O(h\varepsilon_{\text{ANN}})$ will make the global error, summed over $N = O(1/h)$ steps, equal to $E_{\text{global}} = O(h^2) + O(\varepsilon_{\text{ANN}})$. Therefore, the modified Euler method with mean derivatives improves the global accuracy to $O(h^2)$. If an artificial neural network is used to estimate the mean derivative, its error ε_{ANN} can be reduced to a minimum, making the method highly accurate. Thus, this method can be seen as a transition to higher-order Runge–Kutta methods.

7. Results and Analysis

In this section, we perform a numerical and computational analysis of the Universal Numerical Integrator (UNI), which exclusively uses mean derivative functions. As previously described, this is the Euler-Type Universal Numerical Integrator (E-TUNI). Therefore, we present here three case studies: (i) a one-dimensional simple case, (ii) the non-linear simple pendulum (two state variables), and (iii) the non-linear inverted pendulum (four state variables).

Thus, for all experiments that it is presented below, the use of MLP neural networks was standardized with the traditional Levenberg–Marquardt training algorithm [33] from 1994. Concerning the architecture of the neural network used, all experiments were trained using only one inner layer (with thirty neurons with tangent hyperbolic activation function) in an artificial neural network of the Multi-Layer Perceptron (MLP) type. In all experiments, 80% of the total patterns were left for training the MLP neural network, 10% of the patterns for testing, and 10% for validation. Concerning the architecture of E-TUNI, the direct approach was exclusively used. However, it must be said that the indirect or empirical approach of E-TUNI was not tested in this article. Thus, the general algorithm for training and testing the methodology presented in this article can be briefly described as follows:

Step 1. Using a high-order 4-5 Runge–Kutta integrator, over the considered autonomous non-linear ordinary differential equation system, randomly generate p training patterns input/output for E-TUNI concerning the initial instant $y^i(t_0)$. Perform both forward and backward integration.

Step 2. Determine both the values of the positive mean derivatives $tan^{+}_{\Delta t}\,{}^{k}\alpha^{i}_{j}$, as well as the values of the negative mean derivatives $tan^{-}_{\Delta t}\,{}^{k}\alpha^{i}_{j}$ in relation to initial instants $y^i(t_0)$ for $i = 1, 2, \ldots, p$.

Step 3. Train two distinct neural networks. One is to output positive mean derivative functions, and the other is to output negative mean derivative functions. Do this following the graphic diagram in Figure 6.

Step 4. Simulate, for several different Δt integration steps, the performance of E-TUNI both with forward and backward integration. Observe that if starting from an initial instant $y^i(t_0)$, the solution is propagated in n distinct instants forward and, after that, one returns to the same n instants with backward integration because of the uniqueness theorem, one returns perfectly to the original initial instant $y^i(t_0)$. This trick will be used to test the efficiency of E-TUNI when it is propagated backward.

Step 5. Do the same, using the Euler-type first-order integrator, but now using the original instantaneous derivative functions of the dynamical system in question. Then, compare E-TUNI with conventional Euler. Thus, to verify the superiority of E-TUNI concerning the conventional Euler, the accuracy of the discrete numerical solutions obtained must be verified.

Therefore, next, we briefly describe the systems of non-linear differential equations of the three dynamical systems considered here to test the proposed algorithm to perform the backward integration of E-TUNI. Table 1 also summarizes the training data of the eight experiments conducted here to test the proposed methodology.

Example 1. *Simulate the one-dimensional non-linear dynamics problem, given by Equation (35). The variable y was trained on the range $[-1, 13]$. Note that this dynamic has infinite stability points since $sin y = 0$ has infinitely many solutions. Note that the points of stability recovering the initial condition through backward integration is very difficult for any integrator.*

$$\dot{y} = sin(y) \tag{35}$$

Example 2. *Simulate the non-linear simple pendulum problem given by the system of differential Equations (36). Note that this example does not involve control variables. The acceleration values due to gravity constants and the pendulum's length are, respectively, given by $g = 9.81\ m/s^2$ and $l = 0.30\ m$. The variable θ was trained on the range $[-1.2, 1.2]$ rad and the variable $\dot{\theta}$ was trained on the range $[-5.2, +5.2]\ \frac{rad}{s}$.*

$$\begin{aligned} \dot{\theta} &= w \\ \dot{w} &= -\tfrac{g}{l} sin\theta \end{aligned} \quad (36)$$

Example 3. *Do the same for the non-linear inverted pendulum problem described by the system of differential Equations (37). The constants adopted for this problem were* $M = 1.0\,[kg]$, $m = 0.4\,[kg]$, $l = 0.5\,[m]$, $I = 0.05\,[kg \cdot m^2]$, $b = 0.1\,[\frac{N}{m/s}]$, $g = 9.81\,[fracms^2]$, *e* $F = 1[N]$. *This problem has four state variables* ($x_1 = x$, $x_2 = \dot{x}$, $x_3 = \theta$, *and* $x_4 = \dot{\theta}$) *and a constant control* ($u_1 = F = 1[N]$). *The state variables were trained on the intervals* x_1 *between* $[-1, +35][m]$, x_2 *between* $[-1, +7][m/s]$, x_3 *between* $[-1, +1][rad]$, *and* x_4 *between* $[-1.2, +1.2][rad/s]$

$$\begin{aligned} \dot{x_1} &= x_2 \\ \dot{x_2} &= \frac{[F - bx_2 + mlx_4^2 sin(x_3)](I + ml^2) + (ml)^2 g sin(x_3) cos(x3)}{(I + m \cdot l^2)(M + m) - [mlcos(x_3)]^2} \\ \dot{x_3} &= x_4 \\ \dot{x_4} &= \frac{[(F - bx_2 + mlx_4^2 sin(x_3))cos(x_3) + (M + m) g sin(x_3)]ml}{(mlcos(x_3))^2 - (I + ml^2)(M + m)} \end{aligned} \quad (37)$$

Figure 9 graphically illustrates the numerical simulation obtained for Example 1. This figure is not yet the result obtained by E-TUNI, but by Runge–Kutta 4-5, available in Matlab, to numerically solve Equation (35). Therefore, the result obtained by E-TUNI will be compared later, numerically and graphically, with the graphic result of this figure. Also, in Figure 9, the following convention was used: (i) the blue dots in "x" represent the forward propagation, in high precision, of Runge–Kutta 4-5 over the dynamics of Equation (35), (ii) the blue dots in "o" represent the high precision backward propagation of Runge–Kutta 4-5 over the same dynamics, and (iii) the solid red lines represent the slope of the mean derivatives functions between two consecutive points.

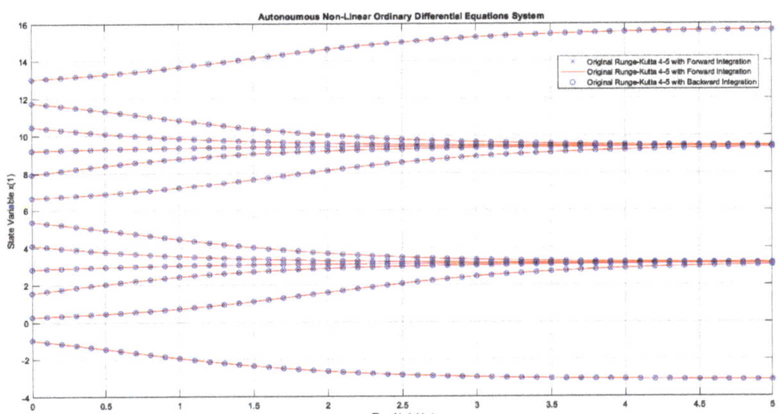

Figure 9. The dynamics of Example 1 solved with Runge–Kutta 4-5, available in Matlab with step automation through the "ode45.m" function, using forward and backward integrations.

Note that the integration step, as graphically presented, was $\Delta t = 0.1$. However, it is essential to notice that the Runge–Kutta 4-5 works internally with a varied integration step much smaller than this one to achieve the high numerical accuracy shown in Figure 9. So, both forward and backward integration were performed from $t_0 = 0$ to $t_f = 5$. In this case, as can be seen, the result obtained is perfect, as the points obtained by backward integration overlapped perfectly over the points with forward integration.

Figure 10 presents the first graphic result of E-TUNI, for the dynamics given by Equation (35). The blue dots represent the results obtained by E-TUNI and follow the same convention as in the previous figure. The green dots represent the results obtained by the conventional Euler Integrator, using the instantaneous derivative functions, also given by Equation (35). The two black dash-dot horizontal lines delimit the E-TUNI training range. Note that within the training range, the E-TUNI result was perfect, with both forward and backward integration. The line in Table 1 with the $Number = 1$ indicates the training data obtained for this case. In this way, 400 training patterns were generated, and 80% of them, 320 patterns, were effectively left for training. Note that in Table 1 the symbols (MSE_F) and (MSE_B) represent, respectively, the mean square error of forward integration and the mean square error of backward integration.

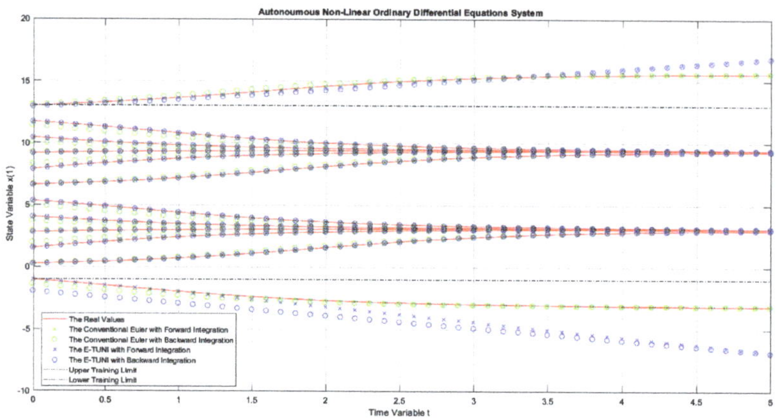

Figure 10. The dynamics of Example 1, comparing the conventional Euler integrator with E-TUNI, using forward and backward integrations with $\Delta t = 0.1$.

Note that outside the training region, E-TUNI has become inaccurate. However, to solve this problem, the training domain of the state variable should be increased. Note also that the conventional Euler presented a slight deviation in the backward integration concerning the forward integration in the given domain. Thus, in conventional Euler, this deviation becomes more critical and accentuated, which increases the integration step. However, in E-TUNI, the result does not deteriorate with the increase of the integration step.

Figure 11 presents the same result as the previous figure, but now using an integration step $\Delta t = 0.5$. The E-TUNI result was perfect, but the conventional Euler result was even worse. This confirms what was said in the previous paragraph. See Table 1 again in line $Number = 2$ to find out about the main parameters used in this training. Figure 12 presents the same result as the previous figure, but now using an integration step $\Delta t = 0.01$. In this case, the result achieved by E-TUNI is still perfect, and the result by conventional Euler is as well. The result, obtained by conventional Euler, was perfect in this case because a tiny integration step was used and equal to $\Delta t = 0.01$. Figure 13 presents a simulation using the integration step $\Delta t = 2 > 1$. Again, E-TUNI presented a perfect result, but the conventional Euler degenerated its solution.

Figures 14 and 15 deserve a little more attention. In Figure 14, as can be seen, the solution obtained by E-TUNI, through backward integration, was degenerate (see the zoom). In this case, the blue circle should lie perfectly on the solid red line. In Figure 15, the backward integration solution obtained by Runge–Kutta 4-5 was also degenerate. Both solutions turned out bad because the integration process was conducted for too long, over a point of stability. The zoom made in Figure 14 will be used to better explain this.

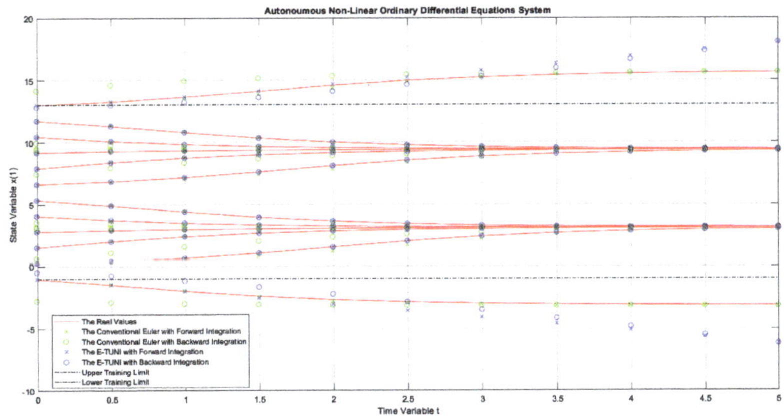

Figure 11. The dynamics of Example 1, comparing the conventional Euler integrator with E-TUNI, using forward and backward integrations with $\Delta t = 0.5$.

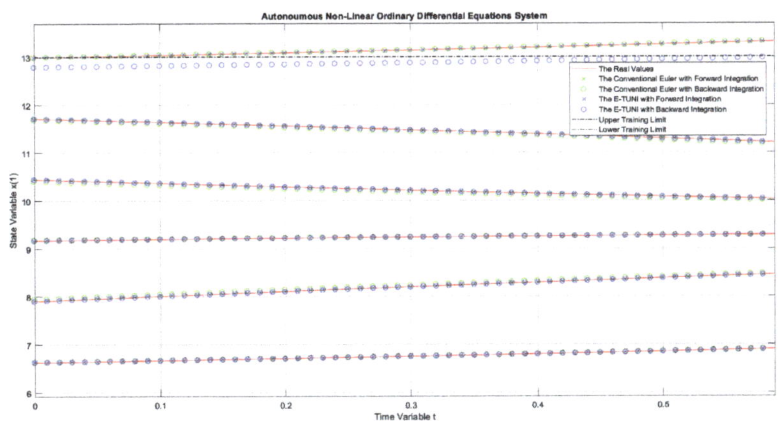

Figure 12. The dynamics of Example 1, comparing the conventional Euler integrator with E-TUNI, using forward and backward integrations with $\Delta t = 0.01$.

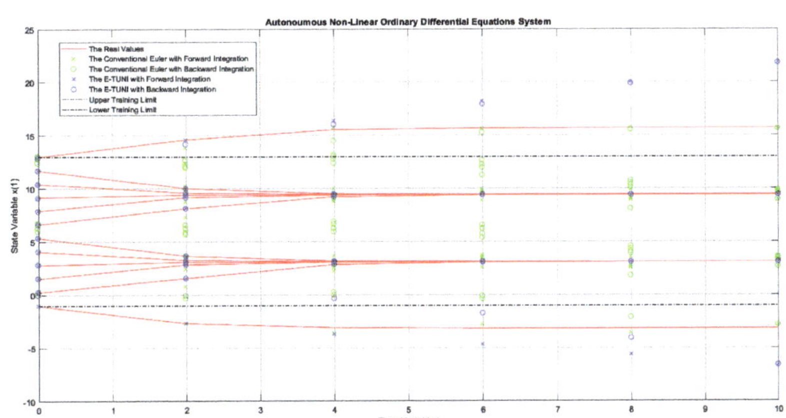

Figure 13. The dynamics of Example 1, comparing the conventional Euler integrator with E-TUNI, using forward and backward integrations with $\Delta t = 2 > 1$ and being integrated up to $t_f = 10$.

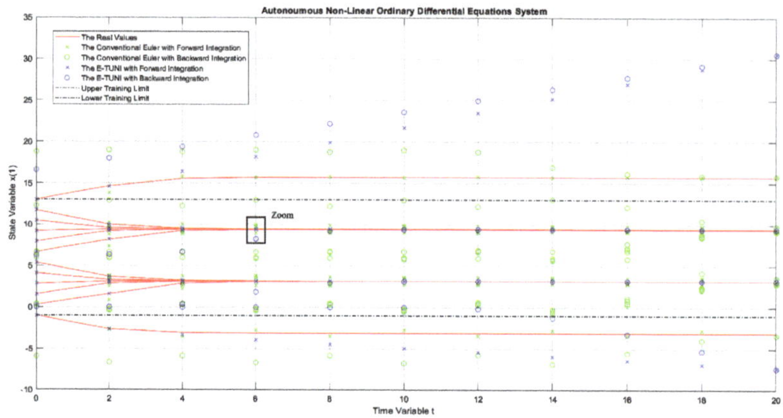

Figure 14. The dynamics of Example 1, comparing the conventional Euler integrator with E-TUNI, using forward and backward integrations with $\Delta t = 2 > 1$ and being integrated up to $t_f = 20$.

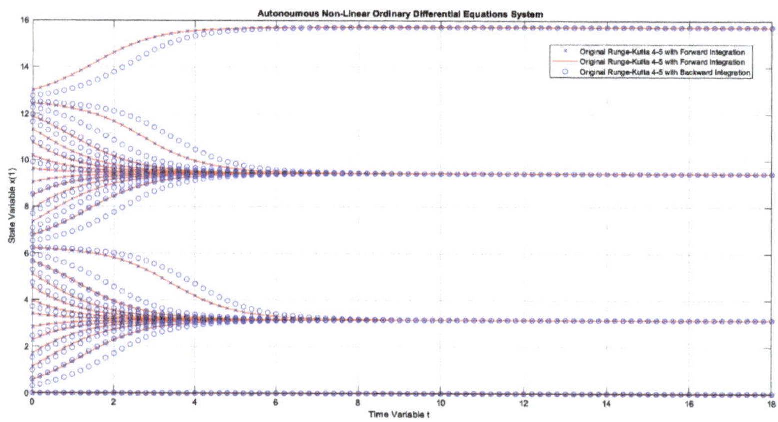

Figure 15. The same example as in Figure 9, but instead of being integrated up to $t_f = 5$, it was integrated up to $t_f = 18$ (notice the dissolution of the solution).

What is explained for Figure 14 is also valid for Figure 15. In Figure 14, the integration process was conducted from $t_0 = 0$ to $t_f = 20$. The biggest problem occurred when returning from $t_f = 20$ to $t_0 = 0$. For example, all families of curves confined between $y(0) = 0$ and $y(0) = 2 \cdot \pi$ at the initial instant $t = 0$ were confined in a much smaller interval than this one at the instant $t_f = 20$. Therefore, to work properly, backward integration would have to be trained with a much smaller mean squared error than the one achieved in Table 1 (line $Number = 5$). However, this is impossible to achieve using just the algorithm in [33]. Note that this task was also impossible for Runge–Kutta 4-5, as schematized in Figure 15. Therefore, the problem presented here is critical, regardless of the integrator used.

Figure 16 presents the first graphic result of E-TUNI for the dynamics given by Equation (36), which represents the dynamics of the non-linear simple pendulum. In this case, the superiority of E-TUNI over the conventional Euler is evident. An integration step $\Delta t = 0.02$ was used in this case. Figure 17 concerns the same previous example, but using an integration step $\Delta t = 5$. The conventional Euler was not presented in this figure because its result was bad, which would impair, therefore, the scale of the graph. Still referring to Figure 17, the main reason the backward integration turned out to be a bit bad at the end of the integration process is that the average training error became slightly oversized (see Table 1 in cell $Number = 7$). To solve this problem, it is enough to reduce the average training error of the artificial neural network used, but that is not always an easy task. Figure 18 demonstrates that, even for Runge–Kutta 4-5, the backward integration process of the simple pendulum can also be imperfect (see blue circles misaligned with the blue "x").

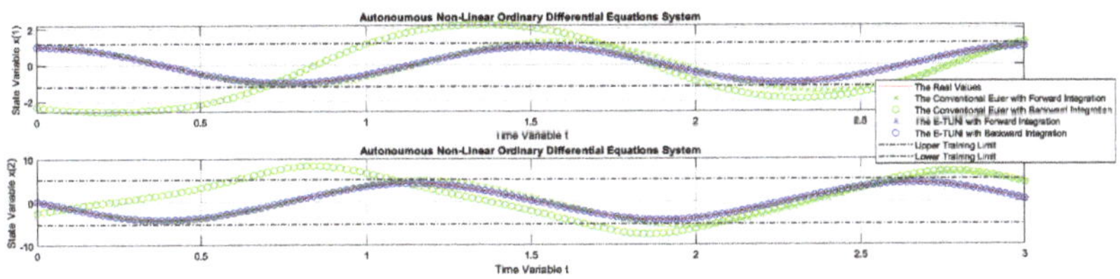

Figure 16. The dynamics of Example 2, comparing the conventional Euler integrator with E-TUNI, using forward and backward integrations with $\Delta t = 0.02$.

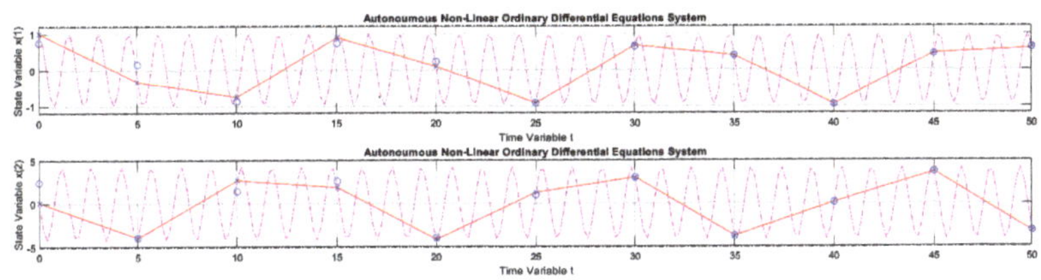

Figure 17. The dynamics of Example 2, comparing the conventional Euler integrator with E-TUNI, using forward and backward integrations with $\Delta t = 5 > 1$.

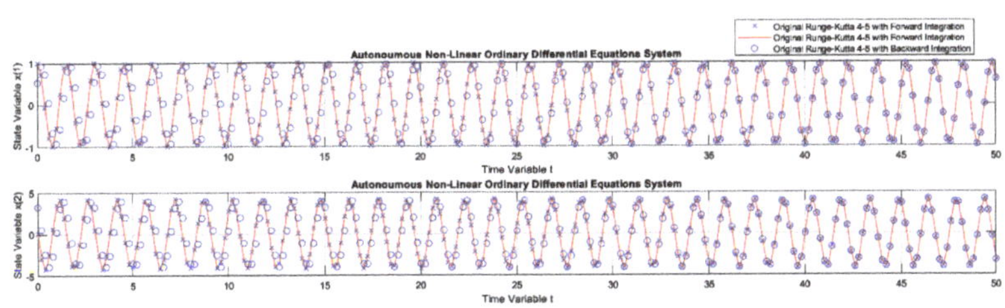

Figure 18. The dynamics of Example 2 solved with Runge–Kutta 4-5, available in Matlab with step automation through the "ode45.m" function, using forward and backward integrations.

Note that the solution from Equation (36), graphically presented in Figure 17, was much worse than the other solutions given in Table 1 (compare lines 6 and 7). This fact can be seen by checking the training mean square errors in Table 1 (line $Number\,7$), which were too high. This was most likely caused by two fundamental reasons. The first reason is that the E-TUNI local error is amplified by the square of the Integration step. However, the analysis of the global error would require further studies. The other reason, which is purely speculative, is the following: it is believed that when the E-TUNI integration step is very large if the solution of the real dynamical system becomes a non-convex function (concerning the line of mean derivatives in this same interval Δt), then the training becomes more difficult. However, this last argument still needs to be verified empirically and theoretically.

Figure 19 presents the first graphic result of E-TUNI, for the dynamics given by Equation (37), which represents the dynamics of the non-linear inverted pendulum. As can be seen, in this figure, Runge–Kutta 4-5 perfectly simulated this dynamic, both for forward and backward integrations. Figure 20 is the same case simulation but performed by

E-TUNI. Theoretically, Figure 20 is the same as Figure 19. They are just on different scales. Notice that in Figure 20 the E-TUNI simulation was perfect. However, the conventional Euler simulation (green dots) became confusing due to the numerical imprecision achieved by it. Furthermore, this caused an exaggerated change in the scale of the figure.

Table 1. Training data summary.

N.	Simul.	(MSE_F)	$(\Delta t)^2 \cdot MSE_F$	(MSE_B)	$(\Delta t)^2 \cdot MSE_B$	Patterns
1	Figure 10	1.951×10^{-10}	1.951×10^{-12}	1.035×10^{-11}	1.035×10^{-13}	320
2	Figure 11	2.157×10^{-13}	5.393×10^{-14}	1.322×10^{-14}	3.305×10^{-15}	320
3	Figure 12	3.097×10^{-12}	3.097×10^{-16}	4.768×10^{-14}	4.768×10^{-18}	320
4	Figure 13	8.636×10^{-12}	3.454×10^{-11}	2.169×10^{-12}	8.676×10^{-12}	320
5	Figure 14	8.636×10^{-12}	3.454×10^{-11}	2.169×10^{-12}	8.676×10^{-12}	320
6	Figure 16	7.921×10^{-11}	3.168×10^{-14}	6.770×10^{-11}	2.708×10^{-14}	580
7	Figure 17	1.845×10^{-6}	4.613×10^{-5}	1.892×10^{-6}	4.730×10^{-5}	580
8	Figure 20	1.774×10^{-10}	1.774×10^{-12}	6.645×10^{-11}	6.645×10^{-13}	640

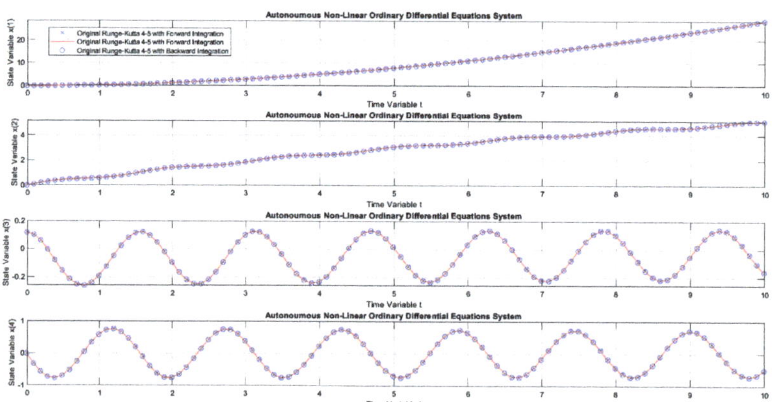

Figure 19. The dynamics of Example 3 solved with Runge–Kutta 4-5, available in Matlab with step automation through the "ode45.m" function, using forward and backward integrations.

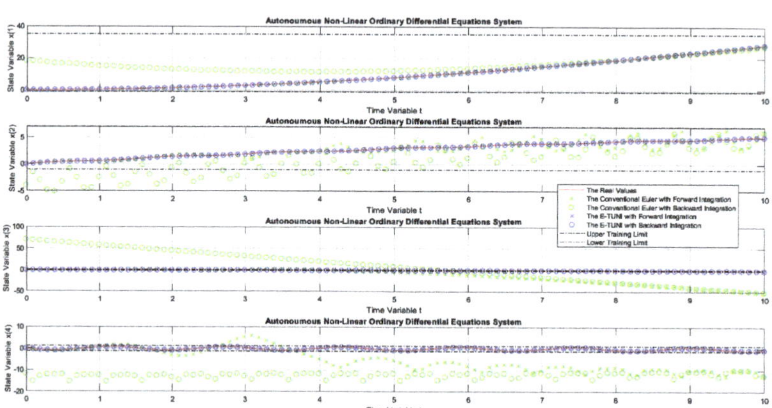

Figure 20. The dynamics of Example 3, comparing the conventional Euler integrator with E-TUNI, using forward and backward integrations with $\Delta t = 0.1$.

8. Conclusions

As far as we know, all previous work on E-TUNI was developed using only forward integration. Therefore, we present here, for the first time, a work that uses E-TUNI in a backward integration process. Three case studies were carried out. Non-linear and autonomous ordinary differential equations govern all three dynamical systems considered in this study.

The Euler-type Integrator designed with instantaneous derivatives is not very accurate. However, the E-TUNI has numerical precision equivalent to that of the highest-order integrators. It is interesting to note that the elegance of the theory of ordinary differential equations can be improved when combined with the theory of universal approximator of functions. This propriety is possible because artificial neural networks allow working with real-world input/output training patterns. This fact enables refining the final solution obtained by the first-order Euler integrator and estimator. Because of this, the E-TUNI can also be used to predict real-world dynamics (e.g., river flow and stock market forecasts, among others).

Additionally, we can call the forward mean derivatives functions positive mean derivatives functions. Equivalently, we can call the backward mean derivatives functions negative mean derivatives functions. Thus, we also conclude that the mean derivative functions depend on the integration step and are asymmetric. This propriety means training two distinct neural networks to simultaneously perform forward and backward integration. Unfortunately, the positive and negative instantaneous derivative functions are symmetric to each other.

Additionally, it would be interesting to carry out a future study of E-TUNI using deep neural networks instead of shallow neural networks, aiming to reach two essential points: (i) to be able to increase the number of training patterns (and, consequently, the domain of state variables) and (ii) try to reduce the training mean squared error, as this quantity is critical, in the case of modeling non-linear dynamic systems designed through artificial neural networks. Interestingly, E-TUNI is an excellent option to replace the NARMAX model and even the Runge–Kutta Neural Network (RKNN).

Finally, as another future contribution, one could consider changing the notation used in this article to something more straightforward, as explained in [34,35]. It is essential to notice that the same notation used in articles [16,26–28,31] was used here. In this sense, the most significant criticism would be not using the over-index i in the algebraic development of E-TUNI. However, in [31], the over-index i was used to help demonstrate the general expression of E-TUNI. Furthermore, E-TUNI could also be tested for dynamic systems using control variables.

Author Contributions: P.M.T. designed the proposed model and wrote the main part of the mathematical model. J.C.M., L.A.V.D. and A.M.d.C. supervised the writing of the paper and its technical and grammatical review. P.M.T. and G.S.G. (supervised by J.C.M., L.A.V.D. and A.M.d.C.) developed the software and performed several computer simulations to validate the proposed model. All authors have read and agreed to the published version of the manuscript.

Funding: This research received no external funding.

Institutional Review Board Statement: Not applicable.

Informed Consent Statement: Not applicable.

Data Availability Statement: The original contributions presented in the study are included in the article, further inquiries can be directed to the corresponding author.

Acknowledgments: I would like to thank my great friend Atair Rios Neto for his valuable tips for improving this article. Finally, I would also like to thank the valuable improvement tips given by the good reviewers of this journal. The authors of this article would also like to thank God for making all of this possible.

Conflicts of Interest: The authors declare no conflicts of interest.

Abbreviations

The following abbreviations are used in this manuscript:

ABNN	Adams-Bashforth Neural Network
E-TUNI	Euler-Type Universal Numerical Integrator
L-MTA	Levenberg–Marquardt Training Algorithm
MSE	Mean Square Error
MLP	Multi-Layer Perceptron
NARMAX	Nonlinear Auto Regressive Moving Average with eXogenous inputs
PCNN	Predictive-Corrector Neural Network
RBF	Radial Basis Function
RKNN	Runge–Kutta Neural Network
SVM	Support Vector Machine
UNI	Universal Numerical Integrator

References

1. McCulloch, W.; Pitts, W. A logical calculus of the ideas immanent in nervous activity. *Bull. Math. Biol.* **1943**, *5*, 115–133. [CrossRef]
2. Cybenko, G. Approximation by superpositions of a sigmoidal function. *Math. Control Signals Syst.* **1989**, *2*, 303–314. [CrossRef]
3. Hornik, K.; Stinchcombe, M.; White, H. Multilayer feedforward networks are universal approximators. *Neural Netw.* **1989**, *2*, 359–366. [CrossRef]
4. Cotter, N.E. The Stone-Weierstrass and its application to neural networks. *IEEE Trans. Neural Netw.* **1990**, *1*, 290–295. [CrossRef]
5. Hanin, B. Universal function approximation by deep neural nets with bounded width and ReLU activations. *Mathematics* **2019**, *7*, 992. [CrossRef]
6. Haykin, S. *Neural Networks: A Comprehensive Foundation*; Prentice-Hall, Inc.: Upper Saddle River, NJ, USA, 1999.
7. Goodfellow, I.; Bengio, Y.; Courville, A. *Deep Learning*; MIT Press: Cambridge, MA, USA, 2017.
8. Henrici, P. *Elements of Numerical Analysis*; John Wiley and Sons: New York, NY, USA, 1964.
9. Lapidus, L.; Seinfeld, J.H. *Numerical Solution of Ordinary Differential Equations*; Academic Press: New York, NY, USA; London, UK, 1971.
10. Lambert, J.D. *Computational Methods in Ordinary Differential Equations*; John Wiley and Sons: New York, NY, USA, 1973.
11. Vidyasagar, M. *Nonlinear Systems Analysis*; Electrical Engineering Series; Prentice-Hall Inc.: Englewood Cliffs, NJ, USA, 1978. [CrossRef]
12. Chen, D.J.L.; Chang, J.C.; Cheng, C.H. Higher order composition Runge-Kutta methods. *Tamkang J. Math.* **2008**, *39*, 199–211. [CrossRef]
13. Misirli, E.; Gurefe, Y. Multiplicative Adams Bashforth-Moulton methods. *Numer. Algor.* **2011**, *57*, 425–439. [CrossRef]
14. Ming, Q.; Yang, Y.; Fang, Y. An optimized Runge-Kutta method for the numerical solution of the radial Schrödinger equation. *Math. Probl. Eng.* **2012**, *2012*, 867948. [CrossRef]
15. Polla, G. Comparing accuracy of differential equation results between Runge-Kutta Fehlberg methods and Adams-Moulton methods. *Appl. Math. Sci.* **2013**, *7*, 5115–5127. [CrossRef]
16. Tasinaffo, P.M.; Gonçalves, G.S.; Cunha, A.M.; Dias, L.A.V. An introduction to universal numerical integrators. *Int. J. Innov. Comput. Inf. Control* **2019**, *15*, 383–406. [CrossRef]
17. Chen, S.; Billings, S.A. Representations of nonlinear systems: The NARMAX model. *Int. J. Control* **1989**, *49*, 1013–1032. [CrossRef]
18. Chen, S.; Billings, S.A.; Cowan, C.F.N.; Grant, P.M. Practical identification of NARMAX models using radial basis functions. *Int. J. Control* **1990**, *52*, 1327–1350. [CrossRef]
19. Narendra, K.S.; Parthasarathy, K. Identification and control of dynamical systems using neural networks. *IEEE Trans. Neural Netw.* **1990**, *1*, 4–27. [CrossRef]
20. Hunt, K.J.; Sbarbaro, D.; Zbikowski, R.; Gawthrop, P.J. Neural networks for control systems—A survey. *Automatica* **1992**, *28*, 1083–1112. [CrossRef]
21. Norgaard, M.; Ravn, O.; Poulsen, N.K.; Hansen, L.K. *Neural Networks for Modelling and Control of Dynamic Systems*; Springer: London, UK, 2000.

22. Wang, Y.-J.; Lin, C.-T. Runge-Kutta neural network for identification of dynamical systems in high accuracy. *IEEE Trans. Neural Netw.* **1998**, *9*, 294–307. [CrossRef] [PubMed]
23. Uçak, K. A Runge-Kutta neural network-based control method for nonlinear MIMO systems. *Soft Comput.* **2019**, *23*, 7769–7803. [CrossRef]
24. Uçak, K.; Günel, G.O. An adaptive state feedback controller based on SVR for nonlinear systems. In Proceedings of the 6th International Conference on Control Engineering and Information Technology (CEIT), Istanbul, Turkey, 25–27 October 2018; pp. 25–27. Available online: https://api.semanticscholar.org/CorpusID:195775331 (accessed on 20 November 2024).
25. Uçak, K. A novel model predictive Runge-Kutta neural network controller for nonlinear MIMO systems. *Neural Process. Lett.* **2020**, *51*, 1789–1833. [CrossRef]
26. Tasinaffo, P.M.; Rios Neto, A. Adams-Bashforth neural networks applied in a predictive control structure with only one horizon. *Int. J. Innov. Comput. Inf. Control* **2019**, *15*, 445–464. [CrossRef]
27. Tasinaffo, P.M.; Rios Neto, A. Mean derivatives based neural Euler integrator for nonlinear dynamic systems modeling. *Learn. Nonlinear Model.* **2005**, *3*, 98–109. [CrossRef]
28. de Figueiredo, M.O.; Tasinaffo, P.M.; Dias, L.A.V. Modeling autonomous nonlinear dynamic systems using mean derivatives, fuzzy logic and genetic algorithms. *Int. J. Innov. Comput. Inf. Control* **2016**, *12*, 1721–1743. [CrossRef]
29. Munem, M.A.; Foulis, D.J. *Calculus with Analytic Geometry (Volumes I and II)*; Worth Publishers, Inc.: New York, NY, USA, 1978.
30. Wilson, E. *Advanced Calculus*; Dover Publication: New York, NY, USA, 1958.
31. Tasinaffo, P.M.; Dias, L.A.V.; da Cunha A.M. A Survey About Universal Numerical Integrators (UNIs): Part II or Quantitative Approach. *Hum.-Centric Intell. Syst. (Preprint)* **2024**, *4*, 1–20. [CrossRef]
32. Ames, W.F. *Numerical Methods for Partial Differential Equations*, 2nd ed.; Academic Press: New York, NY, USA, 1988.
33. Hagan, M.T.; Menhaj, M.B. Training feedforward networks with the Marquardt algorithm. *IEEE Trans. Neural Netw.* **1994**, *5*, 989–993. [CrossRef] [PubMed]
34. Burden, R.L.; Faires, J.D. *Numerical Analysis*, 9th ed.; Brooks/Cole Inc.: Boston, MA, USA, 2011.
35. Cheney, W.; Kincaid, D. *Numerical Mathematics and Computing*, 6th ed.; Thonson Brooks/Cole: Belmont, CA, USA, 2008.

algorithms

MDPI

Communication

Means and Issues for Adjusting Principal Component Analysis Results

Tomokazu Konishi

Graduate School of Bioresource Sciences, Akita Prefectural University, Akita 010-0195, Japan; konishi@akita-pu.ac.jp

Abstract: Background: Principal component analysis (PCA) is a method that identifies common directions within multivariate data and presents the data in as few dimensions as possible. One of the advantages of PCA is its objectivity, as the same results can be obtained regardless of who performs the analysis. However, PCA is not a robust method and is sensitive to noise. Consequently, the directions identified by PCA may deviate slightly. If we can teach PCA to account for this deviation and correct it, the results should become more comprehensible. Methods: The top two PCA results were rotated using a rotation unitary matrix. Results: These contributions were determined and compared with the original. At smaller rotations, the change in contribution was also small and the effect on independence was not severe. The rotation made the data considerably more comprehensible. Conclusions: The methods for achieving this and an issue with this are presented. However, care should be taken not to detract from the superior objectivity of PCA.

Keywords: rotation of PCA; adjustment; unitary matrix

1. Introduction

Much of the data we handle consist of numerous measurement items, requiring multivariate analysis. Among the various methods available, principal component analysis (PCA) is particularly well-suited for scientific studies due to its limited methodological flexibility and high reproducibility [1–9]. The simplicity of PCA ensures that its results are consistent, regardless of the individual performing the analysis. This property is highly valuable in scientific research as it guarantees objectivity.

In PCA, we use singular value decomposition (SVD) to separate the matrix into unitary matrices (U and V) and a diagonal matrix D,

$$M = UDV^*,$$

where V^* denotes the conjugate transpose of V, and M represents the data to be analyzed, often centred or even scaled. The diagonal elements of D are sorted in descending order. Using this decomposition, the principal components (PCs) can be derived as follows:

$$Y = MV = UD \text{ and } Z = M^*U = VD$$

where the column vector of Y is PC for the samples and that of Z represents the PCs for the measurement items (e.g., PC1, PC2, etc.) [8]. Since U and V are unitary matrices, they satisfy the properties $U^*U = I$ and $UU^* = I$. This ensures that the row and column vectors are orthogonal and have a Euclidean norm of 1. Specifically, the inner product of a vector with itself equals 1, while the inner product with other vectors equals 0, confirming orthogonality. As a result, the column vectors of Y and Z are also independent. These vectors can be interpreted as rotations of the original matrix M, with the unitary matrices defining the axes and the diagonal elements of D determining their lengths.

Since the diagonal elements of D are sorted, PC1, PC2, and subsequent components account for the decreasing proportions of the total data variance. PCA thus identifies common directions within M and summarizes them in order of their significance. This ability to effectively reduce the dimensionality of multivariate data is a key advantage of PCA.

The advantage of PCA as a scientific method lies in its objectivity. Due to the limited degree of choice involved in its application, the results remain consistent regardless of who conducts the analysis. Given that science is inherently a collaborative endeavour, it is essential that participants are interchangeable at all times and that the implications of the data are clear and accessible to all. While there are other methods of multivariate analysis, such as cluster analysis and multiple regression analysis, none appear to be as well suited to scientific research as PCA in terms of objectivity. For instance, cluster analysis is inherently less suitable for scientific purposes due to the abundance of options available, which can lead to varying results depending on the choices made. This is because cluster analysis typically presents only one possible interpretation of the data. Additionally, PCA can be viewed as an upwardly compatible method, as it is capable of revealing multiple regression analysis outcomes. Furthermore, PCA has the ability to condense a vast amount of information into a well-defined and interpretable form. To illustrate this, consider a study examining changes in the mammary glands of rodents during pregnancy and childbirth. This study involved dozens of sample measurements and a microarray analysis of tens of thousands of genes [8]. Despite the sheer volume of data, PCA facilitated a clear and concise summary, elucidating the directional trends associated with pregnancy and childbirth, as well as the relationships between individual genes.

However, one of the drawbacks of PCA is its lack of robustness. Even a single outlier can cause errors in SVD. Naturally, noise affects the results. It is common for the identified directions to be slightly off. For instance, group positions or individual Y values may deviate slightly from the axes due to rotation. Since experimental data inherently contain noise, it is expected that noise-sensitive PCA will exhibit such errors. In such situations, there may be a temptation to adjust PCA results or train PCA to correct rotations.

Accordingly, PCA now offers various options for data manipulation. One approach, for instance, involves reducing the dataset to be subjected to SVD by selecting it in a specific way [10]. Another involves altering the direction of rotation derived from SVD [11,12]. Both orthogonal and oblique rotations are available, each offering several methods. Naturally, these variations result in different solutions, thereby compromising the objectivity of PCA. This subjectivity arises because the outcomes depend on the analyst's choices, which poses a significant challenge when analyzing scientific data. Oblique rotations, in particular, introduce a high degree of freedom, potentially leading to arbitrary results.

This study introduces a straightforward method to rotate data in relation to the two principal components while maintaining their orthogonality. The impact of such rotations on the original PCA results is evaluated in terms of the contributions of the principal components. The findings reveal that mild rotations do not significantly alter the results.

2. Materials and Methods

The test data used in this study were obtained from the practical training of students on a soil study. All calculations were performed using R (4.4.0) [13], and both the data and R code are provided as Supplementary Materials. Due to significant variability in the calcium data, the data were z-normalized for each item before applying SVD. Consequently, the centring point corresponded to the mean value of the data; these centring and scaling steps are among the few options available in PCA. The calculation method used for PCA is described in the Introduction. Additionally, since the number of measured items and the sample size differed considerably, I scaled the PCs by the square root of the sample size to facilitate biplots on a common axis [8], specifically $Y_s = Y/\sqrt{n_i}$, where n_i is number of items, and so on.

The angle of rotation, however, needed to be determined on a basis that was intuitive and easily understandable for all. In this case, an angle of 14 degrees was selected because it aligned the potassium (K) component of PC1 horizontally while simultaneously positioning the calcium (Ca) component of PC2 closer to the vertical axis. Alternatively, an averaging method could be employed to achieve an overall alignment of the components.

3. Results

An example of a slight deviation of Z from the axes can be seen in Figure 1 (blue), which represents the PCA of data obtained from measuring substances in soil. Samples P1 to P4 were collected from points found downward, at 50 cm intervals from the surface of the padding field. Overall, soluble Na, K, and Mg appeared to have infiltrated the soil (P3, P4, G3, and G4), while less-soluble Ca remained near the surface (P1, P2, G1, and G2). In unfertilized forest areas, these materials were notably less (F1–F4). The measured items effectively differentiated these samples, demonstrating the impact of human activity on the land—increased calcium levels may alter surface soil, and cations that have penetrated underground could contribute to salinity. However, upon closer examination, the figure appears to be rotated counterclockwise by 14 degrees.

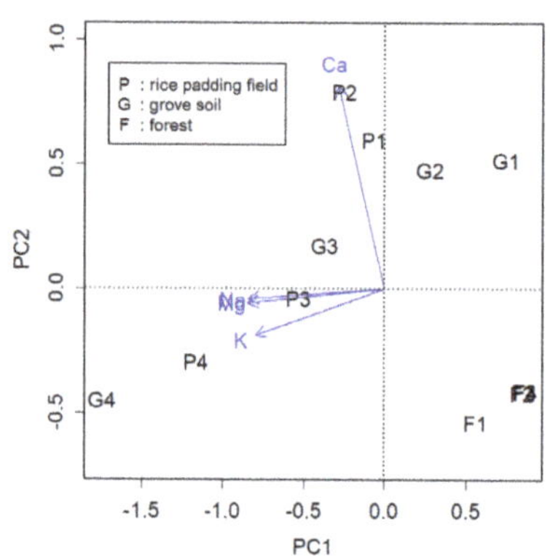

Figure 1. Results of material quantity measurements from soil material. Soil samples were obtained from a rice padding field, the grove soil of dry farmland, and a forest. The black and blue biplots show the PC of the samples, Y, and the PC of the items, Z, respectively. Soluble cations and water-insoluble Ca guided PC1 and PC2, respectively.

For example, when creating a two-dimensional plot using PC1 and PC2 for a matrix of four columns, these two column vectors can be rotated by taking the inner product of them with a rotation matrix, as follows:

$$R(\theta) = \begin{pmatrix} \cos(\theta) & \sin(\theta) & 0 & 0 \\ -\sin(\theta) & \cos(\theta) & 0 & 0 \\ 0 & 0 & 1 & 0 \\ 0 & 0 & 0 & 1 \end{pmatrix}. \quad (1)$$

This is almost the identity matrix, but an alteration has been made in the upper left. This rotation matrix is unitary, so $R(\theta)R(\theta)^* = I$, where I is the identity matrix. Consequently, if we rotate two columns of U, the adjusted U is $U_a = UR(\theta)$. The resulting rotated matrix U_a is also unitary, as $UR(\theta)\ \{UR(\theta)\}^* = UR(\theta)\ R(\theta)^* U^* = UIU^* = I$. Since U and V are related as mirror images, if we rotate one column vector, we need to rotate the corresponding column vector by the same amount. From $M = UDV^*$, we have

$$M = UR(\theta)R(\theta)^* D\left(V R(\theta)R(\theta)^*\right)^* = U_a R(\theta)^* D R(\theta) V_a^*. \tag{2}$$

The matrix that is sandwiched by the two unitary matrixes,

$$R(\theta)^* D R(\theta) = D_a, \tag{3}$$

is not necessarily a diagonal matrix, according to the twice rotations of D. Using D_a, $Y_a = YR(\theta) = MV_a = U_a D_a$ and $Z_a = ZR(\theta) = M^* U_a = V_a D_a$. Hence, the resulting column vectors of Y_a and Z_a are not necessarily independent. The degree of dependence depends on the rotation angle.

The actual result after rotating by 14 degrees is shown in Figure 2. Each item is now displayed closer to the axes (blue). Notably, the high calcium content in P1 and P2, as well as the abundance of soluble cations in G4 and P4, is more clearly visible. The question now is how much independence has been compromised. This becomes evident when examining the contribution of PC1.

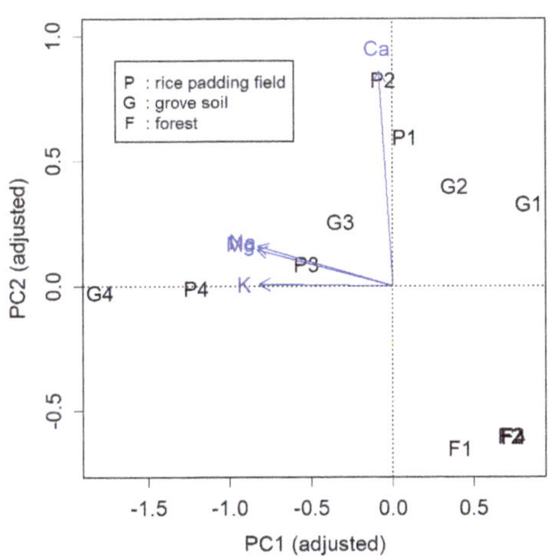

Figure 2. Adjusted results from Figure 1 by rotating the plot 14° clockwise. Each Z (blue) is more along the axis, with the characteristic G4 and P4 in PC1 of the Y (black), and the characteristic P1 and P2 in PC2 also appearing more along their respective axes.

Contributions are often derived from the diagonal elements of D. As D is a diagonal matrix, the contributions can be obtained from the component $\text{diag}(D)/\Sigma(D)$. However, since D_a is not diagonal, we need to calculate the Euclidean distance using the squared sum of each column vector. The contribution is then given by the distance/total distance.

From the perspective of PCA, the goal is to collect contributions primarily from the top PCs. In the case of rotating by 14 degrees, the loss appeared to be relatively small (Figure 3, dashed line). In this context, the most significant change occurred when rotating by 45 degrees, $\pi/4$ (dotted line). At this point, PC1 completely lost its advantage over PC2, and both had equal contributions. In addition, of course, if rotated by 90 degrees,

PC1 and PC2 would have effectively swapped places, and their contributions would have naturally switched as well. As the data's dispersion remained preserved, the sum of all total distances was maintained regardless of the degree of rotations.

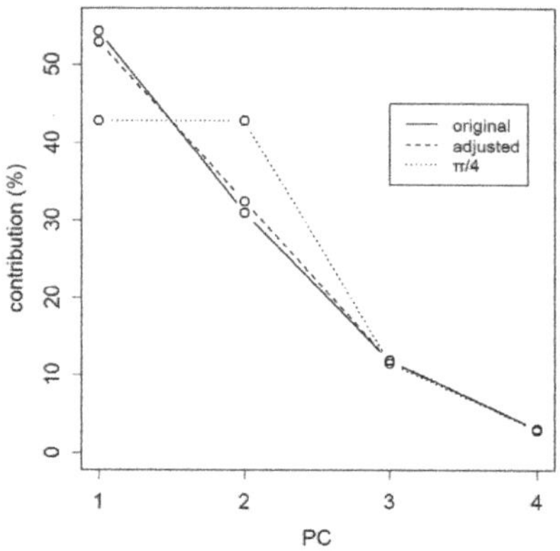

Figure 3. Contribution of each method. The original PCA is the most ideal diagram, with the greatest concentration on PC1; adjusting by 14° rotation weakens this concentration somewhat; finally, rotating by 45°, $4/\pi$, the advantage of PC1 disappears and becomes the same contribution as that of PC2. Rotation by 90 degrees, not shown here, replaces PC1 and PC2.

4. Discussion

In this analysis, PCA revealed two principal directions: PC1, which represented water-soluble ions that permeated the ground in a specific direction, and PC2, which represented a water-insoluble ion that remained on the surface. The samples were differentiated based on their respective depths within the soil, while forested areas that had not been treated were distinctly separated from the treated regions. The application of artificial rotation enhanced the clarity of this representation.

The results of the rotated PCA, albeit by a small angle, were more understandable. This somewhat compromises the priority of higher levels of PCs, but if the angle is not too large, the damage will not be too great. Understanding PCA plots can often be challenging, as PCA merely provides a summary, without revealing the specifics. Interpretation of the plot is left to the analyst. In this regard, enhanced readability could be highly appreciated. Notably, PCA is sensitive to noise. If this effect could be easily mitigated, this technique would be worth considering. To address this, it would be advisable to employ outlier detection methods provided by exploratory data analysis (EDA) [14,15]. This approach could potentially eliminate the need for artificial rotation, which would be a preferable outcome. In any case, introducing rotation complicates the process and reduces its objectivity. Unless there is a clear and compelling justification for its use, it would be more prudent to avoid it altogether.

It should be noted that this constitutes an active intervention by the analyst, potentially compromising PCA's objectivity. The beauty of PCA lies in its impartiality. Diluting this aspect would be regrettable and might even lead to data manipulation. If such adjustments were made, it would be essential to keep the original, unadjusted plot available. This original information is also necessary for others to check whether a rotation was necessary. Alternatively, the rotated plot could serve as supplementary material for explaining the results. Although this analysis focuses primarily on the two main principal components (PCs), there may be instances where it is necessary to rotate subordinate PCs as well. However, this would further diminish the objectivity of the results. In such cases, it is recommended to present visual representations, such as those illustrated in Figure 3, to provide a clear and transparent depiction of the data.

Supplementary Materials: The following supporting information can be downloaded at https://www.mdpi.com/article/10.3390/a18030129/s1: Rscript.txt: R code; and test.txt: the sample data.

Funding: This research received no external funding.

Data Availability Statement: The sample data and R codes are supplied in the Supplementary Data.

Conflicts of Interest: The author declares no conflicts of interest.

Abbreviations

The following abbreviations are used in this manuscript:

PC	Principal component
PCA	Principal component analysis
SVD	Singular value decomposition

References

1. Abdi, H.; Williams, L.J. Principal component analysis. *WIREs Comput. Stat.* **2010**, *2*, 433–459. [CrossRef]
2. Aluja, T.; Morineau, A.; Sanchez, G. Principal Component Analysis for Data Science. Available online: https://github.com/pca4ds/pca4ds.github.io (accessed on 22 February 2025).
3. Bartholomew, D.J. Principal Components Analysis. In *International Encyclopedia of Education*, 3rd ed.; Peterson, P., Baker, E., McGaw, B., Eds.; Elsevier: Oxford, UK, 2010; pp. 374–377.
4. David, C.C.; Jacobs, D.J. Principal component analysis: A method for determining the essential dynamics of proteins. *Methods Mol. Biol.* **2014**, *1084*, 193–226. [CrossRef] [PubMed]
5. Jackson, E. *A Use's Guide to Principal Components*; Wiley: Hoboken, NJ, USA, 1991.
6. Jolliffe, I.T. *Principal Component Analysis*; Springer: Berlin/Heidelberg, Germany, 2002.
7. Jolliffe, I.T.; Cadima, J. Principal component analysis: A review and recent developments. *Philos. Trans. R. Soc. A Math. Phys. Eng. Sci.* **2016**, *374*, 20150202. [CrossRef] [PubMed]
8. Konishi, T. Principal component analysis for designed experiments. *BMC Bioinform.* **2015**, *16*, S7. [CrossRef] [PubMed]
9. Ringnér, M. What is principal component analysis? *Nat. Biotechnol.* **2008**, *26*, 303–304. [CrossRef] [PubMed]
10. Jolliffe, I.T.; Trendafilov, N.T.; Uddin, M. A modified principal component technique based on the LASSO. *J. Comput. Graph. Stat.* **2003**, *12*, 531–547. [CrossRef]
11. Brown, J.D. Choosing the Right Type of Rotation in PCA and EFA. *JALT Test. Eval. SIG Newsl.* **2009**, *13*, 20–25.
12. Jolliffe, I.T. Rotation of principal components: Choice of normalization constraints. *J. Appl. Stat.* **1995**, *22*, 29–35. [CrossRef]
13. R Core Team. *R: A Language and Environment for Statistical Computing*; R Foundation for Statistical Computing: Vienna, Austria, 2024.
14. National Institute of Standards and Technology. NIST/SEMATECH e-Handbook of Statistical Methods. Available online: https://www.itl.nist.gov/div898/handbook/index.htm (accessed on 14 February 2025).
15. Tukey, J.W. *Exploratory Data Analysis*; Addison-Wesley Pub. Co.: Reading, MA, USA; London, UK, 1977.

algorithms

Article

Algorithms for Calculating Generalized Trigonometric Functions

Ivanna Dronyuk

Mathematics and Informatics Department, Jan Dlugosz University in Czestochowa, Waszyngtona Str., 4/8, 42-217 Czestochowa, Poland; i.dronyuke@ujd.edu.pl

Abstract: In this paper, algorithms for calculating different types of generalized trigonometric and hyperbolic functions are developed and presented. The main attention is focused on the *Ateb*-functions, which are the inverse functions to incomplete *Beta*-functions. The *Ateb*-functions can generalize every kind of implementation where trigonometric and hyperbolic functions are used. They have been successfully applied to vibration motion modeling, data protection, signal processing, and others. In this paper, the Fourier transform's generalization for periodic *Ateb*-functions in the form of *Ateb*-transform is determined. Continuous and discrete *Ateb*- transforms are constructed. Algorithms for their calculation are created. Also, *Ateb*-transforms with one and two parameters are considered, and algorithms for their realization are built. The quantum calculus generalization for hyperbolic *Ateb*-functions is constructed. Directions for future research are highlighted.

Keywords: *Ateb*-functions; algorithms; generalization of hyperbolic functions; numerical methods; tabulation of *Ateb*-functions; generalization of Fourier transform; calculation of *Ateb*-transforms; *q*-*Ateb*-functions

1. Introduction

The inspiration for this article is [1]. If the constructions of simple trigonometric functions are fascinating and their formulas elegant, their generalizations should retain these same properties. In this article, algorithms are presented for the generalized trigonometric function in the form of calculation *Ateb*-functions. First introduced in the late nineteenth century in [2], these functions were reintroduced and named *Ateb*-functions in [3]. Though considered rare or specific [4], *Ateb*-functions have been the focus of significant theoretical development and practical implementations since the 1960s, with continuous progress to this day.

The theory of *Ateb*-functions has seen significant advancements as detailed in [5–7]. In these works, the authors demonstrate that periodic *Ateb*-functions serve as solutions to a system of differential equations that model vibrational motion. Additionally, the application of *Ateb*-functions for data protection is explored in [8,9]. The *Ateb*-Gabor filter, an extension of the traditional Gabor filter, was introduced in [10,11] and has proven to be an effective tool for information protection. Initial quantum research findings are discussed in [12].

The theory of Ateb-functions and Ateb-transforms is advanced in this article, making significant contributions to modern applied mathematics. Additionally, a generalization of Ateb-functions for quantum calculus is introduced. The primary goal of this research is to develop algorithms for calculating Ateb-transforms. The research also explores the generalization of hyperbolic Ateb-functions in fractional calculus. The paper is structured as follows: Section 2 provides a brief overview of the Ateb-function theory. Section 3 introduces the well-known definitions and *Ateb*-function properties. The algorithms for the calculation of hyperbolic *Ateb*-functions are developed in Section 4. In Section 5, a Fourier transform generalization named *Ateb*-transform is introduced for the continuous case. *Ateb*-transforms in a discrete case are considered in Section 6. The algorithms for their calculus are developed. In Section 7, the *Ateb*-function generalization for quantum calculus is constructed. The conclusion summarizes the investigation and suggests directions for future research.

2. State of the Art

The concept of *Ateb*-functions is intricately associated with asymptotic techniques in engineering [13], as evidenced in various studies [8,9]. Following the influential publication of [3], significant advancements in *Ateb*-functions throughout the 20th century were primarily made at the University of Novi Sad in Serbia and Lviv Polytechnic National University in Ukraine. More than a hundred scholarly articles by Serbian researchers have enriched this area of study. Although this paper does not aim to provide an exhaustive review of these contributions, it is worth highlighting a few significant works, such as the recent research presented in [7], which offers analytical solutions for a model that illustrates oscillatory motion with two degrees of freedom and Van der Pol coupling. Furthermore, book [6] delves into various aspects of modeling oscillatory motion.

The theory of *Ateb*-functions began to take shape in Ukraine through the work published in [14,15]. The integration and differentiation formulas for these functions are presented in [16]. Their use in generating noise signals is thoroughly examined in [9], highlighting the benefit of being able to modify the characteristics of the noise signal by choosing suitable parameters for the *Ateb*-functions. Furthermore, periodic *Ateb*-functions are utilized for modeling traffic in computer network as discussed in [17]. Reference [18] also investigates how analytical solutions using *Ateb*-functions can be employed to analyze the effects of oscillation amplitude and the elastic properties of board materials on the oscillation frequency of machine control components.

In the 21st century, there has been a notable increase in research surrounding *Ateb*-functions across various regions. Reference [19] discusses these functions using alternative terminology, labeling them as generalized trigonometric functions without specifically mentioning *Ateb*-functions. In [20], the authors derive analytical solutions for nonlinear oscillators that extend an isotonic potential. The relationship between *Ateb*-functions and other forms of generalized trigonometric functions is introduced in [21] and further examined in [22]. Additionally, fractional calculus related to trigonometric and other functions, along with their characteristics, is elaborated upon in [23–26]. Despite their specific properties, *Ateb*-functions find extensive applications in various areas of mathematical modeling. Expanding their framework within fractional calculus is anticipated to greatly enhance their utility for different applications.

3. Definitions and Properties of *Ateb*-Functions

In this section, we show the nonlinear first-order differential equation system solution based on *Ateb*-functions. The results presented in this section are based mainly on references [3,8,9].

The concept of *Ateb*-functions facilitates the analytical solution of differential equation systems that characterize highly nonlinear processes in a medium with one degree of freedom

$$\begin{cases} \dot{x} + \beta y^m &= 0, \\ \dot{y} + \alpha x^n &= 0, \end{cases} \tag{1}$$

where α and β are some real constants, and

$$n = \frac{2\theta_1' + 1}{2\theta_1'' + 1}, \; m = \frac{2\theta_2' + 1}{2\theta_2'' + 1}, \; (\theta_1', \theta_1'', \theta_2', \theta_2'' = 0, 1, 2, \ldots). \tag{2}$$

Ateb-functions are mathematically defined through the inversion of the incomplete *Beta*-function. This approach not only defines these functions but also inspired their name, as *Ateb* is derived from inversing the term *Beta*. An incomplete *Beta*-function is defined by the next formula

$$B_x(p, q) = \int_0^x t^{p-1}(1-t)^{q-1} dt, \tag{3}$$

where p and q are real numbers. In the special case where $x = 1$, Equation (3) is simplified to the first-kind Euler integral:

$$B_1(p, q) = \int_0^1 t^{p-1}(1-t)^{q-1} dt, \tag{4}$$

which represents the *Beta*-function, denoted as $B(p, q)$.

For each x from the interval [0, 1], functions $B_x(p, q)$ and $B_1(p, q)$, defined by expressions (3) and (4), are non-negative and satisfy the following properties:

$$0 \le B_x(p, q) \le B_1(p, q),$$
$$B_x(p, q) = B_1(p, q) - B_{1-x}(p, q).$$

Let us discuss two specific cases:

$$p = \frac{1}{n+1}, \; q = \frac{1}{m+1}; \tag{5}$$

$$p = \frac{1}{n+1}, \; q = \frac{m}{m+1} - \frac{1}{n-1}, \tag{6}$$

where m and n are determined by Formula (2). When $p > 0$ and $q > 0$, then the *Beta*-function is well defined and determined. For other real values of p and q, the Beta function heads to infinity at $t \to 0$ or at $t \to 1$.

Ateb-functions for values (5) are named periodical, and those for values (6) are named hyperbolic or aperiodic *Ateb*-functions. System (1), if parameters m, n satisfy Formula (5), describes oscillatory motion, and, if m, n satisfy Formula (6), it describes hyperbolic or aperiodic motion.

If $m = 1$ and n is defined by (2), then system (1) can be rewritten as:

$$\ddot{x} + c|x| \cdot x^{\theta - 1} = 0, \tag{7}$$

where θ depends on the parameters θ_1' and θ_2' in Formula (2).

Let us evaluate the expression

$$\omega = \frac{1}{2} \int_0^{-1 \le y \le 1} t^{-\frac{n}{n+1}} (1-t)^{-\frac{m}{m+1}} dt. \tag{8}$$

where parameters m, n are determined by (5) and (2). Let us perform the placement of variable

$$t = v^{-n+1}. \tag{9}$$

Equation (8) is transformed into the following expression

$$\omega = \frac{n+1}{2} \int_0^{-1 \le v \le 1} (1 - \bar{v}^{n+1})^{-\frac{m}{m+1}} d\bar{v}. \quad (10)$$

In Formula (10), ω has a dependence from variable v, and from the parameters m and n. For the construction of *Ateb*-functions, we study the inverse dependence of v from ω. This function is unique-valued m and n, and the *Ateb*-sinus has a notation

$$v = sa(n, m, \omega). \quad (11)$$

Analogously, by substitution of the expression $t = 1 - \bar{u}^{m+1}$, from Formula (8) we obtain the following formula

$$-\frac{m+1}{2} \int_1^{-1 \le u \le 1} \left(1 - \bar{u}^{m+1}\right)^{-\frac{n}{n+1}} d\bar{u} = \omega. \quad (12)$$

For function u from ω for integral (12), there is a dependence m and n which is presented as *Ateb*-cosines and is noted as

$$u = ca(m, n, \omega). \quad (13)$$

Then, we prove the equation for *Ateb*-functions with periodical properties

$$ca^{m+1}(m, n, \omega) + sa^{n+1}(n, m, \omega) = 1. \quad (14)$$

From (10) and (12), it is clear: if $n = m = 1$, then we obtain the main trigonometrical identity $u = cos\omega$, and $v = sin\omega$, so *Ateb*-functions are generalizations for simple trigonometrical functions.

Also, it is proven that periodic *Ateb*-functions have period $2\Pi(m, n)$ where

$$\Pi(m, n) = \frac{\Gamma\left(\frac{1}{n+1}\right)\Gamma\left(\frac{1}{m+1}\right)}{\Gamma\left(\frac{1}{n+1} + \frac{1}{m+1}\right)}. \quad (15)$$

In (15), $\Gamma()$ is a Gamma-function.

For the creation of solutions for the differential equation system (1) in the case of (6) conditions, hyperbolic *Ateb*-functions are introduced.

Let us study the next expression

$$\omega^* = \frac{1}{2} \int_0^{0 \le Y \le \infty} t^{-\frac{n}{n+1}} (1 - t)^{-\frac{n}{n+1} - \frac{1}{m+1}} dt, \quad (16)$$

where ω^* is an independent variable $(-\infty \le \omega^* \le \infty)$, and m and n are parametrical variables, that are defined by expressions (2) and satisfy aperiodic conditions:

$$\frac{n}{n+1} - \frac{1}{m+1} \le 0. \quad (17)$$

Let us perform the variable substitution $\bar{V}^{n+1} = t^{-1}$; then, we obtain

$$\omega^* = \frac{n+1}{2} \int_0^{0 \le V \le \infty} \left(1 + \bar{V}^{n+1}\right)^{-\frac{m}{m+1}} d\bar{V}. \quad (18)$$

The dependence V from ω^*, and from the parameters m and n, from the integral (18), is called hyperbolic *Ateb*-sine and is noted

$$V = sha(n, m, \omega^*). \tag{19}$$

In a similar way, by the variable substitution $U^{m+1} = (1-t)^{-1}$, we obtain for the integral (15)

$$\omega^* = \frac{m+1}{2} \int_1^{1 \le U \le \infty} \left(\bar{U}^{m+1} - 1\right)^{-\frac{n}{n+1}} d\bar{U}. \tag{20}$$

The inverse dependence U from variable ω^*, and from the parameters m and n is named hyperbolic *Ateb*-cosines. It is noted as

$$U = cha(m, n, \omega^*). \tag{21}$$

From (18) and (20), we obtain

$$cha^{m+1}(m, n, \omega^*) - sha^{n+1}(n, m, \omega^*) = 1. \tag{22}$$

Hyperbolic *Ateb*-functions are defined in the interval, which can be calculated with the following formula:

$$2\Pi^*(m, n) = \frac{\Gamma\left(\frac{1}{n+1}\right)\Gamma\left(1 - \frac{2+n+m}{(n+1)(m+1)}\right)}{\Gamma(m^2 + m)}. \tag{23}$$

So hyperbolic *Ateb*-functions are defined in the interval $[-\Pi^*, \Pi^*]$.

4. Methods for Implementing Calculations of Hyperbolic *Ateb*-Functions

We use the Fourier series expansion to implement the calculations of *Ateb*-functions. Here is a well-known theorem from mathematical analysis: if a periodic function with period $2T$ is piecewise monotone and bounded on the interval $[-T; T]$, then the Fourier series constructed for this function is convergent at all points in this interval. For hyperbolic *Ateb*-sine and *Ateb*-cosine, these conditions are executed in the interval $[-\Pi^*; \Pi^*]$. So these functions can be expanded on this segment with a Fourier series. Since hyperbolic functions are differentiable, the Fourier series are convergent in the interval $[-\Pi^*; \Pi^*]$. And the hyperbolic cosine $cha(m, n, \omega^*)$ is an even function, so we obtain

$$cha(m, n, \omega^*) = \frac{a_0}{2} + \sum_{k=1}^{\infty} a_k cos\frac{k\pi\omega^*}{\Pi^*}, \tag{24}$$

where

$$\begin{aligned} a_k &= \frac{1}{2\Pi^*(n, m)} \int_{-\Pi^*}^{\Pi^*} cha(m, n, x) cos\frac{k\pi x}{\Pi^*} dx = \\ &= -\frac{m+1}{2\Pi^*(n, m)} \int_{-\Pi^*}^{\Pi^*} cos\frac{k\pi x}{\Pi^*} \int_1^x \frac{d\bar{x}}{(1 - \bar{x}^{m+1})^{\frac{n}{n+1}}} dx, k = 1, 2, \ldots; \end{aligned}$$

$$\begin{aligned} a_0 &= \frac{1}{\Pi^*(n, m)} \int_{-\Pi^*}^{\Pi^*} cha(m, n, x) dx = \\ &= -\frac{m+1}{\Pi^*(n, m)} \int_{-\Pi^*}^{\Pi^*} \int_1^{-1 \le x \le 1} \frac{d\bar{x}}{(1 - \bar{x}^{m+1})^{\frac{n}{n+1}}} dx. \end{aligned} \tag{25}$$

Since the hyperbolic sine $sha(m, n, \omega^*)$ is an odd function, we obtain the following Fourier series

$$sha(n, m, \omega^*) = \sum_{k=1}^{\infty} b_k sin \frac{k\pi\omega^*}{\Pi^*}, \tag{26}$$

Coefficients in this series are calculated according to the formulas

$$\begin{aligned} b_k &= \frac{1}{2\Pi^*(n,m)} \int_{-\Pi^*}^{\Pi^*} sha(m,n,y) cos \frac{k\pi y}{\Pi^*} dy = \\ &= \frac{n+1}{2\Pi^*(n,m)} \int_{-\Pi^*}^{\Pi^*} sin \frac{k\pi y}{\Pi^*} \int_0^{-1 \le y \le 1} \frac{d\bar{y}}{(1-\bar{y}^{n+1})^{\frac{m}{m+1}}} dy. \end{aligned} \tag{27}$$

The algorithm for hyperbolic *Ateb*-sine calculation contains the following stages (see Figure 1)

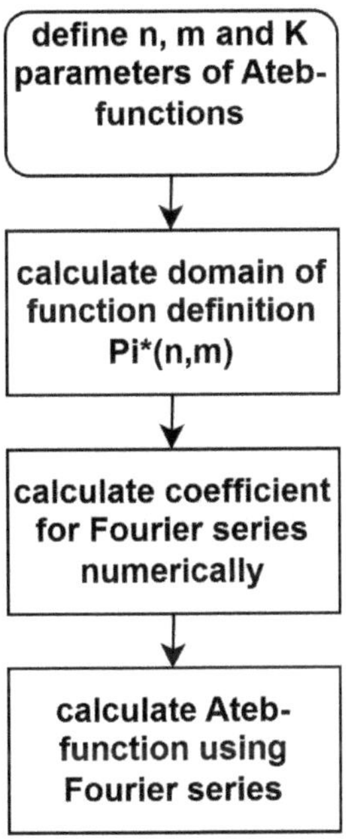

Figure 1. Schema for hyperbolic *Ateb*-function calculations.

1. Define parameters $n, m,$ and K-count of elements in Fourier series;
2. Calculate interval $\Pi^*(n, m)$ according to Formula (23);
3. Define step h for numerical calculation integrals and calculate coefficients of Fourier series according to Formula (27);
4. Calculate $sha(m, n, \omega^*)$ according to Formula (24).

For this algorithm's practical realization, we used $k = 5, h = 0.01$, and quadrature formulas to calculate the defined integral. When we have a value of $sha(m, n, \omega^*)$ to obtain the value of $cha(m, n, \omega^*)$ with the same parameters of n and m, we have two choices. The first one is the realization of the same scheme for calculation:

1. Define parameters $n, m,$ and K-count of elements in Fourier series (this step is the same as for hyperbolic sine);

2. Calculate interval $\Pi^*(n,m)$ according to Formula (23) (this step is also realized for hyperbolic sine);
3. Define step h for numerical calculation integrals for coefficients of Fourier series according to Formula (25);
4. Calculate $cha(m,n,\omega^*)$ according to Formula (26).

The second way for the calculation of hyperbolic cosine is using Formula (22). It is clear that the second way is easier and needs a lower count of calculations.

5. Algorithms for Calculation Space Transform Based on *Ateb*-Functions

Orthogonal trigonometric transform-based methods are widely used in the modeling and development of information transformation and protection systems. A signal $x(t)$ can be converted from the time domain to the frequency domain using a Fourier transform. In this section, at the beginning, we construct Fourier transforms for *Ateb*-functions. After that, we propose the Fourier transform's generalization based on *Ateb*-functions.

5.1. Orthogonal Trigonometric Transforms for Hyperbolic Ateb-Functions

Let us construct orthogonal trigonometric Fourier transforms for *Ateb*-functions.

These formulas are utilized to build a continuous spectrum of *Ateb*-functions. Taking into account the oddness of the hyperbolic *Ateb*-sine $sha(n,m,\omega)$, it has the ability to be depicted as a direct sine Fourier transform $Bs(n,m,x)$

$$Bs(n,m,x) = \int_{-\infty}^{\infty} sha(n,m,\omega)\sin(2\pi x\omega)d\omega. \tag{28}$$

Then, *Ateb*-sine can be depicted by the inverse sine Fourier transform according to the expression

$$sa(n,m,\omega) = \int_{-\infty}^{\infty} Bs(n,m,x)\sin(2\pi x\omega)dx. \tag{29}$$

Operating the property of the hyperbolic *Ateb*-cosine, that $cha(m,n,\omega)$ is even, we represent it in the form of the direct cosine Fourier transform $Ac(m,n,x)$

$$Ac(m,n,x) = \int_{-\infty}^{\infty} cha(m,n,\omega)\cos(2\pi x\omega)d\omega. \tag{30}$$

Then, *Ateb*-cosine is shown by the inverse cosine Fourier transform according to the expression

$$ca(m,n,\omega) = \int_{-\infty}^{\infty} Ac(m,n,x)\cos(2\pi x\omega)dx. \tag{31}$$

Now, we construct the Fourier transform generalization. A method of orthogonal transforms based on periodic *Ateb*-functions is developed. In the following, we will name it orthogonal *Ateb*-transform (OAT). The possibility of constructing OAT is grounded on the following statements. First, in [3], it is shown that *Ateb*-functions are a generalized case of ordinary trigonometric functions. Secondly, in [27], the orthonormality of the system of periodic *Ateb*-functions is proved. In [8], methods and algorithms for calculating *Ateb*-functions depending on the parameters are developed, which allows the proposed OAT method to be successfully used.

We will consider transforms based on periodic *Ateb*-functions.

5.2. Orthogonal Ateb-Transform with One Parameter

Let us consider that $m = 1$; in that condition, *Ateb*-sine and *Ateb*-cosine are presented as $sa(n, 1, t)$ and $ca(1, n, t)$. Let $x(t)$ be a real function; then, *Ateb*-transform can be shown in the following form

$$X(n, \omega) = A(n, \omega) - iB(n, \omega), \tag{32}$$

where

$$A(n, \omega) = \int_{-\infty}^{\infty} x(t) \cdot ca(1, n, \omega t)dt, \tag{33}$$

$$B(n, \omega) = \int_{-\infty}^{\infty} x(t) \cdot sa^n(n, 1, \omega t)dt. \tag{34}$$

If we note that *Ateb*-cosine is even and *Ateb*-sine is odd, we obtain inverse *Ateb*-transform with the following formula

$$x(t) = \frac{1}{\Pi(n,1)} \int_{-\infty}^{\infty} (A(n, \omega)ca(1, n, \omega t) - B(n, \omega)sa(n, 1, \omega t))d\omega, \tag{35}$$

where Π is a half-period of *Ateb*-function. The right part of Formula (35) depends on the parameter n.

The properties, i.e., the rate of increase or decrease, of the period of the *Ateb*-functions $ca(1, n, \omega t)$ and $sa(n, 1, \omega t)$ will vary depending on n. The dependence of the *Ateb*-function on the parameter n allows us to choose the form of $ca(1, n, \omega t)$ and $sa(n, 1, \omega t)$ corresponding to $x(t)$.

For the existence of the *Ateb*-transform for the function $x(t)$, it is sufficient to fulfill the same conditions that are sufficient for the existence of the orthogonal Fourier transform.

5.3. Orthogonal Ateb-Transform with Two Parameters

Let $x(t)$ be a real function; then, we construct a generalization of the known Fourier transform *Ateb*-transform in the form

$$X(m, n, \omega) = A(m, n, \omega) - iB(n, m, \omega), \tag{36}$$

where

$$A(m, n, \omega) = \int_{-\infty}^{\infty} x(t) \cdot ca^m(m, n, \omega t)dt, \tag{37}$$

$$B(n, m, \omega) = \int_{-\infty}^{\infty} x(t) \cdot sa^n(n, m, \omega t)dt. \tag{38}$$

where $ca(m, n, \overline{\omega})$ is the *Ateb*-cosine and $sa(m, n, \overline{\omega})$ is the *Ateb*-sine function. Taking into account the expression (14), we obtain the formula for the inverse transform.

$$x(m, n, t) = \frac{1}{\Pi} \int_{-\infty}^{\infty} \{A(m, n, \omega)ca(m, n, \omega t) + B(n, m, \omega)sa(n, m, \omega t)\}d\omega, \tag{39}$$

where $\Pi(m, n)$ are half-period *Ateb*-functions.

In the case where $n = 1$ and $m = 1$, the introduced Formulas (36)–(38) for *Ateb*-transform become well-known orthogonal Fourier transform formulas. And expression (39) becomes the inverse Fourier transform.

5.4. Method for Calculating Ateb-Transforms

In this section, we describe how to realize algorithms for the calculation of continuous *Ateb*-transform.

1. Define parameters n and m of *Ateb*-transform and function $x(t)$, the spectrum of which we will calculate;
2. Control the periodic conditions ;
3. Calculate the period $\Pi(n, m)$;
4. Define the interval $[-M; M]$ and step h for calculating integrals for $A(n, m, \omega t)$ and $B(n, m, \omega t)$ according to Formulas (37) and (38) and define interval $[-W; W]$ and step h_w for ω;
5. For current point w from the interval $[-W; W]$, calculate the values for $sa(n, m, wt)$ and $ca(n, m, wt)$, then calculate $A(m, n, wt)$ and $B(n, m, wt)$, and then calculate *Ateb*-transform according to Formula (36) .

The cosine and sine Fourier transforms are used for continuous functions. However, for problems related to information technology, it is more appropriate to use discrete functions and transforms. In this case, the discrete Fourier transform is used. Therefore, in the following sections, we will consider the construction of discrete *Ateb*-transforms.

6. Construction of Discrete *Ateb*-Transforms

6.1. One-Dimensional Discrete Ateb-Transform

Let us consider discrete *Ateb*-transforms (DATs). Let the signal be given in the form of a discrete sequence $S(p)$. Let us consider the functions $A(m, n, k)$ and $B(n, m, k)$ given by the following formulas

$$A(m, n, k) = \sum_{p=0}^{N-1} S(p) ca^m(m, n, -i\frac{2\Pi pk}{N}), k = 0, ..., N-1, \quad (40)$$

$$B(n, m, k) = \sum_{p=0}^{N-1} S(p) sa^n(n, m, -i\frac{2\Pi pk}{N}), k = 0, ..., N-1. \quad (41)$$

where p is the harmonic number, N is the sample size, $ca(m, n, \overline{\omega})$ is the *Ateb*-cosine function, $sa(n, m, \overline{\omega})$ is the *Ateb*-sine function.

Then, the direct DAP is given by the formula

$$X(m, n, k) = A(m, n, k) - iB(n, m, k). \quad (42)$$

We obtain an expression for the inverse transform in the form

$$S(m, n, p) = \frac{1}{N} \sum_{k=0}^{N-1} \{A(m, n, k) ca(m, n, -i\frac{2\Pi pk}{N}) + $$
$$+ B(n, m, k) sa(m, n, -i\frac{2\Pi pk}{N})\}, p = 0, ..., N-1. \quad (43)$$

The input signal $S(p)$ is formally transformed into the signal $S(m, n, p)$ under the action of the direct and inverse DAT. However, for fixed values of the parameters m, n, the value of the signal $S(p)$ can be reproduced.

6.2. Algorithms for Calculation of Discrete Ateb-Transform

Here, we will describe the algorithm for the calculation of discrete *Ateb*-transform with two parameters according to Formula (42).

1. Define parameters m and n;
2. Control periodic condition;
3. Define dimension of discrete signal N;
4. Define two N-dimensional arrays S for input signal and X for output signal;
5. Calculate $\Pi(n,m)$ period of function. Define other index k = 0 as array index.
6. Define $SumA = 0, SumB = 0$ the sums for calculation coefficients $A(m,n,k)$ and $B(m,n,k)$ and current index for sum $p = 0$.
7. Calculate elements $Ap = S(p)ca^m(m,n,-i\frac{2\Pi pk}{N})$ and $Bp = S(p)sa^n(n,m,-i\frac{2\Pi pk}{N})$ as current elements for summarizing;
8. Calculate $SumA = SumA + Ap, SumB = SumB + Bp$;
9. Calculate $p = p + 1$;
10. If $p = N$, then $X[k] = sumA - isumB; k = k + 1$; else go to step 6;
11. If $k = N$, then output array X.

As the results of the algorithm realization we have the spectrum $X(n,m,k)$ of discrete signal $S(p)$ created with discrete *Ateb*-transform.

7. Generalization of Hyperbolic *Ateb*-Functions to the Quantum Calculus

At the beginning, we present all definitions from q-analysis, which we need for future constructions. There, we introduced q-analysis, where the q-derivative is defined by the following formula [12]

$$D_q f(x) = (f(qx) - f(x))/(qx - x). \tag{44}$$

The q-analog for a real number, also called the q-bracket or q-number of b, is defined by the following formula [28]

$$[b] = (q^b - 1)/(q - 1). \tag{45}$$

The q-analog of the definite integral on a closed interval $[0;a]$ is defined by the following formula [29]

$$\int_0^a f(x) d_q x = (q-1)a \sum_{i=0}^{\infty} q^i f(q^i a). \tag{46}$$

The analog for the Gamma-function Γ_q-function is constructed as

$$\Gamma_q(t) = \int_0^{[\infty]} x^{t-1} E_q^{-qx} d_q x, \tag{47}$$

where $E_q^z = \prod_{i=0}^{\infty}(1 + (1-q)q^i z)$. An incomplete B_q-function is presented by the following formula

$$B_q(p,s,\omega) = \int_0^{\omega} x^{p-1}(1-qx)_q^{s-1} d_q x. \tag{48}$$

Let us construct the $q-$generalization for hyperbolic q-*Ateb*-functions. The generalization for the quantum calculus in a periodic case is presented in [30]. In conditions (6), we will have an aperiodic (hyperbolic) case. Let us introduce the expression

$$\omega = \frac{n+1}{2} \int_0^{0 \le V \le \infty} (1 + \overline{V}^{n+1})_q^{-\frac{m}{m+1}} d_q \overline{V}. \tag{49}$$

If we consider the inverse dependency V from ω, where conditions (6) are satisfied, we obtain the q-analog of hyperbolic *Ateb*-sine and we propose the following notation

$$V = sha_q(n,m,\omega). \tag{50}$$

Let us introduce the following expression

$$\omega t = -\frac{m+1}{2}\int_{1}^{1\leq U\leq\infty}(\overline{U}^{m+1}-1)_q^{-\frac{n}{n+1}}d_q\overline{U}. \tag{51}$$

In conditions (6), Formula (51) presents the inverse dependency u from ωt; it is named q-analog hyperbolic *Ateb*-cosine, and it is denoted as

$$U = cha_q(m,n,\omega t). \tag{52}$$

It is clear that if $q \to 1, m = 1$, and $n = 1$ in expressions (49)–(52), we obtain in the limit the usual hyperbolic functions. They are clearly the properties below, which follow from the definition of the q-analog of *Ateb*-functions.

$$sha_q(n,m,0) = 0; cha_q(m,n,0) = 1. \tag{53}$$

Extending the functions to the case of quantum calculus will provide new applications of these functions for solving future mathematical modeling problems.

8. Conclusions

The swift evolution of computing power has facilitated the creation of novel mathematical constructs and broadened their applications. A notable instance of this development are the q-*Ateb*-functions. Initially introduced in the 1960s, the computation of *Ateb*-functions as inverses of the incomplete Beta-functions presented considerable difficulties. However, significant advancements occurred around the turn of the century, allowing for the straightforward calculation of *Ateb*-functions on personal computers.

This paper briefly outlines the applications of *Ateb*-functions and proposes generalizations of the Fourier transform that leverage these functions for both continuous and discrete scenarios, accompanied by algorithms for their computation in each case. Additionally, it presents a generalization of hyperbolic *Ateb*-functions applicable to quantum calculus, further enhancing their potential uses. Looking ahead, future research is expected to delve into the applications of q-*Ateb*-functions, with intentions to create a numerical implementation for their calculation and to establish further properties. As scientific inquiry progresses, it is anticipated that new and unforeseen applications for q-*Ateb*-functions will arise.

Funding: This research received no external funding.

Data Availability Statement: The original contributions presented in this study are included in the article. Further inquiries can be directed to the corresponding author.

Acknowledgments: The author would like to thank the Armed Forces of Ukraine for providing security to perform this work. This work has become possible only because of the resilience and courage of the Ukrainian Army.

Conflicts of Interest: The author declares no conflicts of interest.

Abbreviations

The following abbreviations are used in this manuscript:

DAT Discrete Ateb-transform
OAT Orthogonal Ateb-transform

References

1. Kowalenko, V. Algorithms for Various Trigonometric Power Sums. *Algorithms* **2024**, *17*, 373. [CrossRef]
2. Lundberg, E. *Om Hypergoniometriska Funktioner af Komplexa Variabla*; Förf: Stockholm, Norvey, 1879.
3. Rosenberg, R. The Ateb(h) and their proporties. *Quart. Appl. Math.* **1963**, *21*, 37–47. [CrossRef]
4. Abramowitz, M.; Stegun, I. *Handbook of Mathematical Functions*, 9th ed.; Cambridge University Press: New York, NY, USA, 2016; p. 416.
5. Cveticanin, L. Generalized Krylov-Bogoliubov Method for Solving Strong Nonlinear Vibration. In *Lectures on Nonlinear Dynamics*; Springer: Cham, Switzerland, 2024; p. F1825. [CrossRef]
6. Cveticanin, L. Strong Nonlinear Oscillators. In *Mathematical Engineering. Analytical Solution*; Springer: Cham, Switzerland; Berlin, Germany, 2018; pp. 1–296. [CrossRef]
7. Kraljevic, S.; Zukovic, M.; Cveticanin, L. Oscillatory systems with two degrees of freedom and van der Pol coupling: Analytical approach. *Math. Methods Appl. Sci.* **2025**, *48*, 2474–2492. [CrossRef]
8. Nazarkevych, M. *Methods for Increasing the Efficiency of Printing Protection by Means of Ateb-Functions: Monograph*; Publishing House of the National University «Lviv Polytechnic»: Lviv, Ukraine, 2011; 188p. (In Ukrainian)
9. Dronyuk, I. *Information Protection Technologies on Tangible Media: Monograph*; Publishing House of the National University «Lviv Polytechnic»: Lviv, Ukraine, 2017; 200p. (In Ukrainian)
10. Dronyuk, I.; Nazarkevych, M.; Poplavska, Z. Gabor filters generalization based on ateb-functions for information security. *Adv. Intell. Syst. Comput.* **2018**, *659*, 195–206. [CrossRef]
11. Nazarkevych, M.; Logoyda, M.; Troyan, O.; Vozniy, Y.; Shpak, Z. The ateb-gabor filter for fingerprinting. *Adv. Intell. Syst. Comput.* **2020**, *1080*, 247–255. [CrossRef]
12. Kac, V.; Cheung, P. *Quantum Calculus*; Springer: New York, NY, USA, 2002.
13. Andrianov, I.; Awrejcewicz, J. *Asymptotic Methods for Engineers*; CRC Press: Boca Raton, FL, USA, 2024. [CrossRef]
14. Senik, P.M. On Ateb-functions. *Proc. Ukr. Acad. Sci. Ser. A* **1968**, *1*, 23–27.
15. Senik, P.M. Inversion of the incomplete beta function. *Ukr. Math. J.* **1969**, *21*, 271–278. [CrossRef]
16. Drohomyretska, K.T. *Integration of Some Ateb-Functions*; Physical and Mathematical Sciences; Bulletin of the State University «Lviv Polytechnic»: Lviv, Ukraine, 1997; Volume 46, pp. 108–110. (In Ukrainian)
17. Demydov, I.; Dronyuk, I.; Fedevych, O.; Romanchuk, V. Traffic Fluctuations Optimization for Telecommunication SDP Segment Based on Forecasting Using Ateb-Functions. In *Lecture Notes on Data Engineering and Communications Technologies*; Springer: Cham/Berlin, Germany, 2019; Volume 20. [CrossRef]
18. Rebot, D.; Shcherbovskykh, S.; Stefanovych, T.; Topilnytskyy, V. Vibration Effect Modelling Based Ateb-Functions for Printed Circuit Boards of Control Machines. In Proceedings of the IEEE 17th International Conference on Advanced Trends in Radioelectronics, Telecommunications and Computer Engineering, Lviv, Ukraine, 8–12 October 2024; pp. 370–373. [CrossRef]
19. Edmunds, D.E.; Gurka, P.; Lang, J. Properties of generalized trigonometric functions.*J. Approx. Theory* **2012**, *164*, 47–56. [CrossRef]
20. Ghose-Choudhury, A.; Ghosh, A.; Guha, P.; Pandey, A. On purely nonlinear oscillators generalizing an isotonic potential. *Int. J. Non-Linear Mech.* **2018**, *106*, 55–59. [CrossRef]
21. Ghosh, A.; Bhamidipati, C. Action-angle variables for the purely nonlinear oscillator. *Int. J. Non-Linear Mech.* **2019**,*116*, 167–172. [CrossRef]
22. Cveticanin, L.; Vujkov, S.; Cveticanin, D. Application of Ateb and generalized trigonometric functions for nonlinear oscillators. *Arch. Appl. Mech.* **2020**, *90*, 2579–2587. [CrossRef]
23. Cieśliński, J. New definitions of exponential, hyperbolic and trigonometric functions on time scales. *J. Math. Anal. Appl.* **2012**, *44*, 8–22. [CrossRef]
24. Al-Omari, S.K. On a q-Laplace–type integral operator and certain class of series expansion. *Math. Methods Appl. Sci.* **2020**, *44*, 8322–8332. [CrossRef]
25. Al-Omari, S.K. The q-Sumudu transform and its certain properties in a generalized q-calculus theory. *Adv. Differ. Equ.* **2021**, *10*, 247–255. [CrossRef]
26. Alatawi, M.S.; Khan W.A.; Ryoo C.S. Explicit Properties of q-Cosine and q-Sine Array-Type Polynomials Containing Symmetric Structures. *Symmetry* **2022**, *14*, 1675. [CrossRef]
27. Sokil, B.I. Nonlinear Oscillations of Mechanical Systems and Analytical Methods of Their Research. Ph.D. Thesis, National University "Lviv Polytechnic", Lviv, Ukraine, 2001; 36p. (In Ukrainianan)
28. Gosper, R.W. Experiments and Discoveries in q-Trigonometry. In Symbolic Computation, Number Theory, Special Functions, Physics and Combinatorics. In Proceedings of the Conference Held at the University of Florida, Gainesville, FL, USA, 11–13 November 1999; Garvan, F.G., Ismail, M.E.H., Eds.; Kluwer: Dordrecht, The Netherlands, 2001; pp. 79–105.

29. Koekoek, R.; Swarttouw, R.F. The Askey-Scheme of Hypergeometric Orthogonal Polynomials and its q-Analogue. *Delft Fac. Tech. Math. Inform. Rep.* **1998**, *98*, 18–19.
30. Dronyuk, I.M.; Shpak, Z.Y.; Demyda, B.A. Investigation of time scaling for the inverted Beta functions *Ukr. J. Inf. Technol.* **2019**, *1*, 72–75. [CrossRef]

algorithms

MDPI

Article

An Efficient and Accurate Adaptive Time-Stepping Method for the Landau–Lifshitz Equation

Hyundong Kim [1], Soobin Kwak [2], Moumni Mohammed [3], Seungyoon Kang [2], Seokjun Ham [2] and Junseok Kim [2,*]

1 Department of Mathematics and Physics, Gangneung-Wonju National University, Gangneung 25457, Republic of Korea; hdkim@gwnu.ac.kr
2 Department of Mathematics, Korea University, Seoul 02841, Republic of Korea; soobin23@korea.ac.kr (S.K.); heroe2401@korea.ac.kr (S.K.); seokjun@korea.ac.kr (S.H.)
3 MAMCS Group, FST Errachidia, Moulay Ismail University of Meknes, Boutalamine, P.O. Box 509, 52000 Errachidia, Morocco; md.moumni@gmail.com
* Correspondence: cfdkim@korea.ac.kr; Tel.: +82-2-3290-3077

Abstract: This article presents an efficient and accurate adaptive time-stepping finite difference method (FDM) for solving the Landau–Lifshitz (LL) equation, which is an important mathematical model in understanding magnetic materials and processes. Our proposed algorithm strategically selects an adaptive time step, ensuring that the maximum displacement falls within a predefined tolerance threshold. Furthermore, this adaptive approach allows the utilization of larger time steps near equilibrium states and results in faster computations. For example, we introduce a numerical test where the adaptive time step decreases from 3.05×10^{-7} to 3.52×10^{-9}. If a uniform time step is applied, around a 100 times smaller time step must be applied at unnecessary cases. To demonstrate the high performance of our proposed algorithm, we conduct several characteristic benchmark tests. The computational results confirm that the proposed algorithm is efficient and accurate. Overall, our adaptive time-stepping FDM offers a promising solution for accurately and efficiently solving the LL equation and contributes to advancements in the understanding and analysis of magnetic phenomena.

Keywords: adaptive time-stepping algorithm; Landau–Lifshitz equation; finite difference method

1. Introduction

The Landau–Lifshitz (LL) equation, first proposed in 1935 by the distinguished physicists Lev Landau and Evgeny Lifshitz in their seminal work [1], stands as a cornerstone in the realm of theoretical physics, particularly in the study of ferromagnetism. This mathematical framework has evolved into a fundamental tool, serving as a bedrock for understanding and predicting the behavior of magnetic materials, and has found widespread applications, especially within the magnetic recording industry. The LL equation plays a pivotal role in elucidating the dynamic properties of ferromagnetic materials, which are characterized by the alignment of magnetic moments in parallel. Its significance lies in providing a theoretical foundation for describing the evolution of magnetization in response to external perturbations, such as magnetic fields or temperature changes. This predictive capability is invaluable for designing and optimizing magnetic recording technologies, where the precise control of magnetization dynamics is crucial for achieving high-performance data storage devices.

Over the years, advancements in our understanding of condensed matter physics and computational capabilities have led to refinements and extensions of the LL equation.

Researchers have incorporated additional factors, such as quantum mechanical effects and spin transport phenomena, to enhance its accuracy and applicability to a broader range of magnetic materials. This ongoing refinement ensures that the LL equation remains a versatile and reliable tool in addressing contemporary challenges in materials science and technology. Beyond its immediate applications in the magnetic recording industry, the LL equation has contributed to the exploration of novel magnetic phenomena and exotic states of matter. Researchers continue to leverage its theoretical framework to investigate emergent magnetic behaviors in various systems, including spintronics and magnetic nanoparticles. The equation's adaptability and predictive power make it a valuable asset in the quest for new materials with unique magnetic properties, holding promise for future technological innovations.

The LL equation under consideration in this paper is expressed in a particular mathematical form, and it is presented as follows:

$$\frac{\partial \mathbf{m}(x,t)}{\partial t} = -\mathbf{m}(x,t) \times \Delta \mathbf{m}(x,t) + \mathbf{f}(x,t), \;\; x \in \Omega, \;\; 0 < t \leq T \tag{1}$$

In the context of this formulation, the magnetization vector field is represented as $\mathbf{m}(x,t) = (u(x,t), v(x,t), w(x,t))$, where x is a spatial variable and t denotes time. The domain, denoted by Ω and defined as $\Omega = (L_x, \; R_x)$, encompasses the spatial extent of the system. On the boundary of the domain, denoted as $\partial\Omega$, we consider either the zero Neumann boundary or periodic boundary conditions, depending on the specific requirements of the analysis.

The classical LL equation stands as a sturdy theoretical foundation, offering valuable quantitative insights into the intricate dynamics of magnetization within ferromagnetic materials. While analytical solutions for the LL equation [2] are attainable under certain limiting conditions, the inherent non-linearity of the equation demands numerical treatments for a more expansive and realistic comprehension. Expanded models such as the LL–Gilbert–Slonczewski equation [3] also require numerical solutions. The adoption of numerical methods becomes imperative to delve into the nuanced and rich dynamics characterizing the evolution of magnetization. In practical scenarios, where the LL equation captures the complex interplay of magnetic moments in ferromagnets, relying solely on analytical solutions may prove insufficient due to the intricate non-linearities involved. Consequently, numerical methods emerge as indispensable tools, allowing researchers to explore the dynamic evolution of magnetization in a broader parameter space and under diverse conditions. The application of numerical treatments not only enhances the versatility of studying the LL equation but also enables a more comprehensive investigation into the various factors influencing magnetization dynamics. By leveraging numerical methods, researchers can simulate and analyze complex scenarios that may be challenging or impractical to address solely through analytical means. This approach becomes particularly crucial when dealing with real-world materials exhibiting diverse magnetic behaviors, where the robustness and adaptability of numerical methods play a pivotal role in uncovering the full spectrum of magnetization dynamics.

Before immersing ourselves in the intricacies of the adaptive time-stepping method tailored for the LL Equation (1), it is instructive to survey some noteworthy prior investigations in the field. Jeong and Kim, for instance, introduced a Crank–Nicolson scheme and an innovative, robust, accurate, and rapid numerical method as solutions for the LL equation [4,5]. Sharma et al. [6] adopted the adaptive time-step variational integrator to preserve momentum and energy. Moumni and Tilioua [7] contributed to the discourse by presenting a semi-implicit finite difference method (FDM) designed for the mathematical model that encapsulates the dynamics of magnetization, incorporating inertial effects into their framework. Li et al. proposed a Gauss–Seidel projection method with unconditional stability for the numerical solution of the LL equation, employing the Gauss–Seidel method [8]. Janneli [9] proposed an adaptive procedure with a step size selection function to solve time-fractional advection–diffusion–reaction models. Step sizes are adapted according to the behavior of the solution. Wang et al. devised a methodology combining a Gauss–Seidel method of an implicit fractional-step solver for the gyromagnetic term with the projection scheme to address the heat flow of harmonic maps [10]. Adaptive methods can be applied to other areas such as the adaptive signal for time-frequency domain to conduct quilted frames [11]. Meanwhile, Alouges et al. explored the numerical solution using the finite element method (FEM) in their works [12–14]. A Fourier spectral method was employed by Moumni et al. to approximate the solution of the LL equation, showcasing the versatility of different numerical approaches [15]. For a comprehensive exploration of numerical methods applicable to the LL equation, a plethora of references are available. Wang and Wang's work [16], Yang's stability analysis [17], Carstensen's insights [18], Bastos et al.'s magnetic domain modeling [19], and Cai et al.'s exploration of error analysis [20] provide detailed insights into the diverse methodologies employed to tackle the challenges posed by the LL equation. Chen et al. [21] proposed a second-order semi-implicit method based on the backward difference method for the LL equation. They conducted a thorough analysis of their proposed scheme and presented the results of convergence tests. These references collectively offer a rich tapestry of numerical strategies, laying the groundwork for a deeper understanding and development of effective solution methodologies for the LL equation.

In real-world applications, finding solutions to boundary value problems involving partial differential equations often necessitates the application of numerical techniques. Among the predominant methodologies utilized are the FEM [22], finite volume method (FVM), FDM [23–26], and spectral method (SM) [27]. Krivovichev [26] proposed an optimized Runge–Kutta scheme with higher-order derivatives to solve parabolic and hyperbolic partial differential equations. Numerical simulations compared the Mead and Renaut methods with the proposed method by solving the linear advection equation, showing superior stability and applicability. Christou et al. [27] proposed an SM using the Christov functions to solve the problem formulated by the LL and magnetostatic equations. Numerical simulations showed good agreement between the exact and numerical solution. These numerical approaches typically employ a fixed step size, which may not be optimal across a diverse array of problems. Recent developments have introduced alternative techniques, particularly those based on adaptive time-stepping methods, offering distinct advantages over traditional approaches such as FEM, FVM, FDM, and SM. Adaptive time-stepping methods automatically adjust the size of temporal step according to the local characteristics of the problem, allowing for dynamic adaptation to the varying complexities inherent in the solution [28]. Cheng and Shen [29] proposed an adaptive time stepping method based on the energy decreasing scheme, which is an unconditionally energy stable method for the LL equation. As shown through the numerical results, the adaptive time-stepping method is computationally more efficient than a typical semi-implicit method.

Recently, He et al. [30] presented a family of high-order computation methods for the Landau–Lifshitz–Gilbert equation, using Gauss–Legendre quadrature to achieve arbitrary-order accuracy while preserving geometrical properties such as constant magnetization magnitude and Lyapunov structure, validated through theoretical analysis and numerical experiments. Cai et al. [20] analyzed a second-order accurate, linear computational method for the LL equation with large damping parameters, and they provided a rigorous error estimate and addressed the stability challenges of the non-linear projection step, which ensures efficiency by solving only a linear system with constant coefficients at each time step.

The primary purpose of this study is to propose an efficient and simple adaptive time-stepping FDM for solving the LL equation by strategically selecting time steps to maintain displacement within a tolerance, which enables larger steps near equilibrium for faster computations. Unlike traditional adaptive time-stepping methods, the proposed approach does not rely on an iterative process to determine the appropriate time step within a specified tolerance. Instead, the proposed method is a single-step method. Cheng and Shen [29] developed two classes of length-preserving methods for the LL equation using distinct Lagrange multiplier approaches, including efficient higher-order predictor-corrector methods and energy-dissipative schemes, validated through numerical experiments and comparisons with existing methods.

The structure of this paper is delineated as follows: Section 2 introduces the algorithm proposed in this study for the numerical solution. Computational experiments conducted with the proposed method are detailed in Section 3. The paper concludes with summarizing remarks in Section 4.

2. Numerical Method

2.1. Discretization

We shall discretize the given domain $\Omega = (L_x, R_x)$ as $\Omega_h = \{x_i | x_i = L_x + (i - 0.5)h,\ i = 1, \ldots, N_x\}$, where $h = (R_x - L_x)/N_x$ is a space step size and N_x is the number of grid points; see Figure 1.

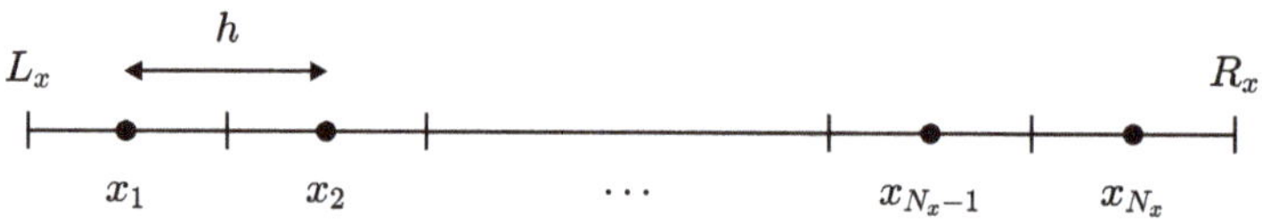

Figure 1. Cell centered computational domain grid.

We simply denote a numerical solution as

$$\mathbf{m}_i^n = \mathbf{m}(x_i, t^n) = (u_i^n,\ v_i^n,\ w_i^n) = (u(x_i, t^n),\ v(x_i, t^n),\ w(x_i, t^n)),$$

where $t^n = t^{n-1} + \Delta t^n$, for $n \geq 1$, Δt^n is the nonuniform time step size, and $t^0 = 0$. The visualization of $\mathbf{m}_i^n$ is shown in Figure 2.

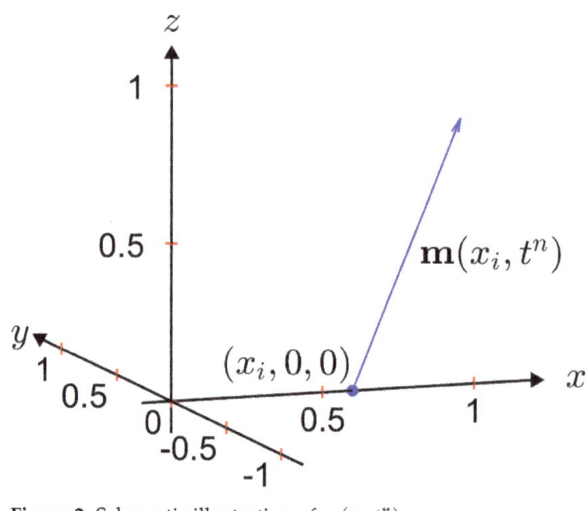

Figure 2. Schematic illustration of $\mathbf{m}(x_i, t^n)$.

Similarly, $\mathbf{f}_i^n = \mathbf{f}(x_i, t^n)$. The explicit Euler scheme is given as

$$\frac{\mathbf{m}_i^{n+1} - \mathbf{m}_i^n}{\Delta t^{n+1}} = -\mathbf{m}_i^n \times \Delta_h \mathbf{m}_i^n + \mathbf{f}_i^n, \ \ 1 \le i \le N_x \text{ and } 0 \le n \le N_t. \tag{2}$$

where the discrete Laplacian is defined as $\Delta_h \mathbf{m}_i^n = (\mathbf{m}_{i+1}^n - 2\mathbf{m}_i^n + \mathbf{m}_{i-1}^n)/h^2$, and N_t is the number of iterations. The periodic boundary condition ($\mathbf{m}_0^n = \mathbf{m}_{N_x}^n$ and $\mathbf{m}_{N_x+1}^n = \mathbf{m}_1^n$) is applied for $n \ge 0$. That is,

$$\begin{aligned} \Delta_h \mathbf{m}_1^n &= \frac{\mathbf{m}_2^n - 2\mathbf{m}_1^n + \mathbf{m}_0^n}{h^2} = \frac{\mathbf{m}_2^n - 2\mathbf{m}_1^n + \mathbf{m}_{N_x}^n}{h^2}, \\ \Delta_h \mathbf{m}_{N_x}^n &= \frac{\mathbf{m}_{N_x+1}^n - 2\mathbf{m}_{N_x}^n + \mathbf{m}_{N_x-1}^n}{h^2} = \frac{\mathbf{m}_1^n - 2\mathbf{m}_{N_x}^n + \mathbf{m}_{N_x-1}^n}{h^2}. \end{aligned}$$

Define the discrete energy function [31] as follows:

$$\begin{aligned} E(\mathbf{m}^n) &= h \sum_{i=1}^{N_x} |\nabla \mathbf{m}_i^n|^2 = h \sum_{i=1}^{N_x} \left| \frac{\mathbf{m}_{i+1}^n - \mathbf{m}_i^n}{h} \right|^2 \\ &= \frac{1}{h} \sum_{i=1}^{N_x} \left[(u_{i+1}^n - u_i^n)^2 + (v_{i+1}^n - v_i^n)^2 + (w_{i+1}^n - w_i^n)^2 \right]. \end{aligned}$$

In particular, the energy function is conserved when the forcing term $\mathbf{f} = 0$ [23].

2.2. Adaptive Time-Stepping Algorithm

Now, we present the adaptive time-stepping method. We set a maximum displacement of the numerical solution within a single time step by a tolerance *tol*. Multiplying both sides of Equation (16) by Δt^{n+1}, we obtain

$$\mathbf{m}_i^{n+1} - \mathbf{m}_i^n = \Delta t^{n+1} \big(-\mathbf{m}_i^n \times \Delta_h \mathbf{m}_i^n + \mathbf{f}_i^n \big), \ \ 1 \le i \le N_x. \tag{3}$$

A maximum norm is defined as follows:

$$\|\mathbf{m}\|_\infty = \max_{1 \le i \le N_x} |\mathbf{m}_i|. \tag{4}$$

Then, from Equation (3), we require that the following condition be satisfied:

$$\|\mathbf{m}^{n+1} - \mathbf{m}^n\|_\infty = \Delta t^{n+1} \| -\mathbf{m}^n \times \Delta_h \mathbf{m}^n + \mathbf{f}^n \|_\infty \le tol. \tag{5}$$

In this study, we use the maximum norm instead of the l^2-norm, which measures the average, because the maximum norm is more effective for assessing the largest individual component in a vector and ensures that no single variable dominates the vector's magnitude. From Equation (5), we have the constraint of the time step sizes:

$$\Delta t^{n+1} \le \frac{tol}{\| -\mathbf{m}^n \times \Delta_h \mathbf{m}^n + \mathbf{f}^n \|_\infty}. \tag{6}$$

Then, we use

$$\Delta t^{n+1} = \min\left(\frac{tol}{\| -\mathbf{m}^n \times \Delta_h \mathbf{m}^n + \mathbf{f}^n \|_\infty}, \ \Delta t_{\max} \right), \tag{7}$$

where $\Delta t_{\max}$ is a given maximum time step size that guarantees stability. From Equation (3), we have the next time solution:

$$\mathbf{m}_i^{n+1} = \mathbf{m}_i^n + \Delta t^{n+1}\big(- \mathbf{m}_i^n \times \Delta_h \mathbf{m}_i^n + \mathbf{f}_i^n\big), \ \ 1 \le i \le N_x. \tag{8}$$

However, generally, $|\mathbf{m}_i^{n+1}| \neq 1$ for some i. We normalize it as

$$\mathbf{m}_i^{n+1} = \frac{\mathbf{m}_i^{n+1}}{|\mathbf{m}_i^{n+1}|}, \ \ 1 \le i \le N_x. \tag{9}$$

Repeat this process while $t^n + \Delta t^{n+1} \le T$ to calculate the numerical approach of $\mathbf{m}(x, T)$. When determining adaptive time steps, t^{n+1} can exceed the desired final time. In order to avoid such circumstance, if $t^{n+1} = t^n + \Delta t^{n+1} > T$, then set $\Delta t^{n+1} = T - t^n$.

We present a detailed numerical algorithm for each step of the proposed method in Algorithm 1.

Algorithm 1: Adaptive scheme for the LL equation

INPUT endpoints L_x, R_x; number of grid points N_x; initial condition; final time T; tolerance *tol*; maximum time step size $\Delta t_{\max}$; forcing term (f_u, f_v, f_w).
OUTPUT approximation of $\mathbf{m}(x, T) = (u(x,T), v(x,T), w(x,T))$.
Step 1 *Initialization*
Set $h = (R_x - L_x)/N_x$ and $t = 0$
For $i = 1, \ldots, N_x$ do
$x_i = L_x + (i - 0.5)h$
$u_i^0 = u_0(x_i), \quad v_i^0 = v_0(x_i), \quad w_i^0 = w_0(x_i)$
Step 2 While ($t < T$), do Steps 3–7.
Step 3 For $i = 1, \ldots, N_x$ do
$\Delta_h u_i^n = (u_{i+1}^n - 2u_i^n + u_{i-1}^n)/h^2;$
$\Delta_h v_i^n = (v_{i+1}^n - 2v_i^n + v_{i-1}^n)/h^2;$
$\Delta_h w_i^n = (w_{i+1}^n - 2w_i^n + w_{i-1}^n)/h^2.$
Use periodic boundary condition
Step 4 Set $s_{u,i}^n = w_i^n \Delta_h v_i^n - v_i^n \Delta_h w_i^n + f_{u,i}^n;$
$s_{v,i}^n = u_i^n \Delta_h w_i^n - w_i^n \Delta_h u_i^n + f_{v,i}^n;$
$s_{w,i}^n = v_i^n \Delta_h u_i^n - u_i^n \Delta_h v_i^n + f_{w,i}^n.$
Step 5 Set $dis = \max\limits_{1 \le i \le N_x} |(s_{u,i}^n, s_{v,i}^n, s_{w,i}^n)|;$
$\Delta t = \min(0.99\, tol/dis, \Delta t_{\max}).$
If $t + \Delta t > T$, then $\Delta t = T - t$.
Step 6 Set $u_i^* = u_i^n + \Delta t\, s_{u,i}^n$
$v_i^* = v_i^n + \Delta t\, s_{v,i}^n$
$w_i^* = w_i^n + \Delta t\, s_{w,i}^n.$
Step 7 Set $u_i^{n+1} = u_i^*/|(u_i^*, v_i^*, w_i^*)|$
$v_i^{n+1} = v_i^*/|(u_i^*, v_i^*, w_i^*)|$
$w_i^{n+1} = w_i^*/|(u_i^*, v_i^*, w_i^*)|.$
$t = t + \Delta t.$
Step 8 OUTPUT $u(x,T), v(x,T), w(x,T)$
STOP.

Remark 1. *We use the maximum norm between $\mathbf{m}^{n+1}$ and $\mathbf{m}^n$ for the criterion for selecting an adaptive time step, which ensures that the maximum displacement falls within a predefined tolerance threshold. The rationale for using the maximum norm between $\mathbf{m}^{n+1}$ and $\mathbf{m}^n$ is to decrease the time step when the temporal evolution is rapid and to increase it when the evolution is slow.*

Remark 2. *The proposed time adaptivity method is different from a well-known method such as the adaptive Runge–Kutta–Fehlberg (RKF) method, which is based on both higher- and lower-order numerical schemes [32]. The adaptive RKF method has been successfully applied for the Allen–Cahn equation [28]. The RKF method is a numerical technique with higher order than our proposed method. If we assume that the numerical solution changes rapidly, the local error generated by the adaptive time-stepping method based on the RKF method will be relatively smaller than that of our proposed method. However, when calculating the time step size adaptively, the adaptive time-stepping method based on the RKF method cannot calculate it at once because it does not know the time step size advance.*

Although our proposed time adaptivity method has lower-order than the adaptive time-stepping method based on the RKF method, it is easy and simple to numerically implement, and it has the advantage of being computationally efficient, because it does not require recomputing numerical solutions when the updated solution does not satisfy a certain condition, as is done in [28]. Our proposed updating algorithm is a one-step method. In addition, our proposed method can continuously reduce the time step size as the numerical solution is updated, which is a drawback that can be compensated for by separately considering the conditions for determining the lower bound. In [33], an optimization of explicit Runge–Kutta schemes up to six-order accuracy was presented for ordinary differential equation. The authors proposed a method for selecting optimal free coefficients based on minimizing residual terms and ensuring interpolational properties.

3. Computational Experiments

We shall study the achievement of the proposed adaptive time-stepping method through several computational experiments. We begin with the comparison study between the numerical and analytic solution for the forcing term.

3.1. Without Forcing Term $\mathbf{f} \equiv \mathbf{0}$

Now, we perform a convergence test when $\mathbf{f} \equiv \mathbf{0}$ on a computational domain $\Omega = (0,1)$ and $h = 1/100$. The analytic solution [4] of the equation can be defined as

$$\begin{aligned} u^e(x,t) &= \sin(\alpha)\cos(kx + tk^2\cos(\alpha)), \\ v^e(x,t) &= \sin(\alpha)\sin(kx + tk^2\cos(\alpha)), \\ w^e(x,t) &= \cos(\alpha), \end{aligned}$$

where $\alpha = 0.25\pi$, $k = 2\pi$. The boundary condition with periodic recurrence is considered as $\mathbf{m}_0 = \mathbf{m}_{N_x}$ and $\mathbf{m}_{N_x+1} = \mathbf{m}_1$. An initial condition is given as follows:

$$(u(x,0), v(x,0), w(x,0)) = (\sin(\alpha)\cos(kx), \sin(\alpha)\sin(kx), \cos(\alpha)).$$

Then, we can observe that $\mathbf{m}(x,t) = (u^e(x,t), v^e(x,t), w^e(x,t))$ meets Equation (1), the initial condition, and the periodic boundary condition.

Figure 3a–c display the snapshots of the computational results of $\mathbf{m}(x,t)$ at $t = 0.01$, 0.07, and 0.1, respectively. Figure 3d–f display the numerical solutions to $u(x,t)$, $v(x,t)$, and $w(x,t)$ with the matching exact solutions at $t = 0.1$, respectively. The differences between the exact solution and the computational solutions $u(x,t)$, $v(x,t)$, and $w(x,t)$, shown in Figure 3g–i, respectively, are evaluated at $t = 0.1$. Here, we use tolerance $tol = 10^{-6}$, $\alpha = 0.25\pi$ and maximum time step size $\Delta t_{\max} = 0.5h^2$. In case $\mathbf{f} = 0$, we verify that the energy is conserved. Figure 3j shows the discrete energy variation over time.

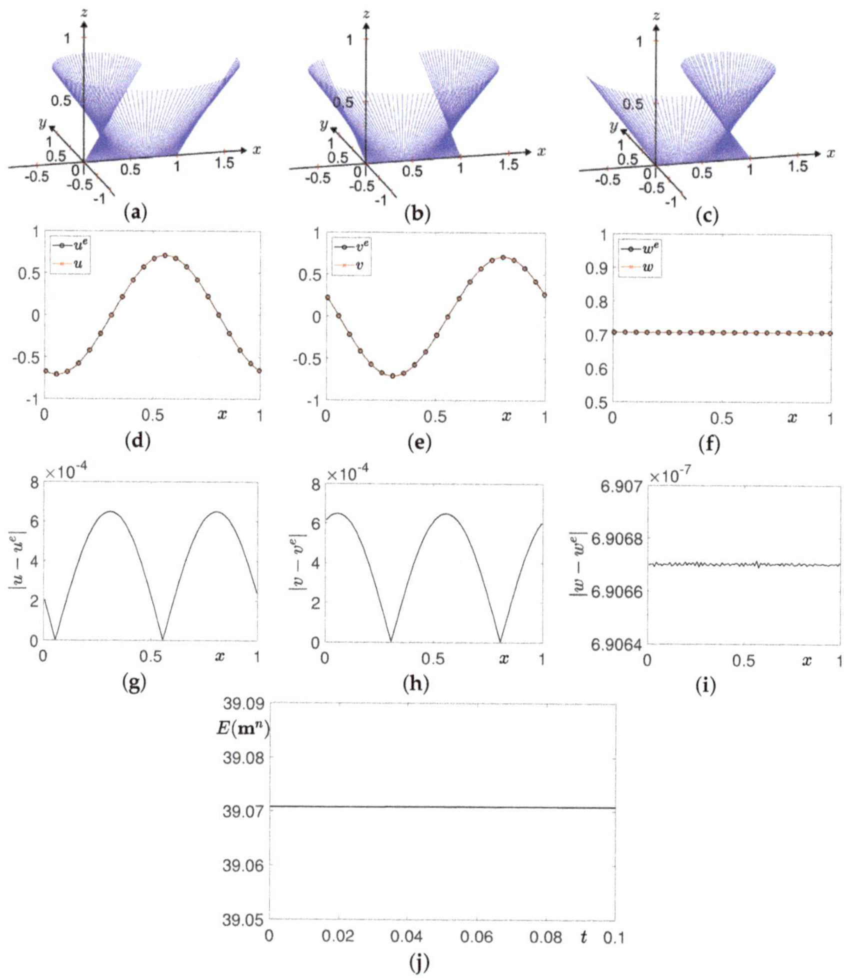

Figure 3. Numerical solutions at (**a**) $t = 0.01$, (**b**) $t = 0.07$, and (**c**) $t = 0.1$. Numerical and analytic solutions of (**d**) $u(x,t)$, (**e**) $v(x,t)$, and (**f**) $w(x,t)$ at $t = 0.1$. The differences between the exact solution and the computational solutions (**g**) $u(x,t)$, (**h**) $v(x,t)$, and (**i**) $w(x,t)$ at $t = 0.1$. (**j**) The time evolution of discrete energy.

3.2. Periodic Forcing Term

We consider a one-dimensional LL equation on domain $\Omega = (0,1)$, $N_x = 100$ and $h = 1/100$ with a forcing term

$$\mathbf{m}_t = -\mathbf{m} \times \mathbf{m}_{xx} + \mathbf{f}, \tag{10}$$

which has an exact solution [4]

$$\mathbf{m}^e(x,t) = \begin{pmatrix} u^e(x,t) \\ v^e(x,t) \\ w^e(x,t) \end{pmatrix} = \begin{pmatrix} \cos(x^2(1-x)^2)\sin(t) \\ \sin(x^2(1-x)^2)\sin(t) \\ \cos(t) \end{pmatrix}. \tag{11}$$

Therefore, a corresponding forcing term is adopted for the governing LL equation. For brevity, we used $X = x^2(1-x)^2$.

$$\begin{aligned} \mathbf{f} &= \mathbf{m}_t + \mathbf{m} \times \mathbf{m}_{xx} \\ &= \begin{pmatrix} \cos(X)\cos(t) + [(X')^2 \sin(X) - X'' \cos(X)] \sin(t)\cos(t) \\ \sin(X)\cos(t) + [(X')^2 \cos(X) + X'' \sin(X)] \sin(t)\cos(t) \\ -\sin(t) + X'' \sin^2(t) \end{pmatrix}. \end{aligned}$$

The computational domain is defined as explained in Section 2.1. For final time $T = 0.1$, tolerance $tol = 10^{-7}$ and maximum time step size $\Delta t_{\max} = 0.5h^2$ are selected as appropriate parameter values. Figure 4a–c show the snapshots of the computational results of $\mathbf{m}(x,t)$ at $t = 0.01, 0.07$, and 0.1, respectively. Figure 4d–f and g–i display the numerical solutions and differences of $u(x,t)$, $v(x,t)$, and $w(x,t)$ with the matching exact solutions at $t = 0.1$, respectively. Computational results are represented by a circle, and analytic solutions are represented by solid lines. We can see that the results from the proposed method show good agreement with the exact solution. See Appendix A Table A1 for enumerated parameters.

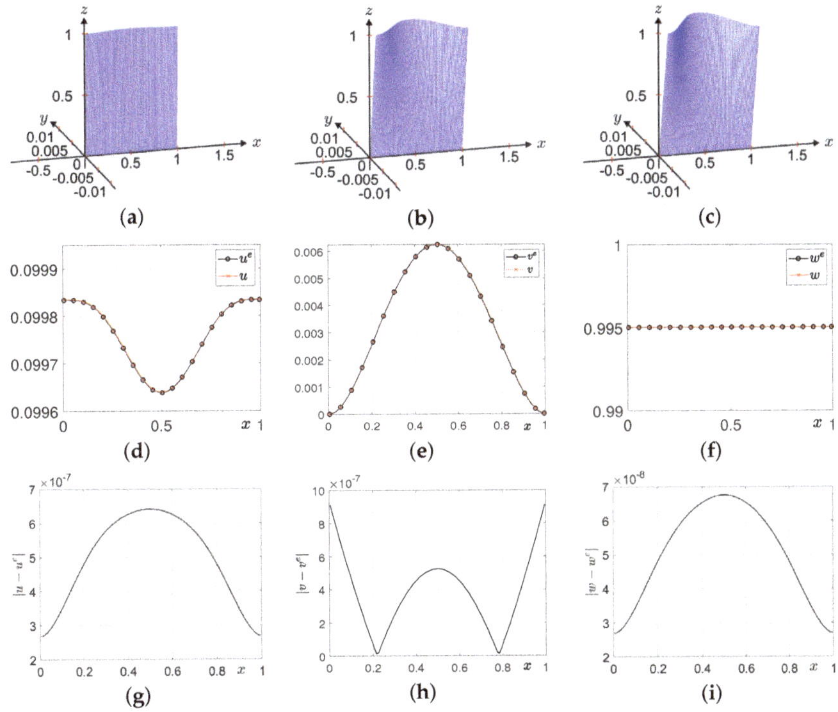

Figure 4. Numerical solution at **(a)** $t = 0.01$, **(b)** $t = 0.07$, and **(c)** $t = 0.1$. Numerical and analytic solutions of **(d)** u, **(e)** v, and **(f)** w at $t = 0.1$. The differences between the exact solution and the numerical solutions **(g)** u, **(h)** v, and **(i)** w at $t = 0.1$.

3.3. Non-Periodic Forcing Term

In this section, we present a computational experiment that rapidly changes over time. The proposed time adaptive approach has its strength where the change of the solution is rapid and diverse during the numerical simulation. Therefore, we apply the following exact solution and corresponding forcing term in Equation (10):

$$\mathbf{m}^e(x,t) = \begin{pmatrix} u^e(x,t) \\ v^e(x,t) \\ w^e(x,t) \end{pmatrix} = \begin{pmatrix} \cos(x^2(1-x)^2)\sin(100t^2) \\ \sin(x^2(1-x)^2)\sin(100t^2) \\ \cos(100t^2) \end{pmatrix}, \tag{12}$$

$$\mathbf{f} = \mathbf{m}_t + \mathbf{m} \times \mathbf{m}_{xx} \tag{13}$$

$$= \begin{pmatrix} 200t\cos(X)\cos(100t^2) + [(X')^2\sin(X) - X''\cos(X)]\sin(100t^2)\cos(100t^2) \\ 200t\sin(X)\cos(100t^2) + [(X')^2\cos(X) + X''\sin(X)]\sin(100t^2)\cos(100t^2) \\ -200t\sin(100t^2) + X''\sin^2(100t^2) \end{pmatrix}. \tag{14}$$

To show the rapid change of the solution over time, Figure 5 illustrates the exact solution $w^e(x,t) = \cos(100t^2)$. The forcing term introduced in this section is no longer periodic. Therefore, we use the homogeneous Neumann boundary condition instead of the periodic boundary condition. Therefore, $\mathbf{m}_0 = \mathbf{m}_1$ and $\mathbf{m}_{N_x+1} = \mathbf{m}_{N_x}$ is applied. On the computational domain $(0,\ 1)$ with $h = 1/128$, we apply tolerance 5×10^{-7}, maximum time step size $\Delta t_{\max} = 0.005h^2$ and find the numerical solution at final time $T = 0.3$. Snapshots of the computational results at $t = 0.01,\ 0.07$ and 0.1 are illustrated in Figure 6a–c, respectively. Figure 6d–i shows the numerical solutions and difference between the numerical solution and exact solution of u, v and w from left to right. For error comparison, we use the discrete maximum error defined as follows:

$$\|\mathbf{m} - \mathbf{m}^e\| = \max\{|u - u^e| + |v - v^e| + |w - w^e|\}.$$

The execution time is 767.9768 s, and the maximum error is 1.5237×10^{-5}.

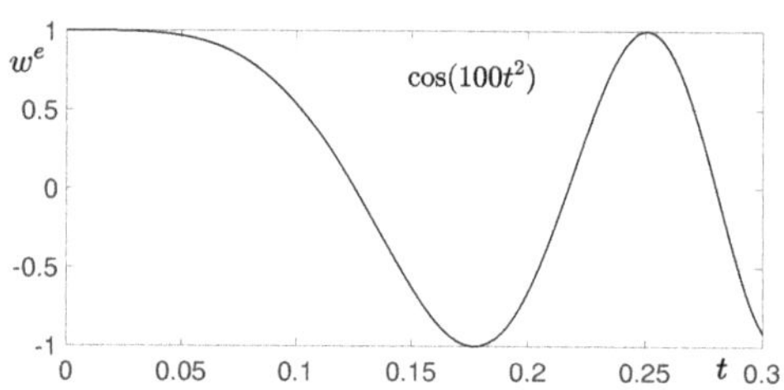

Figure 5. Exact solution $w^e(x,t) = \cos(100t^2)$ in Equation (13)

Figure 7 illustrates the temporal evolution of the adaptive time step until final time T. The time step decreases as evolution processes, and we can find the major advantage of our proposed model. If a constant time step is applied, the minimum value of Δt in Figure 7 must be used, which is unnecessary in most of the evolution. For example, before time $t = 0.05$, the required time step Δt is around six times the size of the initial step size. The time step size applied at $t = 0.3$ is 3.52×10^{-9}, which is approximately 100 times smaller than the initial time step. Assume that a constant time step is applied, which is the minimum step size in Figure 7. Because the adaptive step size decreases exponentially, a smaller time step must be applied for the constant time step method, which will decrease the efficiency of the calculation. Therefore, the proposed adaptive time step not only shows a better performance than the constant time step method but also increases the efficiency as a bigger total time is applied.

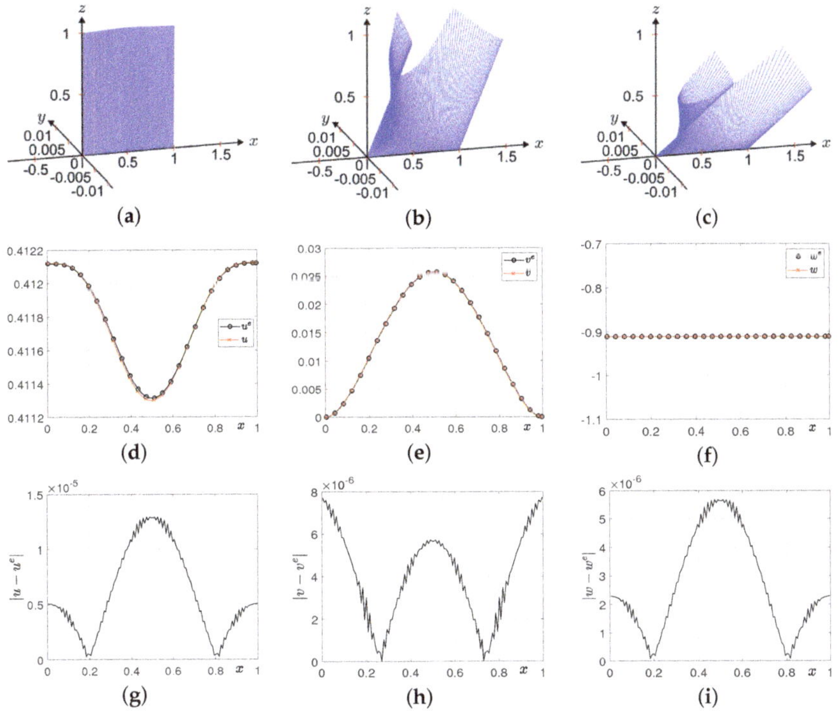

Figure 6. Numerical solutions for the proposed adaptive method at (**a**) $t = 0.01$, (**b**) $t = 0.07$, and (**c**) $t = 0.1$. Numerical and analytic solutions of (**d**) u, (**e**) v, and (**f**) w at $t = 0.3$. The differences between the exact solution and the numerical solutions (**g**) u, (**h**) v, and (**i**) w at $t = 0.3$.

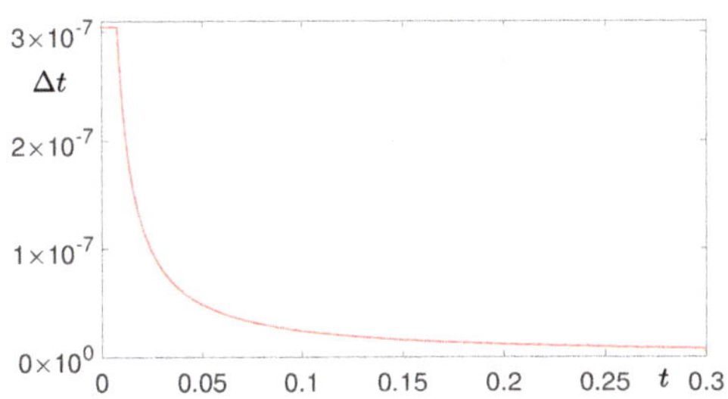

Figure 7. Desired adaptive time step Δt for each time. Adaptive time steps enhance the efficiency of the method.

Next, we present a comparison between the proposed adaptive time step method and the constant time step methods: the explicit method and the Crank–Nicolson method studied by Jeong and Kim [4]. Jeong and Kim proposed a finite difference method for the LL equation using the Crank–Nicolson method and multigrid method for handling nonlinearities.

Figure 8 shows the numerical results for the explicit method with constant time step $\Delta t = 1.3737 \times 10^{-8}$. Figure 8a–c show the temporal evolution of the numerical solutions at $t = 0.01$, $t = 0.07$, and $t = 0.1$, respectively. Figure 8d–f show the numerical and analytic solutions of u, v, and w at $t = 0.3$. Figure 8g–i show the difference between the numerical and analytic solutions for u, v, and w. The execution time is 901.6647 s, and the maximum error is 1.57×10^{-5}.

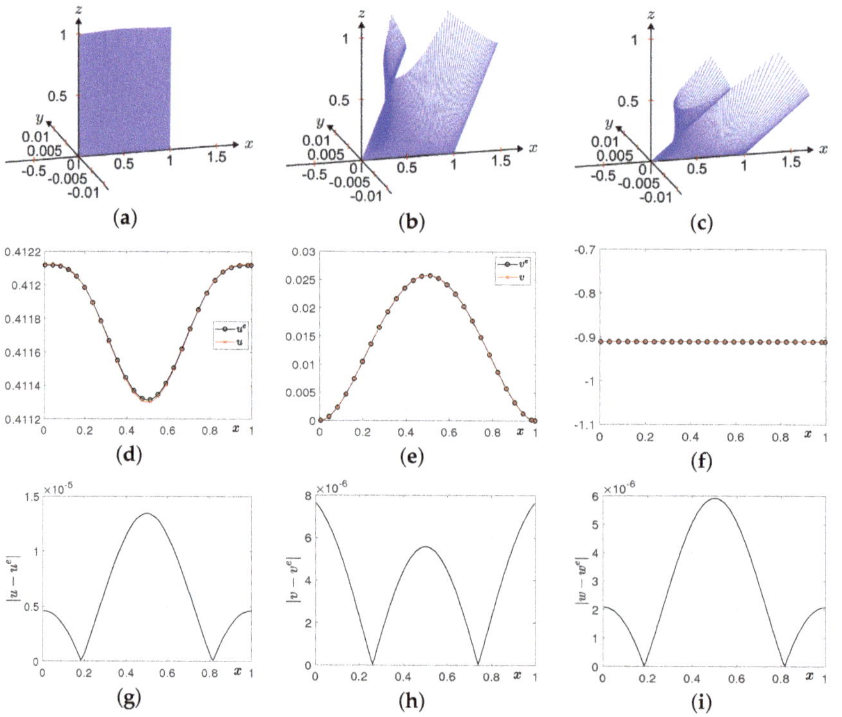

Figure 8. Numerical solutions for the explicit method with constant time step $\Delta t = 1.3737 \times 10^{-8}$ at (**a**) $t = 0.01$, (**b**) $t = 0.07$, and (**c**) $t = 0.1$. Numerical and analytic solutions of (**d**) u, (**e**) v, and (**f**) w at $t = 0.3$. The differences between the exact solution and the numerical solutions (**g**) u, (**h**) v, and (**i**) w at $t = 0.3$.

Under the equal benchmark problem, we applied constant time step $\Delta t = 2 \times 10^{-8}$. Figure 9 shows numerical results for the Crank–Nicolson method with a constant time step. The first row of Figure 9 shows the temporal evolution of the numerical solutions at $t = 0.01$, $t = 0.07$, and $t = 0.1$. The second row of Figure 9 shows the numerical and analytic solutions of u, v, and w at $t = 0.3$. The last row of Figure 9 shows the difference between the numerical and analytic solutions for u, v, and w. The execution time is 1123.6650 s, and the maximum error is 1.02×10^{-5}.

Through Figures 6, 8 and 9, we compared the results of the explicit adaptive time step method, the constant time step method, and the Crank–Nicolson method for a rapidly changing solution. From these results, the adaptive time step method proved to be better than the constant time step method in terms of both execution time and error. While the first-order adaptive time step method showed slightly larger errors compared to the second-order Crank–Nicolson method, it achieve a similar level of error with significantly less execution time. Furthermore, the proposed adaptive method has the advantage that the trial and error of finding a suitable time step is unnecessary. If a desired tolerance is given, the adaptive time step size is automatically given. However, when applying the Crank–Nicolson method, attempts for finding a suitable time step must be previously performed. Therefore, if we include this procedure in account, the proposed method has a superiority compared to the Crank–Nicolson method.

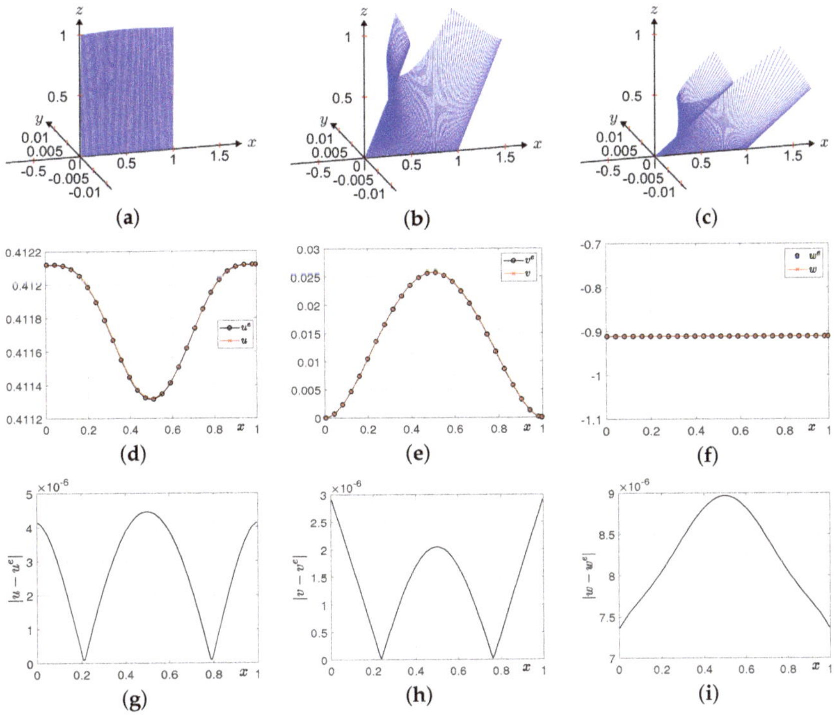

Figure 9. Numerical solutions for the Crank–Nicolson method with constant time step $\Delta t = 2 \times 10^{-8}$ at (**a**) $t = 0.01$, (**b**) $t = 0.07$, and (**c**) $t = 0.1$. Numerical and analytic solutions of (**d**) u, (**e**) v, and (**f**) w at $t = 0.3$. The differences between the exact solution and the numerical solutions (**g**) u, (**h**) v, and (**i**) w at $t = 0.3$.

In concluding this section, we shall provide the maximum error as a function of the tolerance in order to illustrate the behavior of the controller for many levels of accuracy. We used the exact solution and forcing term introduced in this section on the computational domain $(0,\ 1)$ with $h = 1/128$ at final time $T = 0.1$. Under maximum step size $\Delta t_{\max} = 0.5h^2$, maximum errors at tolerance $tol = 10^{-7}, 1.2 \times 10^{-6}, 2.3 \times 10^{-6}, 2.3 \times 10^{-6}, 3.4 \times 10^{-6}, 4.5 \times 10^{-6}, 5.6 \times 10^{-6}, 6.7 \times 10^{-6}, 7.8 \times 10^{-6}, 8.9 \times 10^{-6}, 10^{-5}$ are illustrated in Figure 10. We can see that after the first data, the maximum error linearly grows with the tolerance.

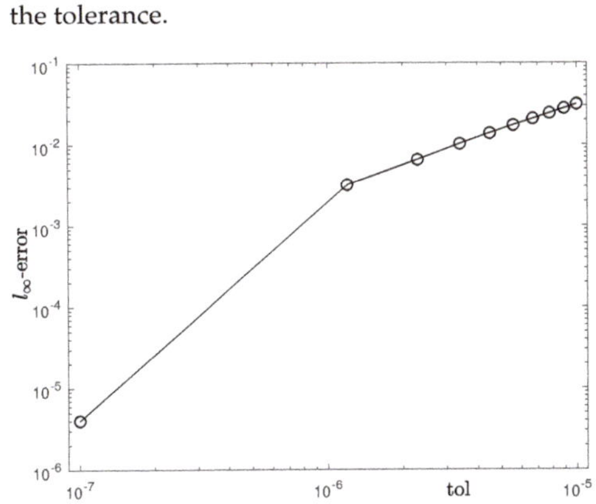

Figure 10. Maximum errors as a function of the tolerance. Tolerance values range from 10^{-7} to 10^{-5}.

3.4. Damping Forcing Term

Next, we consider a one-dimensional LL equation on domain $\Omega = (0, 2\pi)$ with a damping forcing term. The exact solution and corresponding forcing term are given as follows:

$$\mathbf{m}^e(x,t) = \begin{pmatrix} u^e(x,t) \\ v^e(x,t) \\ w^e(x,t) \end{pmatrix} = \begin{pmatrix} \mathrm{sech}(\alpha t)\cos(x) \\ \mathrm{sech}(\alpha t)\sin(x) \\ \tanh(\alpha t) \end{pmatrix},$$

$$\mathbf{f}(x,t) = \mathbf{m}^e_t(x,t) + \mathbf{m}^e(x,t) \times \mathbf{m}^e_{xx}(x,t) = \begin{pmatrix} (v^e(x,t) - \alpha u^e(x,t))w^e(x,t) \\ (u^e(x,t) - \alpha v^e(x,t))w^e(x,t) \\ \alpha[1 - (w^e(x,t))^2] \end{pmatrix}.$$

Figure 11a–c show the snapshots of the computational results of $\mathbf{m}(x,t)$ at $t = 0.0001$, 0.0007, and 0.001, respectively. Figure 11d–f display the numerical approximations of $u(x,t)$, $v(x,t)$, and $w(x,t)$ with the corresponding exact solutions at $t = 0.01$, respectively. Figure 11g–i illustrate the difference of $u(x,t)$, $v(x,t)$, and $w(x,t)$ with the matching exact solutions at $t = 0.01$, respectively. Here, we use $N_x = 100$, $h = 2\pi/N_x$, $\alpha = 1000$, $tol = 10^{-5}$, and $\Delta t_{\max} = 0.5h^2$.

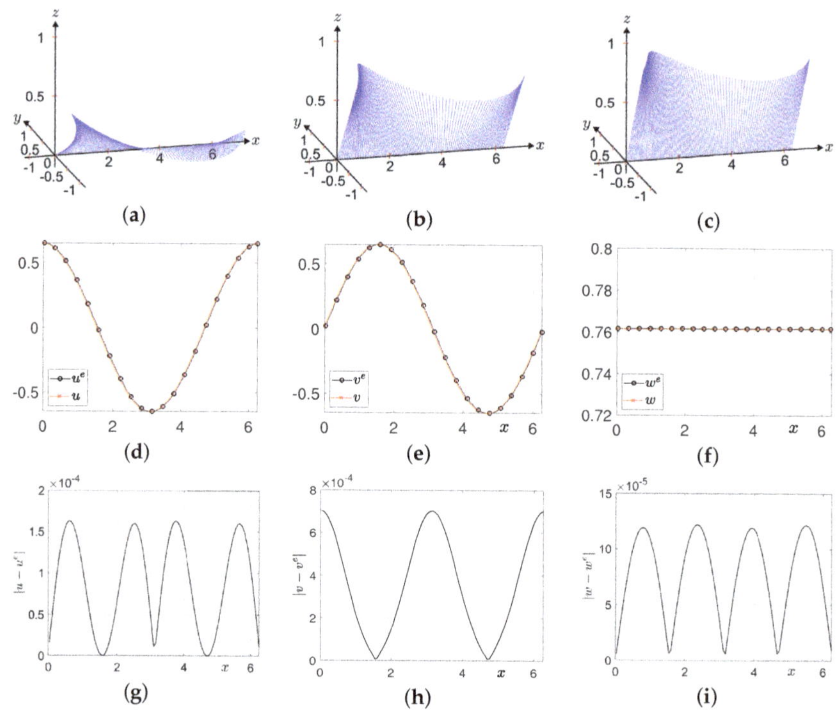

Figure 11. Simulation of damping forcing term. Numerical solution at (**a**) $t = 0.0001$, (**b**) $t = 0.0007$, and (**c**) $t = 0.001$. Numerical and analytic solutions of (**d**) u, (**e**) v, and (**f**) w at $t = 0.001$. The differences between the exact solution and the numerical solutions (**g**) u, (**h**) v, and (**i**) w at $t = 0.001$.

Lastly, we simulate the case where the forcing term is constant, $f = (0,\ 0,\ 1)^T$ with the same computational domain as the last numerical simulation. Tolerance 10^{-7} is applied. The constant forcing term represents the constant one directional external magnetic field that is applied to the dynamics of magnetization. The initial condition is given as $\mathbf{m}(x,0) = (\cos(x)/\sqrt{2},\ \sin(x)/\sqrt{2},\ 1/\sqrt{2})^T$. Figure 12a–c show the snapshots of the computational results of $\mathbf{m}(x,t)$ at $t = 0.001,\ 0.007$, and 0.01, respectively. Figure 12d–f display the numerical approximations of $u(x,t)$, $v(x,t)$, and $w(x,t)$ with the corresponding exact solutions at $t = 0.01$, respectively. We can see the numerical results are stable and therefore capable of simulating this application.

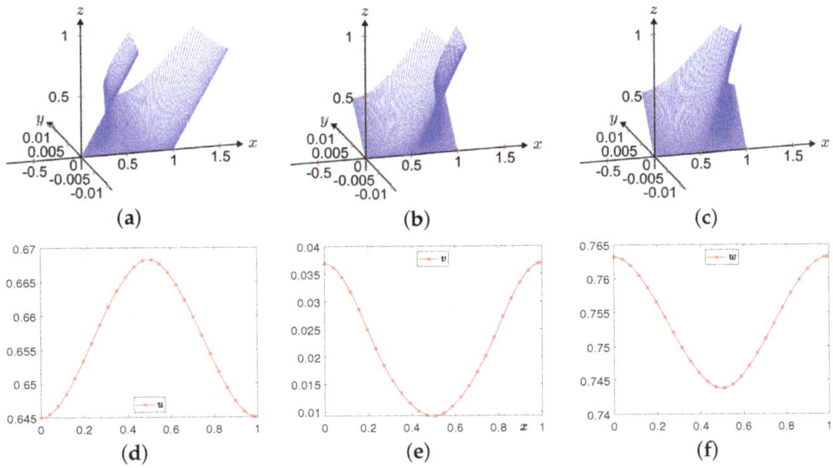

Figure 12. Simulation of constant forcing term. Numerical solution at (**a**) $t = 0.001$, (**b**) $t = 0.007$, and (**c**) $t = 0.01$. Numerical solutions of (**d**) u, (**e**) v, and (**f**) w at $t = 0.01$.

4. Conclusions

The article introduced a new adaptive time-stepping FDM for solving the LL equation, which is crucial for investigating magnetic materials and processes. The method strategically selects time steps to keep displacement within a tolerance and allows larger steps near equilibrium states for faster computations. Benchmark tests demonstrated the algorithm's efficiency and accuracy and showed its potential for advancing magnetic phenomena analysis. We expect that the proposed time-stepping adaptive method can be applied to various equations which can be numerically approximated. Reaction–diffusion equations such as the Allen–Cahn equation can make good use of the proposed method because the displacement of the numerical solution is determined by the time step size. Furthermore, the evolution of the numerical solution varies during the numerical simulation, which indicates that the adaptive time step can be an efficient solution.

In this paper, we considered a one-dimensional LL equation. Extending the proposed method to multi-dimensional problems presents challenges for explicit methods in terms of stability, which is a limitation of this study. Oscillations have already been reported in one-dimensional problems. We expect that adopting an implicit method combined with the adaptive time-stepping method could provide a solution for the multi-dimensional LL problem. In future work, we will present an efficient adaptive time-stepping method for the LL Equation (1) in two- and three-dimensional spaces. As a preliminary model, we consider the two-dimensional case as follows. In two-dimensional space, Equation (1) on $\Omega = (L_x, R_x) \times (L_y, R_y)$ is defined as

$$\frac{\partial \mathbf{m}(x,y,t)}{\partial t} = -\mathbf{m}(x,y,t) \times \Delta \mathbf{m}(x,y,t) + \mathbf{f}(x,y,t), \quad (x,y) \in \Omega, \ 0 < t \leq T. \tag{15}$$

Let N_x and N_y be positive integers. The discrete computational domain is defined as $\Omega_h = \{(x_i = L_x + (i-0.5)h, y_j = L_y + (j-0.5)h) \mid i = 1,2,\ldots,N_x, j = 1,2,\ldots,N_y\}$, where the spatial step size $h = (R_x - L_x)/N_x = (R_y - L_y)/N_y$. We discretize Equation (15) as

$$\frac{\mathbf{m}_{ij}^{n+1} - \mathbf{m}_{ij}^{n}}{\Delta t^{n+1}} = -\mathbf{m}_{ij}^{n} \times \frac{\mathbf{m}_{i+1,j}^{n} + \mathbf{m}_{i-1,j}^{n} + \mathbf{m}_{i,j+1}^{n} + \mathbf{m}_{i,j-1}^{n} - 4\mathbf{m}_{ij}^{n}}{h^2} + \mathbf{f}_{ij}^{n}.$$

We consider the case without the forcing term, where $\mathbf{f} \equiv 0$. An exact solution of Equation (15) is given by [4]

$$\begin{aligned} u^e(x,y,t) &= \sin\left(\frac{\pi}{24}\right)\cos\left(2\pi(x+y) + 8\pi t\cos\left(\frac{\pi}{24}\right)\right), \\ v^e(x,y,t) &= \sin\left(\frac{\pi}{24}\right)\sin\left(2\pi(x+y) + 8\pi t\cos\left(\frac{\pi}{24}\right)\right), \\ w^e(x,y,t) &= \cos\left(\frac{\pi}{24}\right). \end{aligned}$$

The initial condition on the $\Omega = (0,1) \times (0,1)$ is given by

$$(u(x,y,0), v(x,y,0), w(x,y,0)) = \left(\sin\left(\frac{\pi}{24}\right)\cos(2\pi(x+y)), \sin\left(\frac{\pi}{24}\right)\sin(2\pi(x+y)), \cos\left(\frac{\pi}{24}\right)\right).$$

We used the parameters $N_x = N_y = 32$, $tol = 10^{-6}$, $\Delta t_{\max} = 0.2h^2$, and the final time $T = 0.1$. For visualization of the numerical solution at time $t = 0.1$, we used the scaled numerical solution $0.25\mathbf{m}_{ij}$ for $i = 1,3,5,\ldots,31$, $j = 1,3,5,\ldots,31$. Figure 13 shows the scaled numerical solutions at $t = 0$ and $t = 0.1$ using the adaptive time-stepping method.

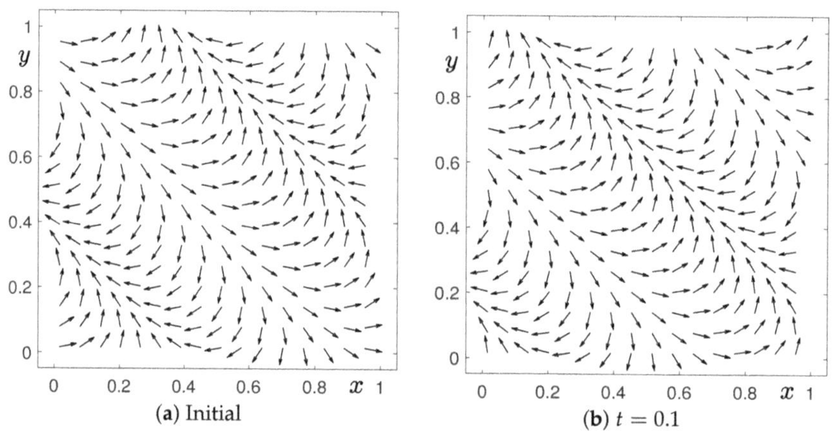

Figure 13. Numerical solution at (**a**) $t = 0$ and (**b**) $t = 0.1$ using the adaptive time-stepping method.

Future work will focus on extending the proposed adaptive method to another class of partial differential equations with a similar structure, particularly those involving fast and slow evolutions such as the Allen–Cahn equation [34], the Black–Scholes equation [35], and the Susceptible–Infected–Recovered (SIR) epidemic model [36].

Author Contributions: Conceptualization, J.K. and H.K.; methodology, J.K., H.K. and S.K. (Soobin Kwak); software, H.K., S.K. (Soobin Kwak), M.M., S.K. (Seungyoon Kang) and S.H.; validation, M.M., S.K. (Soobin Kwak) and S.H.; formal analysis, H.K. and J.K.; investigation, S.K. (Seungyoon Kang) and M.M.; resources, S.K. (Seungyoon Kang) and S.H.; data curation, S.K. (Seungyoon Kang) and S.H.; writing—original draft, H.K., S.K. (Soobin Kwak), M.M., S.K. (Seungyoon Kang), S.H. and J.K.; writing—review and editing, H.K., S.K. (Soobin Kwak), S.H., S.K. (Seungyoon Kang) and J.K.; visualization, S.K. (Soobin Kwak) and S.H.; supervision, H.K. and J.K.; project administration, J.K.;

funding acquisition, H.K. and J.K. All authors have read and agreed to the published version of the manuscript.

Funding: The first author (Hyundong Kim) was supported by the Basic Science Research Program through the National Research Foundation of Korea (NRF) funded by the Ministry of Education (2021R1A6A1A03044326). The corresponding author (J.S. Kim) received support from the Brain Korea 21 (BK 21) FOUR program funded by the Ministry of Education.

Data Availability Statement: The raw data supporting the conclusions of this article will be made available by the authors on request.

Acknowledgments: The authors thank the reviewers for their constructive and helpful comments on the revision of this article.

Conflicts of Interest: The authors declare no conflicts of interest.

Appendix A

The following MATLAB code produces the results shown in Figure 3, and the parameters are enumerated in Table A1. The code can also be downloaded from https://mathematicians.korea.ac.kr/cfdkim/open-source-codes/ (accessed on 23 December 2024). Compared to other programs in the market, MATLAB is highly beneficial in a way that it serves as a unified platform that can provide powerful numerical computation through coding and a comprehensive set of tools for data visualization. Because both functionalities are available, the user can interactively check and modify variables in the workspace and memory and visualize it instantaneously. Moreover, MATLAB boasts an extensive functionality through extensional toolboxes and built-in functions that can boost the work speed of the user.

In this paper, the LL equation in a small scale is simulated through MATLAB. We expect that the proposed method can be expanded to larger-scale problems that handle practical engineering applications with the help of additional computational methods such as parallel computing.

Table A1. Parameters used for the 1D LL equation.

Parameters	Description
Nx	number of grid points on the x-axis
Lx	minimum value on the x-axis
Rx	maximum value on the x-axis
h	space step size
T	final time
maxdt	maximum time step size
tol	tolerance

```
clear;
Nx=100; Lx=0; Rx=1; h=(Rx-Lx)/Nx; x=linspace(Lx+0.5*h,Rx-0.5*h,Nx);
XX=(x.^2).*((1-x).^2); dXX=2*x-6*x.^2+4*x.^3; ddXX=2-12*x+12*x.^2;
ue=@(t) sin(t).*cos(XX);
ve=@(t) sin(t).*sin(XX);
we=@(t) cos(t).*ones(1,Nx);
T=1.e-1; maxdt=0.5*h^2; t=0; u=ue(0); v=ve(0); w=we(0); tol=1.e-7;
while t<T
    Lapu(1)=(u(2)-2*u(1)+u(Nx))/h^2;
    Lapv(1)=(v(2)-2*v(1)+v(Nx))/h^2;
    Lapw(1)=(w(2)-2*w(1)+w(Nx))/h^2;
    for i=2:Nx-1
        Lapu(i)=(u(i+1)-2*u(i)+u(i-1))/h^2;
        Lapv(i)=(v(i+1)-2*v(i)+v(i-1))/h^2;
        Lapw(i)=(w(i+1)-2*w(i)+w(i-1))/h^2;
```

```
    end
    Lapu(Nx)=(u(1)-2*u(Nx)+u(Nx-1))/h^2;
    Lapv(Nx)=(v(1)-2*v(Nx)+v(Nx-1))/h^2;
    Lapw(Nx)=(w(1)-2*w(Nx)+w(Nx-1))/h^2;
    fu=cos(XX).*cos(t)+(dXX.^2.*sin(XX)-ddXX.*cos(XX))*sin(t)*cos(t);
    fv=sin(XX).*cos(t)-(dXX.^2.*cos(XX)+ddXX.*sin(XX))*sin(t)*cos(t);
    fw=-sin(t)+ddXX*sin(t).^2;
    su=v.*Lapw-w.*Lapv-fu;
    sv=w.*Lapu-u.*Lapw-fv;
    sw=u.*Lapv-v.*Lapu-fw;
    en=max(sqrt(su.^2+sv.^2+sw.^2));
    dt=0.99*tol/en; dt=min(dt,maxdt);
    if (t+dt>T)
        dt=T-t;
    end
    t=t+dt;
    nu=u-dt*su; nv=v-dt*sv; nw=w-dt*sw;
    u=nu; v=nv; w=nw;
    A=[u' v' w'];
    for i=1:Nx
        B(i)=norm(A(i,:));
    end
    u=u./B; v=v./B; w=w./B;
end
```

References

1. Landau, L.; Lifshitz, E. On the theory of the dispersion of magnetic permeability in ferromagnetic bodies. *Phys. Z. Sowjetunion* **1935**, *8*, 101–114.
2. Bertotti, G.; Mayergoyz, I.D.; Serpico, C. Analytical solutions of Landau–Lifshitz equation for precessional dynamics. *Physica B* **2004**, *343*, 325–330. [CrossRef]
3. García-Ñustes, M.A.; Humire, F.R.; Leon, A.O. Self-organization in the one-dimensional Landau–Lifshitz–Gilbert–Slonczewski equation with non-uniform anisotropy fields. *Commun. Nonlinear Sci. Numer. Simul.* **2021**, *96*, 105674. [CrossRef]
4. Jeong, D.; Kim, J. A Crank–Nicolson scheme for the Landau–Lifshitz equation without damping. *J. Comput. Appl. Math.* **2010**, *234*, 613–623. [CrossRef]
5. Jeong, D.; Kim, J. An accurate and robust numerical method for micromagnetics simulations. *Curr. Appl. Phys.* **2014**, *14*, 476–483. [CrossRef]
6. Sharma, H.; Borggaard, J.; Patil, M.; Woolsey, C. Performance assessment of energy-preserving, adaptive time-step variational integrators. *Commun. Nonlinear Sci. Numer. Simul.* **2022**, *114*, 106646. [CrossRef]
7. Moumni, M.; Tilioua, M. A finite-difference scheme for a model of magnetization dynamics with inertial effects. *J. Eng. Math.* **2016**, *100*, 95–106. [CrossRef]
8. Li, P.; Xie, C.; Du, R.; Chen, J.; Wang, X.P. Two improved Gauss-Seidel projection methods for Landau–Lifshitz–Gilbert equation. *J. Comput. Phys.* **2020**, *401*, 109046. [CrossRef]
9. Jannelli, A. Adaptive numerical solutions of time-fractional advection–diffusion–reaction equations. *Commun. Nonlinear Sci. Numer. Simul.* **2022**, *105*, 106073. [CrossRef]
10. Wang, X.P.; García-Cervera, C.J.; Weinan, E. A Gauss–Seidel projection method for micromagnetics simulations. *J. Comput. Phys.* **2001**, *171*, 357–372. [CrossRef]
11. Dörfler, M. Quilted Gabor frames—A new concept for adaptive time-frequency representation. *Adv. Appl. Math.* **2011**, *47*, 668–687. [CrossRef]
12. Alouges, F. A new finite element scheme for Landau–Lifshitz equations. *Discrete Contin. Dyn. Syst. Ser. S* **2008**, *1*, 187–196.
13. Alouges, F.; Jaisson, P. Convergence of a finite element discretization for the Landau–Lifshitz equations in micromagnetism. *Math. Models Methods Appl. Sci.* **2006**, *16*, 299–316. [CrossRef]
14. Mohammed, M.; Mouhcine, T. A finite element approximation of a current-induced magnetization dynamics model. *J. Math. Model.* **2022**, *10*, 53–69.
15. Moumni, M.; Douiri, S.M.; Kim, J.S. Fourier-spectral method for the Landau–Lifshitz–Gilbert equation in micromagnetism. *Results Appl. Math.* **2023**, *19*, 100380. [CrossRef]
16. Weinan, E.; Wang, X.P. Numerical methods for the Landau–Lifshitz equation. *SIAM J. Numer. Anal.* **2001**, *39*, 1647–1665.

17. Yang, W.; Wang, D.; Yang, L. A stable numerical method for space fractional Landau–Lifshitz equations. *Appl. Math. Lett.* **2016**, *61*, 149–155. [CrossRef]
18. Cimrák, I. A survey on the numerics and computations for the Landau–Lifshitz equation of micromagnetism. *Arch. Comput. Methods Eng.* **2007**, *15*, 1–37. [CrossRef]
19. Bastos, J.P.A.; Sadowski, N. *Magnetic Materials and 3D Finite Element Modeling;* CRC Press: Boca Raton, FL, USA, 2017.
20. Cai, Y.; Chen, J.; Wang, C.; Xie, C. Error analysis of a linear numerical scheme for the Landau–Lifshitz equation with large damping parameters. *Math. Methods Appl. Sci.* **2023**, *46*, 18952–18974. [CrossRef]
21. Chen, J.; Wang, C.; Xie, C. Convergence analysis of a second-order semi-implicit projection method for Landa–Lifshitz equation. *Appl. Numer. Math.* **2021**, *168*, 55–74. [CrossRef]
22. Yang, Y.B.; Jiang, Y.L. Unconditional optimal error estimates of linearized second-order BDF Galerkin FEMs for the Landau–Lifshitz equation. *Appl. Numer. Math.* **2021**, *159*, 21–45. [CrossRef]
23. Fuwa, A.; Ishiwata, T.; Tsutsumi, M. Finite difference scheme for the Landau–Lifshitz equation. *Jpn. J. Ind. Appl. Math.* **2012**, *29*, 83–110. [CrossRef]
24. Magaletti, F.; Gallo, M.; Perez, S.P.; Carrillo, J.A.; Kalliadasis, S. A positivity-preserving scheme for fluctuating hydrodynamics. *J. Comput. Phys.* **2022**, *463*, 111248. [CrossRef]
25. Daribayev, B.; Mukhanbet, A.; Azatbekuly, N.; Imankulov, T. A quantum approach for exploring the numerical results of the heat equation. *Algorithms* **2024**, *17*, 327. [CrossRef]
26. Krivovichev, G.V. Stability optimization of explicit Runge–Kutta methods with higher-order derivatives. *Algorithms* **2024**, *17*, 535. [CrossRef]
27. Christou, M.A.; Papanicolaou, N.C.; Sophocleous, C. An efficient and highly accurate spectral method for modeling the propagation of solitary magnetic spin waves in thin films. *Comput. Appl. Math.* **2020**, *39*, 205. [CrossRef]
28. Lee, C.; Park, J.; Kwak, S.; Kim, S.; Choi, Y.; Ham, S.; Kim, J. An adaptive time-stepping algorithm for the Allen–Cahn equation. *J. Funct. Spaces* **2022**, *2022*, 2731593. [CrossRef]
29. Cheng, Q.; Shen, J. Length preserving numerical schemes for Landau–Lifshitz equation based on Lagrange multiplier approaches. *SIAM J. Sci. Comput.* **2023**, *45*, A530–A553. [CrossRef]
30. He, J.; Yang, L.; Zhan, J. Temporal High-Order Accurate Numerical Scheme for the Landau–Lifshitz–Gilbert Equation. *Mathematics* **2024**, *12*, 1179. [CrossRef]
31. De Laire, A. Recent results for the Landau–Lifshitz equation. *SeMA J.* **2022**, *79*, 253–295. [CrossRef]
32. Atkinson, K.; Han, W.; Stewart, D.E. *Numerical Solution of Ordinary Differential Equations*, 2nd ed.; John Wiley & Sons: Hoboken, NJ, USA, 2009.
33. Alshina, E.A.; Zaks, E.M.; Kalitkin, N.N. Optimal first-to sixth-order accurate Runge-Kutta schemes. *Comput. Math. Math. Phys.* **2008**, *48*, 395–405. [CrossRef]
34. Ham, S.; Kim, J. Stability analysis for a maximum principle preserving explicit scheme of the Allen–Cahn equation. *Math. Comput. Simul.* **2023**, *207*, 453–465. [CrossRef]
35. Lee, C.; Kwak, S.; Hwang, Y.; Kim, J. Accurate and efficient finite difference method for the Black–Scholes model with no far-field boundary conditions. *Comput. Econ.* **2023**, *61*, 1207–1224. [CrossRef]
36. Dieguez, G.; Batistela, C.; Piqueira, J.R.C. Controlling COVID-19 spreading: A three-level algorithm. *Mathematics* **2023**, *11*, 3766. [CrossRef]

algorithms MDPI

Article

Optimized Analytical–Numerical Procedure for Ultrasonic Sludge Treatment for Agricultural Use

Filippo Laganà [1], Salvatore A. Pullano [1], Giovanni Angiulli [2] and Mario Versaci [3,*]

[1] Department of Health Science, Magna Græcia University, I-88100 Catanzaro, Italy; filippo.lagana@unicz.it (F.L.); pullano@unicz.it (S.A.P.)
[2] Department of Information Engineering, Infrastructures and Sustainable Energy, Mediterranea University, via Zehender, I-89122 Reggio Calabria, Italy; giovanni.angiulli@unirc.it
[3] Department of Civil, Energetic, Environmental and Material Engineering, Mediterranea University, via Zehender, I-89122 Reggio Calabria, Italy
* Correspondence: mario.versaci@unirc.it

Abstract: This paper presents an integrated approach based on physical–mathematical models and numerical simulations to optimize sludge treatment using ultrasound. The main objective is to improve the efficiency of the purification system by reducing the weight and moisture of the purification sludge, therefore ensuring regulatory compliance and environmental sustainability. A coupled temperature–humidity model, formulated by partial differential equations, describes materials' thermal and water evolution during treatment. The numerical resolution, implemented by the finite element method (FEM), allows the simulation of the system behavior and the optimization of the operating parameters. Experimental results confirm that ultrasonic treatment reduces the moisture content of sludge by up to 20% and improves its stability, making it suitable for agricultural applications or further treatment. Functional controls of sonication and the reduction of water content in the sludge correlate with the obtained results. Ultrasound treatment has been shown to decrease the specific weight of the sludge sample both in pretreatment and treatment, therefore improving stabilization. In various experimental conditions, the weight of the sludge is reduced by a maximum of about 50%. Processed sludge transforms waste into a resource for the agricultural sector. Treatment processes have been optimized with low-energy operating principles. Additionally, besides utilizing energy-harvesting technology, plant operating processes have been optimized, accounting for approximately 55% of the consumption due to the aeration of active sludge. In addition, an extended analysis of ultrasonic wave propagation is proposed.

Keywords: sludge treatment for agricultural uses; ultrasound; coupled temperature–humidity–pressure analytical model; FEM analysis

1. Introduction

The adoption of circular business practices is revolutionizing production and consumption patterns, including integrating water services to promote a sustainable and innovative approach. In the waste management and water treatment system, sewage sludge derived from municipal waste requires resources, high costs, and specific procedures for its treatment, being a complex by-product to dispose or manage [1]. However, when reused circularly to extract materials useful to the community, such sludge can be transformed from a liability into a resource. Being composed of carbon (25–35%), nitrogen (4–5%), phosphorus (2–3%), and oxygen (20–25%), along with traces of other useful constituents, reference [2] dry sludge from wastewater treatment has considerable potential for use in agriculture [3–7]. In addition, digestate (the organic residue produced by anaerobic digestion) can be used to improve soil properties and is an excellent source of organic fertilizer, contributing to the nutritional needs of crops while also contributing to the long-term sustainable growth of agriculture [8–11]. Due to the presence of contaminants, such as heavy metals, drugs, microplastics, or flame retardants, the potential use of sludge in agriculture applications is often limited [12,13]. Thus, there is a growing interest in improving contaminant extraction to address resource recovery and pollution prevention in sewage sludge management [12,13]. Untreated sludge has a complex structure and high moisture content, with particles retaining water. Reducing the water content results in a smaller sludge volume for transport and disposal; accordingly, drying becomes a critical step in sludge treatment, lowering its transport and disposal costs. Conditioning facilitates water removal, making dehydration and drying faster and less expensive. Without proper conditioning, these processes would require more resources, making them less sustainable and effective. Recent studies have explored different methods of sludge conditioning using various techniques to improve the effectiveness of treatment [14,15]. A relatively simple technique that can be integrated with other treatment systems, now well established in the literature, is based on physical conditioning that applies mechanical forces to sludge to change its structure and facilitate dewatering and removal of contaminants [16]. While this technique reduces the viscosity of the material and improves drying, it requires large amounts of energy and expensive specialized equipment. However, physical conditioning can be ineffective for some types of sludge, especially in the presence of fine particles or chemical contaminants that require more specific treatments [17,18]. Then, we are helped it their removal by sonication using high-frequency compression and rarefaction sound waves, which create bubbles in the liquid that, when they collapse, cause intense forces that disintegrate the sludge particles and facilitate the release of intracellular and extracellular materials [19]. This technique improves dewatering efficiency by increasing sludge biodegradability, resulting in rapid completion of anaerobic digestion [20,21]. In addition, sonication is particularly effective in reducing viscosity and making the sludge more straightforward to process in subsequent stages. However, the high-energy requirements and the need for sophisticated instrumentation and calibration make this method not always advantageous. In addition, the effectiveness of sonication can be limited by specific characteristics of the sludge, such as the presence of substances resistant to cavitation (the collapse of tiny bubbles that transmit significant mechanical forces to the solid material in suspension), making it less effective in some contexts [22,23]. In addition to the above procedure, a less costly method, the hydrodynamic cavitation, can be used for the same purposes. This method takes advantage of the formation and subsequent collapse of microbubbles of steam in a fluid, creating intense forces that break up the particles in the sludge. Specifically, when liquid passes through a constriction or valve at high velocity, it makes a low-pressure zone that induces bubble formation. The collapse of the bubbles releases enough energy to break down cellular structures and facilitate the solubilization of organic materials. While this technique reduces particle size with low energy consumption and less expensive equipment, it is poorly applicable to high-density slurries and is subject to wear of parts exposed to cavitation [24,25]. Also, intensive heat treatment, which produces sludge dewatering by destroying pathogens, is possible; however, the high energy consumption and possible loss of essential elements limit its use [26,27]. Another technique well established in the literature for dewatering and breaking down sludge structures is microwaves, which provide selective, rapid, and uniform heating while reducing treatment time but require expensive equipment without preventing or limiting the formation of unpleasant odors or toxic compounds [28,29]. As far as contaminant removal is concerned, the application of a suitable electric current to the (very dense and highly conductive) sludge, which, by weakening the binding forces between the particles, helps to separate the solid particles from the aqueous phase, thus reducing the use of any chemical agents [30,31]. Suppose the objective is the degradation of organic matter in low-density sludge. In that case, we are helped by photoanalytical treatment, in which the sludge is exposed to a suitable source of light (constant and prolonged), aided using specific catalysts (usually titanium dioxide) capable of reducing harmful organic compounds and pathogens. However, the continuous exposure to light and the use of expensive catalysts limit its applicability [32,33]. In order to degradate the organic matter in low-density sludge, the photoanalytical treatment can be used. In this case, the sludge is exposed to a suitable source of light (constant and prolonged), aided using specific catalysts (usually titanium dioxide) capable of reducing harmful organic compounds and pathogens [32,33]. Widespread is the mixing of sludge with flocculants/coagulants, which aggregate the particles to form heavy agglomerates that precipitate to the bottom of the tank and rapidly promote dewatering. However, such chemicals are often expensive and produce residues that require further treatment [33–35]. Studies have investigated the combined use of US and ozone to improve sludge conditioning and increase dewatering. Ozone, which is a powerful oxidant, facilitates the rupture of cell membranes and the solubilization of organic matter, therefore enhancing the effect of ultrasound. This combination reduces the sludge's viscosity and its filtration resistance [36]. Other studies have focused on the use of cationic polymers that, when combined with sonication, reduce the concentration of heavy metals and limit the time for sludge conditioning by making them stable during dewatering [15]. Again, the combination of thermo-alkaline conditioning with sonication assists in the degradation of complex organic compounds (due to high temperatures and high pH), facilitating the dewatering of the sludge. The use of ultrasound promotes further solubilization of the compounds and reduces the viscosity of the sludge [37,38]. There is no lack of significant studies on the combined use of microwaves (as a heat source), which can increase the permeability of cell membranes, with ultrasound, which, by causing cavitation, destroys cellular structures and significantly biodegrades sludge [39]. Recently, the combination of ultrasonic techniques with electrocoagulation has been successfully used to remove heavy metals from sludge. Electrical charges destabilize suspended particles, while sonication breaks down cellular structures, facilitating sedimentation of the sludge [40]. These studies strongly suggest that a major line of research must be based on using sonication in combination with chemical or physical treatments to improve sludge quality and manageability significantly. Indeed, combined sonication methods show superior results compared to single treatments, positively impacting process efficiency. Research in this field constantly evolves, with the intent to develop increasingly efficient, sustainable, and environmentally friendly conditioning techniques.

This work introduces an innovative approach that combines sonication with thermal treatment, proposing an advanced physical–mathematical model that couples the thermal and ultrasonic aspects. Such a model allows the reconstruction of detailed maps of temperature, humidity, and pressure on the walls of the treatment tank, providing an accurate and predictive view of system behavior throughout the sludge processing. Integrating this information enables optimized and scientifically based treatment management, reducing operating time and costs. The design of the apparatus was preceded by a detailed numerical simulation using the finite element method (FEM), which allowed the functional characteristics of the tank to be developed and verified virtually, ensuring efficient management of thermal and water variables [41]. The entire apparatus was built and tested only after this software validation, demonstrating complete adherence to regulatory standards for sludge use in agriculture. The proposed system, through integrated sensor monitoring and optimization of operating parameters, has shown the ability to reduce heavy metal content and improve the organic composition of sludge, making it fully compatible with current environmental requirements. The combined drying and sonication technique also enables particle size reduction of up to 50%, contributing to the sustainability and reuse of materials within a circular economy model [42]. This approach emerges as a practical and innovative model of sustainable sewage sludge management, with results that improve environmental and energy efficiency and demonstrate the possibility of valorizing sludge as a safe and certified agricultural resource.

For completeness, with the aim to provide the reader with a comprehensive overview of related work to the present research, we refer to some scientific studies on innovative sludge treatment and valorization techniques, focusing on sustainable methods, advanced technologies, and energy and nutrient recovery processes. Prominent among them are: (a) work on C recovery for bioenergy and N and P recovery for nutrients [43];

(b) on resource recovery for biogas production and P extraction for agricultural reuse [44]; (c) Anaerobic digestion combined with phosphorus recovery from sludge [45]; (d) Chemical/electrochemical methods for removal of heavy metals [46]; (e) Use of thermolysis and sonication for biogas production [47]; (f) on biochar production and C sequestration [48]; (g) on the use of electrodehydration to improve water removal [49]; (h) on the use of phytoremediation to remove heavy metals [50]; (i) the joint use of microwaves and chemical treatments to reduce pathogens in sludge and recover P and N [51]; (l) waste-to-energy for energy resources [52]; (m) hydrothermal carbonization for biofuel production, nutrient recovery, and energy enhancement [53].

The various sludge treatment techniques discussed above, including physical, thermal, chemical, and combined approaches, each present specific advantages and limitations depending on the context of the application. For clarity and to provide a comprehensive overview, the key characteristics, benefits, and limitations of these techniques are summarized in Table 1.

Table 1. Summary of the main sludge treatment techniques, highlighting their key characteristics, advantages, and limitations to provide a comprehensive overview of their applicability and effectiveness in sludge management.

Technique	Main Characteristics	Advantages	Limitations
Physical conditioning	Application of mechanical forces to alter sludge structure and facilitate dewatering.	Reduces sludge viscosity; improves drying.	High energy consumption; ineffective for fine particles.
Sonication	Use of ultrasonic waves to generate cavitation, breaking down particles and structures.	Increases organic material availability; facilitates dewatering.	High energy requirements; less effective for cavitation-resistant sludge.
Hydrodynamic cavitation	Creation and collapse of microbubbles through high-speed fluid flow in low-pressure zones.	Low energy consumption; inexpensive equipment.	Limited applicability to high-density sludge; mechanical wear.
Thermal treatment	Heat application to destroy pathogens and promote sludge dewatering.	Effective pathogen removal; facilitates dewatering.	High energy consumption; potential loss of essential elements.
Microwave treatment	Selective, rapid, and uniform heating via electromagnetic waves.	Uniform heating; reduces treatment time.	High equipment cost; potential odor/toxic compound formation.
Electrocoagulation	Use of electric current to destabilize particles, separating solids from the aqueous phase.	Reduces chemical agents use; effective for conductive sludge.	Limited to conductive sludge; moderate energy costs.
Photoanalytical treatment	Light exposure with catalysts (e.g., TiO_2) to degrade harmful organic compounds.	Removes pathogens and harmful compounds; reduces organic matter.	High catalyst cost; prolonged treatment time required.
Flocculation Coagulation	Addition of chemical agents to aggregate particles, promoting rapid sedimentation.	Facilitates quick dewatering; simple implementation.	High reagent costs; generates secondary residues.
Ozone treatment	Use of ozone to oxidize cell membranes and solubilize organic matter.	Reduces viscosity; enhances sonication efficiency.	High operational costs; complex maintenance.
Thermo-alkaline conditioning	Combination of heat and alkaline treatment to degrade complex organic compounds.	Facilitates solubilization and viscosity reduction.	Requires high temperatures and pH; high energy consumption.

Table 1. *Cont.*

Technique	Main Characteristics	Advantages	Limitations
Combined techniques	Integration of sonication with other treatments (e.g., microwaves, ozone, thermo-alkaline).	Enhances overall treatment efficiency.	Increased operational costs and complexity compared to single methods.

The remainder of the paper is organized as follows: the description of the sample-based sonication technique is given in Section 2. The proposed procedure to enable the production of sludge for agricultural uses is described in Section 3. In Section 4, we discuss the details of how to integrate the proposed approach into the treatment of sludge in sewage treatment plants. In Section 5, a mathematical model that, starting from the quantification of the ultrasonic power, provides a coupled differential model for the spatiotemporal reconstruction of temperature and humidity by also obtaining the pressure distribution inside the sewage tank is formulated. Once the sewage tank has been simulated using the FEM approach (Section 6) and a possible analytical model was proposed to evaluate the pressure exerted by the sludge on it (Section 7), the most important results for the analyses performed in both steady-state and transient regimes, as proposed in Section 8 have been discussed. Section 9 describes the prototype implemented for moisture detection and reduction in a sludge treatment tank, highlighting how sonication significantly improved the performance of the whole process to improve sludge quality (Section 10). Then, a quick roundup of comparisons with known cases in the literature (Section 11) further confirmed that the proposed approach is valid in software and hardware. In the last section, some reflections and possible future developments of the current research are given.

2. Preliminary Laboratory Study: Sonication on a Sample

To test whether the sonication produces sludge that can be used for agricultural purposes, in compliance with European standards EN 12766-1 and EN 12766-2 [54], at the Calabria Service Laboratory we reproduced an ultrasonic bath using the instrumentation shown in Figure 1 capable of applying US waves with a constant frequency of 20 kHz (employing a platinum probe with a tip diameter of 25 mm, favoring cavitation since higher frequencies might not induce the phenomenon mentioned above), for 60 min (with a sampling time of 5 s) on four wastewater sludge samples of 125 mL each, placed in a 1-L beaker. In addition, the percentage of electric current generating the US wave of 20, 40, and 60% with power [W] values of 0.3, 0.8, and 1.6, respectively, were amplified, obtaining a temperature in degrees centigrade of 20, 28, and 36, respectively.

Figure 1. Test apparatus for the sludge pretreatment process by sonication.

During the process, selected parameters allow the transducer to convert electrical energy into mechanical waves, amplified by the booster, which is transmitted to the sludge, generate compression and rarefaction cycles, with the ultimate goal of reducing the sludge volume by at least 15–20%, resulting in a reduction of the maturation time by about 20–30% (reduction from 20 to 14 days) [54–56]. The effectiveness of sludge decomposition and solubilization was monitored by verifying the increase in chemical oxygen demand (COD) in the sludge substrate by titration using a burette, thermoreactor, and digestion vials [57].

ζ Potential and Polydispersity Index (PDI)

An important parameter for the characterization of sludge is represented by the ζ potential, which measures the electric charge on suspended particles. When it has a high absolute value (positive or negative), the particles repel each other, leading to a stable suspension. On the contrary, a low absolute value for it suggests that the particles can aggregate [58]. Furthermore, for the optimization of treatment processes, operators optimize the dosage of coagulants and flocculants by varying the ζ potential. This process ensures efficient particle aggregation and improves the overall efficiency of sludge dewatering and sedimentation processes [18]. To provide a detailed view of the causes of dispersion, aggregation, or flocculation, we measured the particle size of the sonified sludge (and thus the stability of the sludge). We measured the values of the ζ potential [mV], defined as $\frac{\eta u \eta}{\epsilon_0}$, the viscosity of the fluid; u the mobility; ϵ, relative dielectric constant; ϵ_0, permittivity of vacuum) representing the electrical potential at the level of the slipping plane (slipping plane) measuring the magnitude of electrostatic repulsion/attraction or charge between the particles during all the tests performed, showing good stability of the samples, since, for each of them, we obtained $\zeta \gg 40$ mV. PDI values, defined as the ratio of particle size σ^2 to the square of their diameter $\bar{d}^2$, were also evaluated, quantifying size dispersion (a value close to zero indicates a uniform distribution of particles, while a high value reflects a broader and less homogeneous distribution). Specifically, from the initial high values of PDI obtained (ranging between 15 and 20), following treatment, they were reduced between 0.921 ± 0.150 and 0.922 ± 0.150. Both ζ and PDI values were obtained through the Malvern Zetasizer. This instrument measures, with high accuracy, the size, charge, and concentration of particles (by dynamic light scattering (DLS) with a measurement angle of 90 degrees) and their molecular weight, as well as the amount of suspended molecules. The analysis was conducted at different temperatures and durations using appropriate cuvettes.

3. How the Proposed Procedure Enables the Production of Sludge for Agricultural Uses

The US technique tested in the Laboratory was integrated into an established sludge treatment process displayed in Figure 2 (whose steps are included in the red dashed box), while the proposed approach is highlighted with green hatching.

Sludge from wastewater undergoes a first treatment line (water line) that deals with the purification of the water to remove contaminants and return it to the environment following regulatory standards. In contrast, the sludge line manages the sludge produced from the water line processes, aiming to stabilize it, reduce its volume, and valorize it, for example, through biogas production. The water line treats the main water stream, while the sludge line focuses on solid by-product management, working in synergy as sludge comes from the former's processes, and the latter's residues can be recirculated for further treatment. Specifically, the water line processes sludge from wastewater that undergoes initial screening through a screening battery that separates heavy parts (coarse sands and gravels), allowing the filtered sludge to undergo treatment to remove fats and oils. Then, an aerobic digestion chamber facilitates prolonged aerobic treatment (of about 17–20 days) and proceeds with appropriate sedimentation. The fraction of sludge that is insufficiently oxygenated is fed back into the aerobic digestion chamber to repeat the process, while the remainder undergoes NaClO-based treatment to reduce the presence of pathogenic microorganisms, bacteria, viruses, and other contaminants, making the sludge safer for the environment [59]. It is worth noting that in excess flow rates from biological, once the oils and fats are removed, the sludge goes directly to NaClO-based treatment. A further portion of the sludge exiting sedimentation constitutes the input to the sludge line, which, through gravity sludge thickening, aerobic biological stabilization, and sludge dewatering with belt filter press, produces the treated sludges (any supernatant is returned to the water line's head to be fed into the aerobic chamber). Then, before the treated sludge is considered waste (to produce dry sludge for agricultural use) at the end of the sludge line, the proposed procedure subjects it to the sonication process as already described so that the moisture percentage is significantly reduced by appropriate heat treatment. Finally, a monitoring system based essentially on moisture and temperature sensors sets the sonication parameters to optimize the whole process.

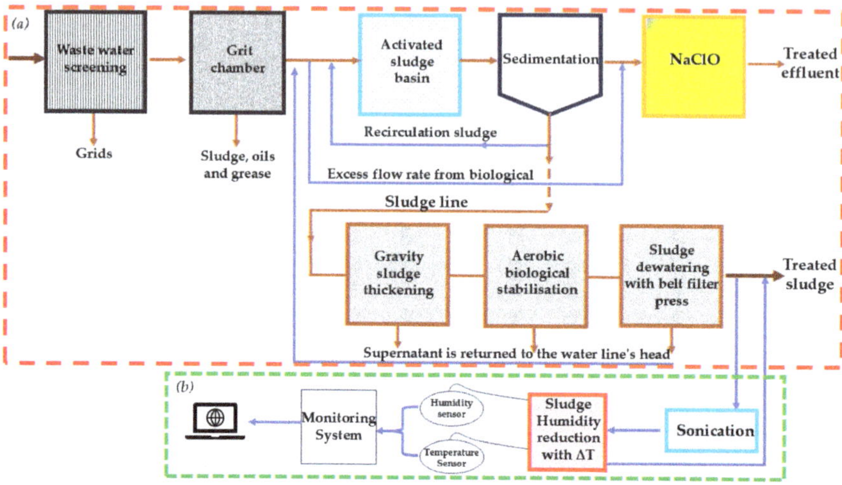

Figure 2. Integration of the proposed approach (enclosed by the green dashed line) into the sludge treatment process within a wastewater treatment plant (red dashed line). Section (**a**) represents the conventional wastewater treatment chain, including pretreatment, sedimentation, biological treatment, and sludge management. Section (**b**) highlights the proposed approach, combining monitoring by humidity and temperature sensors with a sonication system aimed at sludge moisture reduction (sludge humidity reduction with ΔT).

4. Integration of an Innovative Approach in the Treatment of Sludge in Sewage Treatment Plants

Laboratory-tested sonication treatment grafted inside the plant (see Figure 2) lasting up to 150 min, with the usual sampling carried out every 5 min (measuring COD, temperature, and PDI), was performed on an 8-liter sludge sample, applying a 230 V amplitude voltage at 50 Hz (constant frequency throughout the treatment duration), with a maximum flow rate of 50 L/min, with a contact time (total time the slurry remains in contact with a chemical reagent) per liter of 2.40 s. Four units with a peak power of 1.7 A were used to produce US waves to achieve the ideal US frequency of 150 kHz, corresponding to maximum cavitation. As can be seen from Table 2, the data obtained do not reveal any incompatibilities of sludge use for agricultural purposes, both in terms of heavy metals and the possible presence of bacteria (Salmonella). It is worth noting that both the treatment duration (150 min) and the contact time of 2.40 s depend on the sludge composition [60]. The prototype is powered by four sets of US generators, each with a maximum draw of 1.7 A to ensure the ideal frequency of 15 kHz, leading to the maximum detected cavitation (usually achievable between 1.5 A and 1.7 A). Table 3 summarizes the operational parameters of sonication, while the experimental apparatus is displayed in Figure 3.

Therefore, we consider proceeding with sludge humidity reduction using a thermal approach. We propose a physical–mathematical model that couples temperature with humidity to accurately quantify the volume of liquid and condensate inside the sludge treatment tank.

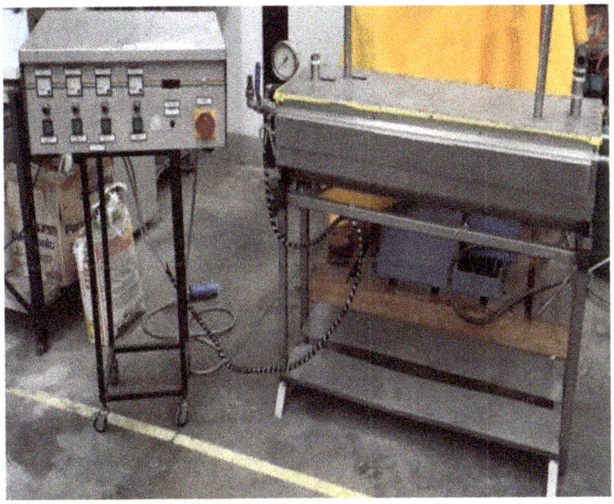

Figure 3. The experimental apparatus for sludge treatment process by ultrasonic sonication. **Left**: the amplifying device with current values increasing in percentage from 0 to 60 A. **Right**: the tank containing the sludge during ultrasonic sonication.

Table 2. Comparison between the parameters given in DL99 for sludge use in agriculture and the data collected on the sludge produced by the plant.

Heavy Metals (mg/kg) and Bacteria (MPN/gSS)	National Decree DL99—29 January 1992	Sludge Analysis of the Plant
arsenic	n.d.	//
copper	1000	700–800
zinc	2500	700–1200
cadmium	20	<1
mercury	10	<1
lead	750	90–160
nickel	300	50–90
organic carbon (% sludge)	20 (minimum)	25–30
phosphorus (% sludge)	20 (minimum)	25–30
nitrogen (% sludge)	1.5 (minimum)	4.5–5.5
salmonella	103 (maximum)	30–60

Table 3. Operating parameter of sludge sonication treatment.

Parameters	Values
Dimensions	445 × 545 × 1560 mm
Electrical supply	230 V, 50 Hz
US frequency	50 kHz, constant
Tank volume	8 L
Maximum input flow rate	3000 L/h, i.e., 50 L/min
Contact time	2.40 s per every sludge sample
Sonication time	0–150 min, sampling time 5 min

5. Temperature–Humidity Coupled Model for Sludge Treatment

5.1. Quantification of the Acoustic Power

Let $Oxyz$ be an ortho-normal Cartesian coordinate system where $\Omega \subset \mathbb{R}^3$ represents the sludge; then, the generic vector $\mathbf{x} = (x, y, z) \subset \Omega$ represents a point on the sludge. The acoustic energy, E, generated and transferred to the sludge sample during US sonication (following pretreatment in an oven at the initial temperature of 373 °C for two hours) is transformed, in part, into heat that produces an increase in temperature $T(\mathbf{x}, t)$ that can be quantified using a calorimetric approach (highlighting the direct proportionality between $T(\mathbf{x},t)$ and P). The idea is based on the thermodynamic principle that P supplied by the US is converted into heat, and thus, the acoustic power can be calculated by measuring the temperature rise in the sludge.

The US energy (expressed in J) that causes an increase in $T(\mathbf{x},t)$ can be expressed as [61–63]:

$$Q = MC_p\Delta T(\mathbf{x},t) \tag{1}$$

where Q and M are the amount of heat absorbed by the slurry and its mass M (kg); C_p is the specific heat capacity (J/kg K); and $\Delta T(\mathbf{x},t)$ is the increment of $T(\mathbf{x},t)$ (K) (experimentally measurable by sensors). Then, the power P, if Δt is the time interval during which heat transfer occurred, takes the form:

$$P = \frac{MC_p\Delta T(\mathbf{x},t)}{\Delta t}, \tag{2}$$

which, in an infinitesimal time frame, becomes:

$$P = MC_p\frac{dT(\mathbf{x},t)}{dt}. \tag{3}$$

5.2. *Fourier's Law of Heat Conduction*

To quantify the heat flux, $\mathbf{q}$ (amount of heat per unit area in unit time measured in W/m^2), in the sludge as a function of $T(\mathbf{x},t)$, we use the well-known Fourier's law:

$$\mathbf{q} = -k\nabla T(\mathbf{x},t), \tag{4}$$

asserting that $\mathbf{q} \propto \nabla T(\mathbf{x},t)$ through k (W/mK) representing the thermal conductivity of the sludge, with obvious heat flow from higher-temperature points to lower-temperature points.

5.3. *General Thermal Balance Equation*

A heat balance equation is essential to describe the thermal behavior in ultrasonic sludge treatment, considering heat transfer mechanisms and internal and external energy sources. This equation allows modeling the interactions between key variables and physical parameters, making it essential to simulate and optimize the process [61–63].

5.3.1. Thermal Storage Term

Together with C_p, it describes the ability of the fluid to store thermal energy. $\frac{\partial T(\mathbf{x},t)}{\partial t}$ measures the rate at which $T(\mathbf{x},t)$ changes over time. Therefore, the contribution due to accumulation can be quantified by the term $\rho C_p\frac{\partial T(\mathbf{x},t)}{\partial t}$. The contribution due to heat accumulation in the sludge can be quantified as $\rho C_p\frac{\partial T(\mathbf{x},t)}{\partial t}$ where ρ is the density of the fluid while C_p denotes the capacity of the sludge to store heat [61–63].

5.3.2. Convective Term

This term represents heat transport by convection, describing how the motion of a slurry at the velocity $\mathbf{u}(\mathbf{x},t)$ transports heat energy, influencing the energy balance with the contribution $\rho C_p\mathbf{u}(\mathbf{x},t)\cdot\nabla T(\mathbf{x},t)$, which quantifies the heat gain or loss in the system [61–63].

5.3.3. Heat Conduction Term

This term represents heat flow by conduction and quantifies how it varies spatially, indicating whether heat enters or leaves a specific region of the fluid, expressed as $\nabla\cdot(-k\nabla T(\mathbf{x},t))$ based on the temperature gradient [61–63].

5.3.4. Heat Sources

Denoted by $Q(\mathbf{x},t)$ and $Q_m(\mathbf{x},t)$, respectively, they represent heat added by an external source (e.g., an external heater) and heat generated inside the system due to internal causes (e.g., chemical reactions or biological processes). Then, the heat generated in the US can act directly by converting P to heat within the sludge; the second allows the mechanical energy generated by the US to break up the particles, facilitating heat diffusion and accelerating the process of temperature homogenization [61–63].

5.4. The Energy Balance Equation

Combining all the contributions, we obtain:

$$\begin{aligned}\rho C_p \tfrac{\partial T(\mathbf{x},t)}{\partial t} + \rho C_p \mathbf{u}(\mathbf{x},t)\cdot\nabla T(\mathbf{x},t) + \nabla\cdot(-k\nabla T(\mathbf{x},t))\\ = Q(\mathbf{x},t) + Q_m(\mathbf{x},t).\end{aligned} \tag{5}$$

representing the parabolic differential equation of the second-order partial derivative that governs the energy balance by describing the evolution of $T(\mathbf{x},t)$, which considers all modes of energy transfer (conduction, convection, internal and/or external heat sources). The model (5) describes the heat transfer and the variation of $T(\mathbf{x},t)$ in the system, influenced directly by P. Heat conduction depends on the energy transferred per unit time and area, a function of P, while ultrasonic convection and turbulence influence heat transport in the fluid. Therefore, the acoustic power determines the thermal behavior of the model [61–65].

5.5. On Moisture Reduction

To calculate the reduction of moisture $W(\mathbf{x},t)$ in a sludge from $T(\mathbf{x},t)$, we use a model based on the Balance Equation (5). $W(\mathbf{x},t)$, representing the water content per unit volume, varies with the evaporative flux, $J_e(\mathbf{x},t)$, described as:

$$\frac{\partial W(\mathbf{x},t)}{\partial t} = -\nabla\cdot J_e(\mathbf{x},t), \tag{6}$$

where $J_e(J_e(\mathbf{x},t)$ is a function of $T(\mathbf{x},t)$ and vapor pressure, and is written as:

$$J_e(\mathbf{x},t) = k_e(T(\mathbf{x},t))\big(p_v(T(\mathbf{x},t)) - p_{v,\text{amb}}\big), \tag{7}$$

with $k_e(T(\mathbf{x},t))$ temperature-dependent evaporation coefficient, $p_v(T(\mathbf{x},t))$ saturated vapor pressure and $p_{v,\text{amb}}$ ambient vapor pressure. The source $Q_m(\mathbf{x},t)$, associated with water evaporation, is related to the latent heat λ and the rate of moisture reduction:

$$Q_m(\mathbf{x},t) = \lambda\frac{\partial W(\mathbf{x},t)}{\partial t}. \tag{8}$$

The overall moisture reduction is calculated by integrating the residual content $W(\mathbf{x},t)$ over time and space, compared with the initial content $W_0(\mathbf{x})$:

$$\Delta W = \int_\Omega \big(W_0(\mathbf{x}) - W(\mathbf{x},t)\big)\,d\mathbf{x}. \tag{9}$$

Then, substituting into the (5) the (8), we obtain:

$$\begin{aligned}\rho C_p \frac{\partial T(\mathbf{x},t)}{\partial t} + \rho C_p \mathbf{u}(\mathbf{x},t)\cdot\nabla T(\mathbf{x},t) + \nabla\cdot(-k\nabla T(\mathbf{x},t))\\ = Q(\mathbf{x},t) + \lambda\frac{\partial W(\mathbf{x},t)}{\partial t}.\end{aligned} \tag{10}$$

5.6. The Coupled System

Considering the balance equation, Equations (6) and (10), the system describing the evolution of temperature and humidity consists of:

$$\begin{cases} \rho C_p \frac{\partial T}{\partial t} + \rho C_p \mathbf{u} \cdot \nabla T + \nabla \cdot (-k \nabla T) = Q + \lambda \dfrac{\partial W(\mathbf{x},t)}{\partial t}, \\ \dfrac{\partial W(\mathbf{x},t)}{\partial t} + \nabla \cdot J_e(\mathbf{x},t) = 0 \\ J_e(\mathbf{x},t) = k_e(T(\mathbf{x},t))\big(p_v(T(\mathbf{x},t)) - p_{v,\text{amb}}\big). \end{cases} \tag{11}$$

5.7. On the Existence, Uniqueness, and Regularity of the Solution: Variational Formulation

We work on $\Omega \subset \mathbb{R}^n$, which is open, restricted, and with edge $\partial\Omega$ sufficiently regular. We define the Cartesian product of function spaces to describe the two coupled variables $T(\mathbf{x},t)$ and $W(\mathbf{x},t)$ [61–63,66]:

$$X = H^1(\Omega) \times H^1(\Omega), \tag{12}$$

where $H^1(\Omega)$ is the Sobolev space of functions belonging to $L^2(\Omega)$ with first-order weak derivatives in $L^2(\Omega)$. Weak solutions of the coupled system will be looked for in $\mathcal{X} = L^2(0,T;X)$, with time derivatives $\dfrac{\partial T(\mathbf{x},t)}{\partial t}, \dfrac{\partial W(\mathbf{x},t)}{\partial t} \in L^2(0,T;X')$, where X' is the dual space of X'. We multiply the budget equation in (11) by a test function $\varphi \in H^1(\Omega)$ and integrate over Ω, obtaining:

$$\int_\Omega \rho C_p \frac{\partial T(\mathbf{x},t)}{\partial t} \varphi \, d\mathbf{x} + \int_\Omega \rho C_p (\mathbf{u} \cdot \nabla T) \varphi \, d\mathbf{x} + \int_\Omega k \nabla T(\mathbf{x},t) \cdot \nabla \varphi \, d\mathbf{x} \\ = \int_\Omega Q \varphi \, d\mathbf{x} + \lambda \int_\Omega \frac{\partial W(\mathbf{x},t)}{\partial t} \varphi \, d\mathbf{x}. \tag{13}$$

To ensure that the first integral in (13) makes sense, we assume $T(\mathbf{x},t) \in L^2(0,T;H^1(\Omega))$ and $\dfrac{\partial T(\mathbf{x},t)}{\partial t} \in L^2(0,T;H^1(\Omega)')$. As for the second equation in (11), we multiply by a test function $\psi \in H^1(\Omega)$ and integrate over Ω, obtaining:

$$\int_\Omega \frac{\partial W(\mathbf{x},t)}{\partial t} \psi \, d\mathbf{x} + \int_\Omega (\nabla \cdot J_e) \psi \, d\mathbf{x} = 0. \tag{14}$$

Using, then, the divergence theorem and imposing a natural boundary condition ($J_e \cdot \mathbf{n} = 0$ on $\partial\Omega$), we can write:

$$\int_\Omega (\nabla \cdot J_e) \psi \, d\mathbf{x} = -\int_\Omega J_e \cdot \nabla \psi \, d\mathbf{x}. \tag{15}$$

Then the second equation of (11) in variational form becomes:

$$\int_\Omega \frac{\partial W(\mathbf{x},t)}{\partial t} \psi \, d\mathbf{x} - \int_\Omega J_e \cdot \nabla \psi \, d\mathbf{x} = 0, \tag{16}$$

that by substituting into it the expression of J_e, we obtain:

$$\int_\Omega \frac{\partial W(\mathbf{x},t)}{\partial t} \psi \, d\mathbf{x} - \int_\Omega k_e(T)\big(p_v(T) - p_{v,\text{amb}}\big) \nabla \psi \, d\mathbf{x} = 0. \tag{17}$$

Then, the problem, in weak form, translates to finding a solution $(T(\mathbf{x},t), W(\mathbf{x},t)) \in L^2(0,T;X)$, such that for each test function $(\varphi,\psi) \in X$ both equations in the variational form are satisfied.

5.7.1. Existence and Uniqueness

We define the paired bilinear operator $\mathcal{A} : X \times X \to \mathbb{R}$ as [61–63]:

$$\begin{aligned}
&\mathcal{A}((T(\mathbf{x},t),W(\mathbf{x},t)),(\varphi,\psi)) \\
&= \int_\Omega k\nabla T(\mathbf{x},t)\cdot\nabla\varphi\,d\mathbf{x} + \int_\Omega \rho C_p(\mathbf{u}\cdot\nabla T(\mathbf{x},t))\varphi\,d\mathbf{x} \\
&\quad + \int_\Omega k_e(T)\big(p_v(T)-p_{v,\mathrm{amb}}\big)\nabla\psi\,d\mathbf{x}. \qquad (18)
\end{aligned}$$

It is simple to verify that the operator $\mathcal{A}$ is continuous, i.e., there exists $C>0$ such that:

$$\begin{aligned}
&|\mathcal{A}((T(\mathbf{x},t),W(\mathbf{x},t)),(\varphi,\psi))| \\
&\leq C(\|T(\mathbf{x},t)\|_{H^1}+\|W(\mathbf{x},t)\|_{H^1})(\|\varphi\|_{H^1}+\|\psi\|_{H^1}). \qquad (19)
\end{aligned}$$

Moreover, $\mathcal{A}$ is coercive under the assumptions of uniform positivity of the coefficients ($k(x)\geq k_0>0$):

$$\begin{aligned}
&\mathcal{A}((T(\mathbf{x},t),W(\mathbf{x},t)),(T(\mathbf{x},t),W(\mathbf{x},t))) \\
&\geq \alpha(\|T(\mathbf{x},t)\|^2_{H^1}+\|W(\mathbf{x},t)\|^2_{H^1}), \qquad (20)
\end{aligned}$$

where $\alpha>0$. The functional associated with the source and coupling terms is:

$$F((\varphi,\psi)) = \int_\Omega Q\varphi\,d\mathbf{x} + \lambda\int_\Omega \frac{\partial W}{\partial t}\varphi\,d\mathbf{x} + \int_\Omega \frac{\partial W}{\partial t}\psi\,d\mathbf{x}. \qquad (21)$$

Under the assumptions of regularity ($Q\in L^2(\Omega)$, $\frac{\partial W}{\partial t}\in L^2(0,T;H^1(\Omega)')$, F is continuous. Then, the Lax-Milgram theorem guarantees the existence and uniqueness of $(T,W)\in L^2(0,T;X)$.

5.7.2. Regularity

The regularity of the solutions $T(\mathbf{x},t)$ and $W(\mathbf{x},t)$ can be analyzed by exploiting the coupled structure of the system. In particular, the time derivative $\dfrac{\partial T(\mathbf{x},t)}{\partial t}$ belongs to $L^2(0,T;H^1(\Omega)')$. This result is ensured by the regularity of $W(\mathbf{x},t)$, which belongs to $L^2(0,T;H^1(\Omega))$, and by the fact that the coupling term $\lambda\frac{\partial W(\mathbf{x},t)}{\partial t}$ is sufficiently regular. Consequently, $T(\mathbf{x},t)$ evolves in time regularly within a weak functional space.

The elliptic structure of the term $-\nabla\cdot(k\nabla T(\mathbf{x},t))$ in the first equation also guarantees that $T(\mathbf{x},t)\in H^1(\Omega)$ at each instant t, provided that k, $\mathbf{u}$, Q are regular. If k is sufficiently regular, e.g., $k\in C^2(\Omega)$, we can conclude that $T(\mathbf{x},t)\in H^2(\Omega)$ for each instant t.

The regularity of the solution $W(\mathbf{x},t)$ depends directly on the regularity of $T(\mathbf{x},t)$ through the nonlinear term $J_e = k_e(T)\big(p_v(T)-p_{v,\mathrm{amb}}big\big)$. If $T(T(\mathbf{x},t)\in H^1(\Omega)$, then $W(\mathbf{x},t)\in H^1(\Omega)$. If moreover $T(\mathbf{x},t)\in H^2(\Omega)$ and the coefficients $k_e(T)$ and $p_v(T)$ are regular, e.g., C^2, then we can conclude that W also belongs to $H^2(\Omega)$.

6. The Numerical Model

6.1. Time Discretization

We apply the implicit Euler's method for the temporal discretization of the terms $\frac{\partial T}{\partial t}$ and $\frac{\partial W}{\partial t}$, obtaining: [61–63]

$$\frac{\partial T}{\partial t}\approx\frac{T^{n+1}-T^n}{\Delta t},\quad \frac{\partial W}{\partial t}\approx\frac{W^{n+1}-W^n}{\Delta t}, \qquad (22)$$

which substituted in the variational formulation, gives, for T^{n+1}:

$$\int_\Omega \rho C_p \frac{T^{n+1}-T^n}{\Delta t}\varphi\,d\mathbf{x} + \int_\Omega \rho C_p(\mathbf{u}\cdot\nabla T^{n+1})\varphi\,d\mathbf{x} + \int_\Omega k\nabla T^{n+1}\cdot\nabla\varphi\,d\mathbf{x}$$
$$= \int_\Omega Q\varphi\,d\mathbf{x} + \lambda\int_\Omega \frac{W^{n+1}-W^n}{\Delta t}\varphi\,d\mathbf{x}, \tag{23}$$

and for W^{n+1}:

$$\int_\Omega \frac{W^{n+1}-W^n}{\Delta t}\psi\,d\mathbf{x} - \int_\Omega k_e(T^{n+1})(p_v(T^{n+1}) - p_{v,\mathrm{amb}})\nabla\psi\,d\mathbf{x} = 0. \tag{24}$$

As for spatial discretization, we partition Ω into a mesh $\mathcal{T}_h$, composed of M finite elements. We approximate the solutions T^{n+1} and W^{n+1} as linear combinations of basis functions $\phi_i(\mathbf{x})$, as follows:

$$T_h^{n+1}(\mathbf{x}) = \sum_{i=1}^{N} T_i^{n+1}\phi_i(\mathbf{x}), \quad W_h^{n+1}(\mathbf{x}) = \sum_{i=1}^{N} W_i^{n+1}\phi_i(\mathbf{x}), \tag{25}$$

where T_i^{n+1} and W_i^{n+1} are the values of the solutions at the nodes of the mesh. The test functions are chosen from the same basis, namely $\varphi = \phi_i$ and $\psi = \phi_j$.
Then, substituting these expansions into the variational equations, we obtain for T^{n+1}:

$$\sum_{j=1}^{N}\left[\int_\Omega \rho C_p \frac{\phi_j\phi_i}{\Delta t}\,d\mathbf{x}\right]T_j^{n+1}$$
$$+\sum_{j=1}^{N}\left[\int_\Omega k\nabla\phi_j\cdot\nabla\phi_i\,d\mathbf{x} + \int_\Omega \rho C_p(\mathbf{u}\cdot\nabla\phi_j)\phi_i\,d\mathbf{x}\right]T_j^{n+1}$$
$$= \int_\Omega Q\phi_i\,d\mathbf{x} + \sum_{j=1}^{N}\left[\int_\Omega \frac{\lambda\phi_j\phi_i}{\Delta t}\,d\mathbf{x}\right]W_j^{n+1} - \int_\Omega \frac{\rho C_p T^n\phi_i}{\Delta t}\,d\mathbf{x}, \tag{26}$$

and for W^{n+1}:

$$\sum_{j=1}^{N}\left[\int_\Omega \frac{\phi_j\phi_i}{\Delta t}\,d\mathbf{x}\right]W_j^{n+1}$$
$$-\sum_{j=1}^{N}\left[\int_\Omega k_e(T^{n+1})(p_v(T^{n+1}) - p_{v,\mathrm{amb}})\nabla\phi_j\cdot\nabla\phi_i\,d\mathbf{x}\right]W_j^{n+1} = \int_\Omega \frac{\phi_i W^n}{\Delta t}\,d\mathbf{x}. \tag{27}$$

6.2. Algebraic Formulation

For computational needs, we define the mass matrix and stiffness matrix for T as:

$$(\mathbf{M}_T)_{ij} = \int_\Omega \rho C_p\phi_j\phi_i\,d\mathbf{x}. \tag{28}$$

and:

$$(\mathbf{A}_T)_{ij} = \int_\Omega k\nabla\phi_j\cdot\nabla\phi_i\,d\mathbf{x} + \int_\Omega \rho C_p(\mathbf{u}\cdot\nabla\phi_j)\phi_i\,d\mathbf{x}. \tag{29}$$

respectively, while, for W, the mass and stiffness matrix (dependent on T), take the following forms:

$$(\mathbf{M}_W)_{ij} = \int_\Omega \phi_j\phi_i\,d\mathbf{x}, \tag{30}$$

$$(\mathbf{A}_W(T))_{ij} = \int_\Omega k_e(T)(p_v(T) - p_{v,\text{amb}}) \nabla\phi_j \cdot \nabla\phi_i \, d\mathbf{x}. \tag{31}$$

Finally, considering the source term:

$$(\mathbf{F}_T)_i = \int_\Omega Q\phi_i \, d\mathbf{x}, \quad (\mathbf{F}_W)_i = \int_\Omega \phi_i W^n \, d\mathbf{x}, \tag{32}$$

our coupled linear system becomes:

$$\begin{cases} \mathbf{M}_T \frac{\mathbf{T}^{n+1} - \mathbf{T}^n}{\Delta t} + \mathbf{A}_T \mathbf{T}^{n+1} = \mathbf{F}_T + \lambda \mathbf{M}_T \frac{\mathbf{W}^{n+1} - \mathbf{W}^n}{\Delta t} \\ \mathbf{M}_W \frac{\mathbf{W}^{n+1} - \mathbf{W}^n}{\Delta t} - \mathbf{A}_W(\mathbf{T}^{n+1})\mathbf{W}^{n+1} = 0. \end{cases} \tag{33}$$

The resolution of the described coupled algebraic system requires numerical methods since it includes nonlinear dependencies and couplings between the variables $\mathbf{T}^{n+1}$ and $\mathbf{W}^{n+1}$. The system (33) can be written in the following form:

$$\begin{bmatrix} \mathbf{M}_T/\Delta t + \mathbf{A}_T & -\lambda \mathbf{M}_T/\Delta t \\ 0 & \mathbf{M}_W/\Delta t - \mathbf{A}_W(\mathbf{T}^{n+1}) \end{bmatrix} \begin{bmatrix} \mathbf{T}^{n+1} \\ \mathbf{W}^{n+1} \end{bmatrix} = \begin{bmatrix} \mathbf{F}_T + \mathbf{M}_T \mathbf{T}^n/\Delta t + \lambda \mathbf{M}_T \mathbf{W}^n/\Delta t \\ \mathbf{M}_W \mathbf{W}^n/\Delta t \end{bmatrix}. \tag{34}$$

It is nonlinear, since $\mathbf{A}_W(\mathbf{T}^{n+1})$ depends on $\mathbf{T}^{n+1}$). Then, using an iterative approach based on Newton-Raphson, we define the residual as:

$$\mathbf{R}(\mathbf{T}, \mathbf{W}) = \begin{bmatrix} \mathbf{M}_T \frac{\mathbf{T} - \mathbf{T}^n}{\Delta t} + \mathbf{A}_T \mathbf{T} - \lambda \mathbf{M}_T \frac{\mathbf{W} - \mathbf{W}^n}{\Delta t} - \mathbf{F}_T \\ \mathbf{M}_W \frac{\mathbf{W} - \mathbf{W}^n}{\Delta t} - \mathbf{A}_W(\mathbf{T})\mathbf{W} \end{bmatrix}, \tag{35}$$

such that we find $(\mathbf{T}^{n+1}, \mathbf{W}^{n+1})$ such that $\mathbf{R}(\mathbf{T}^{n+1}, \mathbf{W}^{n+1}) = 0$. Then, we expand $\mathbf{R}(\mathbf{T}, \mathbf{W})$ around an initial estimate $(\mathbf{T}_k, \mathbf{W}_k)$ at step k using a Taylor series:

$$\mathbf{R}(\mathbf{T}_{k+1}, \mathbf{W}_{k+1}) \approx \mathbf{R}(\mathbf{T}_k, \mathbf{W}_k) + \frac{\partial \mathbf{R}}{\partial \mathbf{T}} \Delta \mathbf{T} + \frac{\partial \mathbf{R}}{\partial \mathbf{W}} \Delta \mathbf{W}, \tag{36}$$

where:

$$\Delta \mathbf{T} = \mathbf{T}_{k+1} - \mathbf{T}_k, \quad \Delta \mathbf{W} = \mathbf{W}_{k+1} - \mathbf{W}_k. \tag{37}$$

6.3. Linearization of the Algebraic System

Linearizing the coupled system, we obtain the following linear system:

$$\begin{bmatrix} \frac{\partial \mathbf{R}_T}{\partial \mathbf{T}} & \frac{\partial \mathbf{R}_T}{\partial \mathbf{W}} \\ \frac{\partial \mathbf{R}_W}{\partial \mathbf{T}} & \frac{\partial \mathbf{R}_W}{\partial \mathbf{W}} \end{bmatrix} \begin{bmatrix} \Delta \mathbf{T} \\ \Delta \mathbf{W} \end{bmatrix} = - \begin{bmatrix} \mathbf{R}_T(\mathbf{T}_k, \mathbf{W}_k) \\ \mathbf{R}_W(\mathbf{T}_k, \mathbf{W}_k) \end{bmatrix}, \tag{38}$$

where:

$$\frac{\partial \mathbf{R}_T}{\partial \mathbf{T}} = \frac{\mathbf{M}_T}{\Delta t} + \mathbf{A}_T, \quad \frac{\partial \mathbf{R}_T}{\partial \mathbf{W}} = -\frac{\lambda \mathbf{M}_T}{\Delta t}, \tag{39}$$

$$\frac{\partial \mathbf{R}_W}{\partial \mathbf{T}} = -\frac{\partial \mathbf{A}_W(\mathbf{T})}{\partial \mathbf{T}} \mathbf{W}, \quad \frac{\partial \mathbf{R}_W}{\partial \mathbf{W}} = \frac{\mathbf{M}_W}{\Delta t} - \mathbf{A}_W(\mathbf{T}) \tag{40}$$

where $\frac{\partial \mathbf{A}_W(\mathbf{T})}{\partial \mathbf{T}}$ is a matrix that is calculated by differentiating $\mathbf{A}_W(\mathbf{T})$ with respect to $\mathbf{T}$. At each iteration, k the system becomes [61–63]:

$$\begin{bmatrix} \frac{\mathbf{M}_T}{\Delta t} + \mathbf{A}_T & -\frac{\lambda \mathbf{M}_T}{\Delta t} \\ -\frac{\partial \mathbf{A}_W(\mathbf{T}_k)}{\partial \mathbf{T}} \mathbf{W}_k & \frac{\mathbf{M}_W}{\Delta t} - \mathbf{A}_W(\mathbf{T}_k) \end{bmatrix} \begin{bmatrix} \Delta \mathbf{T} \\ \Delta \mathbf{W} \end{bmatrix} = - \begin{bmatrix} \mathbf{R}_T(\mathbf{T}_k, \mathbf{W}_k) \\ \mathbf{R}_W(\mathbf{T}_k, \mathbf{W}_k) \end{bmatrix}. \tag{41}$$

from which the updating of solutions is ensured as follows:

$$\mathbf{T}_{k+1} = \mathbf{T}_k + \Delta\mathbf{T}, \quad \mathbf{W}_{k+1} = \mathbf{W}_k + \Delta\mathbf{W}. \tag{42}$$

Obviously, iterations proceed to that some residual, $\epsilon < 0$, satisfies:

$$\|\mathbf{R}_T(\mathbf{T}_{k+1}, \mathbf{W}_{k+1})\| + \|\mathbf{R}_W(\mathbf{T}_{k+1}, \mathbf{W}_{k+1})\| < \epsilon. \tag{43}$$

Then, calculating the matrices $\mathbf{M}_T$, $\mathbf{M}_W$, $\mathbf{A}_T$, and the basic form of $\mathbf{A}_W(\mathbf{T})$, for each time step $n+1$, we initialize $\mathbf{T}_0^{n+1} = \mathbf{T}^n$ and $\mathbf{W}_0^{n+1} = \mathbf{W}^n$ and perform Newton-Raphson iterations until convergence. The solution $(\mathbf{T}^{n+1}, \mathbf{W}^{n+1})$ gives the updated values of the variables at the next time step.

Solution of the Algebraic System

At each iteration, the linear system can be written in the following form:

$$\mathbf{K}\begin{bmatrix}\Delta\mathbf{T}\\ \Delta\mathbf{W}\end{bmatrix} = -\begin{bmatrix}\mathbf{R}_T(\mathbf{T}_k, \mathbf{W}_k)\\ \mathbf{R}_W(\mathbf{T}_k, \mathbf{W}_k)\end{bmatrix}, \tag{44}$$

where:

$$\mathbf{K} = \begin{bmatrix}\mathbf{K}_{TT} & \mathbf{K}_{TW}\\ \mathbf{K}_{WT} & \mathbf{K}_{WW}\end{bmatrix}, \tag{45}$$

with:

$$\mathbf{K}_{TT} = \frac{\mathbf{M}_T}{\Delta t} + \mathbf{A}_T, \quad \mathbf{K}_{TW} = -\frac{\lambda\mathbf{M}_T}{\Delta t}, \tag{46}$$

$$\mathbf{K}_{WT} = -\frac{\partial\mathbf{A}_W(\mathbf{T}_k)}{\partial\mathbf{T}}\mathbf{W}_k, \quad \mathbf{K}_{WW} = \frac{\mathbf{M}_W}{\Delta t} - \mathbf{A}_W(\mathbf{T}_k). \tag{47}$$

Whose known term is:

$$\mathbf{b} = -\begin{bmatrix}\mathbf{R}_T(\mathbf{T}_k, \mathbf{W}_k)\\ \mathbf{R}_W(\mathbf{T}_k, \mathbf{W}_k)\end{bmatrix}. \tag{48}$$

Once the matrices $\mathbf{M}_T$, $\mathbf{M}_W$, $\mathbf{A}_T$, $\mathbf{A}_W(\mathbf{T}_k)$ are constructed by FEM discretization, $\mathbf{K}$ is constructed as a sparse block matrix in which $\mathbf{K}_{TT}$ and $\mathbf{K}_{WW}$ are dominant diagonal matrices. Finally, the paired $\mathbf{K}_{TW}$ and $\mathbf{K}_{WT}$ blocks (calculated from the problem under study). Since the linear system is large with sparse matrices, GMRES is employed. For more complex problems, we can introduce a preconditioner based on the diagonal blocks $\mathbf{K}_{TT}$ and $\mathbf{K}_{WW}$ to speed up convergence.

6.4. Relationship Between $W(\mathbf{x}, t)$ and the Liquid Water Content

To quantify the volume of liquid and condensate inside the sludge treatment tank, starting from temperature $T(\mathbf{x}, t)$ and moisture $W(\mathbf{x}, t)$, it is necessary to implement an approach that integrates the following steps. Since $W(\mathbf{x}, t)$ represents the moisture content per unit volume of the sludge, to obtain the total volume of initial and residual liquid water in the tank, it will be sufficient to calculate:

$$V_{\text{water}}^{\text{inizial}} = \int_\Omega W_0(\mathbf{x})\,d\mathbf{x}, \quad V_{\text{water}}^{\text{residue}}(t) = \int_\Omega W(\mathbf{x}, t)\,d\mathbf{x}, \tag{49}$$

where $W_0(W_0(\mathbf{x})$ is the initial moisture content. During heat treatment, some evaporated water condenses on the inner surfaces of the tank or accumulates as droplets. The volume of condensate can be quantified by balancing the evaporative flux and considering the fraction that turns into condensate. Then, from $J_e(\mathbf{x}, t)$, the total evaporated water flux is calculated:

$$\dot{V}_{\text{evaporate}}(t) = \int_\Omega J_e(\mathbf{x}, t)\,d\mathbf{x}. \tag{50}$$

Assuming that a fraction $\eta_t ext{condensate}$ of the evaporated volume turns into condensate (depending on environmental and system conditions), the total volume of condensate is given by:

$$V_{\text{condensate}}(t) = \int_0^t \eta_{\text{condensate}} \cdot \dot{V}_{\text{evaporate}}(\tau)\, d\tau. \tag{51}$$

The coefficient $\eta_t ext{condensate}$ can be determined experimentally or modeled from the pressure and temperature inside the tank. The total volume of liquid inside the tank, $V_{\text{liquid}}(t)$, includes the residual liquid in the sludge and the accumulated condensate:

$$V_{\text{liquid}}(t) = V_{\text{water}}^{\text{residue}}(t) + V_{\text{condensate}}(t). \tag{52}$$

Integrating the above terms on Ω yields, at each time step, $V_{\text{water}}^{\text{residue}}(t)$, $\dot{V}_{\text{evaporate}}(t)$, and $V_{\text{condensate}}(t)$, Obviously, it is essential to specify the flow and temperature conditions at the surface of the tank to model evaporation and condensation correctly.

6.5. FEM Calculations

To implement the FEM calculation of the volume of liquid and condensate in the tank, since $T(\mathbf{x}, t)$ and $W(\mathbf{x}, t)$ have already been obtained, we proceed as follows. Since the initial and residual volumes of water are calculated by integrating $W_0(\mathbf{x})$ and $W(\mathbf{x}, t)$ on the domain Ω, we can proceed with the following discretization:

$$V_{\text{water}}^{\text{inizial}} \approx \sum_{e=1}^{M} \int_{\Omega_e} W_0^h(\mathbf{x})\, d\mathbf{x}, \quad V_{\text{water}}^{\text{residue}}(t) \approx \sum_{e=1}^{M} \int_{\Omega_e} W^h(\mathbf{x}, t)\, d\mathbf{x}, \tag{53}$$

in which $W^h(\mathbf{x}, t) = \sum_{i=1}^{N} W_i(t)\phi_i(\mathbf{x})$ is the FEM approximation of $\mathbf{x}, t)$, while $\mathbf{x}(\mathbf{x})$ is the shape functions defined on the mesh. For each element of the mesh, Ω_e, we calculate:

$$\int_{\Omega_e} W^h(\mathbf{x}, t)\, d\mathbf{x} \approx \mathbf{W}_e^T \mathbf{M}_e, \tag{54}$$

where $\mathbf{M}_e$ represents the elemental mass matrix, whose generic element is given by:

$$(\mathbf{M}_e)_{ij} = \int_{\Omega_e} \phi_i \phi_j\, d\mathbf{x}. \tag{55}$$

Finally, adding up all the contributions, we will obtain:

$$V_{\text{water}}^{\text{residue}}(t) \approx \sum_{e=1}^{M} \mathbf{W}_e^T \mathbf{M}_e. \tag{56}$$

As for the evaporative flux given by (50), it can be approximated by:

$$\dot{V}_{\text{evaporate}}(t) = \int_{\Omega} J_e^h(\mathbf{x}, t)\, d\mathbf{x}, \tag{57}$$

where $J_e^h(\mathbf{x}, t)$ is the FEM approximation of the evaporative flux:

$$J_e^h(\mathbf{x}, t) = \sum_{i=1}^{N} J_{e,i}(t)\phi_i(\mathbf{x}). \tag{58}$$

Then, for each element Ω_e, we calculate

$$\int_{\Omega_e} J_e^h(\mathbf{x}, t)\, d\mathbf{x} \approx \mathbf{J}_e^T \mathbf{M}_e, \tag{59}$$

where $\mathbf{J}_e$ is the vector of nodal values of J_e on the element. Then, summing the contributions of all the elements, we have:

$$\dot{V}_{\text{evaporate}}(t) \approx \sum_{e=1}^{M} \mathbf{J}_e^T \mathbf{M}_e. \tag{60}$$

To compute the total volume of condensate (51) at each time step, we use the trapezoidal integration method:

$$V_{\text{condensate}}^{n+1} \approx V_{\text{condensate}}^{n} + \frac{\Delta t}{2} \cdot \eta_{\text{condensate}} \cdot \left(\dot{V}_{\text{evaporate}}^{n} + \dot{V}_{\text{evaporate}}^{n+1}\right), \tag{61}$$

where $\dot{V}_{\text{evaporated}}^{n}$ and $\dot{V}_{\text{evaporated}}^{n+1}$ are the evaporative fluxes at the time steps n and $n+1$, respectively, thus providing the total volume in the tank.

7. On the Pressure Exerted by the Sludge on the Tank

If $p(\mathbf{x}, t)$ represents the pressure exerted by the sludge on the tank, being coupled with both $T(\mathbf{x}, t)$ and $W(\mathbf{x}, t)$, its computation requires considering both thermodynamic and mechanical effects of the system. We preliminarily observe that $p(\mathbf{x}, t)$ is generally related to the thermodynamic behavior of the material and depends on the density of the slurry, $\rho(\mathbf{x}, t)$, compressibility $K(T, W)$, as well as $T(\mathbf{x}, t)$ and $W(\mathbf{x}, t)$. Without detracting in generality, we model $p(\mathbf{x}, t)$ by an equation of state describing the behavior of the material:

$$p(\mathbf{x}, t) = p_0 + K(T(\mathbf{x}, t), W(\mathbf{x}, t))[\rho(\mathbf{x}, t) - \rho_0], \tag{62}$$

where p_0 is the reference pressure (referenced to T_0, W_0), ρ_0 is the density of the sludge at T_0 and W_0, $K(T(\mathbf{x}, t), W(\mathbf{x}, t))$ is the compressibility modulus of the sludge. It is worth noting that $\rho(\mathbf{x}, t)$ varies as a function of $T(\mathbf{x}, t)$ and $W(\mathbf{x}, t)$ due to thermal expansion and change in water content, which, to a good approximation, leads to the following formulation:

$$\rho(\mathbf{x}, t) = \rho_0[1 - \beta_T(T(\mathbf{x}, t) - T_0) + \beta_W(W(\mathbf{x}, t) - W_0)], \tag{63}$$

where β_T is the coefficient of thermal expansion and β_W is the coefficient of change in density with respect to moisture. Similarly, for the compressibility of sludge:

$$K(T(\mathbf{x}, t), W(\mathbf{x}, t)) = K_0[1 + \alpha_T(T(\mathbf{x}, t) - T_0) + \alpha_W(W(\mathbf{x}, t) - W_0)], \tag{64}$$

where K_0 is the compressibility modulus at reference conditions, and α_T and α_W are coefficients of variation of K with respect to T and W. Then, the total pressure, $p(\mathbf{x}, t)$, becomes:

$$\begin{aligned} p(\mathbf{x}, t) = p_0 + K_0[1 + \alpha_T(T(\mathbf{x}, t) - T_0) + \\ \alpha_W(W(\mathbf{x}, t) - W_0)] \cdot \rho_0[-\beta_T(T(\mathbf{x}, t) - T_0) + \beta_W(W(\mathbf{x}, t) - W_0)]. \end{aligned} \tag{65}$$

Finally, by expanding and simplifying, we obtain:

$$\begin{aligned} p(\mathbf{x}, t) = p_0 + A(T(\mathbf{x}, t) - T_0) + B(W(\mathbf{x}, t) - W_0) \\ + C(T(\mathbf{x}, t) - T_0)(W(\mathbf{x}, t) - W_0), \end{aligned} \tag{66}$$

where $A = K_0\rho_0\alpha_T - K_0\rho_0\beta_T$, $B = K_0\rho_0\alpha_W + K_0\rho_0\beta_W$, $C = K_0\rho_0(\alpha_T\beta_W + \alpha_W\beta_T)$.
Then, once the distributions of $T(\mathbf{x}, t)$ and $W(\mathbf{x}, t)$ have been obtained, $K(T(\mathbf{x}, t, W(\mathbf{x}, t))$ is computed and then $\rho(\mathbf{x}, t)$ is quantified as specified above.

7.1. *Comsol Multiphysics® Implementation*

The sonication process, in pretreatment, produced a modest decrease in sludge weight, so a prototype software mixer was designed to reduce the weight of heat-treated sludge more significantly. The numerical model described above was implemented in both steady-state and transient regimes to identify areas within the prototype that were less stressed by the pressure and temperature exerted on the sludge. Results regarding moisture and pressure distribution are obtained over a temperature range of 296.96 K to 377.96 K based on the operating characteristics of the sludge treatment tank.

7.1.1. Some Specifications of the Mixing Tank

Geometrically, it is cylindrical and exhibits rotational symmetry about its longitudinal axis (axial symmetry), implying that every plane section passing through the cylinder's axis is identical, regardless of the rotation angle. Such symmetry reduces the 3D geometric problem to analyzing only a single plane section that includes the cylinder's axis. Since this section faithfully represents the geometry of the entire system, it is not necessary to model the entire 3D domain to study its geometric characteristics. In addition to geometric symmetry, the validity of the reduction is also supported by the fact that the physical conditions are also symmetrical concerning the axis. Reducing the problem from 3D to 2D offers computational advantages by requiring fewer resources than 3D by reducing the number of nodes and elements in the mesh. Figure 4 displays the front and top elevation of the (aluminum) sludge mixing tank in which the conduit required to heat the tank (also aluminum), the 1.4301 stainless steel mixing system, and the high-density (28 kg/m^3) polyethylene outer shell with high thermal insulation properties (λ = 0.04) are evident.

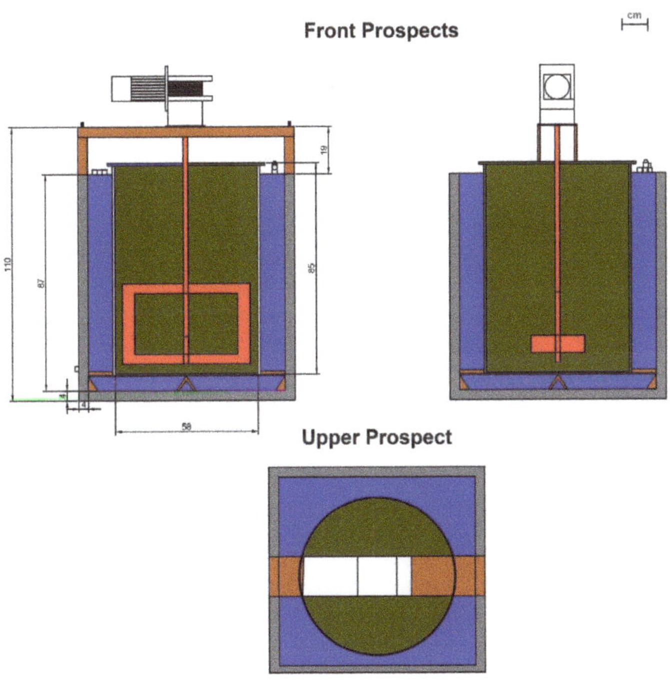

Figure 4. 2D prototype of the sludge treatment tank.

7.1.2. Some Relevant Details About the Designed Mesh

To solve the problem numerically, once the device was implemented geometrically (see Figure 5) under both steady-state and transient conditions, an obtained mesh was constructed using a Delaunay triangulation calibrating it for a fluid dynamics problem whose maximum element size is 0.00335, while their minimum size is around 1.5×10^{-3}. The optimized curvature factor is 0.4, while the maximum element growth ratio is worth 1.2. The obtained mesh has 11,817 degrees of freedom and exhibits high quality since the aspect ratio is ≈1, while the skewness is 0. In addition, the smoothness parameter is gradual, and the condition number is minimal, while the Jacobian determinant is positive and stable. The obtained mesh is characterized by 4448 triangular elements and 560 quadrangular elements. In addition, the number of elements is 588, while those on the vertices are 20. The obtained mesh can be viewed in Figure 6.

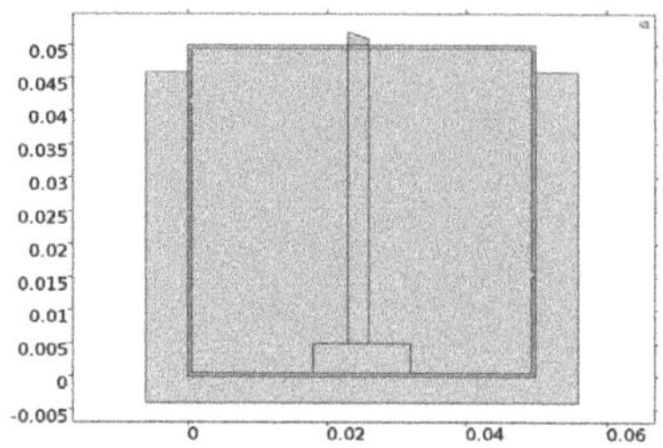

Figure 5. Mixing device designed using FEM for sludge treatment.

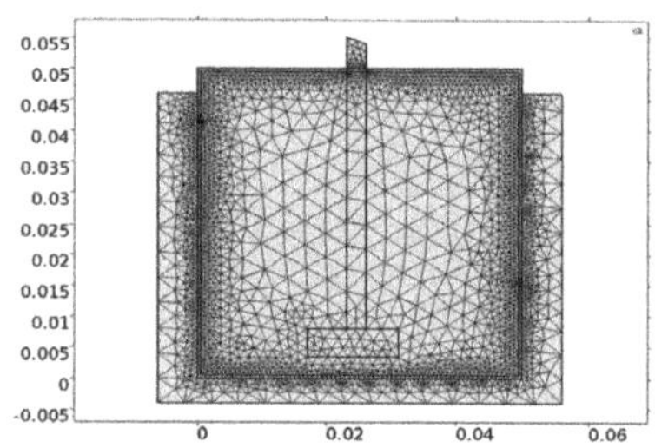

Figure 6. Mesh designed for the analysis of fluid dynamics inside the mixing tank.

Remark 1. *During this study, a preliminary grid independence analysis was performed to ensure that the results obtained using the finite element method were not affected by the density or size of the mesh used. For this purpose, different discretization configurations were considered, varying the maximum size of the grid elements and analyzing the impact on the main parameters of interest, such as temperature, pressure, and humidity distribution within the system. The results showed substantial convergence for an optimized grid, ensuring a balance between accuracy and computational times. Therefore, the chosen mesh configuration was found to be adequate to precisely describe the physical phenomena under consideration without compromising the reliability of the simulations. These checks, although preliminary, confirm the independence of the model with respect to the adopted grid and represent a solid basis for the development of further future studies.*

8. Some Relevant Results

Once the device was implemented, a series of simulations were carried out in both transient and steady state to evaluate the temperature and humidity distribution. However, since the sludge tank is a hermetically sealed aluminum container, to prevent potentially dangerous mechanical instability problems, we equip the pressure control device inside it.

Stationary and Transient Regimes

Simulations in a steady state (temperature and pressure are constant), since the system already reaches the steady state of equilibrium, showed the areas with lower thermal and pressure stresses being less affected by altered environmental conditions, providing valuable indications for the structural stability of the container, eventually.

On the other hand, simulations in the transient regime, during critical phases (startup, heating, and/or cooling of the container as highlighted in Figure 7) showed the evolution of temperature and pressure over time, highlighting how the system responds to rapid or gradual changes in external or internal conditions. In addition, less stressed areas are easily identified as they show fewer thermal and pressure fluctuations, signaling areas of greater thermal and structural stability. The combined analysis identifies critical stresses; by comparing the results of the two regimes, areas that maintain low stresses in both transient and steady state can be identified, suggesting naturally less stressed regions. Areas that show limited changes in stresses during the transient and stabilize these conditions in the steady-state regime are indicators of structural reliability, with a low probability of deformation or failure.

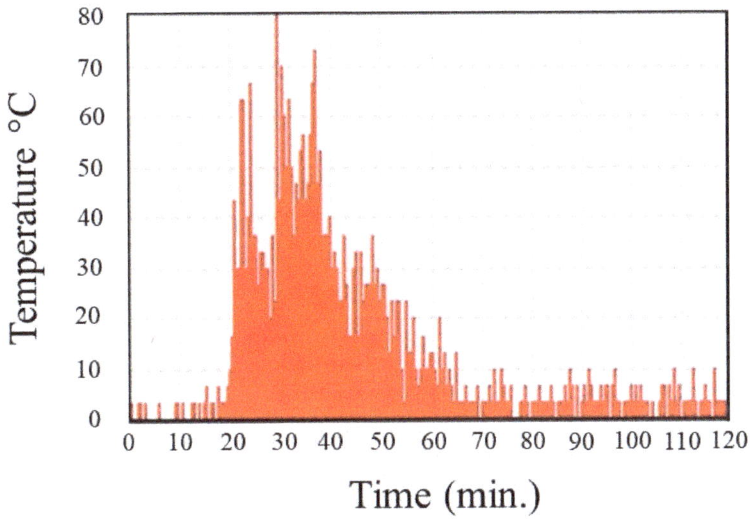

Figure 7. Temperature distribution inside the tank.

Figure 8a displays the areas where the pressure assumes relevant values with apparent overload near the mixer plate (the operating parameters used only listed in Table 4 (please note that the density of the sludge varies with its moisture content during the drying process.). This is in line with expectations since the mixer, being a moving element, undergoes both the action due to the gravity force of the sludge and the effects due to rotation. Obviously, the distribution of the moisture percentage (see Figure 8b) is almost uniform throughout the tank, except in the areas near the mixer plate (tank bottom) where the drying action is more significant.

Table 4. Benchmarks for sludge from wastewater.

Parameter	Value	Unit	Note
p_0	101,325	Pa	Standard atmospheric pressure
ρ_0	1050	kg/m^3	Sludge average density
K_0	2.2×10^9	Pa	Water-like compressibility modulus
T_0	293.15	K	Reference temperature (20 °C)
W_0	0.95	kg/kg	Relative humidity (95%)
β_T	2.1×10^{-4}	K^{-1}	Thermal expansion coefficient
β_W	0.05	(kg/kg)$^{-1}$	Variation of density versus humidity
α_T	0.002	K^{-1}	Coefficient of compressibility modulus vs. temperature
α_W	0.01	(kg/kg)$^{-1}$	Variation of compressibility modulus with respect to humidity

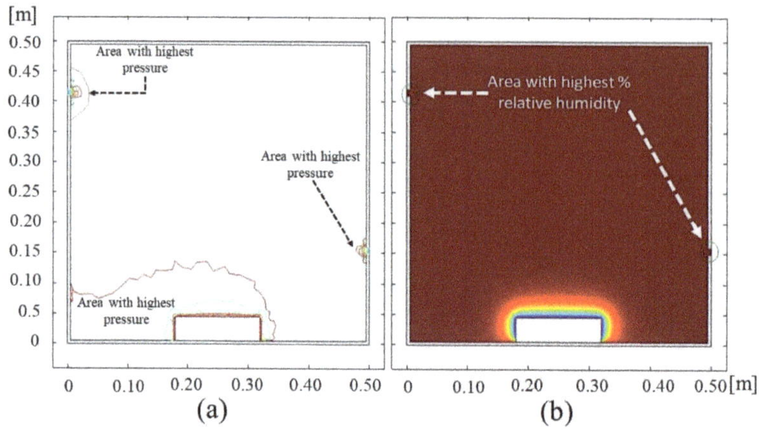

Figure 8. (**a**) Pressure distribution and (**b**) relative humidity inside the sludge-filled tank.

9. Prototype for Moisture Detection and Reduction in a Sludge Treatment Tank

Once the system was designed and tested in software mode, we built the prototype for sludge treatment equipped with mechanical and electronic components for proper operation. Specifically, the tank should be connected to a heat source to heat the sludge. The realized prototype, shown in Figure 9 and consisting of the sludge treatment device (a), mixer (b), and sensors placed inside the tank, is insulated by a layer of polystyrene to prevent heat loss. The sludge, coming from the sonication process, is mixed for about 30 min by a mixer operated by a special mechanical component, which is installed above the tank as per the software design. Sensors to measure the mechanical strength of the sludge (to derive the moisture content) were installed inside the treatment tank and placed at the bottom, middle, and top of the tank, as demonstrated by the software analysis. In addition, temperature sensors have been set up so that it is monitored during the heating of the tank to dehydrate the sludge by decreasing its moisture content, allowing a maximum temperature of 110 °C [67]. Finally, for safety benefits, an automatic pressure relief valve is installed that can raise the internal device, allowing excess vapors to escape. The prototype is equipped with a 3PM-0030 impeller agitator (PRO-DO-MIX® Srl Unipersonale), PAdova, Italy) driven by an 18.5 kW three-phase AC motor that provides the necessary power to operate the agitator under any operating condition. Figures 10 and 11 show, respectively, a general and detailed view of the sludge structure before sonification treatment. In Figure 10, a compact and dense structure is clearly observed, with a high viscosity that prevents effective separation of the solid particles from the liquid matrix. This characteristic is typical of raw sludge, in which the presence of particle aggregates and water retention are significant. In Figure 11, a close analysis of the morphology of the sludge highlights a non-uniform grain size distribution, with the presence of agglomerates of variable dimensions and flocculent structures. The non-homogeneous nature of the particles, combined with the presence of lumps and physical-chemical bonds between the components, confirms the difficulty in the dewatering process of untreated sludge. Figure 12 shows the evolution of the sludge structure during ultrasound treatment. The progressive disintegration of the agglomerates is evident, accompanied by a reduction in the viscosity of the material.

(a) (b) (c)

Figure 9. Details of the proposed prototype: (**a**) Sludge treatment device; (**b**) Wastewater treatment mixer; (**c**) Mixer and Sensors placed inside the sludge treatment tank

Figure 10. Image of raw sludge before ultrasonic treatment. An aggregated and compact structure is observed, a typical characteristic of untreated sludge, with particles of heterogeneous dimensions and high viscosity.

Figure 11. Close-up view of the sludge morphology before sonification. The non-uniform distribution of the particles and the presence of lumps indicate a slightly disintegrated state with a high tendency to sedimentation.

Figure 12. Distribution of sludge structure during ultrasonic treatment. A gradual disintegration of the agglomerates and a reduction in viscosity are observed, indicative of the cavitational effect induced by sonification, which facilitates the breaking of the particles and the release of intracellular and extracellular materials.

10. Experimental Activity: Some Survey Results

10.1. On the Sonication Process

It is evident, as shown in Figure 13, that high electric currents rapidly stabilize the average particle size, exhibiting a marked decrease of up to 55% in particle size at 1.6 W (corresponding to a 60% amplification of the current), between the 20th and 25th minutes of the sonication treatment. However, the reduction is not pronounced by halving the power (corresponding to an amplification of 40% of the current), standing at 49% in the same time interval. By further reducing the power (0.3 W), the size reduction is around 52% with but between the 30th and 45th minutes (corresponding to current amplification of 20%). As for the ζ potential decreases if the negative surface charge does likewise, providing a clear indication of the stability of the colloids present. As highlighted in Table 5, starting from $\zeta = -11.8$ mV, belonging to the usual range from -10 mV to -30 mV, it showed, after sonication pretreatment, a slight fluctuation with a negative trend as the percentage of applied electric current increased. Since the particles tend to repel each other electrostatically in these cases, it is necessary to add flocculating chemical agents.

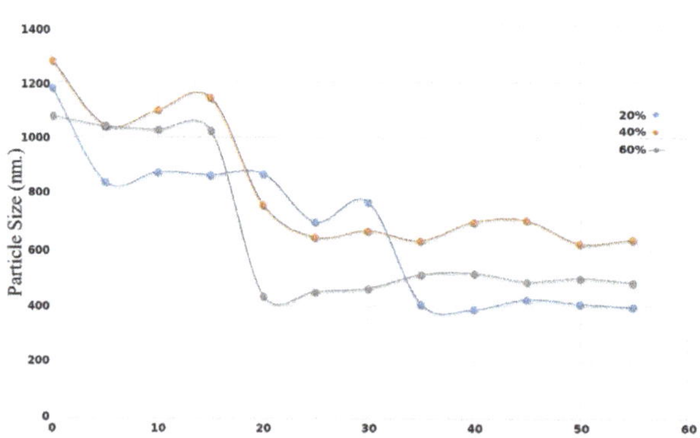

Figure 13. Particle size distribution over time at different amplifications.

Table 5. ζ potential for sludge treated with ultrasound.

Amplification—Treatment Time	Untreated	20% (35 min)	40% (25 min)	60% (25 min)
ζ Potential (mV)	−11.8	−12.2	−11.5	−9.62

Then, as is well known [68], the addition of Ca^{2+} and Mg^{2+} contributes significantly to the flocculation process by neutralizing surface negative charges, as well as by creating ionic bridges between negatively charged particles or between functional groups in the polymer flocculants and the sludge particles by increasing $[Ca^{2+}]$ and $[Mg^{2+}]$ reduces the electric double layer of the particles by decreasing electrostatic repulsion, increasing the attractive van der Waals forces that promote aggregation. However, $[Ca^{2+}]$ and $[Mg^{2+}]$ must be carefully controlled to avoid excess cations that cause very dense or unstable floccules settling rapidly or difficult to separate.

Dispersion agents (non-superactive polymers or highly active substances) added to sludge also prevent sedimentation by deflocculating solids by reducing their viscosity and increasing the amount of dispersible powder material.

To achieve a stable dispersion (ζ potential greater than +30 mV or less than −30 mV), we used the combined effect of Silcosperse HLD5 at 3% v/v, silicon-free high-performance for water-based pigmented systems (total solids: 49.0–51.0%; active agent: 39.0–41.0%; pH: 7.0–9.0, with the ultrasound treatment (Table 6).

Table 6. ζ potential and conductivity for sludges containing a dispersing agent and treated with US.

Current Percentage Treatment Time	20% (35 min)	40% (25 min)	60% (25 min)	Silcosperse (%w/v)	Conductivity (mS/cm)
ζ potential (mV)					
−12.3	−11.8	−11.5	−14.8	1.0	1.28
−11.1	−12.2	−12.1	−15.2	1.5	1.19
−12.5	−11.6	−12.3	−14.9	3.0	1.20

The results confirmed that the above combination of treatments produces stable dispersion by improving the interaction between US and sludge. The additive allows the sludge to become conductive. Since the additive allows the sludge to become conductive, as its concentration increases, conductivity increases.

The effectiveness of sludge disintegration and solubilization was monitored by observing COD trends in the sludge supernatant.

10.2. On COD Values and Specific Gravity Reduction

Treatment of samples with US increases COD value, indicating a high content of oxidizable organic material in the sample due to disintegration. COD is around 2012 mg/L for untreated sludge, while 35 min of sonication increases to 2200 mg/L with ζ of 20%. If we then perform a 25-minute sonication, COD is around 3534 mg/L with ζ of 40% and 3429 mg/L with ζ of 60%. As previously observed in batch experiments, treatment by ultrasound increases COD value, indicating a high content of oxidizable organic material in the sample due to the disintegration process. In the case of the pre-industrial prototype test, a better efficiency of the disintegration process is noted in Table 7.

In the same frequency range, sonication tests were performed to evaluate the impact of the treatment in the sludge drying phase. The disintegration process, induced by sonication, fragments the sludge particles into smaller units, promoting steam migration to the surface and reducing particle aggregation during the drying process. The results, shown in Table 8, show a slight reduction in specific gravity of between 1 and 2% compared to the untreated and dried samples under identical experimental conditions (from 34.02 g to 34.01 g) due to the reduced moisture content of the sonicated sample.

Table 7. COD absolute and percentage change obtained during the pretreatment phase carried out in the laboratory with a sludge volume (sewage sludge) of 125 mL and during the use of the pretreatment prototype industrial installed in the sewage treatment plant for the treatment of a sludge volume equal to 8 L.

	Test in Batch (V = 125 mL)	Testing with Pre-Industrial Prototype (V = 8 L)
COD—Initial (mg/L)	2000	66
COD—Final (mg/L)	3500	552
Variation (%)	+75	+736

Table 8. Sludge drying test comparing untreated sludge and ultrasonically treated sludge (60% amplification).

Sample Type	Initial Weight (g)	Weight Reduction (%)
Untreated sludge	37.52	9.32
Sludge treated with US (60% A)	38.04	10.61

10.3. On the Reduction of Sludge Weight

The results obtained during the measurement campaign showed a further percentage reduction in sludge weight. Specifically, the sludge treated in the tank had an initial weight of 38.05 g and a final weight of 33.52 g, resulting in a percentage reduction in weight of 11.91%. The samples were treated at about 105°C in the sludge treatment tank for 2 h (see Figure 14). Comparing the initial and final weight data of the pretreated, US, and tank-treated sludge, the trend shown in Figure 15 emerges.

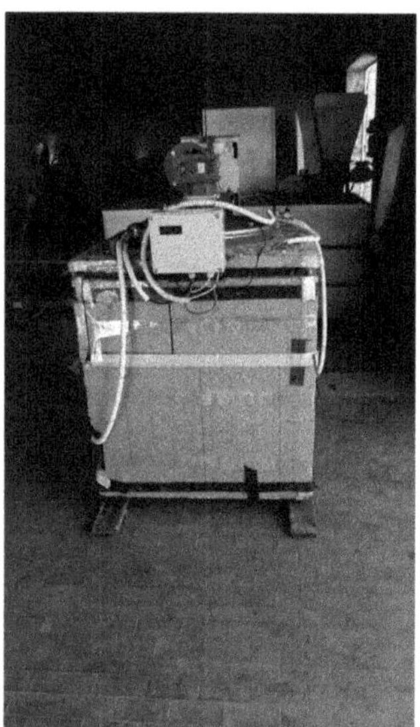

Figure 14. Prototype of a sludge mixing tank. Sludge, once sonicated, is deposited in a conveyor belt and fed into the prototype. Equipped with a temperature sensor and a humidity sensor, the prototype mixing tank heats the already ultrasonically treated sludge, further reducing the amount of water and consequently making it lighter.

The trend shown indicates a slight decrease in the percentage of sludge weight reduction when using the prototype whose exclusive use results in higher energy consumption than the joint use with US pretreatment. As shown in Figure 15, the combination of sonication with heat treatment leads to a significant reduction in the heating rate of the pretreated sludge material.

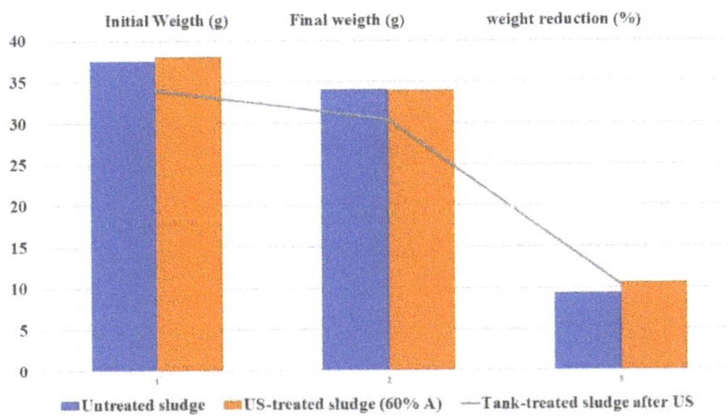

Untreated sludge (Blue) - Sludge treated with ultrasound sonication (Orange) - Sludge treated by increasing temperature (Grey)

Figure 15. Untreated Sludge (Blue)—US (Orange)—Prototype Heat Source (Grey).

10.4. On the Reduction of Water Content

Finally, the final water content of dry sludge was studied and analyzed, revealing that sonication alone is inadequate for effective sludge conditioning, making it necessary to combine with heat treatment by reducing the water content by 9%.

Remark 2. *It is important to note that, in addition to evaluating the ζ potential and conductivity, further sludge characteristics were analyzed to assess the treatment effects. Before sonification, the sludge exhibited a compact morphology with a non-uniform particle distribution and cohesive agglomerates, as shown in Figures 10 and 11. During ultrasound treatment, the cavitational effect progressively disintegrated these structures, facilitating the release of intracellular and extracellular materials (Figure 12). The increase in chemical oxygen demand (COD) observed during sonification indicates enhanced bioavailability of organic components and improved biodegradability, beneficial for subsequent biological processes. Additionally, the combination of sonification and thermal treatment led to a moisture content reduction, resulting in an 11–12% decrease in sludge weight, as highlighted in Figure 12. These findings confirm the process's effectiveness in improving sludge manageability and its suitability for agricultural applications.*

11. Comparison with Some Known Scenarios in Literature

The following simplifications have been considered in our numerical implementation. First, we have not considered some microflows (polymer thickening and dehydration). On the contrary, we considered it appropriate to include both nitrogen dioxide and sulfur dioxide emissions in the combined heat and power production.

Analysis and Optimization of Nutrient and Energy Recovery from Sludge: Comparison of Composting and Anaerobic Digestion

The scenarios studied in [69,70] assumed that all digested compounds and products would be used as fertilizers or soil conditioners for agricultural purposes to calculate the maximum nutrient recovery and energy recovery efficiency. Four processes were selected in combination for composting and soil application: thickening, dewatering, composting, and soil application. After pretreatment, the dewatered sludge is started for composting, requiring a 50% reduction in sludge weight, about 645 kg of reaction oxygen, and a total of 1975 kg of wood chips as filling agent, including 395 kg of raw chips and 1580 recycled chips. In combination with anaerobic digestion, land application, and cogeneration, there are five processes: dewatering, anaerobic digestion, digestion, land application, and cogeneration. According to the first method, raw sludge undergoes pretreatment, reducing the weight of expanded sludge by 1/3 with considerable water expenditure. Next, the sludge is subjected to anaerobic digestion, yielding two main products: 98.6% raw digestate and 1.4% biogas. The sludge output possesses the characteristics shown in Table 9.

Table 9. Characterization of the sludge processed and leaving the plant.

Heavy Metals [mg/Kg]	Sludge Analysis	Heavy Metals [mg/Kg]	Sludge Analysis
Copper	217–247	Zinc	203–357
Cadmium	<1	Mercury	<1
Lead	24–43	Nickel	17–30

Classifying the treated sludge, as opposed to the incoming sludge, allows it to be used in the agricultural sector because it meets the parameters required by current regulations. The raw digestate undergoes further dewatering, and the resulting by-products are transported and spread on agricultural land. At the same time, the generated biogas is directed to a cogeneration plant for energy recovery [71]. The fusion of anaerobic digestion, land application, and biogas involves six processes, of which the first four mirror those of the second method presented. The unique feature lies in the treatment of biogas carried out by this method through the purification of biogas and the subsequent utilization of energy. About 41.3% of the biogas is transformed into biomethane, while 48.7% of the CO_2 is removed. The theoretically required amount of oxygen for the combustion of 41.3% biomethane is four times higher [72]. The disintegration process can be achieved thermally (at 170–190 °C for 30–60 min), resulting in substantial solubilization along with a transformation of the sludge characteristics. This leads to a significant improvement in filterability and a reduction in pathogens [73]. Literature methods indicate that the product of the former method boasts the highest relative nutrient recovery efficiency due to its small volume and low water content compared to digestate. However, composting is constrained by its inherent limitations in that it cannot harness the energy content of sludge, making its energy contribution negligible. This represents a significant disadvantage of composting. The performance of anaerobic digestion is more complete, although its relative nutrient recovery efficiency is lower than that of composting. Compared with composting technology, anaerobic digestion is more energy efficient and has less environmental impact. The latter methodology shares a similar energy recovery efficiency as the former but exceeds it in environmental impact. Therefore, from an overall perspective, the combination of anaerobic digestion, agricultural application, and cogeneration should be considered the most optimal. However, all methods presented require intensive electricity consumption. Contrary to the literature's findings, the research demonstrates both effective sludge weight reduction and reasonable energy consumption. Conventional systems suffer energy losses due to frictional heat, especially with high-pressure pumps and blade mixers that create turbulence during processing. These turbulences lead to friction between the liquid particles and the vibrating parts of the equipment, converting the input energy into frictional heating, which is lost and does not contribute to the dispersion effects. The stronger the cavitation forces that exert stress on the particles, the less energy is required for effective dispersion [74]. Finally, the sludge mixer, designed to reduce the water content in the sludge further, operates based on energy-harvesting techniques [75,76]. It is worth noting that the results obtained meet all normative requirements (UNI EN 13657:2004+ UNI EN ISO 11885:2009 method; UNI 10802-04, UNI 12457-2:04, and UNI EN ISO 11885:09 methods; UNI EN 13657:2004 and UNI EN ISO 11885:2009 methods). Scrupulous adherence to the mentioned standards ensures that the procedures adopted are reliable and consistent with the reference standards, confirming the quality and reliability of the analyses performed.

12. Conclusions

This study introduced an innovative approach for sewage sludge treatment, combining ultrasonic and thermal treatments to optimize sludge management for agricultural purposes. The results demonstrated significant improvements in treatment efficiency, with several key advantages summarized below:

- **Reduction of moisture content and improved stability**: The ultrasonic treatment, combined with thermal techniques, achieved a moisture content reduction of up to 20%. This improvement enhanced material stability, making it more suitable for agricultural use or further processing.
- **Increased energy efficiency**: Compared to traditional methods, the proposed protocol reduced energy consumption by up to 60%, demonstrating that ultrasonic techniques can offer a cost-effective and environmentally sustainable solution for sludge treatment.
- **Environmental benefits**: The method significantly reduced greenhouse gas emissions, human toxicity, and fossil fuel consumption, aligning the process with principles of circular economy and environmental sustainability.
- **Validation at scale and practical applicability**: The protocol was validated both in laboratory and real-plant settings, confirming its feasibility for large-scale implementation in wastewater treatment systems. The proposed methodology adapts to industrial contexts without requiring costly structural interventions.

In addition to these direct benefits, the study highlighted the effectiveness of the developed mathematical model, which integrates information on temperature, humidity, and pressure to optimize operational parameters. This approach enables scientifically supported treatment management, reducing operational costs and improving the quality of the final product. Despite the promising results, the study identified some limitations, including the need to improve the prototype's reliability during operation and address some energy efficiency issues. Future developments will focus on refining the prototype, testing processes on different types of sludge, and implementing advanced monitoring systems based on soft computing technologies to ensure continuous control of the treated material composition. In summary, the presented work addresses existing gaps in the literature, providing an innovative and sustainable solution for sewage sludge treatment. This study offers a solid foundation for further developments and applications in the wastewater treatment sector.

Author Contributions: Conceptualization, F.L., S.A.P., G.A. and M.V.; methodology, F.L., S.A.P., G.A. and M.V.; software, F.L., S.A.P., G.A. and M.V.; validation, F.L., S.A.P., G.A. and M.V.; formal analysis, F.L., S.A.P., G.A. and M.V.; investigation, F.L., S.A.P., G.A. and M.V.; resources, F.L., S.A.P., G.A. and M.V.; data curation, F.L., S.A.P., G.A. and M.V.; writing—original draft preparation, F.L., S.A.P., G.A. and M.V.; writing—review and editing, F.L., S.A.P., G.A. and M.V.; visualization, F.L., S.A.P., G.A. and M.V.; supervision, F.L., S.A.P., G.A. and M.V.; project administration, F.L., S.A.P., G.A. and M.V.; funding acquisition, F.L., S.A.P., G.A. and M.V. All authors have read and agreed to the published version of the manuscript.

Funding: This research has been supported by the Italian Ministry of University and Research under the Program PRIN 2022: "Integration of Artificial Intelligence and Ultrasonic Techniques for Monitoring Control and Self-Repair of Civil Concrete Structures (CAIUS)"—Code 2022AZPLL8.

Institutional Review Board Statement: Not applicable.

Informed Consent Statement: Not applicable.

Data Availability Statement: Data are contained within the article.

Conflicts of Interest: The authors declare no conflicts of interest.

Abbreviations

The following abbreviations are used in this manuscript:

US	Ultrasonic
FEM	Finite Element Method
COD	Chemical Oxygen Demand

References

1. Rajendran, S.; Priya, T.A.K.; Khoo, K.S.; Hoang, K.T.; Ng, H.S.; Munawaroh, H.S.H.; Show, P.L. A Critical Review on Various Remediation Approaches for Heavy Metal Contaminants Removal from Contaminated Soils. *Chemosphere* **2022**, *287*, 132369. [CrossRef]
2. Rabie, G.M.; Abd El-Halim, H.; Rozaik, E.H. Influence of Using Dry and Wet Wastewater Sludge in Concrete Mix on Its Physical and Mechanical Properties. *Ain Shams Eng. J.* **2019**, *10*, 705–712. [CrossRef]
3. Sharma, B.; Sarkar, A.; Singh, P.; Singh, R.P. Agricultural Utilization of Biosolids: A Review on Potential Effects on Soil and Plant Growth. *Waste Manag.* **2017**, *64*, 117–132. [CrossRef]
4. Liu, Y.; Joo-Hwa, T. Strategy for Minimization of Excess Sludge Production from the Activated Sludge Process. *Biotechnol. Adv.* **2001**, *19*, 97–107. [CrossRef] [PubMed]
5. Sodhi, V.; Bansal, A.; Jha, M.K. Minimization of Excess Bio-Sludge and Pollution Load in Oxic-Settling-Anaerobic Modified Activated Sludge Treatment for Tannery Wastewater. *J. Clean. Prod.* **2020**, *243*, 118492. [CrossRef]
6. Corsino, S.F.; de Oliveira, T.S.; Di Trapani, D.; Torregrossa, M.; Viviani, G. Simultaneous Sludge Minimization, Biological Phosphorous Removal, and Membrane Fouling Mitigation in a Novel Plant Layout for MBR. *J. Environ. Manag.* **2020**, *259*, 109826. [CrossRef]
7. Massé, D.I.; Croteau, F.; Massé, L. The Fate of Crop Nutrients during Digestion of Swine Manure in Psychrophilic Anaerobic Sequencing Batch Reactors. *Bioresour. Technol.* **2007**, *98*, 2819–2823. [CrossRef] [PubMed]
8. Wu, B.; Xiaohu, D.; Xiaoli, C. Critical Review on Dewatering of Sewage Sludge: Influential Mechanism, Conditioning Technologies, and Implications to Sludge Re-Utilizations. *Water Res.* **2020**, *180*, 115912. [CrossRef] [PubMed]
9. Collivignarelli, M.C.; Miino, M.C.; Cillari, G.; Bellazzi, S.; Caccamo, F.M.; Abbà, A.; Bertanza, G. Estimation of Thermal Energy Released by Thermophilic Biota during Sludge Minimization in a Fluidized Bed Reactor: Influence of Anoxic Conditions. *Process Saf. Environ. Prot.* **2022**, *166*, 249–256. [CrossRef]
10. Mrozik, W.; Rajaeifar, M.A.; Heidrich, O.; Christensen, P. Environmental Impacts, Pollution Sources, and Pathways of Spent Lithium-Ion Batteries. *Energy Environ. Sci.* **2021**, *14*, 6099–6121. [CrossRef]
11. Øegaard, H. Sludge Minimization Technologies—An Overview. *Water Sci. Technol.* **2004**, *49*, 31–40. 2004.0604. [CrossRef]
12. Bagheri, M.; Bauer, T.; Burgman, L.E.; Wetterlund, E. Fifty Years of Sewage Sludge Management Research: Mapping Researchers' Motivations and Concerns. *J. Environ. Manag.* **2023**, *325*, 116412. [CrossRef] [PubMed]
13. Fiorillo, A.S.; Grimaldi, D.; Paolino, D.; Pullano, S.A. Low-Frequency Ultrasound in Medicine: An In Vivo Evaluation. *IEEE Trans. Instrum. Meas.* **2012**, *61*, 1658–1663. [CrossRef]
14. Liu, Z.; Luo, F.; He, L.; Wang, S.; Wu, Y.; Chen, Z. Physical Conditioning Methods for Sludge Deep Dewatering: A Critical Review. *J. Environ. Manag.* **2024**, *360*, 121207. [CrossRef]
15. Yuan, H.; Zhu, N. Progress of Improving Waste Activated Sludge Dewaterability: Influence Factors, Conditioning Technologies and Implications and Perspectives. *Sci. Total Environ.* **2023**, 168605. [CrossRef] [PubMed]
16. Ma, H.P.; Li, J.P.; Hu, X.P.; Xie, L.; An, G.; Chen, J.Q.; Lv, W.J. On-Site Source-Separation of Microparticles and Reuse of Coal Gasification Wastewater via a Micro-Channel Separator: Performance and Separation Mechanism. *Sep. Purif. Technol.* **2024**, *341*, 126565. [CrossRef]
17. Zhang, X.; Ye, P.; Wu, Y. Enhanced Technology for Sewage Sludge Advanced Dewatering from an Engineering Practice Perspective: A Review. *J. Environ. Manag.* **2022**, *321*, 115938. [CrossRef]
18. Hou, J.; Hong, C.; Ling, W.; Hu, J.; Feng, W.; Xing, Y.; Feng, L. Research Progress in Improving Sludge Dewaterability: Sludge Characteristics, Chemical Conditioning and Influencing Factors. *J. Environ. Manag.* **2024**, *351*, 119863. [CrossRef]
19. Laganà, F.; De Carlo, D.; Calcagno, S.; Pullano, S.A.; Critello, D.; Falcone, F.; Fiorillo, A.S. Computational model of cell deformation under fluid flow based rolling. In Proceedings of the 2019 E-Health and Bioengineering Conference (EHB), Iasi, Romania, 21–23 November 2019; pp. 1–4. [CrossRef]
20. Hao, X.; Chen, Q.; van Loosdrecht, M.C.; Li, J.; Jiang, H. Sustainable Disposal of Excess Sludge: Incineration Without Anaerobic Digestion. *Water Res.* **2020**, *170*, 115298. [CrossRef] [PubMed]
21. Muhlack, R.A.; Potumarthi, R.; Jeffery, D.W. Sustainable Wineries Through Waste Valorisation: A Review of Grape Marc Utilisation for Value-Added Products. *Waste Manag.* **2018**, *72*, 99–118. [CrossRef] [PubMed]
22. Wang, J.; Lai, Y.; Wang, X.; Ji, H. Advances in Ultrasonic Treatment of Oily Sludge: Mechanisms, Industrial Applications, and Integration with Combined Treatment Technologies. *Environ. Sci. Pollut. Res.* **2024**, *31*, 14466–14483. [CrossRef] [PubMed]
23. Askarniya, Z.; Sun, X.; Wang, Z.; Boczkaj, G. Cavitation-Based Technologies for Pretreatment and Processing of Food Wastes: Major Applications and Mechanisms–A Review. *Chem. Eng. J.* **2023**, *454*, 140388. [CrossRef]
24. Hou, T.; Song, H.; Cui, Z.; He, C.; Liu, L.; Li, P.; Jiao, Y. Nanobubble Technology to Enhance Energy Recovery from Anaerobic Digestion of Organic Solid Wastes: Potential Mechanisms and Recent Advancements. *Sci. Total Environ.* **2024**, *931*, 172885. [CrossRef] [PubMed]
25. Wang, T.; Yang, C.; Sun, P.; Wang, M.; Lin, F.; Fiallos, M.; Khu, S.T. Generation Mechanism of Hydroxyl Free Radicals in Micro–Nanobubbles Water and Its Prospect in Drinking Water. *Processes* **2024**, *12*, 683. [CrossRef]
26. Wang, H.; Liu, X.; Zhang, Z. Approaches for Electroplating Sludge Treatment and Disposal Technology: Reduction, Pretreatment and Reuse. *J. Environ. Manag.* **2024**, *349*, 119535. [CrossRef] [PubMed]

27. Zeng, H.; Liu, C.; Wang, F.; Zhang, J.; Li, D. Disposal of Iron-Manganese Sludge from Waterworks and Its Potential for Arsenic Removal. *J. Environ. Chem. Eng.* **2022**, *10*, 108480. [CrossRef]
28. Zeng, S.; Li, M.; Li, G.; Lv, W.; Liao, X.; Wang, L. Innovative Applications, Limitations and Prospects of Energy-Carrying Infrared Radiation, Microwave and Radio Frequency in Agricultural Products Processing. *Trends Food Sci. Technol.* **2022**, *121*, 76–92. [CrossRef]
29. Feng, Y.; Tao, Y.; Meng, Q.; Qu, J.; Ma, S.; Han, S.; Zhang, Y. Microwave-Combined Advanced Oxidation for Organic Pollutants in the Environmental Remediation: An Overview of Influence, Mechanism, and Prospective. *Chem. Eng. J.* **2022**, *441*, 135924. [CrossRef]
30. Yakamercan, E.; Bhatt, P.; Aygun, A.; Adesope, A.W.; Simsek, H. Comprehensive Understanding of Electrochemical Treatment Systems Combined with Biological Processes for Wastewater Remediation. *Environ. Pollut.* **2023**, *330*, 121680. [CrossRef]
31. Ahmed, M.; Mavukkandy, M.O.; Giwa, A.; Elektorowicz, M.; Katsou, E.; Khelifi, O.; Hasan, S.W. Recent Developments in Hazardous Pollutants Removal from Wastewater and Water Reuse Within a Circular Economy. *NPJ Clean Water* **2022**, *5*, 12.. [CrossRef]
32. Pavel, M.; Anastasescu, C.; State, R.N.; Vasile, A.; Papa, F.; Balint, I. Photocatalytic Degradation of Organic and Inorganic Pollutants to Harmless End Products: Assessment of Practical Application Potential for Water and Air Cleaning. *Catalysts* **2023**, *13*, 380. [CrossRef]
33. Ahmadi, Y.; Kim, K.H. Modification Strategies for Visible-Light Photocatalysts and Their Performance-Enhancing Effects on Photocatalytic Degradation of Volatile Organic Compounds. *Renew. Sustain. Energy Rev.* **2024**, *189*, 113948. [CrossRef]
34. Tunçal, T.; Mujumdar, A.S. Modern Techniques for Sludge Dewaterability Improvement. *Dry. Technol.* **2022**, *41*, 339–351. [CrossRef]
35. Kolya, H.; Kang, C.W. Bio-Based Polymeric Flocculants and Adsorbents for Wastewater Treatment. *Sustainability* **2023**, *15*, 9844. [CrossRef]
36. Lin, W.; Liu, X.; Ding, A.; Ngo, H.H.; Zhang, R.; Nan, J.; Li, G. Advanced Oxidation Processes (AOPs)-Based Sludge Conditioning for Enhanced Sludge Dewatering and Micropollutants Removal: A Critical Review. *J. Water Process Eng.* **2022**, *45*, 102468. [CrossRef]
37. Myszograj, S.; Płuciennik-Koropczuk, E. Thermal Disintegration of Sewage Sludge as a Method of Improving the Biogas Potential. *Energies* **2023**, *16*, 559. [CrossRef]
38. Pilli, S.; Bhunia, P.; Yan, S.; LeBlanc, R.J.; Tyagi, R.D.; Surampalli, R.Y. Ultrasonic Pretreatment of Sludge: A Review. *Ultrason. Sonochem.* **2011**, *18*, 1–18. [CrossRef]
39. Djellabi, R.; Su, P.; Ambaye, T.G.; Cerrato, G.; Bianchi, C.L. Ultrasonic Disintegration of Municipal Sludge: Fundamental Mechanisms, Process Intensification and Industrial Sono-Reactors. *ChemPlusChem* **2024**, *89*, e202400016. [CrossRef]
40. Shah, A.A.; Walia, S.; Kazemian, H. Advancements in Combined Electrocoagulation Processes for Sustainable Wastewater Treatment: A Comprehensive Review of Mechanisms, Performance, and Emerging Applications. *Water Res.* **2024**, *252*, 121248. [CrossRef]
41. Angiulli, G.; Calcagno, S.; De Carlo, D.; Laganà, F.; Versaci, M. Second-Order Parabolic Equation to Model, Analyze, and Forecast Thermal-Stress Distribution in Aircraft Plate Attack Wing–Fuselage. *Mathematics* **2019**, *8*, 6. [CrossRef]
42. Gherghel, A.; Teodosiu, C.; De Gisi, S. A Review on Wastewater Sludge Valorisation and Its Challenges in the Context of Circular Economy. *J. Clean. Prod.* **2019**, *228*, 244–263. [CrossRef]
43. Zheng, M.; Hu, Z.; Liu, T.; Sperandio, M.; Volcke, E.I.; Wang, Z.; Yuan, Z. Pathways to Advanced Resource Recovery from Sewage. *Nat. Sustain.* **2024**, *7*, 1395–1404. [CrossRef]
44. Witek-Krowiak, A.; Gorazda, K.; Szopa, D.; Trzaska, K.; Moustakas, K.; Chojnacka, K. Phosphorus Recovery from Wastewater and Bio-Based Waste: An Overview. *Bioengineered* **2022**, *13*, 13474–13506. [CrossRef] [PubMed]
45. Shaddel, S.; Bakhtiary-Davijany, H.; Kabbe, C.; Dadgar, F.; Østerhus, S.W. Sustainable Sewage Sludge Management: From Current Practices to Emerging Nutrient Recovery Technologies. *Sustainability* **2019**, *11*, 3435. [CrossRef]
46. Zeng, Q.; Huang, H.; Tan, Y.; Chen, G.; Hao, T. Emerging Electrochemistry-Based Process for Sludge Treatment and Resources Recovery: A Review. *Water Res.* **2022**, *209*, 117939. [CrossRef] [PubMed]
47. Espinoza, J.R.; Lizama, A.C.; Palma, R.Y.; Hernández-Martínez, G.; Youssef, C.B.; Pedreguera, A.Z. Ultrasonic Pretreatment of Sewage Sludge, an Effective Tool to Improve the Anaerobic Digestion: Current Challenges, Recent Developments, and Perspectives. In *Development in Waste Water Treatment Research and Processes*; Elsevier: Amsterdam, The Netherlands, 2022; pp. 119–138. [CrossRef]
48. Goldan, E.; Nedeff, V.; Barsan, N.; Culea, M.; Tomozei, C.; Panainte-Lehadus, M.; Mosnegutu, E. Evaluation of the Use of Sewage Sludge Biochar as a Soil Amendment—A Review. *Sustainability* **2022**, *14*, 5309. [CrossRef]
49. Zhang, Y.; Ling, Z.; Zhao, M.; Sha, L.; Li, C.; Lu, X. Investigation of the Properties and Mechanism of Activated Sludge in Acid-Magnetic Powder Conditioning and Vertical Pressurized Electro-Dewatering (AMPED) Process. *Sep. Purif. Technol.* **2024**, *328*, 124973. [CrossRef]
50. Mehrez, K.; Fryda, L.; Visser, R.; Kane, A.; Leblanc, N.; Djelal, H. Hydrothermal Processes of Contaminated Biomass: Fate of Heavy Metals and Liquid Effluent Valorization. *Biomass Convers. Biorefin.* **2024**, *8*, 1–16.
51. Pasalari, H.; Farzadkia, M.; Khosravani, F.; Ganachari, S.; Aminabhavi, T.M. Phosphorus Recovery from Sewage Sludge via Chemical and Thermal Technologies. *Chem. Eng. J.* **2024**, *496*, 153869. [CrossRef]

52. Ambaye, T.G.; Djellabi, R.; Vaccari, M.; Prasad, S.; Aminabhavi, T.M.; Rtimi, S. Emerging Technologies and Sustainable Strategies for Municipal Solid Waste Valorization: Challenges of Circular Economy Implementation. *J. Clean. Prod.* **2023**, *423*, 138708. [CrossRef]
53. Nguyen, T.A.H.; Bui, T.H.; Guo, W.S.; Ngo, H.H. Valorization of the Aqueous Phase from Hydrothermal Carbonization of Different Feedstocks: Challenges and Perspectives. *Chem. Eng. J.* **2023**, *472*, 144802. [CrossRef]
54. Leal, C.; del Río, A.V.; Mesquita, D.P.; Amaral, A.L.; Castro, P.M.; Ferreira, E.C. Sludge Volume Index and Suspended Solids Estimation of Mature Aerobic Granular Sludge by Quantitative Image Analysis and Chemometric Tools. *Sep. Purif. Technol.* **2020**, *234*, 116049. [CrossRef]
55. Martínez, E.J.; Rosas, J.G.; Morán, A.; Gómez, X. Effect of Ultrasound Pretreatment on Sludge Digestion and Dewatering Characteristics: Application of Particle Size Analysis. *Water* **2015**, *7*, 6483–6495. [CrossRef]
56. Morabito, F.C. Independent Component Analysis and Feature Extraction Techniques for NdT Data. Mater. Eval. **2000**, *58*, 85–92.
57. Liu, F.; Chen, C.; Qian, J. Film-Like Bacterial Cellulose/Cyclodextrin Oligomer Composites with Controllable Structure for the Removal of Various Persistent Organic Pollutants from Water. *J. Hazard. Mater.* **2021**, *405*, 124122. [CrossRef] [PubMed]
58. Zaki, N.; Hadoudi, N.; Charki, A.; Bensitel, N.; Ouarghi, H.E.; Amhamdi, H.; Ahari, M.H. Advancements in the Chemical Treatment of Potable Water and Industrial Wastewater Using the Coagulation–Flocculation Process. *Sep. Sci. Technol.* **2023**, *58*, 2619–2630. [CrossRef]
59. Rovira, J.; Mari, M.; Nadal, M.; Schuhmacher, M.; Domingo, J.L. Use of Sewage Sludge as Secondary Fuel in a Cement Plant: Human Health Risks. *Environ. Int.* **2011**, *37*, 105–111. [CrossRef]
60. Kebe, X.; Abbt-Braun, G.; Horn, H. Changes in the Characteristics of Dissolved Organic Matter During Sludge Treatment: A Critical Review. *Water Res.* **2000**, *187*, 116441. [CrossRef]
61. Munafò, C.F.; Palumbo, A.; Versaci, M. An Inhomogeneous Model for Laser Welding of Industrial Interest. *Mathematics* **2023**, *11*, 3357. [CrossRef]
62. Versaci, M.; Laganà, F.; Morabito, F.C.; Palumbo, A.; Angiulli, G. Adaptation of an Eddy Current Model for Characterizing Subsurface Defects in CFRP Plates Using FEM Analysis Based on Energy Functional. *Mathematics* **2024**, *12*, 2854. [CrossRef]
63. Versaci, M.; Angiulli, G.; Fattorusso, L.A.; Di Barba, P.; Jannelli, A. Galerkin-FEM Approach for Dyynamic Recovering of the Plate Profile in Electrostatic MEMS with Fringing Field. *COMPEL-Int. J. Comput. Math. Electr. Electron. Eng.* **2024**, *43*, 744–770. [CrossRef]
64. Burrascano, P.; Di Schino, A.; Versaci, M. Efficient Estimation of Synthetic Indicators for the Assessment of Nonlinear Systems Quality. *Appl. Sci.* **2024**, *14*, 9259. [CrossRef]
65. Versaci, M.; Angiulli, G.; La Foresta, F.; Laganà, F.; Palumbo, A. Intuitionistic Fuzzy Divergence for Evaluating the Mechanical Stress State of Steel Plates Subject to Bi-Axial Loads. *Integr. Comput.-Aided Eng. Link Disabl.* **2024**, *31*, 363–379. [CrossRef]
66. Angiulli, G.; Calcagno, S.; La Foresta, F.; Versaci, M. Concrete Compressive Strength Prediction Using Combined Non-Destructive Methods: A Calibration Procedure Using Preexisting Conversion Models Based on Gaussian Process Regression. *J. Compos. Sci.* **2024**, *8*, 300. [CrossRef]
67. Pellicanò, D.; Calcagno, S.; De Carlo, D.; Laganà, F. Analysis and Study of an Integrated System Based on Eddy Current for the Osteogenesis Process. In Proceedings of the 2023 International Workshop on Biomedical Applications, Technologies and Sensors (BATS), Catanzaro, Italy, 28–29 September 2023; pp. 89–94. [CrossRef]
68. Ni, B.J.; Yu, H.Q. Microbial Products of Activated Sludge in Biological Wastewater Treatment Systems: A Critical Review. *Crit. Rev. Environ. Sci. Technol.* **2012**, *42*, 187–223. [CrossRef]
69. Kang, S.; Zhang, J.; Guo, X.; Lei, Y.; Yang, M. Effects of Ultrasonic Treatment on the Structure, Functional Properties of Chickpea Protein Isolate and Its Digestibility In Vitro. *Foods* **2022**, *11*, 880. [CrossRef] [PubMed]
70. Xu, G. Analysis of Sewage Sludge Recovery System in EU-in Perspectives of Nutrients and Energy Recovery Efficiency, and Environmental Impacts. Master's Thesis, Norwegian University of Science and Technology, Taibei, Taiwan, 2014; p. 88.
71. Cofie, O.; Kone, D.; Rothenberger, S.; Moser, D.; Zubruegg, C. Co-Composting of Faecal Sludge and Organic Solid Waste for Agriculture: Process Dynamics. *Water Res.* **2009**, *43*, 4665–4675. [CrossRef] [PubMed]
72. Ammonia Volatilization Losses during Irrigation of Liquid Animal Manure. *Sustainability* **2019**, *11*, 6168. su11216168. [CrossRef]
73. Qian, Y.; Sun, S.; Ju, D.; Shan, X.; Lu, X. Review of the State-of-the-Art of Biogas Combustion Mechanisms and Applications in Internal Combustion Engines. *Renew. Sustain. Energy Rev.* **2017**, *69*, 50–58. [CrossRef]
74. Gahlot, P.; Balasundaram, G.; Tyagi, V.K.; Atabani, A.E.; Suthar, S.; Kazmi, A.A.; Kumar, A. Principles and Potential of Thermal Hydrolysis of Sewage Sludge to Enhance Anaerobic Digestion. *Environ. Res.* **2022**, *214*, 113856. [CrossRef] [PubMed]
75. Yuan, Y.; Liu, T.; Fu, P.; Tang, J.; Zhou, S. Conversion of Sewage Sludge into High-Performance Bifunctional Electrode Materials for Microbial Energy Harvesting. *J. Mater. Chem. A* **2015**, *3*, 8475–8482. [CrossRef]
76. Abdu, N.; Abdullahi, A.A.; Abdulkadir, A. Heavy Metals and Soil Microbes. *Environ. Chem. Lett.* **2017**, *15*, 65–84. [CrossRef]

MDPI AG
Grosspeteranlage 5
4052 Basel
Switzerland
Tel.: +41 61 683 77 34

Algorithms Editorial Office
E-mail: algorithms@mdpi.com
www.mdpi.com/journal/algorithms

www.ingramcontent.com/pod-product-compliance
Lightning Source LLC
Chambersburg PA
CBHW061449210926
51850CB00008B/1656